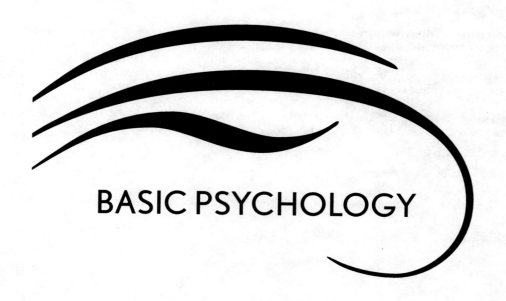

BASIC PSYCHOLOGY

JOSH GEROW

CONTRIBUTING AUTHORS
Roddrick Chatmon • Don Crews

PEARSON
Education

Cover Art: *Blues for Lhasa*, by Michael Wilson

Printed in the United States of America

10 9 8 7 6 5 4 3 2 1

ISBN 0-536-09001-7

2007500209

AK

Please visit our web site at *www.pearsoncustom.com*

PEARSON CUSTOM PUBLISHING
501 Boylston Street, Suite 900, Boston, MA 02116
A Pearson Education Company

CONTENTS

Chapter Nine

Chapter Ten

Chapter Eleven

Chapter Twelve

Chapter Thirteen

This text represents a unique effort for Bent Tree Press. As far as we know, it is unique in all of textbook publishing. You see, *Basic Psychology* has been prepared for a specific audience: the students at Georgia Technical Colleges enrolled in PSY 101—Basic Psychology. Here are the parameters that guided our efforts:

- **The Standards and Course Guide from the Georgia Department of Technical and Adult Education.** There are several guidelines for the content of this course, and those "Standards" were first and foremost in driving any decision about what would be included or excluded from coverage.

- **The content of *Psychology: An Introduction, Eighth Edition*.** The latest edition of this successful introductory psychology text was the source of much of the content for *Basic Psychology*. Existing content has been updated. Much of the content is new. All of it was revised and reviewed.

- **The input from experienced Georgia Technical College instructors.** Contributor/collaborators, **Don Crews** of Southwest Georgia Technical College and **Roddrick Chatmon** of Central Georgia Technical College, read every word of manuscript and made excellent suggestions throughout the process of content preparation. "Standards" are one thing, but the input from these experienced teachers is something else. Their names are on the cover for good reason.

- **Reviewer reactions of Georgia Technical College instructors.** In addition to Professors Crews and Chatmon, the following instructors read and reviewed chapters of the manuscript during preparation. Their input was most welcomed. I only hope that they recognize their good work reflected in the pages that follow. These reviewers were, Yemisi Milledge (Albany Technical College), Michael Young (Valdosta Technical College), Rebecca La Vallee (Central Georgia Technical College), and Susan Walker (Central Georgia Technical College).

FEATURES AND BENEFITS

- **Adherence to the Standards and Course Guide**—A major feature of *Basic Psychology* is that it addresses the requirements of the Georgia Department of Technical and Adult Education. Our goal was to place required content in a single, coherent—and inexpensive—source. We simply wanted to remove any doubt that this was a text appropriate for this course and its students. The one exception to the dogged adherence of "The Standards" is the inclusion of the chapter on **Psychological Disorders and Therapy**. Although not mentioned in the standards, everyone we talked to agreed that this inclusion was consistent with course goals.

- **A Chapter Outline and Preview**—These early entries give a simple, straightforward introduction to the student/reader. The student knows at a glance what is coming and how that information is organized.

- **The use of "everyday life examples"**— As psychologists, we know that personally meaningful information is easier to learn and remember. As has been my goal in all my previous texts, my rule of thumb was to provide everyday life examples and applications at every opportunity. The more we demonstrate psychology's relevance to our lives, the more effective we will be.

- **Highlighted glossary terms**—Beginning psychology is often a matter of vocabulary building. All important terms and concepts are highlighted in the text—with their definitions—and then repeated in a marginal glossary. Simply reviewing the margins for important terms can be an effective last-minute preparation for test taking.

- **Distributing Practice with a "STUDY CHECK"**—Every chapter includes several breaks, or stopping places, each called a Study Check. Psychologists have known for a long time that learning is enhanced if it occurs in short, meaningful sessions—rather than as "massed practice." The Study Check feature provides an excellent marker for pausing and for considering what one has just read. The simple—and effective—notion is that before the student goes on, he or she should reflect on what has just been read and answer the Study Check questions.

- **CYBER PSYCH website suggestions**—These can be found following each Study Check. No text, even a very long one, can cover everything, At the websites provided, students will find additional information on the issues just discussed. I have been using this feature for some time now and have found it very effective. It is more than just an "add on." **A word of caution:** As you well know, websites come and go with unsettling frequency. I do believe all of these sites to be extremely stable. Most have been around for years and are likely to be for many years. Nonetheless, for a multitude of reasons, some may not be accessible at any given moment. Such is life on the Internet, and knowing so from the outset may alleviate concerns later on.

- **CHAPTER SUMMARIES in question-and-answer formats**—Yet another feature that we have found works very well is providing a chapter summary, which repeats the questions posed in the intermittent Study Checks, with answers provided. It is important to note that the answers found in the summary are my simplest attempts to answer the questions. They are not to be taken as definitive.

- **A built-in STUDENT STUDY GUIDE**—Concluding each chapter is a Student Study Guide with four components. 1) A **Study Tip** is provided for each chapter. These are simple, one-page, "how-to-study" reminders. This feature has been very popular with students. 2) The **Key Terms and Concepts** found in the chapter are listed, and space is provided for students to write out their own definitions of important concepts. Students find this "performance" aspect of studying to be quite useful. 3) **Practice Test Questions** are provided as a final review of chapter content. These questions, prepared by the author, give students a chance to test their learning before taking a classroom test. 4) **Answers to Practice Test Questions** are provided in the end matter of the text. Answers are provided in annotated form, letting students know not only the correct answer, but also why it is a better choice than the other alternatives.
- **An extensive Test Bank**—Instructors may obtain a test bank prepared by the author in both print and computerized formats.

ADDITIONAL ACKNOWLEDGMENTS

Any textbook is a collaborative effort, and this one is no exception. In addition to the Georgia Technical College instructors, named above, a few people deserve special mention, along with my sincere expression of appreciation for their timely, professional contributions. I should first mention Jon Fuller, Bent Tree Press publisher. Her enthusiastic support of this rather unusual effort was apparent from the start. Denise Bosma brought her professionalism to this task as its Executive Editor. There is little to be found within the covers of this text that does not reflect her efforts and input. She also has served as lead contact person for getting in touch with Georgia Technical College instructors. Margaret Allyson did the copyediting — the daunting task of transforming my poor keyboard skills and lack of grammatical savvy into coherent text. Our photo researcher was Stacie Lazarcheff, and almost every image in this text reflects her good work. Beverly Baker's layout and design enhance the ease of learning while reflecting the highest standards of book design. And, while folk wisdom has taught us not to place all our faith in book covers: Thank you, Candice Swanson, for this totally gorgeous example. You're a great team.

Psychology Is in Our Lives

Preview

Basic Psychology may well be the best class you'll take. After all, it is about you, your family, and your friends. It's about why people think and feel and behave as they do. It's about how all of us find out about the world and how we learn and remember things. It's about facing problems and stress and finding ways to cope. This class will cover all sorts of issues you've wondered about for a long time. It may not answer all of your questions, and it may even raise a few new ones, but it will set you off on a new path of discovery.

This first chapter is necessarily quite general. It just seems logical to start off with everyone coming to at least a general agreement about what psychology is and what psychologists do. In many ways you can think of this first chapter as an outline, with details to be filled in as we go along. We begin with a rather standard "textbook" definition of psychology, looking at what it is that psychologists study and why we may call their endeavors scientific. We'll take a look at some of the careers that are available to psychologists and to people with training in psychology. We'll end the chapter by making the point that no matter what your chosen career path, learning about matters psychological will be time well spent.

Please be sure to read that section of the Preface called "Features to Help the Student." There you will find a description of several study aids designed to help you get the most out of this text. And don't ignore the "Student Study Guide" at the end of this and every other chapter. It will give you some feedback about what you have learned. So good luck, and enjoy. Please do feel free to contact us at TheCyProf@aol.com if you have any comments or questions. Let's get started!

Psychology's Subject Matter: You and Me and More

psychology the science that studies behavior and mental processes

We will expand on it throughout the rest of this text, but here is a definition of psychology that we can work with for now: **Psychology** is the science that studies behavior and mental processes. This rather simple definition may not tell us a lot just yet, but it does raise a couple of points worthy of our time.

This definition claims that the subject matter of psychology is behavior and mental processes. Before we get into what it means to say that psychology is a science, let's take a closer look at just what it is that psychologists study.

behavior what organisms do—their actions and reactions

Psychologists study behavior. **Behavior** is what organisms do—their actions and reactions. The behaviors of organisms are observable and measurable. If we wonder whether a rat will press a lever in some situation, we can put a rat in that situation and watch to see if it presses the lever. If we are interested in Susan's ability to draw a circle, we can ask her to draw one and observe her efforts. Observable, measurable behaviors offer an advantage as objects of study. Several observers can agree on the behavior or event being studied. We can agree that the rat pressed the lever (or didn't) and even measure the extent, speed, and force with which it did so. We can agree that Susan correctly drew a circle and not a triangle or an oval. If you were interested in the extent to which violent movies contribute to aggression, you

Cognitive processes are "intellectual" mental processes, such as perceiving, remembering, or—in this case—reading.

would most likely focus on observable, aggressive behaviors, rather than on how such movies make a viewer feel or think.

Psychologists also study mental processes. There are two kinds of mental processes: cognitive and affective. **Cognitions** are mental events, such as beliefs, perceptions, thoughts, ideas, and memories. Cognitive (cog′-ni-tiv) processes, then, include such activities as perceiving, thinking, knowing, deciding, and remembering. **Affect** (af′-ekt) is a term that refers to feelings, emotions, or moods. Persons who watch a violent movie might have aggressive thoughts (cognitions) or aggressive feelings (affect) without expressing either in observable behavior.

Here we have a scheme we will encounter repeatedly: the ABCs that make up the subject matter of psychology. Psychology is the science that studies affect, behavior, and cognition. To say that we understand a person at any given time, we must understand what that person is feeling (A), doing (B), and thinking (C).

The major difference between behaviors and mental processes is that while behaviors are directly observable, mental processes are not. A person's affect or cognitions have to be inferred from the observation of behaviors. For example, we may infer that someone is sad (an affective state) if we see him sitting slumped over and crying. We may infer that jurors used certain pieces of evidence when coming to their decision (a cognitive process) on the basis of what they tell us in a post-trial interview.

Here's a point often overlooked: Most of the time, psychologists do focus their study on the behaviors and/or the mental processes of their fellow humans. Although unstated in our definition, psychologists often study non-human animals as well. We will see many examples of psychological research that use animals in an effort to help us understand human behaviors or mental processes. At the same time,

cognitions mental events, such as beliefs, perceptions, thoughts, ideas, and memories

affect a term that refers to feelings, emotions, or moods

Affect is a term that psychologists use when referring to a person's emotional state or mood—such as "happiness."

some psychologists study the behavior and mental activity of animals simply because they find them interesting and worthy of study in their own right.

People in many walks of life can be said to "study behavior and mental processes." Scholars and laypersons alike have studied human nature for centuries. What makes psychology's study unique is its reliance on the methods of science. It is to this issue that we turn now.

✔ STUDY CHECK

What is the subject matter of psychology?

Define affect and cognitions, and provide examples.

CYBER PSYCH

(a) The website, "Psych Web" is hosted by Russ Dewey of Georgia Southern University and is well known to all instructors of psychology. No matter what your concern, a good place to start is http://www.psywww.com.

(b) A huge mega-site is http://www.psych-central.com designed for "psychology students and their professors." It provides hundreds of links to other sites.

(c) The American Psychological Association maintains a website at http://www.apa.org where you will find many links just for students.

Psychology: The Science and the Practice

Our beliefs about ourselves and the world in which we live come from many different sources. Some are formed as a matter of faith (for example, there is a God—or there isn't). Some beliefs come through tradition, passed from generation to generation, accepted because "they say it is so." (For the longest time I believed that if I got my feet wet in the winter I'd catch pneumonia—because that was what my grandmother told me.) Occasionally, our beliefs about the human condition are credited to common sense (for example, "absence makes the heart grow fonder"—but then that same common sense tells us "out of sight, out of mind"). Some of our beliefs derive from art, literature, poetry, and drama (for example, some of our ideas about romantic love may have roots in Shakespeare's *Romeo and Juliet,* or the latest music video from today's hottest recording star). Although all of these ways of learning about behaviors and mental processes have value in some contexts, psychologists maintain that there is a better way: by applying the values and methods of science.

Memories of previous biology or chemistry classes notwithstanding, the goal of science is to make the world easier to understand (Mitchell & Jolley, 2001, p. 3). Scientists do this by generating scientific laws about their subject matter. Simply put, scientific laws are statements about one's subject matter that one believes to be true—not on the basis of faith, tradition, or common sense, but through logical reasoning and observation. So a discipline is a **science** if it can demonstrate two things: 1) an organized body of knowledge (a set of scientific laws), and 2) the use of scientific methods. How does psychology rate on these two criteria?

science a discipline that can demonstrate: 1) an organized body of knowledge (a set of scientific laws), and 2) the use of scientific methods

Over the years, psychologists have accumulated a great deal of information about the behaviors and mental processes of organisms. Granted, many intriguing questions remain unanswered. Some of the knowledge that psychologists have accumulated about some very important, relevant questions is incomplete and tentative. And not having all the answers can be frustrating, but that is part of the excitement of psychology today—there are still so many things to discover! The truth remains, however, that psychologists have learned a lot, and what they know is reasonably well organized. In fact, you have in your hands one version of the organized body of knowledge that is psychology. That's right—your textbook!

Psychology also meets the second requirement of a science because what is known in psychology has been learned through **scientific methods**—methods that involve observing a phenomenon, formulating hypotheses about it, making more observations, refining and re-testing hypotheses (Bordens & Abbott, 2002). The scientific method reflects an attitude or an approach to discovery and problem-solving. It is "a process of inquiry, a particular way of thinking," rather than a prescribed set of procedures that must be followed rigorously (Graziano & Raulin, 1993, p. 2). Science involves an attitude of being both skeptical and open-minded about one's work.

scientific methods methods that involve observing a phenomenon, formulating hypotheses about it, making more observations, refining and re-testing hypotheses

There might not be specific rules to follow, but there *are* guidelines. The process goes something like this: The scientist (the psychologist) makes some observations about her subject matter. For example, she notices that her son and his close friends seem to be doing better in first grade than are most of the other students. On the basis of that preliminary observation, the scientist develops a hypothesis. A **hypothesis** is a tentative explanation of some phenomenon that can be tested and then either accepted or rejected. It is essentially an educated guess about one's subject matter. In our example, the psychologist might hypothesize that the reason that

hypothesis a tentative explanation of some phenomenon that can be tested and then either accepted or rejected

Some beliefs we have about the world, such as "If you get your feet wet, you'll catch a cold," come from tradition, passed on from one generation to the next.

her son and his friends are doing so well in school is because they spent at least two years in a daycare center. In this case, a causal factor (time in daycare) is tentatively linked to behavior (success in first grade).

No matter how reasonable this hypothesis may sound to the scientist—or to others—it cannot be accepted as an explanation. The hypothesis must be tested under carefully controlled conditions. First, how much time *did* her son and his friends spend in daycare? How will performance in first grade be measured? New observations need to be made.

Let us assume for a moment that the psychologist's son and his friends did indeed spend significantly more time in daycare than did their classmates. Let us assume further that these children performed at a higher level on each of the tests of academic achievement used in this study. It looks as though the psychologist's hypothesis has been confirmed: At least two years of daycare produces superior academic achievement in first grade.

An interesting reality about scientific research is that once a hypothesis is confirmed, the research process does not stop. In fact, more questions are often raised than are answered, and these new questions serve as a basis for generating new hypotheses and new research. In our example, for instance, are there any other characteristics of those students who did well in first grade other than the fact that they had similar daycare experiences? What factors other than daycare might account for these results? Will the differences in achievement hold up through second grade? Can these results be replicated with any other group of youngsters? What is there about being in daycare that might account for superior academic achievement at any level? Many new hypotheses could be developed and tested. In this way, the acquisition of knowledge becomes an ongoing process of trying to refine explanations of behavior and mental processes.

Here is an important point to remember about science, the scientific method, and hypotheses. A scientific hypothesis may be rejected because there is no data to support it. On the basis of evidence, a hypothesis may be supported, but it cannot be "proven" as true. No matter how much evidence one finds to support a hypothesis, scientists—always open-minded—realize that new hypotheses may come along that can do a better job of explaining what has been observed. Thus, psychologists avoid statements or claims that their research proves something. As an example, evidence—based on some pretty good science of the day—once indicated that stomach ulcers were caused by stress and stress alone. We now understand that many types of ulcers are caused by infection, not stress at all.

The goal of many psychologists is to use scientific methods to learn about their subject matter. But, while all psychologists are scientists, most are *scientist-practitioners*. Sometimes these psychologists are called "service providers." This means that they are not so much involved in discovering new laws about behavior and mental processes as they are in applying what is already known. Of those psychologists who are practitioners, most are clinical or counseling psychologists. Their goal is to apply what is known to help people deal with problems that affect their ability to adjust to the demands of their environments, including other people.

Psychological practitioners can be found in many places, not just clinical settings where therapy and treatment are conducted. Even before the dust settled after

Many psychologists are scientist-practitioners, applying knowledge of psychological principles to real-world issues—such as how best to present evidence to juries during a trial.

the World Trade Center bombings of September 2001, psychologists (and other mental health professionals) were rushing to New York City to try to offer some relief from the pain and suffering of that horrendous trauma.

Other scientist-practitioners apply psychological principles to situations that arise in the workplace; these are industrial-organizational, or I/O, psychologists. Sports psychologists use what they know about affect, behavior, and cognition to improve the performance of athletes. Other practitioners advise attorneys on how to present arguments in the courtroom. Some intervene to reduce ethnic prejudice or to teach others how differing cultural values affect behaviors. Some establish programs to reduce litter or to increase the use of automobile safety belts, while others help people train their pets.

Thus, we can say that, as a discipline, psychology has two inter-related goals: 1) to use scientific methods to understand the behaviors and mental processes of organisms, and 2) to apply that understanding to help solve problems in the real world. The science of psychology and the practice of psychology are not mutually exclusive. Many practitioners in clinical, industrial, or educational settings are also active scientific researchers. And much of the research in psychology originates as a response to problems that arise in the real world.

✔ **STUDY CHECK**

Why does psychology qualify as a science?

In general terms, what are scientific methods?

What do psychologists who are scientist-practitioners do?

CYBER PSYCH

(a) A very engaging essay (by a physicist) on the misperception of "the scientific method can be found at http://www.lhup.edu/~dsimanek/scimeth.htm.

(b) The site http://www.punaridge.org/doc/teacher/method/default.htm is actually a site about the scientific method designed for children, but it is well worth a look.

The Methods of the Science of Psychology

reliability consistency, dependability, or repeatability

Before psychologists can explain what people do (much less why they do it), they first must make reliable and valid observations of just what it is that people do. **Reliability** refers to consistency, dependability, or repeatability—in psychology as in any other context. For observations to be worthwhile, they must be reliable. They must be stable, and a number of people have to agree on the observations under study. If you observe today that Tommy is actively aggressive, but others do not see that aggressiveness, or if he never appears aggressive again, then your observation lacks reliability. A test that indicates today that Rolanda's intelligence is well below average, but next week indicates that she is almost mentally gifted is not a reliable test.

validity the extent to which an observation reflects what is actually happening

Validity refers to the extent to which an observation reflects what is actually happening. A test, for example, is said to be valid if it measures what it claims to be measuring. Several observers notice Jason acting in a very friendly, supportive, caring manner in the presence of members of another race or ethnic group. The observers conclude that Jason has little or no prejudice toward that ethnic group. It may be, of course, that Jason's behaviors were shaped by that particular social

All research in psychology begins with reliable, valid observations. Before we can examine the impact of daycare on child development, we need careful observations of just what happens in the daycare setting.

situation—and the fact that he knew that he was being watched. He may, in fact, have extreme prejudices toward that group. In such a case, the original observation lacks validity. A test that claims to be measuring intelligence, but is actually just a mechanism for sorting people on the basis of race is not a valid test. (For example, a test that calls itself a measure of "Mental Abilities" on which African-American children do poorly—regardless of their intelligence—and on which Caucasian children do well—regardless of their ability—is simply not a valid test.)

Sometimes having good, reliable, valid observations about peoples' affects or cognitions or behaviors is an acceptable end in itself. It may be valuable to know, for example, just how many registered voters intend to vote for a given candidate. It might make a difference if the cafeteria on your campus had reliable and valid information about the food preferences of the student body. How many hours a week, on average, *do* children watch television, and how many hours do they spend playing outside? How many times a month *do* most married couples engage in sexual intercourse? How many Iraqi civilians *have* been wounded in the current conflict? Good questions—requiring carefully made, reliable, valid observations.

Although the range of specific research techniques available to psychologists is vast, in general terms, we can divide methods into two categories: correlational or experimental. In **correlational research**, one looks for a lawful relationship between variables that are observed and measured, but not manipulated. A variable is anything that can take on different values—as opposed to a constant, which has but one value. Correlational research depends on measuring the values of variables and looking for relationships between or among them. It's not all that complicated.

correlational research a method in which one looks for a lawful relationship between variables that are observed and measured, but not manipulated

There is clearly a correlation between gymnastic ability and overall body size, but if all we know is that these two variables are correlated, we cannot make any conclusions regarding cause and effect.

For example, if you were interested in the play patterns of boys and girls in a day-care center, you could observe their play times and categorize their behaviors (e.g., being aggressive or helping, playing with others or alone). Correlational methods could then tell you if there were lawful relationships between those variables you observed. You might find that boys tend to engage in aggressive play with others, while girls tend to play alone.

This sort of study can be useful in many situations. If it is not possible (or proper) to manipulate a variable of interest, then correlational research is the way to go. For instance, in a study of the relationship between birth defects and alcohol consumption, you surely would not want to encourage pregnant women to drink alcohol—particularly if it were your own hypothesis that doing so would have negative consequences! But you might be able to find women who *did* drink to varying degrees during their pregnancies and use that information to see if it is related to birth defects. Correlational research is often used in the early stages of an investigation just to see if relationships between selected variables do exist. For example, based on the early correlational data concerning alcohol consumption and birth defects, subsequent experimental research (using animal participants) might further explore the biological link between alcohol and birth defects. Research that involves the age of the persons involved is correlational by necessity; after all, you cannot manipulate a person's ages.

Whenever you encounter correlational research, there are two very important points to keep in mind:

1. No matter how strongly two variables are correlated, one cannot make predictions for individual cases; there always will be exceptions. For example, there is a very strong correlation between high school grades and college grades, but that relationship is not perfect. As you may know from your own experience, some students who do well in high school flunk out of college, while other students who did poorly in high school end up doing very nicely

in college. That is, there are exceptions, even though it is generally true that students who earned good high school grades will tend to earn good college grades.

2. No matter how logical it may be, if all you know is that two variables are correlated, you cannot infer a cause-and-effect relationship between them. After all, good high school grades do not cause good college grades—they simply are related to each other, or co-related (correlated).

In **experimental research**, investigators actually manipulate a variable and then look for a relationship between that manipulation and changes in the value of some other variable. Say, for example, that a researcher was interested in factors that influence children's willingness to donate candy to needy children. The researcher has one group of children watch a pro-social television program (say an episode of *Mr. Rogers' Neighborhood* portraying generosity). At the same time, a second group watches a "neutral" show, perhaps a series of standard cartoons. Afterward, all the children are asked to play a game in which part of their winnings are donated to needy children. In this case, the researcher manipulates one variable (the nature of a television show) and measures another (the number of pieces of candy donated in a game) to see if there is a relationship between the two.

> **experimental research** a method in which investigators manipulate a variable and then look for a relationship between that manipulation and changes in the value of some other variable

When researchers perform an experiment, they are no longer content just to discover that two measured observations are related; they want to be able to claim that, at least to some degree, one *causes* the other. To determine if such a claim can be made, researchers manipulate the values of one variable to see if those manipulations cause a measurable change in the values of another variable. An **independent variable** is the variable that the experimenter manipulates. The experimenter determines its value, and nothing the participant in the experiment does will affect its value. For example, if you were interested in the effects of alcohol on birth defects, you could give three groups of pregnant mice different amounts of alcohol in their diets (0.0 oz. per day. 0.5 oz. per day, or 1.0 oz. per day). As the experimenter, you determine which groups get which dosage; i.e., the alcohol is your independent variable. On the other hand, a **dependent variable** provides a measure of the participants' behavior. In general, an experimental hypothesis is that values of the dependent variable will, indeed, *depend* upon the independent variable manipulation the participants received. In our example, some measure of the number and/or extent of birth defects would be the dependent variable.

> **independent variable** the variable that the experimenter manipulates

> **dependent variable** one that provides a measure of the participants' behavior

In its simplest form, an experiment has two groups of participants. Those in the **experimental group** are exposed to some value of the independent variable. For example, in an experiment on the effects of a new drug on the maze-learning ability of rats, ten rats in the experimental group are given an injection of a certain amount of the new drug. These rats are then given a series of trials in which they are placed in a complicated maze. The number of errors (wrong turns) that the rats make in getting from the start box of the maze to the end of the maze are recorded. We discover that these rats make very few errors and quickly learn to get through the maze without error after just seven exposures (trials). Is there any way we can claim that the drug they were given can account for this rapid maze learning? No, not really. Why not? Well, there are lots of reasons. For one thing, these ten rats might be among the best maze-running rats in the laboratory. Maybe the maze is just easier than the experimenters thought it was. To show that it was the new drug causing the good maze-running performance, you need a second group of rats—rats in all known ways the same as the first ten—who receive an injection

> **experimental group** those in an experiment who are exposed to some value of the independent variable

An experiment can support or refute the hypothesis that taking a "Study Skills" course will improve classroom performance.

control group participants in an experiment who receive a zero level of the independent variable

of, say, saline solution, with no active ingredient. Their behaviors (errors) in the maze are measured and compared to those of the first group of rats. Rats in this latter group comprise the control group. If the rats in the control group do just as well as those in the experimental group, we surely cannot claim any maze-running enhancement caused by the new drug. In general, a **control group** receives a zero level of the independent variable. You may think of the control group as the baseline against which the performance of the experimental group is judged. Even in the simplest of experiments, one must have at least two levels of the independent variable, where one will be zero.

Now let's work through an example, just to be sure we have our terminology straight. While checking out "study skills" on the internet, you read an article claiming that students can do better on exams simply by learning how to take tests. (Remember, all good science begins with observation.) You decide to test this idea experimentally. Your hypothesis: Taking a class on test-taking skills will have a positive influence on classroom exams.

You get some volunteers from your psychology class and divide them into two groups. One group (A) agrees to take a three-hour class on test-taking strategies, while the other group (B) takes a three-hour class on making and sticking to a budget while in college. At the end of the semester, with the students' permission, you will compare the exam scores of the two groups.

Now for some terminology: Your *hypothesis* is that training on test-taking strategies will improve performance in a psychology class. You have manipulated whether the participants in your study get that training, so getting the training is your *independent variable* (which in this example has two values, either training or no training). You believe that such training will improve performance. What will you measure to see if this is so—that is, what will be your *dependent variable?* You observe the scores the students in your study earn on classroom exams throughout the term. You discover that Group A (those who had the training) score, on the average, nearly a whole letter grade better than do the students in the control group who did not have the training (Group B). It looks as though you have confirmed your hypothesis.

Before we get too carried away, there is yet one more type of variable to consider. **Extraneous variables** are those factors, other than the independent variables, that can influence the dependent variable of an experiment. To conclude that changes in the dependent variable are caused by the manipulations of the independent variable, extraneous variables need to be controlled for or eliminated. Such factors should be considered and dealt with before an experiment begins. In our example, what extraneous variables might be involved? Other than just taking a test-taking class, what factors might have produced the demonstrated effect? For one obvious thing, we'd better be able to show that the students in both our groups were of essentially the same academic ability before we began. We would have a serious problem if we discovered that the students in Group A were honor students, while those in Group B were struggling to get by in all their classes. When we do an experiment and find measurable differences in our dependent variable, we want to be able to claim that these differences were caused by our manipulation of the independent variable and nothing else. Indeed, the quality of an experiment is determined by the extent to which extraneous variables are anticipated and then eliminated.

extraneous variables those factors, other than the independent variables, that can influence the dependent variable of an experiment

✔ STUDY CHECK

What are reliability and validity?

Compare and contrast correlational and experimental methods.

Using an example, define the three major variables involved in an experiment.

CYBER PSYCH

(a) A site that begins with correlation and then moves on to other methods is http://psychology.about.com/library/weekly/aa051502a.htm.

(b) A wonderful piece on "Psychological Experiments on the Internet," including many links is http://psych.fullerton.edu/mbirnbaum/web/IntroWeb.htm.

Careers in Psychology— Psychology in Your Career

Most careers in psychology require a graduate degree. In fact, in most states a person cannot publicly claim to be "a psychologist" unless he or she has an earned doctorate degree. That certainly does not mean that decent jobs in psychology are available only to persons with a Ph.D. in psychology—to the contrary.

With a baccalaureate or an associate degree, there are several career options within psychology, but they are likely to be in supportive roles. You will not be able to open your own office as a psychotherapist, but you may find relevant employment in a psychological clinic, rehabilitation center, nursing home, or hospital. You may not get a job as a school psychologist, but there are several places within most school systems that would love to have someone with any background in psychology. You may not get hired as an industrial/organizational psychologist, but most human resources offices of companies look for people with training in psychology.

There are many jobs
or careers for which a
knowledge of psychology is
a real benefit.

In the 2002–2003 academic year, (the latest for which statistics are available) a survey of college freshmen indicated that psychology was the most popular choice of major.

As with most generalizations, it is not fair to divide careers in psychology into only specialty areas of "researcher" and "practitioner." As we said earlier, many psychologists in applied settings engage in scientific research, and many research psychologists become involved in projects that are applied or practical in nature. Still, for the sake of generating a list of subfields in psychology, let's start with those that are *primarily* scientific/research oriented and then move to those that are *primarily* applied or practical in focus.

SCIENTIFIC/RESEARCH AREAS IN PSYCHOLOGY:

- **Cognitive psychologists** study how people perceive the world and form memories of their experiences. They do research on matters such as thinking, problem-solving, and intelligence.
- **Physiological psychologists** focus on the biological organism, filled with tissue, fibers, nerves, and chemicals that underlie all of our thoughts, feelings, and behaviors.

- **Social psychologists** look at how a person's psychological functioning is influenced by others. They are concerned about people as they really live, as social organisms in a world of others.
- **Health psychologists** are concerned with how psychological processes influence physical health, and vice versa, how one's physical health influences affect, behavior, and cognition.
- **Developmental psychologists** study the psychological development of the individual throughout the life span, looking for milestones of development at all age levels.
- **Psychometric psychologists** explore how best to measure the subtleties of psychological functioning, developing and evaluating psychological tests and devising ways to design and analyze experimental and correlational data.

APPLIED/PRACTITIONER AREAS IN PSYCHOLOGY:

- **Industrial/organizational psychologists** aim to improve both the quality of work life and worker productivity, dealing with issues such as personnel selection, training, and motivation.
- **Rehabilitation psychologists** tend to work with persons with disabilities, both physical and mental, in an effort to help such people function at the best possible level.
- **Educational, or instructional, psychologists** apply psychological principles to the processes of teaching and learning in an effort to maximize the efficiency of both.
- **Clinical psychologists** have a Ph.D. in psychology from a program that provides practical, applied experience in therapeutic techniques, as well as research. Clinicians complete a one-year internship, usually at a mental health center or psychiatric hospital, and have extensive training in psychological testing and assessment. Some clinical psychologists have a Psy.D. (pronounced "sigh-dee"), which is a Doctor of Psychology, rather than the Doctor of Philosophy degree. Psy.D. programs take as long to complete as Ph.D. programs, but tend to emphasize more practical, clinical work.
- **Counseling psychologists** usually have a Ph.D. in psychology. The focus of study (and required one-year internship) is generally with patients with less severe psychological problems. For instance, rather than spending an internship in a psychiatric hospital, a counseling psychologist is more likely to spend time at a university's counseling center.
- **Occupational therapists** usually have a master's degree (less frequently, a bachelor's degree) in occupational therapy, which includes many psychology classes and internship training in aiding the psychologically and physically handicapped.
- **Psychiatric nurses** often work in mental hospitals and clinics. In addition to their R.N. degrees, psychiatric nurses have training in the care of mentally ill patients.
- **Pastoral counseling** is a specialty of those with a religious background and a master's degree in psychology or educational counseling.
- **Mental health technicians** usually have an associate degree in mental health technology (MHT). MHT graduates seldom provide unsupervised therapy, but they may be involved in the delivery of many mental health services.

- **Psychiatry** is a specialty area in medicine. In addition to work required for the M.D., the psychiatrist does a psychiatric internship (usually one year) and a psychiatric residency (usually three years) in a hospital where psychological disorders are treated. A psychiatrist is the only type of psychotherapist permitted to use biomedical treatments, such as drugs).

Even if you pursue a career in some area not directly related to psychology, you will find that training in psychology is relevant for nearly *every* job you can imagine. Think about it: Psychology seeks to understand feelings, beliefs, and behaviors. For what position is even a basic understanding of such matters not a relevant skill or talent? Psychology may be most valuable for careers in which you would interact with others—as clients, customers, or fellow workers. And no matter what your chosen line of work, the better you can understand yourself, your affect, cognitions, and behaviors, the better off you will be.

The workplace today is significantly different from what it was when your parents—much less your grandparents—entered the world of work. Manufacturing jobs, or work that requires sitting or standing alone in assembly lines, are becoming fewer and fewer. Most jobs today are "service industry" positions and require an interaction with (servicing) the public (customer). They are positions that require active listening, tact, interpersonal communication skills, and empathy. In short, they require good psychology.

The workplace today also requires self-understanding, flexibility, and stress management. Seldom can a young adult enter the workforce with any reasonable expectation of retiring in the same position at the same company. In many companies, large and small, *flextime* allows workers to schedule their work shifts to accommodate personal needs—at least up to a point. Job-sharing is becoming a recognized way for employers to keep valued workers who do not want full-time employment. The nature of one's job can change. Companies change: Some expand, some downsize. Being open and ready for change is a powerful asset—as is being open to retraining. We will get back to these issues later, in Chapter 13.

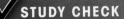

STUDY CHECK

For what jobs or careers is the study of psychology a relevant experience?

CYBER PSYCH

(a) By far, the best place to go for information about careers in psychology is http://www.apa. org/students/brochure/brochurenew.pdf part of the site of the American Psychological Association. Here you will find a 40-page brochure on psychology careers for the 21st century.

(b) A listing of links to careers in psychology is at http://psychology.about.com/od/careerarticle.

Chapter Summary

What is the subject matter of psychology?

Psychologists study the behavior and mental processes of organisms (human and non-human), where mental processes are categorized as affects and cognitions.

Define affect and cognitions and provide examples.

In psychology, "affect" refers to feelings, moods, and emotional states, whereas cognitions are understood to be ideas, beliefs, perceptions, knowledge and understanding. You may know that a high-fiber cereal is good for you (a cognition), but you may hate the taste of such a cereal (affect). Sometimes your emotions (affect) may be so powerful that you find it difficult to express those feelings in words (a cognitive process).

Why does psychology qualify as a science?

Psychology is a science because it meets the two defining conditions: a) an organized body of knowledge and b) the application of scientific methods.

In general terms, what are scientific methods?

Not so much a list of rules to be followed, scientific methods reflect an attitude to discovery and problem-solving. Science involves observing, forming hypotheses, testing hypotheses and then observing some more, always being both skeptical and open-minded.

What do psychologists who are scientist-practitioners do?

Scientist-practitioners take present knowledge—as incomplete and possibly flawed as it may be—and apply that knowledge in the real world in attempts to solve real-world problems. Many are clinical or counseling psychologists, helping people deal with personal problems, but psychological service providers can be found in many other settings, including the law, sports, education, business, and industry.

What are reliability and validity?

An observation, measurement, or event is reliable if it is consistent, repeatable, or stable. It is said to be valid if it truly reflects what it claims to be observing or measuring.

Compare and contrast correlational and experimental methods.

Correlational methods seek reliable relationships between measured observations. If two variables are correlated, one can be used to predict the other. High school grades can be used to predict college grades, for instance. Predictability will never be perfect, however, because exceptions are always present. Importantly, no matter how well two variables may be correlated, we cannot reach any cause-and-effect conclusions about them. Experimental methods do allow for cause-and-effect conclusions. If an experiment is well done, it may be said that changes in the independent variable have caused measured changes in the dependent variable.

Using an example, define the three major variables involved in an experiment.

Your hypothesis is that learning is enhanced by the use of audio-visual (AV) aids. You have three third-grade classes. One gets all the AV aids you can find. A second gets videotapes and movies, while the third gets no AV aids. You have manipulated the amount of AV aids; therefore, it is the independent variable. After six weeks of instruction, the three classes are given a test, and you find that the first class gets the best (average) score, while the third class gets the worst score. You have measured learning with a test; the test scores, then, are the dependent variable. In order to conclude that the AV aid differences caused the measured differences in test scores, you have to show that you have eliminated or controlled all extraneous variables—any other events (like differences in the skill of the teachers involved) that might have produced the differences in test scores.

For what jobs or careers is the study of psychology a relevant experience?

The study of psychology will surely be required for anyone wanting a job as a scientist-practitioner, either in a clinical setting, an educational setting, or an industrial or organizational setting. One could also argue the case that the study of psychology is relevant for every job or career imaginable—particularly for those that involve interacting with others.

Student Study Guide

STUDY TIP #1 Now's the Time

At the beginning of the Student Study Guide for each chapter, I will share some thoughts on how to maximize your performance in this course. The suggestions and advice come directly from psychology itself and have been tested over generations of college students.

You are about to begin a new course and a new semester. It's all rather exciting, really. The beginning of a new semester can be nearly magical—filled with promise, high hopes, and good intentions. There are new people to meet, new experiences to be relished, new things to be learned.

What I would like you to start thinking about immediately is that right now is the very best time to get started with your studying. The points you earn on your first classroom test are just as valuable as the points you'll earn on your final exam. Too many students approach finals week wishing that they had done better on their classroom quizzes earlier in the semester because now they have figured out that they must do a truly superior job on the final exam. That's putting unnecessary pressure on oneself at finals time.

Recent research demonstrates that procrastinators—people who tend to put things off "until later"—are healthy and happy people at the beginning of a semester. Toward the end of the semester, however, because they have neglected so much work, they are unhappy, stressed, and suffer an abnormally high incidence of physical ailments and illnesses.

So get to it—not this weekend or tomorrow or the day after, but right now, today. As the semester goes by, you'll be glad you got off to a good start. I wish you well. If at any time during this course you have any questions at all, please feel free to contact me at TheCyProf@aol.com.

Josh R. Gerow

KEY TERMS AND CONCEPTS

psychology _____

_____

behavior _____

_____

cognitions _____

_____

affect _____

_____

science _____

_____

scientific methods _____

_____

hypothesis _____

_____

reliability _____

_____

validity_____

_____

correlational research _____

_____

experimental research _____

_____

independent variable _____

_____

dependent variable _____

_____

experimental group _____

_____

control group_____

_____

extraneous variable _____

_____

Practice Test Questions—Chapter One

MULTIPLE CHOICE

1. If you feel queasy, apprehensive, or nervous at the sight of exam papers, you are experiencing

_____ a. cognition.   _____ c. insight.

_____ b. affect.   _____d. conflict.

2. Which of the following best describes psychology's subject matter?

_____ a. what people do, normally and abnormally

_____ b. the actions of people when they are stimulated

_____ c. the mental activities and behaviors of organisms

_____ d. what people think about the things that affect them

3. When a researcher develops a tentative explanation for some phenomenon that can be tested and either rejected or supported, that researcher has developed

_____ a. a scientific method.   _____ c. a hypothesis.

_____ b. empirical evidence.   _____ d. an operational definition.

4. Clinical psychologists and industrial/organizational psychologists are often referred to as "scientist-practitioners" because they

_____ a. seldom have a Ph.D. in psychology.

_____ b. work in clinics and hospitals.

_____ c. usually do not use the scientific method in their work.

_____ d. work to apply psychological knowledge in the real world.

5. The basic, or first, step of all of the specific research methods in psychology is

_____ a. the formation of correct hypotheses.

_____ b. knowing ahead of time if one's theory is accurate.

_____ c. making careful observations of one's subject matter.

_____ d. choosing to use people rather than animals in one's research.

6. Although there are many varieties and types of research in psychology, research methods tend to fall into one of which two categories?

_____ a. experimental and correlational

_____ b. meta-analyses and baseline designs

_____ c. unilateral and multilateral

_____ d. physical or social

7. The quality or value of the results of an experiment mostly depend upon

_____ a. the extent to which extraneous variables have been controlled or eliminated.

_____ b. the number of independent variables that have been manipulated.

_____ c. the extent to which the independent and the dependent variables are correlated with each other.

_____ d. whether humans or non-humans were used as participants in the experiment.

8. If you want to experimentally test the usefulness of a new drug for treating some psychological disorder, the independent variable in your experiment will be

_____ a. the extent to which patients show improvement after taking the drug.

_____ b. the amount of the drug administered to the patients.

_____ c. the type of psychological disorder being treated.

_____ d. other forms of treatment or therapy that the patients are receiving.

9. In most states, to advertise oneself as a "psychologist," one must

_____ a. be a graduate of an accredited medical school.

_____ b. hold a doctorate degree in psychology.

_____ c. pass an interview process held by the state's Board of Examiners.

_____ d. have majored in psychology as an undergraduate.

TRUE/FALSE

1. _____ True _____ False Science is the only way to gain insight into the nature of human behavior.

2. _____ True _____ False Psychologists study the ABCs; Affect, Behavior, and Cognition.

3. _____ True _____ False Clinical and counseling psychologists may be referred to as "scientist–practitioners."

4. _____ True _____ False Experiments are the only scientific methods used by psychologists.

5. _____ True _____ False Psychology is not a popular choice for a college major.

Childhood

Preview

From conception to death, human beings share many developmental events and experiences that unite us as one species. On the other hand, each of us is unique, distinct from all others. Developmental psychologists are interested in both the common patterns of development *and* the ways in which we differ as we grow and develop throughout our lives. Growth and development begin well before birth, so that is where we will start. We will see that, even before birth, many factors can affect the developmental process.

The centerpiece of any discussion of the psychology of children is usually their cognitive development. Because it is such a classic and has inspired so many, the approach of Jean Piaget is a reasonable place to begin. Then we'll turn to moral reasoning. How do children come to appreciate the differences between what is right and what is wrong? Finally, we'll consider a significant concern not only for psychologists, but also for makers of public policy: the development of social attachments, their possible benefits, and how secure attachments can be fostered by society's institutions.

Throughout this chapter we will use growth and development to mean different things. *Growth* refers to simple enlargement—getting bigger—while *development* refers to a differentiation of structure or function. Something develops when it first appears and then remains. For example, the nervous system develops between week two and week eight after conception.

Prenatal Development

Human development begins at conception, when the father's sperm cell unites with the mother's ovum, or egg cell. At that time, all of the genes on the 23 chromosomes from each parent's cell pairs off within a single new cell, called the *zygote*. We have in that one action the transmission of all inherited characteristics. The period of development between conception and birth is called the **prenatal period.** From the one cell that defines conception until birth the newborn human will have grown to include about 200 billion cells (Shaffer, 2002, p. 105).

prenatal period the period of development between conception and birth

The prenatal stage, between two weeks after conception through week eight, is called the *embryonic stage*. During this period, the embryo (as the developing organism is now called) develops at a rapid rate, and all of the organ systems of the body are laid in place. It is during the embryonic stage that the unborn child is most sensitive to environmental influences. If any prenatal problems occur, they are most likely to develop during this stage.

Two months after conception, the embryonic stage draws to a close. The 1-inch-long embryo now has enough of a primitive nervous system to respond to a light touch, exhibiting a simple reflex movement. The stage of the *fetus* has begun. Now the most noticeable change, at least to the mother, is the significant increase in weight and movement of the fetus. Sometime in the seventh month, most fetuses reach the point of *viability*—the time when it could survive if it were born. At this point, however, if the fetus were to survive outside the mother, it would almost certainly do so only with medical intervention and care. Birth in the seventh month

Child psychologists study the ways in which children grow and develop. They look for common patterns that apply to all children and also for ways in which children differ from one another.

often leads to difficulties later on. After nearly 270 days, the fetus is ready to enter the world as a *newborn*.

In a vast majority of cases, the growth and development of the human organism from conception through birth progresses smoothly, according to the blueprint laid down in the genes. However, in the prenatal period, the human organism is not immune to influences from the environment. Most external influences on prenatal development have negative consequences.

Never meant to be taken literally, the old expression "You are what you eat" does have some truth to it. By the same token, before we are born, we are what our mothers eat. Maternal malnutrition leads to an increase in miscarriages, stillbirths, and premature births. Newborns with low birth weight (four pounds or less) who do survive have a significantly greater risk of cognitive deficits, even as they approach adolescence. What works best is a balanced, sensible diet.

There is no doubt that cigarette smoking has harmful effects on the smoker. A mother's smoking during pregnancy is harmful to the developing fetus as well, associated with low birth weight and premature birth. Infants born to smokers have a higher risk of hearing defects. Children whose mothers smoked at least a pack of cigarettes a day during pregnancy have a 75 percent increase in the risk for mental retardation, even when other risk factors (e.g., the mother's age, education, and alcohol use) are controlled. As they get older, the children of mothers who smoked during pregnancy have higher rates of behavioral problems such as aggression and hyperactivity (Mick et al., 2002). So the bad news is that smoking during pregnancy relates to a wide range of problems. And yet many expectant mothers continue to smoke. There is some good news, however. If a mother stops smoking early in pregnancy, at least some of the negative effects of smoking can be avoided.

Alcohol is a drug that can be extremely injurious to unborn children. Alcohol is quickly and directly passed from the mother to the fetus. Alcohol then collects in organs that have a high water content, most ominously in the gray matter of the

Protecting the unborn is often just a matter of common sense and maintaining a healthy lifestyle. Exercising may not be as vigorous, but stretching and walking can be very helpful.

brain. To make things worse, the fetus eliminates alcohol at half the rate of the mother. The bottom line is that alcohol gets into the fetus easily and stays in for a long time.

Heavy drinking (three drinks or more per day) significantly increases the chance of having smaller babies with retarded physical growth, poor muscle tone, poor coordination, intellectual retardation, and other problems, collectively referred to as *fetal alcohol syndrome* (FAS). Children whose mothers drank even small amounts of alcohol during pregnancy are at an increased risk for behavior problems later in life (Sood et al., 2001). Such children are significantly more likely to be diagnosed with attention-deficit hyperactivity disorder (Mick et al., 2002) and are at a greater risk of having alcohol-related problems, even at the age of 21 (Baer et al., 2003). There are racial/ethnic differences in the rates of alcohol-related birth complications. African-American mothers who drink have a far higher rate of alcohol-related fetal deaths than do Caucasian mothers who drink.

Mothers who use or abuse psychoactive drugs such as heroin, cocaine, or crack cocaine during pregnancy may cause considerable complications for their unborn children. For example, 70 percent of newborns of mothers who used heroin during pregnancy showed symptoms of drug withdrawal (e.g., tremors, irritability, hyperactivity, and respiratory problems) after birth. (Weintraub et al., 1998). These newborns are also more likely than normal newborns to have a low birth weight and retarded fetal growth. Even aspirin has become suspect as a cause of prenatal complications. There also is an association between caffeine and the risk of miscarriage. Women who consume an amount of caffeine equivalent to five or more cups of coffee per day nearly doubled the rate of miscarriage.

Alongside all of this should be a word of caution against over-reactions. Yes, taking a potentially harmful substance such as alcohol during pregnancy does raise the likelihood of birth defects and mental retardation. But there are a few things to bear in mind. First, some mothers and fetuses are simply more resilient than others. Second, the physical health of the mother is important. Harmful substances are less harmful when the mother is otherwise healthy. Third, exposure to multiple harmful substances is more damaging than exposure to one. In other words, just because a mother is exposed to a harmful substance does not guarantee that birth defects or mental retardation will result. The best advice is to avoid as many harmful substances as possible, get good prenatal care, eat a healthy diet, and follow a doctor's advice.

 STUDY CHECK

In general terms, describe the major events of prenatal development.

What are some possible consequences of a pregnant mother's behavior?

CYBER PSYCH

(a) A website with the address http://www.child developmentinfo.com certainly sounds relevant, doesn't it? And this one is.
(b) A general site crammed with useful information is http://www.babycenter.com.
(c) The website at http://www.srcd.org is from the Society for Research in Child Development and provides many useful links—particularly to their publications.

Cognitive Development

Cognitive development refers to age-related changes in learning, memory, perception, attention, thinking, and problem-solving. From the moment a person is born, several changes are taking place in the basic psychological processes underlying cognition.

cognitive development age-related changes in learning, memory, perception, attention, thinking, and problem-solving

Jean Piaget proposed a comprehensive theory that describes the course of cognitive development from birth through adolescence. In 1919 he left his native Switzerland and went to France. There, although he was not trained as a psychologist, Piaget worked with Alfred Binet to help develop the first IQ test and became fascinated with the *incorrect* answers children gave to items on the test. He noticed that children of about the same age gave very similar incorrect answers. His observations eventually led Piaget to conclude that cognitive development was represented by qualitative changes in the ways that children think.

Piaget claimed that intelligence has two aspects: structure (what is known) and function (how one comes to know it). Structures of cognitive knowledge are **schemas**—mental representations that children construct in order to make sense of the world in which they live. Functions are the mechanisms that help children understand and adapt to their environments. They are the processes by which the child comes to discover the objects and events of his or her world and to create new or different schemas. One major cognitive function for Piaget is **adaptation**—developing

schemas mental representations that children construct in order to make sense of the world in which they live

adaptation the development of appropriate schemas so that one can manage the demands of the environment

Piaget's sensorimotor stage of cognitive development lasts from birth to age 2. In this stage children assimilate and accommodate information about their environments by sensing—tasting, touching, smelling, seeing, and hearing—and by actively interacting with their worlds.

the appropriate schemas so that one can manage the demands of the environment. How does a child get along in the world? By using the appropriate schemas. Where do these schemas come from? Adaptation.

Piaget's theory is a stage theory, maintaining that a child passes through four qualitatively different stages of cognitive development. A child moves through these stages in this order and with no turning back. Piaget further argued that these stages were universal across cultures. All children pass through these stages, with each stage building on the one before. Although Piaget allowed for no variation in the order of cognitive development, he did observe that there certainly were large individual differences in how rapidly children moved from one stage to the next. Let's take a brief look at Piaget's stages of cognitive development.

sensorimotor stage (birth to two years), Piaget's stage in which children learn about the world by sensing (sensori-) and by doing (motor)

In the **sensorimotor stage** (birth to two years), children learn about the world by sensing (sensori-) and by doing (motor). A child may come to appreciate, for example, that a quick pull on a dog's tail (a motor activity) reliably produces a loud yelp (a sensory experience), perhaps followed, in turn, by parental attention. One of the most useful schemas to develop in the sensorimotor stage is that of causality. Infants gradually come to realize that events may have knowable causes and that some behaviors cause predictable reactions. Pushing a bowl of oatmeal off the high chair causes a mess and gets Mommy's attention: if A, then B—a very practical insight.

An important discovery that occurs near the end of this developmental stage is that objects may exist even when they are not immediately in view. Early in this stage, an object that is out of sight is more than out of mind. The object ceases to exist. By the end of the sensorimotor period, children have learned that objects can still exist even if they are not physically present and that their reappearance can be anticipated. Another useful skill acquired in the sensorimotor period is imitation. If it is within its range of abilities, a baby will imitate almost any behavior it sees. A cognitive strategy has developed, one that will be used for a lifetime: trying to imitate the behaviors of a model.

Throughout most of the **preoperational stage** (two to seven years), a child's thinking is self-centered (technically, *egocentric*. According to Piaget, the child has difficulty understanding life from someone else's perspective. In this usage, egocentrism was never meant to imply a selfish, emotional sort of reaction. It simply refers to a limitation on children's thinking when they are in the early years of preoperational thought. Imagine a 4-year-old child seated at a table upon which is placed a large paper maché mountain. Clearly in the child's view are several small plastic sheep "grazing" on the mountainside. At the other end of the table sits another child looking at the same mountain, but on this side there are no sheep. This situation creates great difficulties for the two children because each assumes that the other has exactly the same view of the same object, either with or without sheep.

In the preoperational stage, children begin to develop symbols, usually in the form of words, to represent concepts. At this stage, children do not yet know how to manipulate symbols in a consistent, rule-governed way. It's not until the end of this period that they can play word games or understand why riddles about rabbits throwing clocks out of windows in order to "see time fly" are funny. It is similarly true that children at this stage have great difficulty with many "abstract" concepts, such as religious beliefs. On the other hand, they seem quite capable of playing "make believe," pretending to be mommies and daddies, for instance.

Children in the **concrete operations stage** (seven to 11 years) begin to form many new concepts and show that they can manipulate those concepts. For example, they can organize objects into categories of things: balls over here, blocks over there, plastic soldiers in a pile by the door, and so on. Each of these items is recognized as a toy, ultimately to be put away in the toy box and not in the closet, which is where clothes are supposed to go. It is in this period that rule-governed behavior begins. The concrete, observable objects of the child's world can be classified, ranked, ordered, or separated into more than one category, according to rules.

As its name suggests, in the concrete operations stage, children begin to use and manipulate (operate on) concepts and ideas. But their manipulations are still very concrete—tied to real objects in the here and now. An 8-year-old can be expected to find her way to and from school, even if she throws in a side trip along the way. What she will have difficulty doing is telling you with any precision just how she gets from one place to another. Drawing a sensible map is difficult for her. If she stands on the corner of Maple Street and Sixth Avenue, she knows where to go next to get home. Dealing with the concrete reality, here and now, is easy. Dealing with such knowledge in abstract terms is tough.

The last of Piaget's stages is **formal operations** (12 and older) and involves the logical manipulation of abstract, symbolic concepts. The key to this stage, usually begun in adolescence, is abstract, symbolic reasoning. By the age of 12, most children can develop and mentally test hypotheses—they can work through problems mentally.

In the stage of formal operations, youngsters can reason through hypothetical problems: "What if you were the only person in the world who liked rock music?" "If nobody had to go to school, what would happen?" Now they are able to deal with questions that are literally contrary to fact: "What if John F. Kennedy or Ronald Reagan were still president of the United States?" The stages of Piaget's theory and the cognitive milestones associated with each are summarized in Figure 2.1.

There can be no doubting the significance of Piaget's influence. His observations and insights about intellectual development spanned decades. Considerable

preoperational stage (two to seven years), Piaget's stage in which a child's thinking is self-centered

concrete operations stage (seven to 11 years) Piaget's stage in which children begin to form many new concepts and show that they can manipulate those concepts

formal operations stage (12 and older) Piaget's stage that involves the logical manipulation of abstract, symbolic concepts

FIGURE 2.1

Piaget's Stages of
Cognitive Development

1. **Sensorimotor stage (ages birth to two years)**
   "Knows" through active interaction with environment
   Becomes aware of cause-effect relationships
   Learns that objects exist even when not in view
   Crudely imitates the actions of others

2. **Preoperational stage (ages two to six years)**
   Begins by being very egocentric
   Language and mental representations develop
   Objects are classified on just one characteristic at a time

3. **Concrete operations stage (ages seven to 12 years)**
   Develops conservation of volume, length, mass, etc.
   Organizes objects into ordered categories
   Understands relational terms (e.g., bigger than, above)
   Begins using simple logic

4. **Formal operations stage (ages over 12)**
   Thinking becomes abstract and symbolic
   Reasoning skills develop
   A sense of hypothetical concepts develops

research has supported many of these insights. Finding evidence of Piaget's stages is one of the success stories of cross-cultural research. That evidence tells us that the stages just reviewed can be found in children around the world. As Piaget predicted, there will be some individual differences, of course.

There are two major criticisms of Piaget's theory: First, the borderlines between his proposed stages are much less clear-cut than his theory suggests, and, secondly, Piaget underestimated the cognitive talents of preschool children. As one example, the egocentrism said to characterize the child in the preoperational stage may not be as flagrant as Piaget believed. In one study (Lempers et al., 1977), children were shown a picture pasted inside a box. They were asked to show the picture to someone else. In showing the picture, they turned it so that it would be right side up to the viewer. Every child over two years old indicated such an appreciation of someone else's point of view. More than that, more recent research makes it clear that young children (18 months old) readily ascribe goals and intentions to the action of others. That is, preschoolers can observe someone else doing something and appreciate what it is they are trying to do.

It may be the case that some of Piaget's observations and assumptions have come under attack. This is to be expected in science, particularly for so grand a theory. Nonetheless, Piaget made some important contributions. He focused attention on the social and emotional development of children and had considerable influence on the American educational system (Shaffer, 1999). He showed that children are not just passive receptacles during the development process but rather are active participants in their own cognitive development. One of the most important contributions of Jean Piaget is that he developed a theory of cognitive development in children that was so detailed, so thought-provoking, that it will continue to challenge researchers for years to come.

✓ **STUDY CHECK**

Describe the basic features of Piaget's theory of cognitive development.

What are the approximate ages of, and characteristics of, Piaget's four stages of cognitive development?

CYBER PSYCH

http://www.piaget.org is the website for "The Jean Piaget Society," and it may be excused for being a little less than totally objective about Piaget. It is difficult to imagine what you might want to learn about Piaget that you could not find here.

Moral Development

How children learn to reason and make judgments about what is right and wrong is an aspect of cognitive development that has received considerable attention in psychology. Piaget included the study of moral development in his theory, saying that morality is related to cognitive awareness and that children are unable to make moral judgments until they are at least three or four years old (Piaget, 1932/1948). Lawrence Kohlberg (1963, 1985) has offered a major theory of moral development. Like Piaget's approach, Kohlberg's is a theory of stages—of moving from one stage to another in an orderly fashion. Kohlberg's original data came from young boys who responded to questions about stories involving a moral dilemma. A commonly cited example concerns whether a man should steal a drug in order to save his wife's life after the pharmacist who invented the drug refuses to sell it to him. Should the man steal the drug? Why or why not?

On the basis of responses to such dilemmas, Kohlberg proposed three levels of moral development, with two stages (or "orientations") at each level. The result is the six stages summarized in Figure 2.2. For example, a child at the level of **pre-conventional morality** would focus on the rewards and punishments that come from breaking a rule. Thus, he might reason that the man should not steal the drug because "he'll get caught and be put in jail" or that he should steal the drug because "the drug didn't cost all that much." A child who says the man should steal the drug because "it will make his wife happy, and most people would do it anyway," or that he shouldn't steal the drug because "you always have to follow rules, even if the situation is serious" is reflecting a type of reasoning at the second level. This is the level of **conventional morality,** where judgments are based on an accepted social convention—social approval and disapproval matter as much as or more than anything else.

The argument that he should steal the drug because "human life is more important than a law," or that "he shouldn't steal the drug for a basically selfish reason, which in the long run would promote more stealing in the society in general" is an example of moral reasoning at the highest level. This **postconventional morality** reflects complex, internalized standards—what matters are not the choices the child makes, but the reasoning behind those choices.

The evidence suggests that the basic thrust of Kohlberg's theory has merit (Rest, 1983). It also has cross-cultural application. To varying degrees, Kohlberg's descriptions are valid for several cultures, including Israel, India, Turkey, and Nigeria (Snarey, 1987). Remember: What matters is not the choice that is made, but how the choice is made. For example, the level of conventional morality depends

preconventional morality
Kohlberg's stage of moral reasoning in which one focuses on the rewards and punishments that come from breaking a rule

conventional morality
Kohlberg's stage of moral reasoning in which judgments are based on an accepted social convention—social approval and disapproval matter as much as or more than anything else

postconventional morality
Kohlberg's stage of moral reasoning that reflects complex, internalized standards — what matters are not the choices made, but the reasoning behind those choices

It's a very hot day. The signs say "No Trespassing." No one else is in the fountain. But the fountain looks so inviting. Sould I? Should I not? A minor moral conflict, perhaps, but not unlike those used by Kohlberg.

largely on accepted social convention, and surely there are differences from culture to culture in what is "accepted as social convention."

Problems with the theory also exist. For one thing, there may be a "disconnect" between how people reason, how they feel about a given circumstance, and how they actually behave (Shaffer, 2000). Just because someone "knows what's right" and "feels what's right" does not mean that person will actually *do* what is right. Among other things, the nature of the situation (particularly the social pressures of that situation) may overpower internal moral cognitions (Thoma & Rest, 1999). And, "although people occasionally make moral judgments in their everyday lives to reveal solutions to moral dilemmas, as Kohlberg's model assumes, they more often make moral decisions that advance their adaptive interests" (Krebs, 2000, p. 132).

It also turns out that few people (including adults) operate at the higher stages of moral reasoning described by the theory. This is particularly true in cultures that emphasize communal or group membership more than individuality, such as the Israeli kibbutz or tribal groups in New Guinea.

This brings us to a key concept in cross-cultural psychology: the dimension of **individualism–collectivism** (e.g., Triandis, 1990, 1993). People in some cultures are socialized from early childhood to take others (the family, the tribe, the neighborhood, the society) into account when setting any goals or making decisions. Such a tendency toward collectivism is more likely to be found in Asia, Africa, and South America. People in many other cultures are socialized to think more about themselves and their own individual behaviors, a sort of "pull yourself up by your own boot straps; make it on your own; you get what you deserve" mentality. This

individualism-collectivism a way of classifying cultural orientation where the focus is either on the person (individualism) or the group or community (collectivism)

Level 1

1. Obedience and punishment orientation

Preconventional morality

Rules are obeyed simply to avoid punishment: "If I take the cookies, I'll get spanked."

2. Naive egotism and instrumental orientation

Rules are obeyed simply to earn rewards: "If I wash my hands, will you let me have two desserts?"

Level 2

3. Good boy/girl orientation

Conventional (conforming) morality

Rules are conformed to in order to avoid disapproval and gain approval: "I'm a good boy 'cause I cleaned my room, aren't I?"

4. Authority-maintaining orientation

Social conventions blindly accepted to avoid criticism from those in authority: "You shouldn't steal because it's against the law, and you'll go to jail if the police catch you."

Level 3

5. Contractual-legalistic orientation

Postconventional morality

Morality is based on agreement with others to serve the common good and protect the rights of individuals: "I don't like stopping at stop signs, but if we didn't all obey traffic signals, it would be difficult to get anywhere."

6. Universal ethical principle orientation

Morality is a reflection of internalized standards: "I don't care what anybody says—what's right is right."

tendency toward individualism is common in North America and Western Europe. Please keep in mind that we're talking about a dimension of comparison here; even within the same culture and the same community, individualism and collectivism exist to varying degrees. This discussion relates to Kohlberg's theory because most measures of moral reasoning put a high value on the sort of thinking found in individualistic (largely Western) cultures and devalue the sorts of thinking typical of collective cultures. This does not mean that Kohlberg was wrong, of course. It just means that what is true for one culture may not be for another, and neither is necessarily any "better" or more moral.

A similar argument has been raised about Kohlberg's theory as it applies to females. Remember: All of Kohlberg's original data did come from the responses of young boys. Later, when girls were tested, some studies seemed to suggest that the girls were less advanced in moral development than were boys. Carol Gilligan (1982) argues that comparing the moral reasoning of females and males is problematic because the moral reasoning of females is simply different from the moral reasoning of males. Males (at least in Western cultures) are concerned with rules, justice, and an individual's rights. As a result, they approach moral dilemmas differently than do females, who characteristically are more concerned with caring, personal responsibility, and interpersonal relationships. The issue is not a judgmental one in the sense of trying to determine if men or women are more or less moral in their thinking. The question is whether women and men develop different styles of moral reasoning. So far, most studies have shown that any differences between men and women in resolving moral conflicts are small (Darley & Schultz, 1990;

Judgments concerning what constitutes moral reasoning need to take into account gender and cultural differences. Members of some cultures in Japan, for instance, or other Asian or South American countries, place a strong emphasis on collectivism, on adherence to the values and goals of the group, the family, the tribe, or the society.

Gilligan, 1993) and that males and females both consider justice and concern for others when reasoning about moral issues.

✓ STUDY CHECK

Summarize Kohlberg's approach to the development of moral reasoning.

What cultural and gender issues may be related to moral reasoning?

CYBER PSYCH

(a) A simple summary of Kohlberg's theory can be found at the unlikely site: http://www.awa.com/w2/erotic_computing/kohlberg.stages.html.

(b) Notes attributed to Kohlberg about his stages of moral development are at http://www.xenodochy.org/ex/lists/moraldev.html.

(c) The relationship between Kohlberg's stages of morality and theology can be found at http://www.aggelia.com/htdocs/kohlberg.shtml.

Developing Social Attachments

attachment a strong and reciprocal emotional relationship between a child and mother or primary caregiver

To a large degree, we adapt and thrive in this world to the extent that we can profit from interpersonal relationships. The roots of social development can be found in early infancy—in the formation of attachment. **Attachment** is a strong and reciprocal emotional relationship between a child and mother or primary caregiver. Attachment has survival value, "increasing the chances of an infant being protected by those to whom he or she keeps proximity" (Ainsworth, 1989). A well-formed attachment provides a child with freedom to explore the environment, curiosity, adaptive problem-solving, and competence when interacting with peers.

Forming an attachment between infant and mother (for example) involves regular interaction and active give-and-take between the two. Strong attachments are most likely to be formed if the parent is optimally sensitive and responsive to the needs of the child. Sensitivity refers to the parent's ability to correctly read the signals coming from an infant (for example, correctly identifying when the infant is hungry—as opposed to sleepy—by the nature of the infant's crying pattern). Responsiveness refers to how the parent responds to the child's signals—for example, picking up the infant when he or she cries, changing the diaper as soon as it is soiled, feeding on a regular basis, and so on. Interestingly, there is an optimal level of sensitivity and responsiveness that relates to positive, secure attachments. Too much or too little can result in negative, insecure attachment.

Simply spending time with an infant is seldom adequate to produce successful attachment. Spontaneous hugging, smiling, eye contact, and vocalizing promote attachment. It is fostered by qualities such as warmth and gentleness. When the process is successful, we say that the child is "securely attached." Forming an attachment is a two-way street. Attachment will be most secure when the baby reciprocates by smiling, cooing, and clinging to mother when attended to. About 65 percent of American children become securely attached by the age of one year—a percentage close to that found in seven other countries (van Ijzendoorn & Kroonenberg, 1988).

Fathers can make significant contributions to the attachment of their children.

Are there long-term benefits of becoming securely attached? Yes. Secure at-tachment is related to: a) sociability (less fear of strangers, better relationships with peers, more popularity, and more friends), b) higher self-esteem, c) better relation-ships with siblings, d) fewer tantrums; less aggressive behaviors, e) less concern by teachers about controlling behaviors in the classroom, f) more empathy and concern for the feelings of others, g) fewer behavioral problems at later ages, and h) better attention spans (from Bee, 1992). Securely attached children also show greater per-sistence at problem-solving and are less likely to seek help from adults when disap-pointed or injured. It is also becoming increasingly clear that attachment patterns set in early childhood retain their influences indefinitely (Fraley, 2002).

Let us be clear on one point: Infants can and do form attachments with per-sons other than their mothers. Father-child attachments are quite common and are beneficial for the long-term development of the child (Grych & Clark, 1999). One researcher found that she could predict the extent to which a child showed signs of attachment to its father simply by knowing how often Dad changed the baby's diaper (Ross et al., 1975). There is no evidence that fathers are less sensitive to the needs of their children than are mothers, although they may be a little more physical and a little less verbal in their interactions (Parke & Tinsley, 1987).

Finally, we need to consider attachment formation for those children who spend time—sometimes a lot of time—in daycare facilities. In the United States, more than half the mothers of children younger than three are employed, and the care of those children is taken over, at least in part, by others. There is evidence that children placed in high-quality daycare benefit cognitively and socially (Burchi-nal et al., 2000; NICHD, 2002). How do these children fare with respect to at-tachment? It depends to a large extent on the quality of the care the children are given—no matter where they get it. Children who receive warm, supportive, at-tentive care; adequate stimulation; and opportunities for exploration demonstrate secure attachment. The impact of daycare depends on the likelihood that the child would have received good, warm, supportive, loving care at home. Additionally, the quality of daycare and quality of maternal care combine to affect attachment security. Children who experience both low-quality daycare *and* insensitive or un-responsive parenting show the poorest attachment security.

The benefits or harm of non-parental childcare may also depend on the age of the child. "There is little dispute about the conclusion that children who enter day care at 18 months, two years, or later show no consistent loss of security of attach-ment to their parents" (Bee, 1992, p. 510). In fact, the debate centers on children less than one year old, and there is some evidence that secure attachment is less likely among those children who are not cared for at home during their first year. Other studies suggest that early infant daycare has little or no effect on a child's later social and emotional development. In a study done in France, there was no differ-ence in the amount of aggression and other behavior problems between children three to four years old who had attended daycare during the first three years of life and those who had not (Balleyguier & Meihuish, 1996). Early daycare has also been found not to affect mother–infant interactions or cognitive outcomes for the child. Thus, it appears that there is no consistent relationship between early infant daycare and later social and emotional development.

It may tentatively be concluded that forming secure attachments is important for the later development of the child. There are long-term benefits (ranging from improved emotional stability to improved problem–solving skills) to be derived

Research indicates that daycare may enhance or diminish a child's degree of attachment, depending on the quality of the care received.

from the development of strong attachments formed early in childhood. Further, attachments formed with the father or other caregivers seem as useful for long-term development as do attachments to the mother.

✓ STUDY CHECK

In child development, what is "attachment," and how is it fostered?

How does daycare outside the home impact a child's attachment?

CYBER PSYCH

(a) A comprehensive website on attachment can be found at the website http://www.attachmentparenting.org.

(b) Another good source on this issue is http://www.kidsource.com/kidsource/content/infant_care.html.

Chapter Summary

In general terms, describe the major events in prenatal development.

Prenatal development begins at conception and ends (about 270 days later) at birth. The period between two and eight weeks after conception is the *embryonic stage,* during which development is rapid and the organs of the body are laid in place. From two months after conception until birth is the *stage of the fetus,* during which weight gain is rapid. Survival is possible if the fetus is born after the seventh month, the point of *viability.*

What are some possible consequences of a pregnant mother's behavior?

To avoid the negative consequences of low birth weight, miscarriage, and retarded mental and physical development, it is important that a pregnant woman eat a balanced, nutritious diet, avoid smoking, alcohol, and drugs—even being careful with aspirin and caffeine.

Describe the basic features of Piaget's theory of cognitive development.

Piaget theorized that a child's mental development involves the formation of cognitive structures *(schemas)* of what is known and functions (how one comes to know it). An important cognitive function is *adaptation,* developing schemas to help meet the demands of the environment. Piaget proposed that development takes place in four successive stages and that these stages are universal.

What are the appropriate ages of, and characteristics of, Piaget's four stages of cognitive development?

During the *sensorimotor stage* (birth–2 years) a baby develops schemas through an interaction with the environment by sensing and doing. The baby begins to appreciate cause-and-effect relationships, imitates the actions of others, and by the end of the period, develops a sense of object permanence. Egocentrism is found in the *preoperational stage* (2–7). The child appears unable to view the world from anyone else's perspective. In addition, children begin to develop and use symbols in the form of words to represent concepts. In the concrete operations stage (7–11), a child organizes concepts into categories, begins to use simple logic and understand relational terms. The essence of the *formal operations stage* (12–older) is the ability to think, reason, and solve problems symbolically or in an abstract rather than a concrete, tangible form.

Summarize Kohlberg's approach to the development of moral reasoning.

Kohlberg claims that moral reasoning develops through three levels of two stages each. First, a person decides between right and wrong on the basis of avoiding punishment and gaining rewards *(preconventional morality),* then by conforming to authority or accepting social convention *(conventional morality),* and finally on the basis of one's understanding of the common good, individual rights, and internalized standards *(postconventional morality)*.

What cultural and gender issues may be related to moral reasoning?

Although much of the theory has been supported, there is evidence that many individuals never reach the higher levels of moral reasoning. Kohlberg's notion of morality seems most appropriate for children in *individualistic cultures,* where people tend to think more of themselves and their own behaviors, as opposed to *collectivist* cultures, where the focus is more on the group, the family, and so on. Also, there may be deficiencies in applying the theory equally to both genders or to all cultures, wherein what is "moral" or "right" may vary. There is some evidence that women are more concerned with caring and relationships, while men focus more on rules, justice, and individual rights. It also seems to be the case that how a child or adult reasons about moral issues need not be reflected in actual behaviors.

In child development, what is "attachment," and how is it formed?

Attachment is a strong emotional relationship formed early in childhood between the child and primary caregiver(s). It has survival value in an evolutionary sense, keeping the child in proximity to those who can best care for him or her. Secure attachment in childhood has been associated with improved cognitive performance and self-esteem later in life. A secure attachment is most likely to occur if the parents (or other caregivers) are optimally sensitive and responsive to the infant and develop a reciprocal pattern of behavior with the infant. Fathers as well as mothers can demonstrate appropriate attachment-related behaviors.

How does daycare outside the home impact a child's attachment?

To date, most evidence is that daycare for children (particularly for those older than two) does not have negative consequences (depending mostly on the quality of care). At the very least, quality daycare has consequences for attachment that are not significantly better or worse than for children who do not use daycare.

Student Study Guide

STUDY TIP #2 "How Much Should I Study?"

One of the main reasons some students do not do as well in their college courses as they would like is that they simply do not have—or do not make—enough time for studying. If you were to ask me how much time you should spend studying psychology, I'd likely say something like, "You should be studying every waking minute of every day." As it happens, of course, I know better. I know you have other classes that require your time and a multitude of commitments pulling at you for your attention. Nonetheless, if you are going to succeed at this business of being a college student, it is important to understand that being successful is going to be time-consuming. Almost certainly, the amount of time you spent studying in high school will be inadequate now that you are in college.

My students chuckle—or laugh out loud—when I tell them that the standard rule of thumb regarding study time is to schedule three hours outside of class for every hour spent in class. Note what that means: If yours is a 5-credit-hour psychology class, you should set aside **15 hours a week** to study psychology! That's right: 15 hours studying psychology in addition to the time you spend in class.

This rule of thumb is valid at the beginning of the quarter. A few weeks' experience may suggest that more or less time will be needed depending on the difficulty of the classes you are taking. Some classes may require even more time, while a few may take less. The implications here are significant. If you are taking a full-time load, or nearly so, let's say 12-15 credit hours, I'm suggesting that as an average student, you will need 36 to 45 hours *each week* for study time. Yes. That's like a full-time job, and thinking about your college experience as a full-time job is a reasonable thing to do. You will be in class or studying from 48 to 60 hours each week. Additionally, you will need time for sleeping, relationships, eating, dressing, driving, a part-time job, perhaps, and—I would hope—some fun! There are only 168 hours in each week. Time management is an important issue for college students.

KEY TERMS AND CONCEPTS

prenatal period _____

_____

cognitive development_____

_____

adaptation _____

_____

sensorimotor stage _____

preoperational stage _____

_____

concrete operations stage _____

_____

formal operations stage_____

_____

preconventional morality_____

_____

conventional morality _____

_____

postconventional morality_____

_____

attachment _____

_____

Practice Test Questions – Chapter Two

MULTIPLE CHOICE

1. Which of these developmental periods lasts the longest?

    _____ a. embryonic period   _____ c. prenatal period

    _____ b. period of conception   _____ d. fetal period

2. At which stage, or at what time, is the developing human at greatest risk of a physical defect?

    _____ a. as a zygote   _____ c. as a growing fetus

    _____ b. during the embryonic stage _____ d. during the birth process

3. Which of these typically has the most adverse effect on the developing human organism?

    _____ a. the mother's inability to gain weight during pregnancy

    _____ b. inadequate calcium intake during pregnancy

    _____ c. having to take antibiotics, such as penicillin, during pregnancy

    _____ d. alcohol use or abuse during pregnancy

4. On what basis were Piaget's stages of development determined?

_____ a. the actual, chronological age of the child

_____ b. whether the child uses adaptation or not

_____ c. the extent to which the child is egocentric or social

_____ d. how schemas are formed or modified with experience

5. During which of Piaget's stages of cognitive development does the child demonstrate that he or she can manipulate abstract concepts?

_____ a. sensorimotor

_____ b. preoperational

_____ c. concrete operations

_____ d. formal operations

6. Of the several criticisms of Piaget's theory of development, which is LEAST reasonable?

_____ a. It lacks attention to cognitive processing.

_____ b. The divisions between stages are not as clear as Piaget asserted.

_____ c. Piaget underestimated the abilities of preschool children.

_____ d. It lacks a significant concern for cross-cultural differences.

7. Melanie is 9 years old. She can easily get to school and back, a distance of six city blocks. On the other hand, she has great difficulty telling you how she manages the trip to school and back each day. Melanie is in Piaget's ____ stage of cognitive development.

_____ a. sensorimotor   _____ c. concrete operations

_____ b. preoperational   _____ d. formal operations

8. Kohlberg's theory of development focuses mainly on the development of

_____ a. cognitive representations, called schemas.

_____ b. strategies that children use to learn.

_____ c. morality and a sense of right and wrong.

_____ d. how children and adolescents interact with each other.

9. If secure attachment is going to occur, it will occur for most children (nearly two-thirds) when they are

_____ a. born.   _____ c. five years old.

_____ b. one year old.   _____ d. about to become teenagers.

TRUE/FALSE

1. _____ True _____ False Fetal alcohol syndrome includes the likelihood of intellectual retardation.

2. _____ True _____ False Because of its beneficial effects on cardiovascular functioning, pregnant women are now being advised to drink at least one, but no more than three glasses of red wine each day.

3. _____ True _____ False In developing his theories of cognitive development, Piaget seems to have underestimated the cognitive skills of very young, preschool children.

4. _____ True _____ False Carol Gilligan has argued that with regard to moral development, there are no sex differences in morality, but that males and females approach moral dilemmas differently.

5. _____ True _____ False Whether a child will become securely attached depends on the behaviors of the child as well as the behaviors of the caregiver.

Adolescence and Adulthood

Preview

A timeline of the development of an individual tells us that the most rapid development and most dramatic changes occur between conception and around 11 years of age. So much happens during this time span—physical growth, the development of memory, language, and social relationships—that it is easy to lose sight of the fact that development is a lifelong process. Although the changes we see in development after childhood are not as rapid or dramatic as those seen during childhood, development progresses until the day we die. This chapter continues the story of human development past childhood, through adolescence, and into early, middle, and late adulthood.

For more than 100 years, psychologists have struggled to determine how best to characterize that period of life called adolescence. We begin our discussion with a look at some of those characterizations. Interestingly, most of the research on the development of adolescents has focused on their troubles, conflicts, and problems. Indeed, there is simply little to say about what we might consider the "normal" development of teenagers. There has been a sort of collective focus that implies that, if we can understand how adolescents adjust (or fail to adjust) to the demands put upon them, we will come to appreciate how it is that most of us manage to get through the period with few lasting negative consequences. We will follow this lead, addressing the issues of physical maturation and identity formation.

We will divide our discussion of adulthood (somewhat artificially) into three sub-stages: early, middle, and late. Although there are no sharp dividing lines, each sub-stage does reflect a rather different set of challenges and adjustments, involving family, career, retirement and—ultimately—one's own mortality.

What it Means to Be an Adolescent

adolescence a period of transition from the dependence of childhood to the independence of adulthood; it begins at puberty (sexual maturity) and lasts through the teen years

Adolescence is a period of transition from the dependence of childhood to the independence of adulthood. It is the period of development that begins at puberty (sexual maturity) and lasts through the teen years—essentially the second decade of life.

Adolescence can be viewed from several different perspectives. As noted in our definition, in biological terms, adolescence begins with puberty—sexual maturity and an ability to reproduce—and concludes with the end of physical growth, which is usually late in the teen years. A psychological perspective emphasizes the development of the cognitions, feelings, and behaviors that characterize adolescence. Such approaches stress the development of problem-solving skills and increased reliance on the use of symbols, logic, and abstract thinking. Psychological perspectives emphasize the importance of identity formation and the appreciation of self and self-worth. A social perspective looks at the role of adolescents in their societies and defines adolescence in terms of being "in between"—not yet an adult, but no longer a child. In this context, adolescence usually lasts from the early teen years through the highest educational level, when a person is thought to enter the adult world.

Actually, whether we accept a biological, psychological, or social perspective, we are usually talking about people who, in our culture, are between the ages of 12 and 20. An intriguing issue in the psychology of adolescence today is how to characterize this stage of development in a general way. Is it a time of personal growth, independence, and positive change? Or is adolescence a period of rebellion, turmoil, and negativism?

The view that adolescence can be best described in terms of turmoil, storm, and stress is actually the older of the two, attributed to G. Stanley Hall (who wrote the first textbook on adolescence in 1904) and to Anna Freud (who applied psychoanalytic theory to adolescents). This position claims that normal adolescence involves many difficulties of adjustment. "To be normal during the adolescent period is by itself abnormal" (Freud, 1958, p. 275). "Adolescents may be expected to be extremely moody and depressed one day and excitedly 'high' the next. Explosive conflict with family, friends, and authorities is thought of as commonplace" (Powers et al., 1989, p. 200). Actually, the teen years often *do* present pressures and conflicts that require difficult choices, and some teenagers react to those pressures in maladaptive ways.

Adolescence requires making adjustments, but those adjustments are usually made in psychologically healthy ways (Steinberg & Morris, 2001). As adolescents struggle for independence and for means of self-expression, some engage in behaviors that may be considered risky or reckless. Such behaviors are often a reflection of the socialization process of the teenagers' culture. Nonetheless, the majority of teenagers weather the challenges of the period without developing significant social, emotional, or behavioral difficulties (Steinberg, 1999).

At least we can describe adolescence as a stage of development that presents the individual with a series of challenges. In the following sections, we'll examine two of the challenges faced by an adolescent: puberty and identity formation.

✓ STUDY CHECK

What are the major—and conflicting—views of adolescence that have been put forward in psychology?

CYBER PSYCH

Here are two rather general articles on the nature of adolescence, both as downloadable pdf files.

(a) http://www.apa.org/pi/pii/develop.pdf is from the American Psychological Association and has many pages of reference citations.

(b http://jea.sagepub.com/cgi/reprint/24/1/45.pdf is "The Scientific Study of Adolescence: A Brief History," first published in the *Journal of Early Adolescence*.

Adolescent Development—Challenges of Puberty

The onset of adolescence is marked by two biological changes. First, there is a marked increase in height and weight, known as a *growth spurt,* and second, there is sexual maturation. The growth spurt of adolescence usually occurs in girls at an earlier age than it does in boys. Girls begin their growth spurt as early as age nine or ten and then slow down at about age 15. Boys generally show increased rates of growth between the ages of 12 and 17. Males usually don't reach adult height until

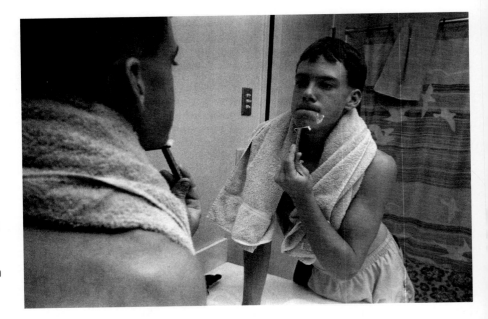

Adolescence begins with puberty, a period during which there are many physical changes for both boys and girls. For boys, the pitch of the voice begins to drop and facial hair begins to appear.

their early twenties; females generally attain maximum height by their late teens (Roche & Davila, 1972; Tanner, 1981).

At least some of the challenge of early adolescence may be a direct result of the growth spurt. It is common to find increases in weight and height occurring so rapidly that they are accompanied by real, physical growing pains, particularly in the arms and legs. The spurt of adolescent growth seldom affects all parts of the body uniformly, especially in boys. Boys around the ages of 13 and 14 often appear incredibly clumsy and awkward as they try to coordinate their large hands and feet with the rest of their bodies. One of the most noticeable areas of growth in boys is that of the larynx and vocal cords. As the vocal cords lengthen, the pitch of the voice lowers. This transition is seldom a smooth one, and a teenage boy may suffer through weeks of a squeaking, cracking change of pitch in his voice.

Puberty occurs when a person becomes physically capable of sexual reproduction. With the onset of puberty, there is a marked increase in levels of sex hormones—androgens in males and estrogens in females. (Everyone has androgens and estrogens. Males simply have more androgens; females have more estrogens.) Boys seldom know when their puberty begins. For some time they have experienced penile erections and nocturnal emissions of seminal fluid. Puberty in males begins with the appearance of live sperm in the semen, and most males have no idea when that happens; that requires a laboratory test. In females, the onset of puberty is quite recognizable. It is indicated by the first menstrual period, called **menarche**.

With puberty, adolescents are biologically ready to reproduce. Dealing with that readiness and making the adjustments that we associate with psychological maturity, however, do not come automatically with sexual maturity. Some boys and girls reach puberty before or after most of their peers and are referred to as early or late bloomers. Reaching puberty well before or after others of the same age may have some psychological effects, although few are long-lasting.

puberty the period that occurs when a person becomes physically capable of sexual reproduction

menarche the first menstrual period

Let's first get an idea of what early and late puberty means. The age range during which the major developments associated with puberty may be expected to occur are between ten and 15 years of age for girls and between 11 and 16 for boys. This age range is quite large and is subject to change. In the United States 150 years ago, the average age of menarche was 16; now it's close to 12. However, the trend of menarche appearing at younger and younger ages is apparently leveling off (Shaffer, 2002). It may be that earlier maturation is related to the quality of family relationships. Families that are characterized by stress, conflict, and a lack of closeness among its members tend to see their children reaching puberty at younger ages (Kim & Smith, 1998).

What are the advantages and disadvantages of early maturation? A girl who enters puberty early will probably be taller, stronger, faster, and more athletic than other girls (and many boys) in her class at school. She is more likely to be approached for dates, have earlier sexual encounters, and marry at a younger age than her peers. She may have self-image and self-esteem problems and be more susceptible to emotional problems, especially if she puts on weight and shows marked breast development (Ge, Conger, & Elder, 1996).

Because of the premium put on physical activity in boys, the early-maturing boy is at a greater advantage than the early-maturing girl. He will have more dating and sexual experiences than his peers, which probably will raise his status among his peers. He'll have a better body image and higher self-esteem. Also, physically mature adolescents are *expected* by parents, teachers, and friends to show higher levels of social and emotional maturity (Jaffe, 1998). This presents the physically mature adolescent with quite a challenge, because physical development usually progresses more quickly than social and emotional development. Indeed, early-maturing boys (often influenced by others who are older than they) are at greater risk for all sorts of problems, including delinquency and drug and alcohol use (Dick et al., 2000; Williams & Dunlap, 1999).

For teens of both sexes, being a late bloomer is more negative in its impact (at the time) than is being an early bloomer. Late-maturing boys may carry a sense of inadequacy and poor self-esteem into adulthood. Late maturity for girls has virtually no long-term negative consequences. Some feel, at least in retrospect, that being a late bloomer was an advantage because it allowed them to develop other, broadening interests, rather than becoming "boy-crazy" like so many of their peers in early adolescence.

✔ STUDY CHECK

What characterizes the onset of puberty?

What are the consequences of reaching puberty before or after one's age-mates?

CYBER PSYCH

(a) http://www.teenpuberty.com is, frankly, a rather strange website, but the links are well done. It seems aimed primarily at a teenage audience.

(b) The American Academy of Pediatrics has an authoritative website that is updated regularly at http://www.aap.org/family/puberty.htm.

(c) The University of Michigan Health Systems maintains a very useful site on early puberty at http://www.med.umich.edu/1libr/yourchild/puberty.htm.

Adolescent Development—Challenges of Identity Formation

Adolescents around the world give the impression of being great experimenters. They experiment with hairstyles, music, religions, drugs, sexual outlets, fad diets, part-time jobs, part-time relationships, and part-time philosophies of life. It often appears that most of a teenager's commitments are made on a part-time basis. Teens are busy trying things out, doing things their own way, off on a grand search for Truth.

This perception of adolescents as experimenters is not without foundation. It is consistent with the view that one of the major tasks of adolescence is the resolution of an **identity crisis**—the struggle to define and integrate the sense of who one is, what one is to do in life, and what one's attitudes, beliefs, and values should be. The concept of identity formation is associated with psychologist Erik Erikson (1963), in whose view the search for identity is a stage of psychosocial development that occurs during the adolescent years. During adolescence we come to grips with questions like "Who am I?" "What am I going to do with my life?" "What is the point of it all?" Needless to say, these are not trivial questions.

For many young people, resolving their identity crisis is a relatively simple and straightforward process. In such cases, the adolescent years bring very little confusion or conflict in terms of attitudes, beliefs, or values. Many teenagers are able and willing to accept the system of values and the sense of self they began to develop in childhood. For many teenagers, however, the conflict of identity formation is quite real. They have a sense of giving up the values of parents and teachers in favor of new ones—their own. Physical growth, physiological changes, increased sexuality, and the perception of societal pressures to decide what they want to be when they "grow up" may lead to what Erikson calls *role confusion,* the state in which wanting to be independent, to be one's own self, does not fit in with the values of the past, of childhood. As a result, the teenager experiments with various possibilities in an attempt to see what works best, often to the obvious dissatisfaction of bewildered parents. It seems that most of the process of forging a new and independent sense of self takes place rather late in adolescence. Most of the conflicts between parents and teenagers over independence occur early in adolescence and then gradually decline (Smetna & Gaines, 1999). Further, there is evidence that black adolescents are more likely to develop a sense of self-esteem and identity adjustment than are white adolescents and that developing a sense of ethnic identity is one of the contributing factors to this observation (Gray-Little & Hafdahl, 2000).

A slightly different perspective on identity formation comes from the work of James Marcia (1980). According to Marcia, identity development begins in infancy but becomes a dominant theme in adolescence. At this point the teenager works to develop a plan for movement into adulthood. Marcia has identified four ways that identity issues can be resolved during adolescence: identity achievement, foreclosure, identity diffusion, and moratorium. *Identity achievers* have reached a decision-making period during which they have settled on a career and ideological path that they have chosen for themselves. A person in *identity foreclosure* is also set on a career and ideological path. However, that path was chosen by someone else—most likely the parents. *Identity diffusers* are individuals who have not yet set a career or ideological path, even if they have gone through a decision-making process. Finally, those in *moratorium* are in a state of struggle over their futures. These individuals can be characterized as being in "crisis."

identity crisis the struggle to define and integrate the sense of who one is, what one is to do in life, and what one's attitudes, beliefs, and values should be

Alan Waterman (1985) looked at identity status across eight cross-cultural studies of individuals of varying ages. Waterman found that identity achievement is most frequently found for college juniors and seniors. Foreclosure and identity diffusion are most common for younger children (sixth to tenth grade). Moratorium was less common for most age groups, except for individuals in their first two years of college where around 30 percent were in moratorium. Finally, once an identity has been formed, it may not be stable. Individuals typically fluctuate among identity statuses (for example, between moratorium and identity achievement).

 STUDY CHECK

What is meant by "identity formation" in adolescence, and what factors influence its development?

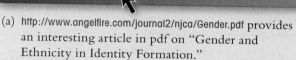 **CYBER PSYCH**

(a) http://www.angelfire.com/journal2/njca/Gender.pdf provides an interesting article in pdf on "Gender and Ethnicity in Identity Formation."
(b) A very intriguing—and huge—website (subtitled "a continuing study of American youth") can be found at http://monitoringthefuture.org.

Development in Early Adulthood

The changes that occur during our adult years may not seem as striking or dramatic as those of our childhood and adolescence, but they are no less real. Many adjustments that we make as adults go unnoticed as we accommodate physical changes and psychological pressures. As an adult, one's health may become a concern for the first time. Psychological adjustments need to be made to marriage, parenthood, career, retirement, the death of friends and family, and, ultimately, one's own death.

Following the lead of Erikson (1968) and Levinson (1986), we will consider adulthood in terms of three overlapping periods, or seasons: early adulthood (roughly ages 18 to 45), middle adulthood (ages 45 to 65), and late adulthood (over age 65). Presenting adult development in this way can be misleading, so we'll have to be careful. Although there is some support for developmental stages in adulthood, these stages may be better defined by the individual adult than by the developmental psychologist.

If anything marks the transition from adolescence to adulthood, it is choice and commitments made independently. The sense of identity formed in adolescence now needs to be put into action. In fact, the achievement of a sense of self by early adulthood is a good predictor of the success of intimate relationships later in adulthood. With adult status, there are new and often difficult choices to be made. Advice may be sought from elders, parents, teachers, or friends, but as adults, individuals will make their own choices. Should I get married? Which job/career should I pursue? Do I need more education? What sort? Where? Should we have children? How many? Most of these issues are first addressed in adolescence, during identity formation. But for the adult, these questions are no longer abstract. They now are real questions that demand a response.

Levinson calls early adulthood the "era of greatest energy and abundance and of greatest contradiction and stress" (1986, p. 5). In terms of our physical development, we are at something of a peak during our twenties and thirties, and we are apparently willing to work hard to maintain that physical condition. On the one hand, young adulthood is a season for finding our niche, for working through aspirations of our youth, for raising a family. On the other hand, it is a period of stress, finding the "right" job, taking on parenthood, and maintaining a balance among self, family, job, and society at large. Let's take a look at two important decision-making tasks of young adulthood: the choice of mate and family and the choice of job or career.

MARRIAGE AND FAMILY

Erikson suggests that early adulthood revolves around the choice of intimacy or isolation. Failure to establish close, loving, intimate relationships may result in loneliness and long periods of social isolation. Marriage is not the only source of interpersonal intimacy, to be sure, but it is the first choice of most Americans. More young adults than ever before are postponing marriage plans, but 85 percent of us eventually marry (at least once).

Young adults may value marriage, but the choice of whom to marry is of no small consequence. Psychologists have learned over the past 40 years that mate selection is a complex process. At least three factors influence the choice of a marriage partner. The first deals with *availability*. Before we can develop an intimate relationship with someone, we need the opportunity to establish the relationship in the first place. The second factor is *eligibility*. Here, matters of age, religion, race, politics, and background come into play. Once a partner is found who is avail-

It is usually in early adulthood that couples make choices about a mate, marriage, and beginning a family.

FIGURE 3.1

Characteristics Sought in Mates

Rank (most important)	Male choices	Female choices
1	Kindness and understanding	Kindness and understanding
2	Intelligence	Intelligence
3	Physical attractiveness	Exciting personality
4	Exciting personality	Good health
5	Good health	Adaptability
6	Adaptability	Physical attractiveness
7	Creativity	Creativity
8	Desire for children	Good earning capacity
9	College graduate	College graduate
10	Good heredity	Desire for children
11	Good earning capacity	Good heredity
12	Good housekeeper	Good housekeeper

able and eligible, a third factor enters the picture: *attractiveness*. Attractiveness in this context does mean physical attractiveness, but as we all know, judgments of physical beauty depend on who's doing the judging. Attractiveness also involves psychological traits, such as understanding, emotional supportiveness, and similarity in values and goals.

Psychologist David Buss reviewed the evidence on mate selection with a focus on the question of whether opposites attract. He concluded that, in marriage, they do not. He found that "we are likely to marry someone who is similar to us in almost every variable" (Buss, 1985, p. 47). The most important factors are (in order) age, education, race, religion, ethnic background, attitudes and opinions, mental abilities, socioeconomic status, height, weight, and even eye color. Buss and his colleagues found that men and women are in nearly total agreement on the characteristics they seek in a mate. Figure 3.1 presents 12 such characteristics ranked by men and women. Note that there is a significant difference in ranking for only two: good earning potential and physical attractiveness.

Let's pause here and remind ourselves of two important points. First, the conclusions of the studies just cited are true only in general, on the average. There may be happy couples that share few of the traits listed in Figure 3.1. Second, these general conclusions are valid only in Western, largely Anglo, North American cultures. Buss and many others have been studying global preferences in selecting mates. In one report of their efforts, people from 33 countries on six continents were studied. There were some similarities among all of the cultures studied, but cultures tended to show significantly different rankings of preferences for mates. The trait that varied most across cultures was chastity.

Samples from China, India, Indonesia, Iran, Taiwan, and Palestine placed great importance on chastity in a potential mate. Samples from Ireland and Japan placed moderate importance on chastity. In contrast, samples from Sweden, Finland, Norway, the Netherlands, and West Germany generally judged chastity to be irrelevant or unimportant. (Buss et al., 1990, p. 16). You'll note that chastity is nowhere to be found on the list of preferred characteristics presented in Figure 3.1.

Choosing a marriage partner is not always a matter of making sound, rational (cognitive) decisions, regardless of one's culture. Several factors, including romantic love and the realities of economic hardship, sometimes affect such choices. As sound and sensible as choices at the time of marriage may seem, approximately 50 percent of all first marriages end in divorce, and 75 percent of second marriages suffer the same fate. The average life span of a first marriage in the United States is about ten years.

Just as men and women tend to agree on what matters in choosing a mate, so do they agree on what matters in maintaining a marriage, listing such things as liking one's spouse as a friend, agreeing on goals, having similar attitudes and interests, and sharing a mutual concern for making the marriage work. One of the best predictors of a successful marriage is the extent to which marriage partners were able to maintain close relationships (such as with parents) before marriage (Wamboldt & Reiss, 1989).

Beyond establishing an intimate relationship, becoming a parent is often taken as a sure sign of adulthood. For many couples, parenthood is more a matter of choice than ever before because of more available means of contraception and new treatments for infertility. Having a family fosters the process of generativity, which Erikson associates with middle adulthood. **Generativity** reflects a concern for family and for one's impact on future generations. Although such concerns may not become central until a person is over age 40, parenthood usually begins much sooner.

generativity a concern for family and for one's impact on future generations

There is no doubt that having a baby around the house significantly changes established routines. Few couples have a realistic vision of what having children will do to their lives. The freedom for spontaneous trips, intimate outings, and privacy is in large measure given up in trade for the joys of parenthood. As parents, men and women take on the responsibilities of new social roles—of father and mother. These new adult roles add to the already-established roles of being male or female, son or daughter, husband or wife. It seems that choosing to have children (or at least choosing to have a large number of children) is becoming less popular. Although many people see the decision not to have children as selfish, irresponsible, even immoral, there is no evidence that such a decision leads to a decline in well-being or satisfaction later in life.

What changes occur in a relationship when a child is born? There is overwhelming evidence that marital satisfaction tends to drop during the child-rearing years of a marriage. The good news is that marital satisfaction increases again once the children leave the nest. There has been no newer data to contradict Glenn's (1990) review of the literature in this area, in which he concluded that the U-shaped curve representing marital satisfaction before, during, and after the child-rearing years is one of the most reliable in the social sciences. Nearly all indicators of marital satisfaction tend to go down, although not tremendously, in the months immediately following the birth of a first child.

Why does dissatisfaction increase after the birth of a child? The most likely explanation is that role conflict (a person having to play more than one role at a time, such as wife and mother) and role strain (when the demands of a role are higher than a person's abilities) both increase (Bee, 1996). The competing demands of multiple roles and constantly changing demands on one's role as parent contributes to high levels of stress and dissatisfaction.

✓ **STUDY CHECK**

How do psychologists characterize "early adulthood"?

What factors tend to influence the choice of a mate?

What are the consequences of young adults starting a family?

CYBER PSYCH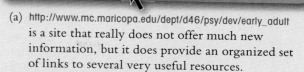

(a) http://www.mc.maricopa.edu/dept/d46/psy/dev/early_adult is a site that really does not offer much new information, but it does provide an organized set of links to several very useful resources.

(b) A great 76-page article, "A Portrait of Well-being in Early Adulthood" provides a great review at http://www.hewlett.org/Archives/Publications.

CAREER CHOICE

By the time a person has become a young adult, it is generally assumed that he or she has chosen a vocation or life's work. In today's marketplace, a person's initial career choice is not likely to be a life-long decision, as multiple career changes are commonplace. Choice of occupation, and satisfaction with that choice, go a long way toward determining self-esteem and identity. For women in early adulthood, being employed outside the home is a major determinant of self-worth (Stein et al., 1990). These days, dual-career families, in which both the woman and the man are pursuing lifelong careers, are becoming quite common (Barnett & Hyde, 2001). Women now constitute about half of the *professional* labor force in this country.

Selection of a career is driven by many factors; family influence and the potential for earning money are just two. Choosing a career path involves several stages. The following terminology is that of Turner & Helms (1987).

1. *Exploration:* There is a general concern that something needs to be done; a choice needs to be made, but alternatives are poorly defined, and plans for making a choice are not yet developed.
2. *Crystallization:* Some real alternatives are being weighed: Pluses and minuses are associated with each possibility, and although some are eliminated, a choice is not yet made.
3. *Choice:* For better or worse, a decision is made. There is a sense of relief that at least a person knows what he or she wants, and an optimistic feeling develops that everything will work out.
4. *Career clarification:* The person's self-image and career choice become intertwined. Adjustments and accommodations are made. This is a matter of fine-tuning the initial choice: "I know I want to be a teacher; but what do I want to teach, and to whom?"
5. *Induction:* The career decision is implemented, presenting a series of potentially frightening challenges to a person's own values and goals. "Is this really what I want to do?"
6. *Reformation:* A person discovers that changes need to be made if he or she is to fit in with fellow workers and do the job as expected. "This isn't going to be as simple as I thought it would be. I'd better take a few more classes or sign up for in-house training."
7. *Integration:* The job and the work become part of a person's self, and the person gives up part of himself or herself to the job. This is a period of considerable satisfaction.

I hardly need to point out that this list is idealized. Sometimes situational factors simply overpower a rational, well-thought-out procedure. "This farm (or business or shop) has been in this family for generations, and when we die, you will not abandon it. Period." Occasionally a person makes a poor career decision (a few seem to do so habitually). This is most likely to occur in the third stage of choosing a career path but probably won't be recognized until the fourth or fifth stage. In such cases, there is little to do but begin again and work through the process, seeking the self-satisfaction that comes at the final stage.

✔ STUDY CHECK

What factors may be involved in making a decision about one's career?

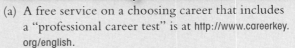

CYBER PSYCH

(a) A free service on a choosing career that includes a "professional career test" is at http://www.careerkey.org/english.
(b) A site of links to other sites is http://www.careerplanning.about.com/od/careerchoicechan. It has links that deal both with choosing a career and with changing job choices.

Development in Middle Adulthood

As the middle years of adulthood approach, many aspects of life have become settled. By the time most people reach the age of 40, their place in the framework of society is fairly set. They have chosen their lifestyle and have grown accustomed to it. They have a family (or have decided not to). They have chosen their life work. "Most of us during our forties and fifties become 'senior members' in our own particular worlds, however grand or modest they may be" (Levinson, 1986, p. 6). In reality, the notion of a mid-life crisis is mostly a myth (McCrae & Costa, 1990).

By middle adulthood, most persons have chosen their career paths and have developed a lifestyle that allows for some leisure time. At the very least, this picture of adulthood is presented as part of the American dream.

There are several tasks that a person must face in the middle years, and one of the first is adjusting to physiological changes. Middle-aged persons can surely engage in many physical activities, but they may have to be selective or modify the vigor with which they attack such activities. Heading out to the backyard for pickup basketball with the neighborhood teenagers is something a 45-year-old may have to think twice about.

While career choices have been made, in middle age one comes to expect satisfaction with work. If career satisfaction is not attained, a mid-career job change is possible. Of course, there are also situations in which changing jobs in middle age is more a matter of necessity than choice. In either case, the potential exists for crisis and conflict or for growth and development.

A major set of challenges that middle-aged persons face is dealing with family members. At this stage in life, parents are often in the throes of helping their teenagers adjust to adolescence and prepare to "leave the nest," while at the same time caring for their own parents. Adults in this situation have been referred to as "the sandwich generation." Individual responsibility and concern for the care of the elderly has not lessened in recent years. In fact, 80 percent of all day-to-day health care for the elderly is provided by family members.

One task of middle adulthood is similar to Erikson's stage, or crisis, of generativity versus stagnation. People shift from thinking about all they have done with their life to thinking about what they will do with what time is left for them and how they can leave a mark on future generations.

Although all the "tasks" noted above are interdependent, this is particularly true of these last two: relating to a spouse as a person and developing leisure-time activities. As children leave home and financial concerns diminish, there may be more time for a person's spouse and for leisure. In the eyes of adults, these tasks can amount to enjoyment: enjoying each other, status, retirement, vacations, and travel. In truth, taking advantage of these opportunities in meaningful ways provides a challenge for some adults whose lives have previously been devoted to children and career.

 **STUDY CHECK**

How would you characterize the developmental stage of middle adulthood?

CYBER PSYCH

(a) http://www.successfulaging.ca is a most pleasant and positive website from Canada. There are links to serious issues, but I'll admit to spending too much time on the humor and recipe links.

(b) A much more academic website is the one from The Center for Successful Aging at California State University Fullerton. If nothing else, visit "Related Links" at http://hdcs.fullerton.edu/csa.

Development in Late Adulthood

The transition to late adulthood generally occurs in our early to mid-sixties. Perhaps the first thing to acknowledge is that persons over the age of 65 constitute a sizable and growing proportion of the population. By the year 2030, nearly 20 percent of Americans will be over 65—about 66 million persons (Armas, 2003). According to a Census Bureau report, by the year 2050, the number of persons of age 65-plus years will be 78.9 million—with an average life span of 82.1 years. The census data also tell us that aging is disproportionably a women's issue. The vast majority of those over age 80 are women, and the number of older ethnic minority adults is increasing more rapidly than for the population in general.

Ageism is the name given to discrimination and prejudice against a group on the basis of age. Ageism is particularly acute in our attitudes about the elderly. One misconception about the aged is that they live in misery. We cannot ignore some of the difficulties that come with aging, but matters may not be as bad as many believe they are. Sensory capacities, for example, are not what they used to be. But as Skinner (1983) suggested, "If you cannot read, listen to book recordings. If you do not hear well, turn up the volume of your phonograph (and wear headphones to protect your neighbors)." Some cognitive abilities decline with age, but others develop to compensate for most losses (Grady et al., 1995). Some apparent memory loss may reflect more of a choice of what one wants to remember than an actual loss. Mental speed is reduced, but the accumulated experience of living often outweighs any advantages of speed.

Children have long since left the nest, but they're still in touch, and now there are grandchildren with whom to interact. Further, the children of the elderly have reached adulthood themselves and are more able and likely to provide support for aging parents. Indeed, most older adults live in family settings. In fact, only about 13 percent of Americans over the age of 65 live in nursing homes (AAHSA, 2003). However, the number of elderly living in nursing homes increases with age, reaching about 25 percent for individuals aged 85 and older.

Some individuals dread retirement, but most welcome it as a chance to do things they have planned for years (Kim & Moen, 2001). Many people over the age of 65 become more physically active after retiring, perhaps from a job in which they sat at a desk all day long. Three factors contribute to one's sense of well-being once retired: a) the extent of available economic resources; b) social relationships with a spouse, family, and friends; and c) personal resources, such as physical health, education, and self-esteem (Moen, Kim, & Hofmeister, 2001). Until recently, almost all research on the effects of retirement focused on males. As more women enter the workforce and then retire from it, the study of retirement is changing. Two tentative conclusions seem warranted: First, women appear to have more negative attitudes toward retirement. Second, having an employed spouse extends the working life of both members of the couple.

Many people assume that old age necessarily brings with it the curse of poor health. However, only 28 percent of elderly individuals report their health to be fair or poor. That compares to a 10 percent rate for non-elderly individuals. Also, only 5 percent of individuals between the ages of 65 and 69 reported needing assistance for important daily activities (AARP, 1995). That's not to say that older people do not have health problems; of course they do. But what matters most—as is true for all of us—is the extent to which problems can be managed successfully (Brod et al., 1999). Acute short-lived illnesses actually occur less frequently among older Americans (but when they do occur, they tend to be more severe). More common are chronic illnesses, such as arthritis, rheumatism, osteoporosis, arteriosclerosis, and hypertension (Cavenaugh & Blanchard-Fields, 2002). Another medical issue that is more of a concern for the elderly than for younger folks is over-medication

ageism the name given to discrimination and prejudice against a group on the basis of age

There is little doubt that late adulthood can bring health problems, as well as cognitive and sensory loss. However, for many—who engage in "successful aging"—it also can be a stage for retirement, reflection, relaxation, and exploration.

and drug interactions. The average 85-year-old individual takes eight to ten pre-scription medications (Giron et al., 2001). Not only is this an expensive reality, but it also can produce "adverse drug events" (ADEs). When ADEs do occur, they usually are the result of an accumulation and interaction of several drugs rather than any one medication (Tune, 2001).

Developmental psychologists find it useful to think about persons over 65 as member of one of two groups: the *young-old* and the *old-old*. This distinction is not made on the basis of actual, chronological age, but on the basis of psychologi-cal, social, and health characteristics. The distinction reinforces the notion that aging is not some sort of disease. The young-old group is the large majority of those over 65 years of age (80 to 85 percent). They are "vigorous and competent men and women who have reduced their time investments in work or home-making, are relatively comfortable financially and relatively well-educated, and are well-integrated members of their families and communities" (Neugarten & Neugarten, 1989).

The concept of successful aging is one that, until recently, seldom got much attention. Most research on the elderly has focused on average age-related losses. But, in fact, the declines, deficits, and losses of the elderly are not the result of ad-vanced age but of factors over which we all can exercise some degree of control. The major contributors to decline in old age include such things as poor nutrition, smoking, alcohol use, inadequate calcium intake, failure to maintain a sense of con-trol over life circumstances, and lack of social support (as long as the support does not erode self-control). Attention to these factors may not lengthen the life span but should extend the "health span, the maintenance of full function as nearly as pos-sible to the end of life" (Rowe & Kahn, 1987, p.149). Research suggests that close family relationships and involvement in effective exercise programs predict success-ful aging. If it comes from the initiative of the individual, a growing dependency on others can be a positive, adaptive strategy for successful aging.

Of the two sure things in life, death and taxes, the former is the surer. There are no loopholes. About 55 million people die each year, worldwide, nearly 2.4 million in the United States. Dealing with the reality of our own death is the last major crisis we face in life. A century ago, most people died in their homes, and death was an experience witnessed by everyone, even children. Now a majority of Americans die in hospitals and nursing homes, and children occasionally see grandparents entering such places and being brought back dead (Leming & Dickinson, 2002, p. 3). Many people never have to deal with their own deaths in psychological terms. These are the people who die young or suddenly. Still, many individuals do have time to contemplate their own deaths, and this usually takes place in late adulthood.

Much attention was focused on the confrontation with death in the popular book, *On Death and Dying* by Elisabeth Kübler-Ross (1969, 1981). Her description of the stages one goes through when facing death was based on hundreds of interviews with terminally ill patients who were aware that they were dying. (Kübler-Ross herself died on August 24, 2004.) She suggested that the process commonly takes place in five stages:

1. *denial*—a firm, simple avoidance of the evidence; a sort of "No, this can't be happening to me" reaction;
2. *anger*—often accompanied by resentment and envy of others, along with a realization of what is truly happening; a sort of "Why me? Why not someone else?" reaction;
3. *bargaining*—a matter of dealing, or bartering, usually with God; a search for more time; a sort of "If you'll just grant me a few more weeks, or months, I'll go to church every week—no, every day" reaction;
4. *depression*—a sense of hopelessness that bargaining won't work, that a great loss is imminent; a period of grief and sorrow over both past mistakes and what will be missed in the future; and
5. *acceptance*—a rather quiet facing of the reality of death, with no great joy or sadness, simply a realization that the time has come.

Kübler-Ross' description may be idealized. Many dying patients do not fit this pattern at all. Some may show behaviors consistent with one or two of the stages, but seldom all five. Although she never meant her stages to be taken as a prescription, there has been some concern that this pattern of approaching death may be viewed as the "best" or the "right" way to go about it. The concern is that caretakers may try to force dying people into and through these stages, instead of letting each face the inevitability of death in his or her own way (Kalish, 1985).

Although elderly people have to deal with dying and death, they are less morbid about it than are adolescents. Older people may fear the process of dying, but have much less concern about the event of death (Leming & Dickinson, 2002). In one study, adults over age 60 did report thinking about and talking about death more frequently than did the younger adults in the survey. However, of all of the adults in the study, the oldest group expressed the least fear of death, some even saying they were eager for it (Fortner & Neimeyer, 1999).

STUDY CHECK

Summarize the major aspects of the last stage of human development, late adulthood.

CYBER PSYCH

(a) There are many websites on the Internet devoted to the topics of death and dying. http://www.nlm.nih.gov/medlineplus/deathanddying.html is my candidate for the top of the list. For one thing, it professes no point of view. It is kept current and has scores of links to matters statistical, legal, practical and so much more.

(b) For practical advice on how to prepare for and cope with the reality of death and dying, it is difficult to imagine a better, more experienced group than the folks at Hospice. Their website is http://www.hospicenet.org.

Chapter Summary

What are the major—and conflicting—views of adolescence that have been put forward in psychology?

Physically, adolescence begins with puberty (attainment of sexual maturity) and lasts until the end of physical growth. Historically, the period has been seen as one of stress, distress, and abnormality. More contemporary views see adolescence as a period of challenges, but a period that most teenagers survive with no lasting negative consequences.

What characterizes the onset of puberty?

Two significant physical developments mark adolescence: a spurt of growth, seen at an earlier age in girls than in boys, and the beginning of sexual maturity, a period called *puberty*. As adolescents, individuals are for the first time physically prepared for sexual reproduction and begin to develop secondary sex characteristics.

What are the consequences of reaching puberty before or after one's age-mates?

The consequences of reaching puberty early are more positive for males than females. Being a late bloomer is more negative in its impact on teens of both sexes, although the long-term consequences for both are few and slight.

What is meant by "identity formation" in adolescence, and what factors influence its development?

The challenge of identity formation is to establish a personal identity (sense of self) that is separate from the parents. A major task of adolescence, then, is to define and integrate the sense of who one is, what one is to do in life, and what one's attitudes, beliefs, and values should be. According to James Marcia, there are four stages of identity formation: identity achievement, foreclosure, identity diffusion, and moratorium. Resolution through identity achievement means that a person has gone through a period of decision-making and has settled on a self-chosen career and ideological path. An individual in foreclosure has had an ideological and career path chosen by someone else, most likely the parents. Individuals who have not yet chosen an ideological or career path, but may have gone through a decision-making phase, are said to be identity diffusers. Those in moratorium are in "crisis" and are in a state of struggle over the future. Identity achievement is most common among college juniors and seniors. Foreclosure and identity diffusion are most often seen in younger children in sixth to tenth grades.

How do psychologists characterize "early adulthood"?

Early adulthood (ages 18 to 45) is characterized by commitments and choices made independently. The young adult assumes new responsibilities and is faced with decisions about career, marriage, and family. For Erikson, the period is marked by the conflict between social relationships and intimacy on the one hand, and social isolation on the other.

What factors tend to influence the choice of a mate?

Mate selection and marriage are two issues that most young adults face. Individuals tend to "match" on a variety of characteristics (e.g., age, race, or education). Many marriages do fail, but most adults list a good marriage as a major source of happiness in their lives. Many factors determine the choice of a mate. There is little support for the notion that opposites attract, and the characteristics of desired mates vary among cultures.

What are the consequences of young adults starting a family?

There is a U-shaped function relating family status and marital satisfaction. Before the birth of the first child, marital satisfaction is high. During the child-rearing years, marital satisfaction declines, but recovers again after the children leave the home. The birth of a child adds stress to a marriage via role conflict and role strain.

What factors may be involved in making a decision about one's career?

Choosing a career or occupation is a decision of early adulthood. Choosing the right career contributes in positive ways to self-esteem and identity. It is a process that often goes through several stages: exploration, crystallization, choice, career clarification, induction, reformation, and integration. From time to time, a person makes a poor career choice and may have to begin the process all over again.

How would you characterize the developmental stage of middle adulthood?

Middle adulthood (ages 45 to 65) may be troublesome for some, but most adults find middle age to be a period of great satisfaction and opportunity. Toward the end of the period, the person begins to accept his or her own mortality in several ways. Tasks of middle age involve adapting to one's changing physiology, occupation, aging parents and growing children, social and civic responsibilities, and the use of leisure time.

Summarize the major aspects of the last stage of human development, late adulthood.

The number of elderly is growing rapidly—approaching nearly 66 million by the year 2030 in the United States alone. Although there may be sensory, physical, and cognitive limits forced by old age, fewer than 30 percent of elderly people rate health problems as a major concern. Although some elderly are isolated and lonely, fewer than 13 percent live in nursing homes. Older people may be concerned about death, but they are neither consumed by it nor morbid about it. With good nutrition, the development of a healthy lifestyle, proper social support, and the maintenance of some degree of autonomy and control over one's life, "successful aging" can become even more common than it is today. This is another way of saying that we can increase the already large percentage (80 to 85 percent) of those over the age of 65 who have been characterized as young-old, as opposed to old-old.

Worldwide, over 55 million people die each year. Kübler-Ross has described five stages of the dying process. The first is denial—involving avoidance of evidence of impending death. The second stage is anger, which is often accompanied by resentment and envy of others who are not dying. Bargaining is the third stage, in which the dying person tries to make a deal with God for more time. The fourth stage is depression, or a sense of hopelessness that bargaining won't work, along with sorrow over past mistakes and what will be missed in the future. The final stage is acceptance, in which the dying person finally accepts the reality of death with no great joy or sadness. As Kübler-Ross acknowledged, not all patients who are dying progress through the five stages of death she outlined. There is also the danger that caretakers might force people to go through the stages. Elderly people have to deal with death (their own and that of others) more than individuals of other ages. They tend to be less morbid about it than adolescents, but they think about it more than younger adults. However, elderly people express less fear of death than younger individuals, which is not to say that they are not anxious about the process of dying. Some even express eagerness for death.

Student Study Guide

STUDY TIP #3 "When Should I Study?"

I've already made the point that doing well in college is going to require a lot of study time. I also have acknowledged that there are other things for you to do each week in addition to studying. How do you best schedule your study time? Fortunately, many decades of research on this issue provide some guidance.

As you will see when we discuss memory, "distributed practice is superior to massed practice." What that means is that cramming doesn't work. It means that there is an optimal balance between study and rest, study and rest. It means that you should not even think about sitting down to study anything for three hours on a Sunday afternoon or for four hours on a Tuesday evening. That's too much time "massed" together to be effective.

For most college students and most course work, a concentrated, focused study effort of about 45 minutes duration is best. Then there should be a rest, a "break," of 15–20 minutes before resuming study. In fact, what the data show us is that just 10–15 minute episodes of good, solid study can be very useful. Another—and nearly obvious—point about scheduling study time is that (usually) daylight study is superior to studying in the evenings or night time, when you are more likely to be tired and unable to focus attention. Now put those two ideas together. An excellent time to study is during short periods of opportunity throughout the day. If a class gets out a little early, what a great chance to review some notes or go over some vocabulary or start to think about what will happen in your next class.

Perhaps you got by in high school with studying on the weekends and an occasional evening or two. Unless you're awfully lucky or remarkably bright, that's not likely to be the case in college.

KEY TERMS AND CONCEPTS

adolescence _____

_____

puberty _____

_____

menarche _____

_____

identity crisis _____

_____

generativity _____

_____

ageism _____

_____

Practice Test Questions

MULTIPLE CHOICE

1. Which of these observations about adolescence is most valid?

    _____ a. It is a developmental stage through which many individuals will not pass successfully.

    _____ b. It is a developmental stage defined in terms of stress, turmoil, and abnormality.

    _____ c. It is a developmental stage through which most pass in psychologically adaptive ways.

    _____ d. It is a developmental period—the only one—defined in biological terms.

2. Which "biological" phenomenon is LEAST associated with the onset of adolescence?

    _____ a. penile erections and nocturnal emissions in boys

    _____ b. a growth spurt in both boys and girls

    _____ c. menarche in girls

    _____ d. the appearance of secondary sex characteristics

3. Which observation concerning menarche is TRUE?

    _____ a. It is found more commonly in boys than in girls.

    _____ b. It occurs, on average, at a younger age than it did 100 years ago.

    _____ c. It generally occurs two to three years before puberty begins.

    _____ d. It is produced, or triggered, by an increased level of androgens.

4. At the time of their puberty, or in their early adolescence, who seems to benefit the MOST?

    _____ a. early-blooming males   _____ c. late-blooming males

    _____ b. early-blooming females   _____ d. late-blooming females

5. Which of Piaget's stages of development is best associated with adolescence?

    _____ a. identity formation   _____ c. identity achieved

    _____ b. postconventional reasoning _____ d. formal operations

6. What two concepts, taken together, best characterize the beginning of adulthood?

   _____ a. independence and interdependence

   _____ b. death and dying

   _____ c. growth and development

   _____ d. assimilation and accommodation

7. For Erikson, early adulthood is best characterized in terms of

   _____ a. competence vs. inferiority.

   _____ b. ego–identity vs. despair.

   _____ c. intimacy vs. isolation.

   _____ d. generativity vs. stagnation

8. The evidence suggests that—in general, of course—a woman is most likely to choose to marry someone who

   _____ a. she believes to be most like herself.

   _____ b. she believes will earn the most money in his lifetime.

   _____ c. is physically most attractive.

   _____ d. is most unlike, or opposite from, her father.

9. Of all the concerns that one might have about the characteristics of a mate, the one trait that varies most widely from culture to culture seems to be

   _____ a. chastity.   _____ c. earning potential.

   _____ b. intelligence or wisdom.   _____ d. kindness.

10. Which of the following best characterizes the elderly in the United States?

    _____ a. Most of them (more than 50%) require supervision of the sort found in nursing homes.

    _____ b. Most of them (more than 50%) are preoccupied with thoughts of their own deaths.

    _____ c. Most (more than 75%) are vigorous and healthy.

    _____ d. Most (nearly 65%) list their health as a serious problem.

11. According to Kübler-Ross, the final stage in facing one's own death is the stage of

    _____ a. anger.   _____ c. acceptance.

    _____ b. denial.   _____ d. joy.

TRUE/FALSE

1. _____ True _____ False   Most adolescents are seriously troubled, rebellious, and uncooperative.

2. _____ True _____ False   Boys profit from early maturity more than girls do, and they suffer more from late maturity.

3. _____ True _____ False   Most Americans (male and female) experience a real mid-life crisis, accompanied by the realization that "time is running out" and that they may not get to do all that they wanted to do.

Sensation and Perception

Preview

This chapter on sensation and perception actually begins our discussion of learning and memory. Before you can learn about or remember some event in the world you must perceive that event. You must select, organize, and interpret the event. And before you can do that, you must first sense the event. That is, you must gather information about the event and put it in a form your brain can appreciate. Your senses take energy from the world around you (in the form of light, sound, tastes, smells, physical pressures, etc.) and change that energy into the only energy there is in your brain: the impulses of energy called "neural impulses."

In brief: We cannot remember what we have not learned, we cannot learn that which we have not perceived, and we cannot perceive that which we have not sensed.

Processing information begins with sensation, the topic now before us. We'll review three important concepts that are relevant to all the human senses: transduction, thresholds, and adaptation.

The scientific study of the human senses—and your own personal experience—should tell you just how incredibly sensitive sense receptors are. Here is the problem that such sensitivity produces: Our senses are so good that they present to us much more information, more detail, than we can possibly process or deal with—and that is where perception comes in. Perception allows us to pay attention and react to only a small number of stimuli, selected from the massive amounts of incoming signals. Once attended to, these stimuli can be made meaningful; can be recognized, organized, interpreted, and remembered.

Much of the discussion that follows comes from the work of German psychologists, who began their study of perception at the beginning of the twentieth century. It was their insight that there is a difference between what we *sense* and what we *perceive.* Imagine a foggy evening. Imagine two very similar lights, only slightly separated, blinking on and off alternately. As one blinks on, the other goes off. We may *sense* the reality of two separate lights, but what we perceive, what we *experience,* is one light moving back and forth.

Perception is largely a matter of selection and organization. To select some aspects of sensory input while ignoring others relies on our paying attention to the world around us. Some of what we attend to is determined by characteristics of the stimulus events in our environment. Some of what we perceive is determined by who we are. Once information is attended to and selected for processing, we tend to organize that information in sensible, meaningful ways. The factors that guide that process are the subject matter of the remainder of the chapter.

You'll find that there are many glossary terms in this chapter. Please do not let this bother you. You already know most of these terms. It is likely, for example, that you first studied basic sensory processes in grade school and then again in middle school and in high school. So although they are technical terms, many should be familiar.

A Preliminary Distinction

In this chapter, we begin our discussion of information processing—how we find out about the world, make judgments about it, learn from it, and remember what we have learned. Although they are very much related, and cannot be separated in our personal experience, I'll divide our discussion of the initial stages of information processing into two sub-processes: sensation and perception.

Sensation is the act of detecting external stimuli and converting those stimuli into nervous-system activity. Sensation provides our immediate experience of the stimuli in our environment. The psychology of sensation deals with how our various senses do what they do. Sense receptors are the specialized nerve cells in the sense organs that change physical energy into neural impulses. That is, each of our sense receptors is a **transducer**—a mechanism that converts energy from one form to another. A light bulb is a transducer. It converts electrical energy into light energy (and a little heat energy). Your eye is a sense organ with sense receptors that transduce light energy into neural energy (neural impulses). Your ears are sense organs that contain receptors that transduce the mechanical energy of sound waves into neural energy.

Compared to sensation, perception is a more active, complex, even creative, process. It acts on the stimulation received by the senses. **Perception** is a process that involves the selection, organization, and interpretation of stimuli. Perception is a more cognitive and central process than sensation. We may say that senses present us with information about the world in which we live, and that perception represents (re-presents, or presents again) that information, often flavored by our motivational states, our expectations, and our past experiences. In other words, "we sense the presence of a stimulus, but we perceive what it is" (Levine & Shefner, 1991, p. 1).

sensation the act of detecting external stimuli and converting those stimuli into nervous-system activity

transducer a mechanism that converts energy from one form to another

perception a process involving the selection, organization, and interpretation of stimuli

---

✓ STUDY CHECK

How do the processes of sensation and perception differ?

CYBER PSYCH

(a) It is a very long URL. It goes to The Mind Project at Illinois State University. And it provides a nice discussion and demonstration. http://www.mind.ilstu.edu/curriculum2/perception/Intro_to_perception_1.html

---

Basic Sensory Processes

Before we get into the story of how each of our senses transduces physical energy from the environment into the neural energy of the nervous system, we need to consider a few concepts common to all of our senses.

Think about some electronic device that runs on a solar battery—for example, a calculator. If you use it in the dark, it will not work. In dim light, you might see some signs of life from the calculator, but in bright light, the calculator functions fully. The display is bright and easy to read, and all of its features work properly. The calculator's power cell requires a minimal amount of light to power the calculator sufficiently. This is the threshold level of stimulation for that device. Light intensities below the threshold will not allow the electronics of the calculator to work. Light intensities at or above threshold allow the calculator to operate properly.

Your sense organs operate in a manner similar to the photoelectric cell in the calculator. A minimal intensity of a stimulus must be present for the receptor cells within the sense organ to transduce the external physical stimulus from the

Difference thresholds are relevant in everyday life, whether you are painting a roof ("Are these really the same color?") or making a sauce (Do you think that anyone will notice that we used the cheap seasonings?").

sensory threshold the minimal intensity of a stimulus needed to operate a sense organ

environment (for example, light, sound, pressure on your skin) into a neural impulse that your nervous system can interpret. This intensity is known as the **sensory threshold**, or the minimum intensity of a stimulus needed to operate a sense organ. Notice that threshold level is actually a measure of *sensitivity*. If a receptor has a *low* threshold, then—by definition—very little energy is needed to stimulate it. In other words, that receptor is very sensitive. As threshold levels go down, sensitivity increases. As threshold levels go up, sensitivity decreases.

What good is the concept of sensory threshold? Determining sensory thresholds is not just an academic exercise. Threshold levels as a measure of sensitivity are used to determine if one's senses are operating properly and detecting low levels of stimulation (which is what happens when you have your hearing tested, for example). Engineers who design sound systems need to know about sensory thresholds; stereo speakers that do not reproduce sounds above threshold levels aren't of much use. Warning lights must be well above visual (sensory) threshold to be useful. How much perfume do you need to use for it to be noticed? How low must you whisper so as not to be overheard in a classroom? Do you really smell natural gas in the house, or is it your imagination? Can one basil leaf in the tomato sauce be detected, or will two be required? These are questions about sensory thresholds that pertain to everyday experiences outside the laboratory. As it happens, our sense receptors are remarkably sensitive, as you can see from the examples in Figure 4.1.

There is another sort of sensory threshold that is important in our everyday lives. These are *difference thresholds*. We often are called upon to detect differences between stimuli that are above our sensory thresholds. The issue now is not whether

FIGURE 4.1

Vision	A candle flame seen from a distance of 30 miles on a clear, dark night
Hearing	The ticking of a watch under quiet conditions from a distance of 20 feet
Taste	One teaspoon of sugar dissolved in two gallons of water
Smell	One drop of perfume in a three-room apartment
Touch	The wing of a bee dropped on your cheek from a height of one centimeter

From Galanter, 1962

Examples of absolute threshold values for five senses (i.e., these stimuli will be detected 50 percent of the time)

the stimuli can be detected, but whether they are in some way *different* from each other. So, a **difference threshold** is the smallest difference between stimulus attributes that can be detected.

difference threshold the smallest difference between stimulus attributes that can be detected

Here's an example: You are presented with two tones. You hear them both (they are above your sensory threshold), and you report that they are equally loud. If the intensity of one of the tones is gradually increased, it will reach a point (eventually) at which you can just detect that it has become louder. This difference is the amount of change in a stimulus that makes it just detectably different from what it was.

The concept of difference threshold is relevant in many contexts. A parent tells a teenager to "turn down that stereo!" The teenager reduces the volume, but not by a noticeable amount from the parent's point of view, and an argument could erupt. Does the color of the shoes match the color of the dress closely enough? Can anyone tell the difference between the expensive ingredients in the stew and the cheaper ones? While painting a room, you run out of paint. Does the newly purchased paint (from a different batch) match the old paint closely enough to be below the difference threshold?

Sensory adaptation occurs when our sensory experience decreases with continued exposure to a stimulus. There are many examples of sensory adaptation. When we jump into a pool or lake, the water may feel very cold. After a few minutes we adapt and are reassuring our friends to "Come on in; the water's fine." When we walk into a house in which cabbage is cooking, the odor is nearly overwhelming, but we soon adapt and then fail to notice it. When the refrigerator turns on, the compressor motor seems to make a terribly loud noise. In a few minutes, we no longer notice the noise—until it stops and silence returns to the kitchen.

sensory adaptation a process that occurs when our sensory experience decreases with continued exposure to a stimulus

There is an important psychological insight in these examples of sensory adaptation: The ability to detect a stimulus depends largely on the extent to which our sense receptors are being newly stimulated or have adapted. In fact, sense receptors respond best to changes in stimulation (Rensink, 2002). The constant stimulation of a receptor leads to adaptation and less of a chance that the stimulation will be detected.

There is an exception to this use of the term "adaptation." What happens when you move from a brightly lit area to a dimly lit one? Say you enter a darkened movie theater on a sunny afternoon. At first you can barely see, but in a few

dark adaptation the process in which visual receptors become more sensitive with time spent in the dark

minutes, you can see reasonably well. What happened? We say that your eyes have "adapted to the dark." Here the term "adaptation" is being used differently. **Dark adaptation** refers to the process in which visual receptors become *more* sensitive with time spent in the dark. You are also familiar with light adaptation, which occurs when you move from a darkened area to a lighted one. For example, imagine you need to use the bathroom in the middle of the night. You stumble out of bed and head to the bathroom. Without thinking, you reach for the light switch and are nearly blinded by the light, which, as you know, can even be painful. After a very short period of time, you adapt to the light and are no longer bothered by it. This occurs because while you are asleep, your eyes are maximally dark-adapted (that is, they are very sensitive to light). When the light comes on, the visual sense receptors in your eyes all fire at once, flooding your brain with visual stimulation. It takes a much shorter period of time for your eyes to light-adapt than it takes them to dark-adapt.

 STUDY CHECK

What are sensory thresholds?

In sensation, what is a difference threshold?

What is sensory adaptation?

CYBER PSYCH

(a) A website that will tell you everything you would want to know about the relationship between the physical characteristics of stimuli and our psychological experience of them is http://www.psychophysics.org.

(b) http://www.sweetmarias.com/article.sensory-evaluation.html is a website that is basically about coffee, how it is grown, how it is ground, and how it should be brewed. And it is a commercial site. But tucked away here is a great little article on sensory thresholds a wonderful application of science in action!

(c) A website with links to tell you all you want to know about subliminal perception is from the University of Michigan and is at http://www.umich.edu/~onebook/pages/frames/psychF.html.

Perceptual Selection: A Matter of Paying Attention

To help guide our discussion of perceptual processes, consider the following true story of a classroom demonstration observed by your author when he was in graduate school.

In a grand old lecture hall at the University of Tennessee, nearly 600 students settled down to listen to the day's lecture on perception. Suddenly a student burst through the closed doors at the rear of the hall. Unknown to the class, he was the lecturer's student assistant. This student stomped down the center aisle of the classroom, screaming obscenities at the professor. "You failed me for the last time, you so-and-so!" The class was stunned. No one moved as the student leaped over

A standard rule of thumb for building billboards is "The bigger; the better" if you want others to pay attention to your message. This one covers the entire side a large building!

the lectern to grab the professor. The two struggled briefly, then—in full view of everyone—a chrome-plated revolver appeared. Down behind the lectern they fell. Kaboom! The class sat frozen in their seats as the professor lay moaning on the floor and the student ran from the room through the same side door from which the professor had entered just minutes ago. Six hundred students just sat there, silent, unmoving. At just the proper dramatic moment, the professor slowly drew himself up to the lectern. And in a calm, soft voice he said, "Now I want everyone to write down exactly what you saw."

You can guess what happened. The "irate student" was described as being from 5′4″ to 6′3″ tall, weighing between 155 and 230 pounds, wearing either a blue blazer or a gray sweatshirt. The most remarkable misperception had to do with the pistol. When the professor first reached the lectern, he reached into his suit-coat pocket, removed the gun, and placed it on top of his notes. When the "irate student" crashed into the room, the first thing the professor did was to reach for the revolver and point it at the student. In fact, the student never had the gun. It was the professor who fired the shot that startled the class, sliding the gun to the floor as he fell. In fact, fewer than 20 of the 600 students in class that day reported the events as they occurred. The overwhelming majority of witnesses claimed that a crazy student had burst into the classroom with a gun in his hand.

Try to imagine how you might have reacted if you had been in class that morning. You sit in class listening to your professor lecture, and from time to time, your mind wanders (we hope not too frequently). You think that wearing your new shoes was not a good idea. Your feet hurt. To your left, a student rips open a bag of chips. You turn your head, annoyed. You smell someone's perfume and think what a pleasant fragrance it is. You can feel the pen in your hand as you write. Your senses are being bombarded simultaneously by all sorts of information: sights, sounds, tastes, smells, even pain. Suddenly, someone enters the room and begins arguing with your professor. A scuffle breaks out. You see a gun and hear a shot. Your heart is pounding, you are breathing heavily, and you don't know what to do next.

What determines which stimuli attract our attention and which get ignored? One thing is for sure: You cannot attend to every stimulus at once. Typically, we select a very few details to which we attend. The competition among stimuli to be selected or ignored is not just an academic exercise. For one example, this is precisely the issue involved in the debate over the use of cellular telephones while driving. There are nearly 120 million cell-phone users in the United States, and 85 percent of them report using their phones, at least occasionally, while driving. One series of research studies concluded that cellular-phone use disrupts driving behaviors by diverting attention from important details (road conditions, traffic, etc.) to other tasks (listening to the phone) (Strayer & Johnston, 2001).

Now let's consider some of the important variables that influence what we attend to and what we ignore. These variables are of two general types: stimulus factors and personal factors. By *stimulus factors* I mean those characteristics that make some stimuli more compelling than others no matter who the perceiver is. By *personal factors* I mean those characteristics of the perceiver that influence which stimuli get attended to or perceived. Personal factors may be short-lived, such as the emotional arousal that accompanies witnessing an accident. Or personal factors can be more stable, such as poor vision or personal prejudices.

STIMULUS FACTORS IN PERCEPTUAL SELECTIVITY

contrast the extent to which a stimulus is physically different from the other stimuli around it

The most important stimulus factor in perceptual selection is **contrast**, the extent to which a stimulus is physically different from the other stimuli around it. One stimulus can contrast with other stimuli in a variety of ways. For example, we are more likely to attend to a stimulus if its *intensity* is different from the intensities of other stimuli. Generally, the more intense a stimulus, the more likely we are to select it for further processing. We are more likely to attend to an irate student in a classroom if he is shouting rather than whispering. In other contexts, a bright light is more attention-grabbing than a dim one; an extreme temperature is more likely to be noticed than a moderate one. This isn't always the case, however, as context can make a difference. A shout is more compelling than a whisper, unless everyone is shouting; then it may be the soft, quiet, reasoned tone that gets our attention. If we are faced with a barrage of bright lights, a dim one, by contrast, may be the one we process more fully.

The same argument holds for the stimulus characteristic of physical size. In most cases, the bigger the stimulus, the more likely we are to attend to it. There is little point in building a small billboard to advertise your motel or restaurant. You want to construct the biggest billboard you can in hopes of attracting attention. Still, faced with many large stimuli, contrast effects often cause us to attend to the one that is smaller. The easiest player to spot on a football field is often the place-kicker, who tends to be smaller and does not wear as much protective padding as the other players.

A third dimension for which contrast is relevant is motion. Motion is a powerful factor in determining visual attention. Walking through the woods, you may nearly step on a chipmunk before you notice it, as long as it stays still—an adaptive camouflage that chipmunks do well. If it moves to escape, you easily notice it as it scurries across the leaves. Again, it is the contrast created by movement that is important.

Although intensity, size, and motion are three characteristics of stimuli that readily come to mind, there are others. Indeed, any way in which two stimuli are different can provide a dimension that determines which stimulus we attend to. A red leaf on a tree of otherwise green leaves will "stand out" and get our attention. (Even a small grease spot can easily grab attention if it is right in the middle of a solid yellow tie.) Because contrast so often guides attention, key terms are printed in **boldface type** throughout this book—so you will notice them, attend to them, and recognize them as important stimuli. There is no doubt that every student in that Tennessee classroom the morning the "crazed" student rushed the lectern attended to several salient details of the situation. The events of that class session surely contrasted with normal classroom expectations.

There is another stimulus characteristic that determines attention, but for which contrast is not relevant: *repetition*. The more often a stimulus is presented, the more likely it will be attended to, with all else being equal, of course. Note that we have to say "all else being equal," or contradictions will arise. If stimuli are repeated too often, we adapt to them, because they are no longer new or novel. Even so, there are many examples that convince us of the value of repetition in getting someone's attention. Instructors who want to make an important point seldom mention it just once; they repeat it. This is why we repeat the definitions of important terms in the text, in the margin, and again in the glossary. People who schedule commercials on television want you to attend to their messages, and obviously repetition is one of their main techniques.

There are many ways in which stimuli differ. The greater the contrast between any stimulus and others around it, the greater the likelihood that that stimulus will capture our attention. All else being equal, the more often a stimulus is presented, the greater the likelihood that it will be perceived and selected for further processing.

✔ STUDY CHECK

What stimulus factors influence which stimuli are selected or attended to?

CYBER PSYCH

(a) This website is well described by its URL. Do click on the link, "Color & Science." http://www.colormatters.com

(b) I think you'll like this short article from "The Monitor," a monthly publication of the APA: http://www.apa.org/monitor/apr01/blindness.html.

A trained and experienced bird-watcher is going to perceive (attend to) many more birds than will someone out bird-watching for the first time.

PERSONAL FACTORS IN PERCEPTUAL SELECTIVITY

Sometimes attention is determined less by the physical characteristics of the stimuli present than by personal characteristics of the perceiver. Imagine two students watching a football game on television. Both are viewing identical stimulation from the same screen. One asks, "Wow, did you see that tackle?" The other responds, "No, I was watching the cheerleaders." The difference in perception here is hardly attributable to the nature of the stimuli because both students received the same sensory information from the same TV. The difference is due to personal factors, categorized as motivation, expectation, or past experience.

After each classroom exam, an instructor collects answer sheets from the students and then goes over the multiple-choice test, sharing what she believes is the best answer. Students have marked their answers on the exams and thus can get immediate feedback. One student is particularly worried about item #2. It was a difficult item for which he chose alternative D. The instructor gets to item #2 and clearly says, "The answer to number two is B." The student responds, "Yes! I knew I got that one right!" But wait a minute! The instructor said "B," but the student wanted to hear her say "D" so badly that that was what he perceived. He selected (attended to) a stimulus that was not even there.

Just as we often perceive what we want to perceive, we often perceive what we expect to perceive. We may not notice, or process, stimuli when they are present simply because we did not "know" that they were coming—we didn't expect them. When we are psychologically predisposed, or expect, to perceive something, we have formed a **mental set**.

Here is an example from the research of Mack and Rock (1998). Participants in this study gaze at a screen upon which a simple cross pattern is flashed very quickly. The stimulus is rather like a large plus (+) sign. They are to report which arm of the cross is longer, the horizontal line or the vertical line. After a few presentations, and without warning, a small figure (a square, a circle, a triangle, or a slanted line) is added to the stimulus of the cross pattern. Participants are asked to identify the small figure that was added. Even though they looked right at it, *none* could recognize the figure at a rate any better than guessing, because they simply were not expecting such a stimulus to appear.

Take a second to glance quickly at the message in Figure 4.2. What does the message say? (If you have seen this before, you'll have to try it with someone who hasn't.) Many people say the message is "Paris in the spring." In fact, there are two "thes" in the triangle: "Paris in the the spring." Most people familiar with the English language (and with this phrase) do not expect to see two adjacent "thes." Given their mental set, they report seeing only one. Others may develop a different mental set. Their reasoning may go something like this: "This is a psychology text, so there's probably a trick here, and I'm going to find it." In this instance, such skepticism is rewarded. There *is* a trick, and if their mental set is to find one, they do.

The inability to change a mentally set way of perceiving a problem can interfere with finding a solution to that problem. What we call "creative" problem-solving is often a matter of perceiving aspects of a problem in new or unexpected ways. Thus, even as complex a cognitive process as problem-solving can be, it often hinges on basic perceptual processes.

When we say that what we attend to is a result of motivation and expectation, we are claiming that what we perceive is often influenced by our past experiences. Much of our motivation and many of our expectations develop from past experiences. We are likely to perceive, or be set to perceive, what we have perceived in the past. Perhaps a personal example will make this clear. I once took a course in comparative psychology that examined the behaviors of non-human organisms. One of the teachers of the course was an ornithologist (a scientist who studies birds). Participation in early morning bird-watching was a requirement of the course. The memory is still vivid: cold, tired, clutching the thermos of coffee, slopping through the marshland looking for birds as the sun was just rising. After 20 minutes of this unpleasantness, the instructor had identified 10 or 11 different birds. I wasn't certain, but I thought I had seen a duck. The differences in perception between my instructor and me that cold, wet morning can be explained in terms of motivation (he did care more than I), but I suspect his ability to spot birds so quickly also reflected his past experience. He knew where to look and what to look for.

To review: Our perception of stimuli in the world usually happens without conscious effort. The process can be influenced by several factors, some of which depend on the stimuli themselves. What we perceive is determined to some extent by the bits and pieces of information we receive from our senses. We may attend to a particular stimulus because it is significantly larger, smaller, more colorful, louder, or slower than the other stimuli around it. We then try to organize, identify, and

mental set a psychological predisposition, or expectation, to perceive something (or not to)

FIGURE 4.2

How we perceive the world is determined at least in part by our mental set or our expectations about the world. How many THEs did you see when you first glanced at this figure? Why?

bottom-up processing the attempt to organize, identify, and store stimuli in our memory based on information derived from our senses

store that stimulus in our memory based on information derived from our senses; this is called **bottom-up processing**. On the other hand, how stimuli are perceived also can be influenced by the motivation, expectations, and experiences of the perceiver. In this case, selection of stimuli is a matter of applying concepts and information already processed. When what one selects and perceives depends on what the perceiver already knows, this is called **top-down processing**.

 STUDY CHECK

What personal factors influence which stimuli are selected or attended to?

 CYBER PSYCH

(a) An interesting article on paying attention that is accessed by clicking on the links: http://psychcentral.com/psypsych/Face_perception.

(b) This URL is to a classic piece on top-down processing and how values influence perception: http://psychclassics.yorku.ca/Bruner/Value.

(c) Here is a relevant piece on "Paying attention in the classroom": http://www.studygs.net/classr.htm.

top-down processing the process of selecting and perceiving stimuli based upon what the perceiver already knows

Organizing Our Perceptual World

A basic task of perception is to select certain stimuli from among all those that strike our receptors for further processing. A related perceptual task is to organize and interpret those bits and pieces of experience into meaningful, organized wholes. We

Stimuli that are alike in some way tend to be organized together as part of the same figure against a background.

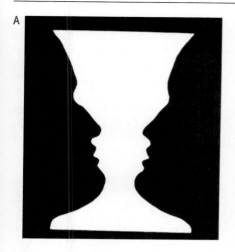

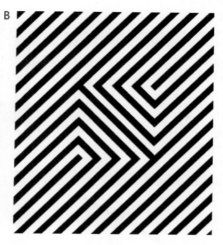

FIGURE 4.3

(A) A classic reversible figure-ground pattern. What do you see here? A white vase or two black profiles facing each other? Can you see both figures clearly at the same time? (B) After a few moments' inspection, a small square should emerge as a figure against a ground of diagonal lines.

do not hear individual sounds of speech; we perceive words, phrases, and sentences. Our visual experience is not one of bits of color and light and dark, but of identifiable objects and events. We do not perceive a warm pat on the back as responses from hundreds of individual receptors in our skin. Our view of the world falls onto a two-dimensional surface at the back of our eyes, but our experience of that world is in three dimensions.

A basic principle of perceptual organization is the **figure-ground relationship**: Stimuli that are attended to and grouped together are figures, whereas all the rest are the ground. As you focus your attention on the words on this page, they form figures against the ground (or background, if you'd prefer) provided by the rest of the page and everything else within your field of vision. When you hear your instructor's voice during a lecture, it is the figure against the ground of all other sounds in the room. The irate student who barged into the classroom to confront a professor became a perceptual figure rather quickly. Figure 4.3 provides a couple of visual examples of the figure-ground relationship.

figure-ground relationship the notion that stimuli that are attended to and grouped together are figures, whereas all unattended to become part of the ground (background)

GROUPING STIMULI WITH BOTTOM-UP PROCESSING

As with perceptual selection, many factors influence how we organize our perceptual world. Again, it will be useful to consider both stimulus factors (bottom-up processing) and personal factors (top-down processing).

Bottom-up processing occurs when we select stimuli as they enter our senses and process them on up "higher" into our cognitive systems by organizing them, interpreting them, making them meaningful, and storing them in our memories. When we talk about bottom-up processing in this context, we are talking about organizing stimuli together based solely on the characteristics of the stimuli themselves. These "stimulus factors" include: proximity, similarity, continuity, common fate, and closure.

FIGURE 4.4

Four Gestalt psychology examples of grouping. (A) These Xs are organized as two groups, not as four rows or four columns, because of proximity. (B) Here we see two columns of Os and two columns of Xs because of similarity. (C) We tend to see this figure as two intersecting lines—one curved, the other straight—because of continuity. (D) This figure is perceived as the letter R, not because it is a well-drawn representation, but because of closure.

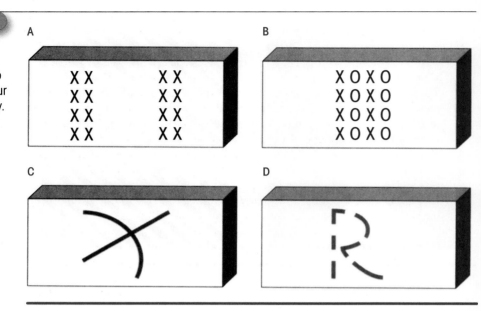

proximity (or contiguity) the principle claiming that events occurring close together in space or time are perceived as belonging together and part of the same figure

similarity the principle claiming that stimuli that are alike or share properties tend to group together in perception

continuity (or good continuation) the principle claiming that we tend to see things as ending up consistent with the way they started

1. *Proximity.* Glance quickly at Figure 4.4(A). Without giving it much thought, what did you see? A bunch of Xs, yes; but more than that, there were two identifiable groups of Xs, weren't there? The group of Xs on the left seems somehow separate from the group on the right, whereas the Xs within each group seem to go together. This illustrates what psychologists called **proximity**, or contiguity—events occurring close together in space or time are perceived as belonging together and part of the same figure.

    Proximity operates on more than just visual stimuli. Sounds that occur together (are contiguous) in speech are perceived together to form words or phrases. In written language there are physical spaces between words on the printed page. Thunder and lightning often occur together, thunder following shortly after the lightning. As a result, it is difficult to think about one without also thinking about the other.

2. *Similarity.* Now glance at Figure 4.4(B) and describe what you see there. A collection of Xs and Os are clearly organized into a simple pattern: two columns of Xs and two of Os. Perceiving rows of alternating Xs and Os is possible, but difficult, which demonstrates the principle of **similarity**. Stimuli that are alike or share properties tend to group together in perception—a "birds of a feather are perceived together" sort of thing. For example, most of us perceive Australian koalas as bears because they look so much like bears, when, in fact, they are related to kangaroos and wallabies.

3. *Continuity.* The principle of **continuity** (or good continuation) is operating when we see things as ending up consistent with the way they started. Figure 4.4(C) illustrates this point with a simple line drawing. The clearest, easiest way to organize this drawing is as two separate but intersecting lines, one straight, the other curved. It's difficult to imagine seeing this figure any other way.

    Continuity may account for how we organize some of our perceptions of people. Aren't we surprised when we hear that a hardworking, award-winning high school honor student does poorly in college and flunks out? That's not the way we like to view the world. We would not be as surprised to find that a student who barely made it through high school fails to pass at college. We want things to continue as they began, as in "as the twig is bent, so grows the tree."

4. *Common fate.* **Common fate** is our tendency to group together in the same figure those elements of a scene that appear to move together in the same direction and at the same speed. Common fate is like continuity, but it applies to moving stimuli. Remember our example of a chipmunk sitting motionless in the woods? As long as both the chipmunk and the leaves remain still, the chipmunk isn't noticed. When it moves, all the parts of the chipmunk move together, sharing a common fate, and we see a chipmunk (not disconnected legs and ears and a torso) scurrying away.

common fate the tendency to group together in the same figure those elements of a scene that appear to move together in the same direction and at the same speed

5. *Closure.* One of the most commonly encountered principles of grouping, or organization, is **closure**, the process by which we fill in gaps in our perceptual world. Closure provides an excellent example of perception as an active process. It underscores the notion that we constantly seek to make sense out of our environment, whether that environment presents us with sensible stimuli or not. This concept is illustrated by Figure 4.4(D). At a glance, we see this figure as the letter R, but, of course, it is not. That's not the way to make an R. Because of closure, however, we perceive an R.

closure the process by which a perceiver fills in gaps in the perceptual world

As an example of closure, make an audiotape of a casual conversation with a friend and write down exactly what you both say. A truly faithful transcription will reveal that many words and sounds were left out. Although they were not actually there as stimuli, they were not missed by the listener, because he or she filled in the gaps (closure), and you both understood what was being said.

A phenomenon that many psychologists believe to be a special case of closure is the perception of **subjective contours**, in which arrangements of lines and patterns enable us to see figures that are not actually there. If that sounds a bit strange, look at Figure 4.5, in which we have an example of subjective contour. In this figure, you "see" a solid triangle that is so clear it nearly jumps off the page. There is no accepted explanation for subjective contours, but it seems to be another example of our perceptual processes filling in gaps in our perceptual world in order to provide us with sensible information.

subjective contours arrangements of lines and patterns that enable us to see figures that are not actually there

✓ STUDY CHECK

What are the characteristics of stimuli that guide our bottom-up organization of information presented by our senses?

FIGURE 4.5

An example of subjective contour.

GROUPING STIMULI WITH TOP-DOWN PROCESSING

Remember that when we refer to top-down processing, the implication is that we take advantage of motivations, expectations, and previously stored experiences in order to deal with incoming stimuli. In terms of perceptual organization, this

FIGURE 4.6

THE CAT SAT BY THE DOOR.

means that we often perceive stimuli as going together, as part of the same figure, because we want to, because we expect to, or because we have perceived them together in the past.

I can think of no better example than the one used at the beginning of this chapter. Nearly 600 students claimed to have perceived something that did not really happen. They saw a student with a gun try to shoot their professor. The problem was not one of perceptual selection. Everybody saw the gun. The problem was one of organization—with whom did they associate the gun? No one was mentally set for the professor to bring a gun to class. No one wanted to see the professor with a gun. And no one had experienced a professor with a gun in class before. (Seeing crazed students with guns is not a common experience either, but with television and movies and similar events showing up in the daily news, it is certainly a more probable one.)

Here is another simple example of how top-down processing can influence our perception of reality. Examine the short sentence presented in Figure 4.6. Even at a glance, you have little difficulty with the meaning of this short phrase. The cat sat by the door. Now note that the "H" in both instances of the word "THE" and the "A" in the words "CAT" and "SAT" are identical. Your senses could not discriminate between these two figures, except that they occurred in a meaningful context. Without past experience with the English language and a passing knowledge of cats, doors, and sitting, the stimuli of Figure 4.6 would make little sense.

Hidden in all these examples of perceptual selection and organization is one of the most important principles of psychology as it affects our lives. It is the central importance of perception in our everyday lives. Simply put: What matters most to you and me is not what actually happened in the world. What matters most is what *we perceive to have happened.* Yes, it was the professor who had the pistol. But—for many reasons—most of those people present saw the irate student with the gun. And *that* is what they processed. *That* is how they organized their worlds. And *that* is what they remembered—not what actually happened, but what they perceived to have happened. We shall return to this powerful observation in the chapter on memory.

✔ STUDY CHECK

How does top-down processing influence how incoming sensory messages are organized or grouped together?

CYBER PSYCH

(a) A brief summary piece on perceptual organization can be found at: http://www.webrenovators.com/psych/GestaltPsychology.htm.

(b) A true classic: Max Wertheimer's 1923 paper on perceptual organization. It is surprisingly readable and contains many examples found in today's texts: http://psychclassics.yorku.ca/Wertheimer/Forms/forms.htm.

(c) Visual illusions are great fun and show what happens when our usual sense of perceptual organization gets fooled. Two wonderful sites for illusions are: http://www.grand-illusions.com and http://www.sandlotscience.com.

PERCEIVING DEPTH AND DISTANCE

Perception requires that we select and organize stimulus information. One of the ways in which we organize visual stimuli is to note where they happen to be in the world. We perceive the world as three-dimensional. As long as we pay attention (surely a required perceptual process), we won't fall off cliffs or run into buildings. We know with considerable accuracy just how far we are from objects in our environment. What is remarkable about this ability is that light reflected from objects and events in our environment falls on two-dimensional retinas at the back of our eyes. Thus, the depth and distance in our world is not something we directly sense; it is something we perceive.

The ability to judge depth and distance accurately is an adaptive skill that plays an important role in determining many of our actions. Our ability to make such judgments reflects the fact that we are simultaneously responding to a large number of cues to depth and distance. Some cues are built into our visual systems, while others rely on our appreciation of the physical environment. We'll also see that one's culture plays a role in the perception of depth and distance.

Some of the cues we get about distance and depth reflect the way our eyes work. Cues that involve both eyes are called binocular cues (bi means "two"). For example, when we look at a nearby three-dimensional object, each eye gets a somewhat different view of it. Hold a pen with a clip on it a few feet in front of your eyes. Rotate the pen until the clip can be viewed by the left eye, but not by the right. (Just close one eye, then the other, as you rotate the pen.) Now each eye (retina) gets a different (disparate) view of the same object. This phenomenon is called **retinal disparity**. It is a cue that what we are looking at must be solid or three-dimensional. Otherwise, each eye would see the same image, not two disparate ones (Figure 4.7).

Another binocular cue to depth and distance is **convergence**—our eyes turning toward each other when we view something up close. As we gaze off into the distance, our eyes aim outward in almost parallel fashion. As we focus on objects up close to us, our eyes come together, or converge, and we interpret that convergence as an indication that what we are looking at is nearby. Convergence is also illustrated in Figure 4.7. If you consider convergence and retinal disparity together, you get a hint about the depth-perception abilities of certain animals. Those with their two eyes located at the front of their heads (dogs, cats, frogs, and primates, for example) have significantly better depth perception than do those animals with one eye located on each side of their heads (such as horses, rabbits, birds, and fish).

The remaining depth-perception cues are monocular, implying that they require only one eye to have their influence. (Even the physical cues that follow are monocular cues because they can be appreciated with only one eye.) A unique monocular cue, at least for relatively short distances, is **accommodation**. This process is the changing of the shape of the lens by the ciliary muscles to focus images on the retina. When we focus on distant objects, accommodation flattens our lens, but when we focus on nearby objects, our lens gets rounder or fatter. Although the process is reflexive and occurs automatically, our brains react to the activity of our ciliary muscles in terms of the distance of an object from our eyes. Accommodation does not function well as a cue for distances much beyond arm's length because the changes in the activity of the ciliary muscles are too slight to be noticed ("below

retinal disparity the cue to depth derived from the fact that each eye (retina) gets a different (disparate) view of the same three-dimensional object

convergence the observation that a perceiver's eyes turn inward toward each other when viewing something up close

accommodation the process of the changing of the shape of the lens by the ciliary muscles to focus images on the retina

This two-dimensional image provides an excellent example of the use of linear perspective to give rise to the perception of distance.

FIGURE 4.7

When looking at a three-dimensional object, such as a pen, the right eye sees a slightly different image than does the left eye—a phenomenon called retinal disparity. This disparity gives us a cue that the object we are viewing is three-dimensional. Here we also note convergence—our eyes turn toward each other when we view an object that is close to us.

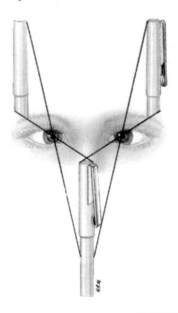

threshold," right?). But it is within arm's length that decisions about distance are often critical.

The physical cues to distance and depth are those we get from the structure of our environment. These are sometimes called *pictorial cues* because artists use them to create the impression of three-dimensionality on a two-dimensional canvas or paper. Here are some of the most important.

1. *Linear perspective:* As you stand in the middle of a road, looking off into the distance, the sides of the road, which you know to be parallel, seem to come together in the distance. Using this pictorial cue in drawing takes some time and experience to develop.

2. *Interposition:* This cue to distance reflects our appreciation that objects in the foreground tend to cover, or partially obscure, objects in the background, and not vice versa. One of the reasons a professor knows that people sitting in the back of a classroom are farther away than people sitting in the front row is the information that he or she gets from interposition. People (and other objects) in the front partially block the view of the people sitting behind them.

3. *Relative size:* This is a commonly used clue to our judgment of distance. Very few stimuli in this world change their size, but a lot of things get nearer to or farther away from us. Objects that are near to you cast a larger image on your retina than objects that are farther away. So, all else being equal, we tend to judge the object that produces the larger retinal image as closer.

4. *Texture gradient:* Standing on a gravel road, looking down at your feet, you can clearly make out the details of the texture of the roadway. You can see individual pieces of gravel. As you look on down the road the texture gradually changes, and details give way to a smooth blend of a surface without texture. We interpret this gradual change (gradient) in texture as a change in distance. Here is a related observation, known well by golfers: People tend to overestimate the distance of an object (e.g., a flag in the center of a green) when it is

observed across a gap, such as a steep ravine or valley. The same distance can be judged much more accurately if viewed over flat or even rolling terrain, where the ground is continuously in view—allowing for texture gradient effects to operate (Sinai, Ooi, & He, 1998).

5. *Patterns of shading:* Drawings that do not use shading look flat and two-dimensional. Children eventually learn that if they want their pictures to look lifelike, they should shade in tree trunks and apples and show them casting shadows. Two-dimensional objects do not cast shadows, and how objects create patterns of light and shade tells us a great deal about their shape and solidity.

6. *Motion parallax:* This rather technical label names something with which we are all familiar. The clearest example may occur when we are in a car, looking out a side window (as the passenger, not the driver). Even if the car is going at a modest speed, nearby utility poles and fence posts seem to race by. Objects farther away from the car seem to move more slowly, while mountains or trees way off in the distance seem hardly to be moving at all. This difference in apparent motion is known as motion parallax.

Even something as "natural" as perceiving depth and distance can be susceptible to cultural constraints. Here is a classic example: Turnbull (1961) reported that the Bambuti people of the African Congo live much of their lives in the dense Ituri Forest where they seldom see much farther than 100 feet. When Turnbull first took his Bambuti guide out of the forest onto the open plains, the guide, Kenge, was disoriented with regard to cues for distance. Kenge thought that buffalo grazing a few miles away were, in fact, tiny insects. Kenge was responding more to retinal size than to relative size as a cue to distance. Interestingly, with just a little training in how the real, physical world can be represented, most cultural differences in the perception of depth disappear.

✓ STUDY CHECK

List and describe the cues that allow us to perceive depth and distance.

CYBER PSYCH

(a) Why not to drink and drive—depth perception. This article is from the BBC: http://news.bbc.co.uk/1/hi/health/4135233.stm.

(b) Excellent examples of the cues for the perception of depth and distance can be found at: http://webvision.med.utah.edu/KallDepth.html.

(c) Here is a commercial website, trying to sell you all sorts of things, but if you maintain attention, you will find all sorts of great examples of illusions http://www.grand-illusions.com.

Chapter Summary

How do the processes of sensation and perception differ?

Sensation is the process of receiving information from the environment and changing it into nervous-system activity. The process of transforming external stimuli into a form that the nervous system can interpret is known as transduction. Perception is the process that involves selection, organization, and interpretation of stimuli. Sensation and perception differ in that perception is a more active, cognitive, and central process than sensation.

What are sensory thresholds?

Sensory thresholds refer to the minimum amount of stimulus intensity or energy necessary to trigger a reaction from a sense organ.

In sensation, what is a difference threshold?

A difference threshold is the minimal difference between stimuli that can be detected. Difference thresholds can be determined for any stimulus characteristics, not just intensity.

What is sensory adaptation?

Sensory adaptation occurs when sensory experiences decrease as a result of continued exposure to a stimulus. For example, when you first walk down a city street, the noise of the traffic may seem very loud. As you continue to stroll, even though the noise level is unchanged, you tend not to notice the sounds because of adaptation. Sense organs are best able to detect changes in stimulation, not continuous stimulation.

What stimulus factors influence which stimuli are selected or attended to?

Characteristics of the stimuli in our environments can determine which will be attended to. We are more likely to attend to a stimulus if it *contrasts* with others around it in terms of intensity, size, motion, novelty, or any other physical characteristic. The *repetition* of a stimulus also increases the likelihood that we will attend to it.

What personal factors influence which stimuli are selected or attended to?

The selection of stimuli is partly based on characteristics of the perceiver. Such factors as *motivation, expectation* (or mental set), and *past experience* often determine which stimuli become selected for further processing. When characteristics of the perceiver are influential, we say that information is processed from the "top down" rather than from the "bottom up."

What are the characteristics of stimuli that guide our bottom-up organization of information presented by our senses?

How we organize or group objects and events in our experience depends in part on the characteristics of the available stimuli themselves, such as *proximity* (occurring together in space or time), *similarity* (the extent to which stimuli share physical characteristics), *continuity* (the extent to which stimuli appear to end as they began), *common fate* (seeing together elements of a scene that move together), and *closure* (filling in gaps in our perceptual world in a sensible way). When these factors influence organization, we have bottom-up processing, moving from stimulus input up to higher cognitive processing (organizing, storing, and remembering).

How does top-down processing influence how incoming sensory messages are organized or grouped together?

These factors originate in our cognitive (largely memory) systems and are referred to as personal factors. The personal factors that affect perceptual organization are the same as those that influence attention: motivation, mental set, and past experience. Simply put, we perceive stimuli as belonging together because we want to perceive them together, we expect them to be together, or we have experienced them being grouped together in the past.

List and describe the cues that allow us to perceive depth and distance.

We are able to perceive three-dimensionality and distance, even though we sense the environment on two-dimensional retinas at the back of our eyes, because of the many cues with which we are provided. Some have to do with the visual system. *Retinal disparity* refers to the fact that each eye gets a slightly different view of three-dimensional objects. *Convergence* occurs when we look at something near our eyes and they move in toward each other. Retinal disparity and convergence are called binocular cues because they require both eyes. *Accommodation,* a monocular cue requiring only one eye, occurs when our lenses change shape to focus images as objects move toward or away from us.

Cues for depth and distance also come from the environment, and include such phenomenon as *linear perspective* (parallel lines seem to come together in the distance), *relative size* (everything else being equal, the smaller the stimulus, the farther away we judge it to be), *interposition* (near objects partially obscure our view of more distant objects), *texture gradients* (details of texture that we can see clearly up close are difficult to determine at a distance), *patterns of shading,* and *motion parallax* (as we move toward stationary objects, those close to us seem to move past us more rapidly than do objects in the distance). Depth and distance perception have been found to be susceptible to cultural influences.

Student Study Guide

STUDY TIP #4 "Where Should I Study?"

There's a good chance that this Study Tip's title may strike you as too silly to bother with. Bear with me. It's not as silly as it sounds—and there's good psychology to back me up.

A lot of research tells us that the best place to study is in the very location where you will be tested. Scuba divers learn some material at poolside. They learn different material while sitting on the bottom of the pool in their scuba gear. Some time later, they are tested on what they can remember. Material learned at poolside is remembered significantly better there than when it is tested under water. Materials learned under water are recalled better there than at poolside. So where is the best place to study for a psychology exam? In the classroom in which the exam is to be given!

It's not likely that you'll be able to spend a great deal of time studying in the psychology classroom (but even a minute or two would help). So then where do you go? A designated place. There should be someplace at home, on campus, or in the public library that you can set aside, designate as the main place where you will study. Do as little else there as possible. Make it your special "study place." The problem with trying to study at the kitchen table, for example, is that the kitchen table is already associated with other non-study activities like eating.

If you are living at home, getting your own designated study area may cause a bit of family friction. You're going to need some cooperation in this regard. You can't be expected to study successfully if you are sitting in the living room, watching TV, and looking after a younger brother or sister at the same time.

KEY TERMS AND CONCEPTS

sensation _____

_____

transducer _____

_____

perception _____

_____

sensory threshold _____

_____

difference threshold _____

_____

sensory adaptation _____

_____

dark adaptation _____

_____

contrast _____

_____

mental set _____

_____

figure-ground relationship _____

_____

proximity _____

_____

similarity _____

_____

continuity_____

_____

common fate _____

_____

closure_____

_____

subjective contours _____

_____

retinal disparity _____

_____

convergence _____

_____

accommodation _____

_____

Practice Test Questions—Chapter Four

MULTIPLE CHOICE

1. Which term is most descriptive of the process of sensation?

_____ a. transportation   _____ c. selection

_____ b. interpretation   _____ d. transduction

2. Which terms are most descriptive of the process of perception?

_____ a. selecting and organizing   _____ c. learning and memory

_____ b. seeing and hearing   _____ d. detecting and feeling

3. The notion of sensory adaptation suggests that what we tend to experience most readily are

_____ a. lights and sounds, not smells and tastes.

_____ b. stimuli that have remained the same for a very long time.

_____ c. objects or events that we are used to, or have adapted to.

_____ d. changes in level or type of stimulation.

4. Factors that direct our attention to some stimuli and not to others are classified in the text as being either

_____ a. stimulus or personal.   _____ c. primary or secondary.

_____ b. learned or inherited.   _____ d. sensory or perceptual.

5. When we say that someone is likely to perceive something that he or she expects to perceive, we are saying that

_____ a. figures and grounds are often confused.

_____ b. some stimuli are inherently more attention-grabbing than others.

_____ c. our motivational states often direct our attention.

_____ d. we can form a mental set that influences attention.

6. We tend to hear the individual speech sounds of a word organized together and separate from other words largely because of the organizational principle of

_____ a. proximity.   _____ c. continuity.

_____ b. novelty or familiarity.   _____ d. similarity.

7. What makes our perception of the world as being three-dimensional remarkable is that

_____ a. it is a skill or ability found only in humans.

_____ b. it is a perception with no particular survival function.

_____ c. images of the world are inverted by the lens of the eye to appear upside-down.

_____ d. the retina of the eye records visual experiences in only two dimensions.

8. Research from cross-cultural psychology would suggest that persons with the best ability to discern great distances would be people who have spent most of their lives in

_____ a. downtown New York City.

_____ b. the Sahara Desert.

_____ c. the African Congo.

_____ d. the Amazon River Valley.

TRUE/FALSE

1. _____ True _____ False As one's sensory threshold goes up, one's sensitivity in that sense goes down.

2. _____ True _____ False Common fate is a Gestalt organizational principle that is applicable only to objects in motion.

3. _____ True _____ False Motion parallax is an example of a common illusion of motion—seeing motion when there is really none there to be seen.

Learning

Preview

Directly or indirectly, learning has an impact on every aspect of our being. Learning affects how we perceive the world, how we interact with it as we grow and develop, how we form social relationships, and how we change during the course of psychotherapy. Who we are as unique individuals is a reflection of the interaction of our biological/genetic constitution and our learning experiences. Indeed, the human organism is poorly suited to survive without learning. If we are to survive, much less prosper, we must profit from our experience.

We begin by considering how psychologists define learning. Learning surely produces changes in an organism's psychological functions (affect, behavior, and/or cognition), but we'll see that some such changes can be attributed to processes other than learning. Then we focus on a simple form of learning, *classical conditioning*. (Although learning and conditioning are technically not synonymous, they can be used interchangeably. We follow common usage here by referring to the most basic and fundamental types of learning as "conditioning.") The basic processes of classical conditioning are straightforward. So that we can fully understand those processes, we will spend most of our discussion talking about dogs learning to salivate when bells ring. Don't worry. Before we are through, we will see how important salivating dogs are to our everyday human experience.

We then turn our attention to operant conditioning and observational learning. In operant conditioning, what matters most are the consequences of an organism's behaviors. The basic premise of operant conditioning is that behaviors are shaped by the consequences they have produced in the past. In this case, learning is a matter of increasing the rate of those responses that produce positive consequences and decreasing the rate of those behaviors that produce negative consequences. We shall see that a great deal of human behavior can be explained in terms of operant conditioning.

As we did with classical conditioning, we'll take a close look at a laboratory demonstration of operant conditioning, and, because the concept of reinforcement is so central in operant conditioning, we'll spend a good deal of time examining some of the principles of reinforcement—and punishment.

This chapter ends with a brief discussion of some approaches to basic learning procedures that are more cognitive in nature. Classical conditioning and operant conditioning both focus entirely on the behavior of organisms and changes in those behaviors. By definition, cognitive approaches consider relatively permanent changes that take place within an organism and may or may not be reflected in that organism's behavior. We'll focus on Bandura's "observational learning" and see that it has both cognitive and social aspects.

What Is Learning?

There is little doubt that learning is a critically important psychological process, but how shall we define it? Psychologists say that **learning** is demonstrated by a relatively permanent change in behavior that occurs as the result of practice or experience. This is a standard definition, and it raises some important points that we should explore.

learning demonstrated by a relatively permanent change in behavior that occurs as the result of practice or experience

Some of our personal characteristics may have an inherited basis, but who we are in the world reflects our ability to profit from experience—i.e., to learn.

When I say that learning is *demonstrated* by a change in behavior, I mean that learning (like many other psychological processes) cannot be observed directly. In a literal sense, there is no way that anyone can directly observe or measure what you have learned. Therefore, we have to make a distinction between "learning," which is an internal process that is not observable, and "performance," which is overt, observable behavior. All we can measure directly is your performance, or your behavior. To determine if you have learned something, we ask you to perform, to do something, and then make inferences about your learning on the basis of your performance. Unfortunately, there are times when performance does not adequately reflect underlying learning. For example, you may learn a great deal while studying for a test. However, you may perform poorly on that test because you are ill, anxious, or otherwise distracted. Note that this example can work both ways. Occasionally a student who barely studies and who learns little may do well on a multiple-choice test simply with the good luck of guessing.

A second aspect of our definition that takes a bit of explaining is that learned changes in behavior are *relatively permanent*. They are not fleeting, short-lived, or cyclical changes such as those due to fatigue or brief shifts in motivation. Consider, for example, the change in keyboarding behavior that occurs, even for a skilled typist, between 8 and 10 each morning. There is likely to be a significant improvement in behavior that we ought not attribute to learning, but to "warm-up." That same person might not function as well at the end of the day—a change in behavior better attributed to fatigue than to forgetting. These are important changes in behavior, but they are not due to learning. Learned changes are relatively permanent.

Another term in our definition reminds us that there are other changes in behavior that do not result from learning. Learned changes in behavior result from *practice* or *experience*. Some behavioral changes may be due to maturation. The fact that birds fly, salamanders swim, or humans walk has more to do with genes and physical development than with learning. In addition, some changes in our behaviors are due to automatic physiological processes, such as sensory adaptation and are not learned. When we enter a darkened theater, we don't "learn" to see in the dark. Our vision improves, and our behaviors change as our eyes adapt to the change in lighting.

One final point about learning: We often fall into the habit of thinking that learning is a good thing. Clearly, this is not always true. We can learn maladaptive, ineffective habits just as readily as we learn good, adaptive ones. No one I know honestly claims to have enjoyed the first cigarette that he or she smoked. Yet many people have learned the habit, which is hardly an adaptive one. Learning is simply reflected in a change in behavior, be it for better or worse.

When we put these ideas together, we have our definition: Learning is demonstrated by (inferred from) a relatively permanent change in behavior that occurs as the result of practice or experience.

STUDY CHECK

How do psychologists define learning?

CYBER PSYCH

(a) More than providing a definition, this site provides 44 links to other sites about learning. It is from "The Encyclopedia of Psychology." http://www.psychology.org/links/Environment_Behavior_Relationships/Learning/.

Classical Conditioning: The Basics

When most people think about learning, they typically think about such activities as memorizing the Bill of Rights, studying for an exam, or learning to do things, such as drive a car. But our study of learning begins over a hundred years ago in the laboratory of a Russian physiologist who taught dogs to salivate in response to tones. How salivating dogs could be relevant to college students may be difficult to imagine, but please be patient; the relevance will soon become apparent.

Late in the nineteenth century, Ivan Pavlov was studying processes of digestion—work for which he would be awarded a Nobel Prize in 1904. Pavlov focused on the salivation reflex in dogs. He knew that he could get his dogs to salivate by forcing food powder into their mouths. He measured the number of drops of saliva that were produced each time food was introduced. Salivation is a **reflex**—an unlearned, automatic response that occurs in the presence of a specific stimulus. Every time Pavlov presented the food powder, his dogs salivated.

reflex an unlearned, automatic response that occurs in the presence of a specific stimulus

Pavlov then made an observation that led him to one of the most important discoveries in psychology. He noticed that his dogs sometimes began salivating before food was put in their mouths. They would salivate at the sight of the food or at the sight of the laboratory assistant who usually delivered the food. With this observation, Pavlov went off on a tangent that he pursued for the rest of his life. The phenomenon he studied is now called **classical conditioning**, (or sometimes Pavlovian conditioning), a learning process in which a neutral stimulus is paired with a stimulus that elicits an unconditioned response. After conditioning, the neutral stimulus alone elicits a new, conditioned response, much like the original unconditioned response. In an abstract summary statement, that may not make much sense, but as we go through the process step by step, you will realize that the process is straightforward and simple.

To demonstrate classical conditioning, we first need a stimulus that reliably, or consistently, produces a predictable response. The relationship between this stimulus and the response it elicits is usually an unlearned, reflexive one. Given this stimulus, the same response always follows. Here is where the food powder comes in. If we present the food powder to a dog, the salivation response follows. We call the stimulus an *unconditioned stimulus (UCS)* and the response to it an *unconditioned response (UCR)*. A UCS (food powder) produces a UCR (salivation) with no prior learning. A dog does not need to learn to salivate at food. It happens naturally with no learning involved.

Now we need a neutral stimulus that, when presented, produces a minimal response, or a response of no particular interest. For this neutral stimulus, Pavlov chose a tone. At first, when a tone is sounded, a dog *will* respond. It will, among other things, perk up its ears and try to orient toward the source of the sound. We call this response an **orienting reflex**, a simple, unlearned response of attending to a new or unusual stimulus. Imagine students sitting in class while repairs are going on in the hallway. From time to time the sound of a pounding hammer snatches everyone's attention as they reflexively orient toward the noise.

Pavlov found that after hearing the tone for a while, the dog would get used to it and ignore it. Essentially, the dog learns not to orient toward the tone. (And students in the classroom soon get used to the hammering in the hallway and no longer orient toward it.) We're ready to go. We have two stimuli: a tone that produces a minimal response and food powder (UCS) that reliably produces salivation (UCR).

Neutral Stimulus (NS)   **No Response**
(a tone)   (no salivation)

UCS ⟶ **UCR**
(food powder)   (salivation)

Once we get our stimuli and responses straight, the rest is easy. The two stimuli are paired. That is, they are presented at about the same time—the tone first, then the food. The salivation then occurs automatically in response to the food. We have a neutral stimulus, then a UCS, followed by the UCR (or tone-food-salivation).

Neutral Stimulus (NS)   +   **UCS** ⟶ **UCR**
(a tone)   (food powder)   (salivation)

Each pairing of the two stimuli may be considered a conditioning *trial*. If we repeat this procedure several times—for several trials—conditioning will (eventually) take place. There is a relatively permanent change in behavior as a result of this experience. After a number of trials, when we present the tone alone, the dog

classical conditioning (Pavlovian conditioning), a learning process in which a neutral stimulus is paired with a stimulus that elicits an unconditioned response. After conditioning, the neutral stimulus alone elicits a new, conditioned response, much like the original unconditioned response

orienting reflex a simple, unlearned response of attending to a new or unusual stimulus

Not unlike Pavlov's dogs, sometimes we salivate at the very sight of attractive-looking foods.

salivates, something it did not do before. Now the dog salivates not just in response to the food powder, but to the tone as well. The tone is no longer "neutral." It produces a response, so we call the tone a conditioned stimulus (CS). To keep the salivation response that it elicits separate from the salivation in response to the food powder, we call it a conditioned response (CR), indicating that it has been conditioned, or learned. Thus, anytime you see the term "conditioned," you will know that you are dealing with the learned component of classical conditioning.

CS ⟶ **CR**
(a tone)   (salivation)

Let's review:

1. We start with two stimuli: the neutral stimulus (soon to be the CS), which elicits no UCR, and the UCS, which elicits the UCR.
2. We repeatedly present the CS and UCS together.
3. As a result, when we present the CS alone, it now elicits a CR.
4. Or, as I say, Pavlovian conditioning is basically ding-poof-slobber.

The same type of stimulus—say a bell's tone—can be either a neutral stimulus (before learning occurs) or a conditioned stimulus (when it elicits a learned response). Similarly, the same type of response (salivation, for example) can be either an unconditioned response (if it is elicited without learning) or a conditioned response (if it is elicited as the result of learning).

If you have a pet, you have no doubt seen this process in action. You may have noted a range of excited, anticipatory behaviors every time your pet hears you open the cabinet where its food is kept. The open door (CS) has been paired with the food inside (UCS), which produces the same sort of reaction (CR) that was originally reserved for the food (UCR).

Let me make it clear that classical conditioning is not something that occurs only in dogs and cats. You demonstrate a classically conditioned salivation response when you see pictures or smell the aromas of your favorite foods (particularly if you're hungry). If you respond with anxiety at the sight of your instructor entering the classroom with exam papers, you're displaying a classically conditioned response.

✔ STUDY CHECK

Describe the steps involved in demonstrating the classical conditioning of the salivation response in dogs to the tone of a bell.

CYBER PSYCH

(a) http://nobelprize.org/medicine/laureates/1904/pavlov-bio.html is a website that provides a wealth of information, including a nice biography and a speech given by Pavlov. In addition, there is a game (teaching a dog to drool) and a link to the Pavlov Institute of Physiology.
(b) This site has a biography and links to 23 of Pavlov's lectures http://www.ivanpavlov.com.
(c) An essay on all manner of things related to classical conditioning, with internal links to pursue (some are no longer available, but give it a try anyway). http://evolution.massey.ac.nz/lecture9/lect900.htm.

Classical Conditioning in Everyday Life

It is time to leave our discussion of dogs, salivation, and Pavlov's laboratory and turn our attention to the practical application of classical conditioning. There are examples of classically conditioned human behaviors everywhere. Many of our physiological reactions have been classically conditioned to stimuli in our environments. The sights or aromas of certain foods can cause a CR of salivation or of hunger pangs. The sight, sound, or mention of some (often food-related) stimuli may produce a rumbling nausea in the pit of the stomach. Certain stimuli can make us sleepy. And in each case the response is not naturally occurring but has been learned, or classically conditioned.

One of the most significant aspects of classical conditioning is its role in the development of emotional responses to stimuli in our environment. There are few stimuli that naturally, or instinctively, produce an emotional response. Yet think of all the things that directly influence how we feel.

For example, very young children seldom seem to be afraid of spiders, snakes, or airplane rides. (Some children actually seem to enjoy them.) Yet how many adults do you know who are afraid of these things? Many stimuli in our environments evoke fear. There are stimuli that produce feelings of pleasure, calm, and relaxation. What scares you? What makes you feel relaxed? Why? Might you feel upset in a certain store because you once had an unpleasant experience there? Might you anticipate a trip to the beach because of a very enjoyable vacation you had there as a child? Do you shudder at the sight of a police car or smile at the thought of a payroll envelope? In each case, we are talking about classical conditioning. (Not all our learned emotional reactions are acquired through classical conditioning alone. As we will see, there are other possibilities.)

THE CASE OF LITTLE ALBERT

In 1920, psychologist John B. Watson and his student assistant, Rosalie Rayner, published a summary research article about a series of experiments they had performed with "Little Albert." Albert's experiences have become well known. Although Watson and Rayner's summary of their own work tended to oversimplify matters (Samuelson, 1980), the story of Little Albert provides a good model for the classical conditioning of emotional responses—in this case, fear.

Eleven-month-old Albert was given many toys. Among other things, he was allowed to play with a live white rat. Albert showed no apparent sign of fearing it. At this point, the rat was a neutral stimulus (NS) with respect to fear. Then conditioning began. One day, as Albert reached for the rat, one of the experimenters (Rayner) made a sudden loud noise by striking a metal bar with a hammer. The loud noise frightened Albert. Two months earlier Watson and Rayner had established that a sudden loud noise would frighten Albert—at least he behaved in a way that Watson and Rayner felt indicated fear.

After repeated pairings of the rat and the loud noise, Albert's reaction to the rat underwent a relatively permanent change. Albert would at first start to reach toward the rat, but then would recoil and cry out, often trying to bury his head in his blanket. He was making emotional responses to a previously neutral stimulus (NS) that did not elicit those responses before it was paired with a sudden loud noise. This sounds like classical conditioning: The rat is the CS, and the sudden loud noise is the UCS that elicits the UCR of an emotional fear response. After repeated pairings of the rat and the loud noise (CS and UCS), the rat elicits the same sort of fear response (or CR). Figure 5.1 presents a diagram of the procedures used to condition Little Albert to be afraid of a white rat.

Watson and Rayner then demonstrated that Albert's fear of the white rat generalized to all sorts of stimuli: a dog (in fact, a brown spotted dog, not a white one), a ball of cotton, even a Santa Claus mask with a white beard and mustache. Through classical conditioning, Watson and Rayner demonstrated that an emotional response to several stimuli could be learned.

Several issues have been raised concerning Watson and Rayner's demonstration of learned fear—not the least of which is the unethical treatment of Albert. It is unlikely that anyone would even attempt such a project today. Watson had previously argued (1919) that emotional experiences of early childhood can affect an individual for a lifetime, yet he purposely frightened a young child (and without the advised consent of the boy's mother). Albert's mother removed him from the hospital before Watson and Rayner had a chance to undo the conditioning. They were convinced that they could reverse Little Albert's fear, but as fate would have it, they never got the chance.

Even so, it is easy to see how the Little Albert demonstration can be used as a model for describing how fear or any other emotional response can develop. When the project began, Albert didn't respond fearfully to a rat, a cotton ball, or a Santa Claus mask. After a few trials of pairing a neutral stimulus (the rat) with an emotion-producing stimulus (the loud noise), Albert appeared to be afraid of all sorts of white fuzzy objects.

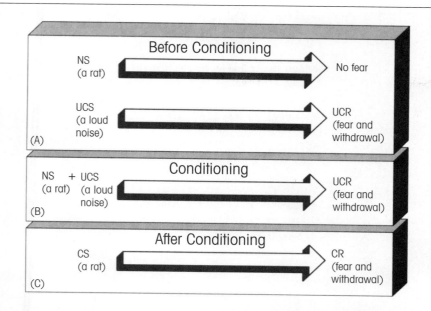

FIGURE 5.1

Conditioning Albert to fear a neutral stimulus (NS) by pairing it with a fear-producing stimulus (UCS). The NS becomes a CS when it has been associated with the UCS and will come to elicit a learned fear response (CR).

TREATING PHOBIAS

Classical conditioning surely is relevant to our everyday lives. It continues to intrigue psychologists searching to understand the underlying processes involved (Lavond et al., 1993; Pearce & Bouton, 2001). Psychologists also are interested in finding new ways to apply conditioning in the real world. In this section, we briefly explore an example of such an application.

There are many things in this world that are life-threatening and downright frightening. Being afraid of some stimuli is often a wise, rational, and adaptive reaction. Occasionally, however, people experience distressing fears of stimuli that are *not* threatening in any real or rational sense. Some people are intensely afraid of heights, spiders, the dark, riding on elevators, or flying. Psychologists say that these people are suffering from a **phobic disorder**—an intense, irrational fear of an object or event that leads a person to avoid contact with it. There are many explanations of how phobic disorders or phobias occur, but one possibility is classical conditioning. This accounting for phobias suggests that a previously neutral stimulus (a spider, for example) is associated with a fear-inducing event (perhaps a painful spider bite). Through a process of association, the previously neutral stimulus (the CS) comes to elicit a fear response that, through generalization, also may be elicited by all sorts of spiders and bugs.

An effective way to treat such fears and phobias is to make use of the principles of classical conditioning. Mary Cover Jones (1924) made one of the earliest attempts to apply classical conditioning to the elimination of a fear. Jones worked with a young boy who had a fear of rabbits. Jones began pairing a pleasing food with the presence of the rabbit. The food by itself did not elicit fear, but rather feelings of pleasure. By pairing the food with the fear-producing rabbit, Jones was able to condition the boy to substitute the feelings of pleasure for the feelings of fear that had been associated with the rabbit. Over 30 years later, the application of classical

phobic disorder an intense, irrational fear of an object or event that leads a person to avoid contact with it

Some adults are terribly afraid of flying. Few children are. This is probably one fear that is learned—through classical conditioning.

systematic desensitization a therapeutic technique whose goal is to gradually teach a patient to associate positive feelings of relaxation with a previously feared stimulus

conditioning to the treatment of fears was elaborated by Joseph Wolpe (1958, 1997). Wolpe's technique is called **systematic desensitization**. Its goal is to gradually teach a patient to associate positive feelings of relaxation with a previously feared stimulus.

In its standard form, systematic desensitization occurs in three stages. First, the therapist instructs or trains the client to relax. As you might know from your own experience, this is not always easy to do at first, but after a few hours of training, the client learns how to enter a relaxed state quickly. The second stage is to construct an "anxiety hierarchy"—a list of stimuli that gradually decrease in their ability to elicit anxiety. The most-feared stimulus is placed at the top of the list (for example, giving a formal speech to a large group, being called on in class, talking to a small group of strangers, being introduced to two or more people, talking with friends, talking to a friend on the phone, etc.). The third stage involves conditioning.

The client relaxes completely and thinks about the stimulus that is lowest on the anxiety hierarchy. The client is then to think about the next highest stimulus, and the next, and so on, all the while remaining as relaxed as possible. As they move up the list toward the anxiety-producing stimuli at the top, the therapist constantly monitors the client's level of tension or relaxation. When anxiety seems to be overcoming relaxation, the client is told to stop thinking about that item on the hierarchy and to think about an item lower on the list.

Systematic desensitization is more than the forgetting of a previously conditioned fear response. A new response (relaxation) is being acquired to "replace" an old one (fear). This process is called *counter-conditioning*. The logic is that a person cannot be relaxed and anxious at the same time. These are incompatible responses. If one pairs a stimulus with the feelings of being relaxed, classical conditioning produces a reaction of calm, not the response of tension and anxiety. For many people, this technique can be effective. It works best for fears or anxieties associated with specific, easily identifiable stimuli; it is less successful for a diffuse, generalized fear, for which it is difficult to generate anxiety hierarchies.

STUDY CHECK

Briefly describe how Watson and Rayner classically conditioned fear in Little Albert.

How can classical conditioning be used in the treatment of phobias?

CYBER PSYCH

(a) Check out http://psychclassics.yorku.ca/Watson/emotion. htm for a copy of Watson and Rayner's 1920 Journal of Experimental Psychology article of Little Albert.

(b) A critical reappraisal of the Little Albert project can be found at http://faculty.concord.edu/rockc/articles/ albert.html.

(c) A brief piece on using classical conditioning for the treatment of phobic disorders is at http://www. phobialist.com/treat.html.

(d) A nice article on systematic desensitization can be found at http://www.guidetopsychology.com/sysden.htm.

(e) And finally, a wonderful site on using classical conditioning techniques to help fearful dogs: http://www.hswv.com/tips/fearful.html.

Operant Conditioning: The Basics

Most of the early research on operant conditioning was done by Harvard psychologist B. F. Skinner, although he really did not discover it. The techniques of operant conditioning had been in use for hundreds of years before Skinner was born. What Skinner did was bring that earlier work—most of it casual, some of it scientific—into the laboratory. There he studied the process of operant conditioning with a unique vigor that helped the rest of us realize the significance of the process.

Skinner used the term "operant" to refer to a behavior or behaviors an organism uses to operate on its environment in order to produce certain effects. Operant behaviors are controlled by their consequences: They will maintain or increase their rate if they are reinforced; they will decrease their rate if they are not reinforced or if they are punished (Staddon & Ceruti, 2003). Thus, **operant conditioning** changes the rate, or probability, of responses on the basis of the consequences that result from those responses. Note that Skinner is careful not to claim here that the future governs what happens in the present, but rather that past experiences influence present ones. Skinner put it this way: "…behavior is shaped by its consequences, but only by consequences that lie in the past. We do what we do because of what has happened, not what will happen" (Skinner, 1989).

Examples of operant conditioning are all around us. You don't need any special apparatus to observe the principle. Imagine a father rushing through a supermarket with his toddler seated in a shopping cart. The youngster is screaming at the top of his lungs, "I wanna candy bar! I wanna candy bar!" Father is doing a good (and an appropriate) job of ignoring this unruly behavior until he spies a neighbor coming down the next aisle. The neighbor has her three children with her, all of whom are acting like perfect angels. What's a parent to do? He races by the checkout lanes, grabs a candy bar, and gives it to his child. He has reinforced the child's tantrum by

operant conditioning a learning technique that changes the rate or probability of responses on the basis of the consequences that result from those responses

In some circumstances a simple piece of blue cloth with some writing on it can be very reinforcing indeed!

giving the child the candy. Does one have to be an expert in psychology to predict what is likely to happen on the next visit to the store? Screaming "worked" this time, so it will be tried again. Reinforced behaviors tend to recur.

To demonstrate operant conditioning in the laboratory, Skinner built a special apparatus that he called an *operant chamber.* Although Skinner never used the term and said he didn't like it, some psychologists continue to call this device a "Skinner box." Figure 5.2 shows a standard operant chamber. The chamber pictured here is designed for rats. The box is empty except for a small lever that protrudes from one wall and a small cup that holds a piece of rat food. Food pellets are dispensed, one at a time, through a tube into the food cup when the lever is pressed all the way down.

Now that we have our chamber, we need a learner. If we put a hungry rat into the chamber and do nothing else, the rat will occasionally press the lever. There is, after all, little else for it to do in there. Rats naturally explore their environments and tend to manipulate objects in them. The rate at which the rat freely presses the lever is called its base rate of responding. Typically, a rat will press the lever eight to ten times an hour.

After a period of observation, we activate the dispenser so that a food pellet is delivered every time the lever is pressed. As predicted, the rate of the lever-pressing response increases. The rat may reach the point of pressing the lever at a rate of 500 to 600 times an hour. Learning has taken place. There has been a relatively permanent change in behavior as a result of experience.

FIGURE 5.2

A drawing of a typical operant chamber.

Here is a little subtlety: Has the rat learned to press the lever? In any sense can we say that we have taught the rat a lever-pressing response? No. The rat "knew" how to press the lever and did so long before we introduced the food pellets as a reward for its behavior. The change in behavior that took place was a change in the *rate* of the response, not in the nature of the response.

 STUDY CHECK

How does one demonstrate operant conditioning?

CYBER PSYCH

(a) A website hosted by the B. F. Skinner Foundation presents an overview of everything Skinnerian at http://www.bfskinner.org.
(b) A biography can be found at http://ww2.lafayette.edu/~allanr/autobio.html.
(c) And from the man himself, one of B. F. Skinner's classic articles on the necessity of theories is at http://psychclassics.yorku.ca/Skinner/Theories.

REINFORCEMENT

Clearly, reinforcement is a crucial concept in operant conditioning. At this point, it is useful to make a distinction between *reinforcement* and a *reinforcer*. **Reinforcement** refers to the process of increasing the rate or probability of a response. Any time you see the term "reinforcement," you should know that someone is talking about a procedure for increasing the probability of a behavior. A **reinforcer** refers to the actual stimulus used in the process of reinforcement that increases the probability or rate of a response.

reinforcement the process of increasing the rate or probability of a response

reinforcer the actual stimulus used in the process of reinforcement that increases the probability or rate of a response

Skinner and his students have long argued that we should define reinforcers only in terms of their effect on behavior. Reinforcers are stimuli. If a stimulus presented after a response increases the strength of that response, then that stimulus is a reinforcer regardless of its nature or its "quality." For example, imagine the following scenario: A parent spanks his 4-year-old child each time the child pulls the cat's tail. The parent then notices that instead of pulling the tail less, the child is actually pulling the cat's tail more often. If the operant behavior we are trying to influence is pulling of the cat's tail, then the spanking is serving as a reinforcer because the frequency of the operant behavior has increased. This is despite the fact that the parent sees the spanking as negative. The intent was to punish the tail-pulling behavior. Perhaps the child is being reinforced by the attention from the parent attached to the spanking! In short, identifying which stimuli will function as reinforcers may be difficult to do ahead of time. We need to observe the effect of a stimulus on the level of a behavior before we can really know if that stimulus is a reinforcer. The intent of the person trying to do the reinforcing is simply not relevant.

Culture can influence what will or will not be reinforcing. In many cultures (mostly Eastern, South American, and African), the group is valued above the individual. In such cultures, reinforcing an individual person's achievements will have less effect than in those cultures (European and North American) in which individual effort and achievement are valued. For example, in traditional Hawaiian culture, the sense of family is very strong, and personal independence is not a sought-after goal. Thus "the Hawaiian child may not be motivated by individual rewards (gold stars, grades) to the extent that his or her Caucasian counterpart may be" (Cushner, 1990). The point is that we cannot tell whether a stimulus will be reinforcing until we try it. It is reinforcing only if it increases the rate or the likelihood of the response it follows.

So, reinforcers are defined in terms of their effects on behavior—events that increase the rate of the behaviors that they follow are said to be reinforcing. When psychologists distinguish between primary and secondary reinforcers, the issue is the extent to which those reinforcers are natural and unlearned or acquire their reinforcing capability through learning or experience.

Primary reinforcers are unlearned and do not require previous experience to be effective. In some way, they are related to the organism's survival and are usually physiological or biological in nature. Food for a hungry organism or water for a thirsty one are common examples. Providing a warm place by the fire to a cold, wet dog involves primary reinforcement. A **secondary reinforcer** may be referred to as a conditioned, acquired, or learned reinforcer. There is nothing about secondary reinforcers that implies that they are inherently reinforcing in any biological sense, yet they increase response rates.

In fact, most of the reinforcers that you and I work for are of this sort. Money, praise, high grades, and promotions are good examples. Money in itself is not worth much. But previous experiences have convinced most of us of the reinforcing nature of money, largely because it can be traded for something we need (such as food) or value (such as a new car). Thus, money can serve to increase the rate of a variety of responses.

The use of secondary reinforcers and operant conditioning can be illustrated by a type of psychotherapy called *contingency contracting*. Contingency contracting usually involves setting up a system called a *token economy* that provides secondary reinforcers for appropriate behaviors. For example, a child earns a checkmark on the calendar for each day he or she makes the bed, takes out the trash, walks the dog,

primary reinforcers stimuli whose reinforcing properties are unlearned and do not require previous experience to be effective

secondary reinforcer a conditioned, acquired, or learned reinforcer, whose reinforcing qualities are due only to experience

or clears the table. The "economy" hinges on the extent to which the checkmarks serve as secondary reinforcers. The child first must learn that a certain number of checkmarks can be exchanged for something that already reinforces his or her behaviors (for example, an extra dessert, an extra hour of TV viewing, or a new toy). Techniques such as this, when applied consistently, can be very effective in modifying behaviors.

Perhaps because of their effectiveness, examples such as this one often disturb students and parents. "Why, this isn't psychology," they argue. "You're just bribing the child to behave." There are at least two reasons why we need not be overly concerned. First, bribery involves contracting to reward someone for doing something that both parties view as inappropriate. People are bribed to steal, cheat, lie, change votes, or otherwise engage in behaviors they know are wrong. Token economies, on the other hand, reinforce behaviors judged in the first place to be appropriate. Second, as Skinner argued for many years, the long-term hope is that the child (in our example) will come to appreciate that having trash removed, walking the dog, or having a clean room is a valued end in itself and can be its own reward. The hope is that the use of reinforcers will no longer be needed as appropriate behaviors become reinforced by more subtle, intrinsic factors.

Now that we have a general idea of what a reinforcer is, and have distinguished primary from secondary, we can make one more distinction. A **positive reinforcer** is a stimulus given to an organism after a response is made that increases (or maintains) the rate of a response it follows. This sounds familiar and even redundant: If something is positive, it ought to be reinforcing. Examples include such stimuli as food for hungry organisms, water for thirsty ones, high grades for well-motivated students, and money, praise, and attention for most of us. Remember, the intention of the person doing the reinforcing does not matter at all.

A **negative reinforcer** is a stimulus that increases (or maintains) the rate of a response that precedes its removal. To increase the rate of a response with negative reinforcement, one presents an aversive stimulus before the behavior to be learned is emitted. For example, you could give a weak electric shock to a rat in an operant chamber. Any behavior that immediately precedes the removal of the negative reinforcer will increase in rate. So, if we want the rat to learn to press a lever, we make termination of the negative reinforcer contingent upon the lever press. When the animal presses the lever, the shock is terminated. It is the removal of an aversive event that is reinforcing.

"Negative reinforcer" is a strange term, isn't it? If something is negative, how can it be a reinforcer? Remember that the key word here is *reinforcer,* and reinforcers increase the rate of responses. Negative reinforcers must produce some sort of satisfying state of affairs. They do. The reinforcement comes not from the delivery or presentation of negative reinforcers, but from their removal.

So negative reinforcers are stimuli that increase the probability of a response when they are removed. They may include such stimuli as shocks, enforced isolation, or ridicule—exactly the sorts of things a person would work to avoid or escape. It may not sound like it, but negative reinforcement is desirable. If one is offered negative reinforcement, "one should accept the offer. It is always good to have bad things terminated or removed" (Michael, 1985). Figure 5.3 illustrates how positive and negative reinforcers work.

Consider a few examples. A rat in an operant chamber is given a constant shock (through the metal floor of the chamber). As soon as the rat presses a lever, the shock is turned off. The lever press has been reinforced. Because a painful

positive reinforcer a stimulus given to an organism after a response is made that increases (or maintains) the rate of a response it follows

negative reinforcer a stimulus that increases (or maintains) the rate of a response that precedes its removal

The major differences
between positive and
negative-reinforcement

Positive Reinforcement

Behavior to be strengthened or maintained (e.g., a child cleaning her room, a rat pressing a lever)	Provide, or Deliver (+)	Stimulus to serve as a positive reinforcer (e.g., a piece of candy, a pellet of food)	If Effective	Behavior is strengthened or maintained (e.g., a child cleaning her room more often, a rat pressing a lever more frequently)

Negative Reinforcement

Stimulus to serve as a negative reinforcer (e.g., isolation from playmates, mild foot shock)	Remove, or Eliminate (−)	Behavior to be strengthened or maintained (e.g., a child stops throwing a tantrum, a rat pressing a lever)	If Effective	Behavior is strengthened or maintained (e.g., a child stops throwing a tantrum, a rat pressing a lever more frequently)

avoidance conditioning a
process demonstrating negative
reinforcement, in which an
organism learns to get away from
(avoid) a painful, unpleasant,
aversive situation before it occurs

stimulus was terminated, negative reinforcement occurred. The negative reinforcer was the shock, and the learning was operant conditioning. You take an aspirin when you have a headache and are reinforced: The pain stops. You will be likely to try aspirin the next time you have a headache. When a prisoner is released early "for good behavior," the good behavior is being reinforced. The process is negative reinforcement. A child who learns to clean up his or her room just to prevent constant parental nagging may be said to have engaged in escape conditioning.

In **avoidance conditioning**, an organism learns to get away from (avoid) an unpleasant, painful, aversive situation before it occurs. A dog is placed in a long box divided into a left and right compartment by a chest-high barrier in the middle. Now in the left compartment, a light (signal) turns on. Five seconds later a strong, painful shock is delivered to the floor of the box. The dog hops around, squeals, barks, and eventually jumps into the right compartment where there is no shock. The dog has been negatively reinforced for jumping. Now a light comes on in the right compartment, followed five seconds later by a shock to the floor. Yelping, barking, and scratching occur again, but the dog rather quickly jumps back to the left compartment. One more trial: light, five-second delay, shock, jump. Now the dog is again in the right compartment of the box. The next time the light comes on, the dog jumps into the left side of the box within five seconds, thus avoiding the shock. On each subsequent trial, the dog jumps the barrier when the light comes on. It has learned to avoid the shock.

This example is impressive in a couple of ways. Here, the removal of a painful stimulus is used to bring about a relatively permanent change in behavior. In just three trials we have trained a dog to jump over a hurdle when a light comes on. One of the most noteworthy aspects of avoidance conditioning is that responses acquired this way are highly resistant to extinction. After all, once the jump is made to the signal light, the shock is no longer required. Our dog will continue to jump for a very long time. Remember, though, we are here using a shock as a negative reinforcer, not as punishment. We are not shocking the dog for doing anything in particular. Indeed, when the appropriate response is made, the shock is avoided. It's also important to realize that a response for avoiding the shock is readily available. There is something that the dog can do to avoid the shock. All it has to do is jump to the other side. When dogs, for example, are shocked at random intervals in a situation from which there is no escape nor any way to avoid the shock, an unusual thing happens. The dogs eventually reach a state where they appear to give up. They just lie down and passively take the administered shock. This behavior pattern is called *learned helplessness.*

Are there examples of avoidance conditioning in human behaviors? Of course there are. As you drive down the road on a day when there is good visibility and little traffic, do you see if you can go just as fast as your car will take you? One would hope not. You probably keep your speed fairly close to the posted limit, trying to avoid the consequences of being stopped and given a ticket. This is most likely the scenario if you have received a speeding ticket (or tickets) in the past. When Wayne says "uncle" to get Ken to stop twisting his arm, Ken stops, thereby reinforcing Wayne's saying "uncle." If this negative reinforcement is effective, in order to avoid the pain of arm-twisting, Wayne will be more likely to say "uncle" in the future when Ken asks him to. (Note that Ken could have used a positive reinforcer to get Wayne to say "uncle," perhaps by offering him five dollars to do so.)

Here's one more hint for you. Don't think of positive and negative reinforcement in terms of good and bad, but in terms of plus (+) and minus (–). When using positive reinforcement, one adds (+) a stimulus, and in negative reinforcement one takes away, or subtracts (–), a stimulus. And any time you see the terms "reinforcement" or "reinforcer," you know that the intention is to increase the rate of a behavior.

✓ STUDY CHECK

Define the concepts of reinforcement and reinforcer, distinguishing between primary and secondary reinforcers and between positive and negative reinforcers.

CYBER PSYCH

(a) http://www.psy.pdx.edu/PsiCafe/KeyTheorists/Thorndike.htm is a rich offering from "The Psi Café" on E. L. Thorndike— who spoke of operant conditioning techniques even before Skinner. Click on the links to the right!

(b) A site on the crusty topic of "negative reinforcement": http://www.mcli.dist.maricopa.edu/proj/nru.

(c) A slight diversion from academic websites is one called "An Animal Trainer's Introduction to Conditioning," with an emphasis on positive reinforcement: http://www.wagntrain.com/OC.

PUNISHMENT

Punishment occurs when a stimulus delivered to an organism *decreases* the rate, or probability, of the response that preceded it. Punishment is usually hurtful or painful, either physically (e.g., a spanking) or psychologically (e.g., ridicule). It is a painful, unpleasant stimulus presented to an organism after some response is made.

punishment a process that occurs when a stimulus delivered to an organism decreases the rate or probability of the response that preceded it

Determining ahead of time which stimuli will be punishing is as difficult to do as determining ahead of time which stimuli will serve as reinforcers. Once again, intentions are irrelevant. We'll know for sure that something is a punisher only after observing its effect on behavior. We may think we are punishing Jon by sending him to his room when he begins to throw a temper tantrum. It may be that "in his room" is exactly where Jon would like to be. We very well may have reinforced Jon's temper tantrum behaviors simply by attending to them. The only way to know for certain is to note the effect on behavior. If Jon's tantrum-throwing behaviors become less frequent, sending him to his room may indeed have been a punishing thing to do.

Commonly, punishment is a matter of presenting a painful, unpleasant stimulus (e.g., a slap on the hand) following an inappropriate response. On other occasions, punishment involves removing a valued, pleasant stimulus (e.g., "No TV for a week!") following an inappropriate response. Another example of this approach is the use of "time out" sessions, which work well with children in groups. If one child begins acting inappropriately (say, by yelling and bullying others), that child is taken aside and placed away from the other children in a quiet setting for a prescribed period of time. The notion here is that one is removing the valued, positive opportunity for social interaction and play, and so we have negative punishment.

Is punishment an effective means of controlling behavior? Does it really work? Yes, it can. Punishment can be an impressive modifier of behavior. A rat has learned to press a lever in order to get food. Now you decide that you no longer want the rat to press the lever. You pass an electric current through the lever so that each time the rat touches the lever it receives a strong shock. What will happen? Actually, several things may happen, but—if your shock is strong enough—there is one thing of which we can be sure: The rat will stop pressing the lever. If punishment is effective, why do psychologists so often argue against its use, particularly the punishment of children for their misbehavior?

There are many potential problems, or side effects, connected with the use of punishment, even when it is used correctly, and often it is not. Let's review some of what we know about the use of punishment in general, and then we'll see about spanking.

1. *To be effective, punishment should be delivered immediately after the response.* The logic is clear. Priscilla is caught in mid-afternoon throwing flour all over the kitchen. Father counts to ten in an attempt to control his temper (a good reaction) and then says, "Just wait until your mother gets home" (not so good). For the next three hours, Priscilla's behavior is angelic. By the time mother gets home, what gets punished, Priscilla's flour-tossing or the appropriate behaviors that followed?

2. *For punishment to be effective, it needs to be administered consistently.* If one chooses to punish a certain behavior, it should be punished whenever it occurs, and often that is difficult to do. Threatening punishment ("If you do that one more time...," "I'm warning you...," "You'd better stop right now, mister") but not delivering on the threat simply reinforces a child to ignore the caregiver.

3. *Punishment may decrease (suppress) overall behavior levels.* Although an effectively punished response may end, so may other responses as well. For example, that rat who has been shocked for pressing the bar will not only stop pressing the

Sometimes punishment can be more psychologically painful than physically hurtful. It also may involve the removal of valued opportunities.

bar, but will also cower in the corner of the operant chamber, doing very little of anything.

4. *When responses are punished, alternatives should be introduced.* Think about your rat for a minute. The poor thing knows what to do when it is hungry: Press the lever. Indeed, you reinforced the rat for making that response. Now it gets shocked for doing that very thing. Without an alternative response to make in order to get food, the rat is in a conflict that has no solution. There is no way out. The result may be fear, anxiety, and even aggression. In other words, punishment does not convey any information about what to do; it only communicates what not to do. Rubbing your puppy's nose in a "mess" it just made on the living room carpet doesn't give the dog much of a sense of what it is supposed to do the next time it feels a need to relieve itself; taking it outside will.

Now let's consider the use of the physical punishment of children—spanking—as a separate case. There are fewer issues related to child-rearing that can get so many people emotionally engaged than whether hitting or spanking a child is always, never, or occasionally warranted (Kazdin & Benjet, 2003). Spanking is an issue that involves religious beliefs ("spare the rod and spoil the child" [Proverbs 13:48]); political actions (hitting a child as a disciplinary action has been outlawed in several countries, including Israel, Sweden, Austria, and Germany [Gershoff, 2002]), and family traditions ("My folks beat up on me, and I turned out okay"). If nothing else, corporal punishment is common in the United States, where 74 percent of parents of children younger than 17 years of age and 94 percent of parents of 3- and 4-year-olds use spanking as a discipline technique (Benjet & Kazdin, 2003; Gallop, 1995; Straus, Sugarman, & Giles-Sims, 1997).

spanking a punishment that is a) physically non-injurious; b) intended to modify behavior; and c) administered with an opened hand to the extremities or buttocks

Before we go any further, let's define **spanking** as punishment that is "a) physically non-injurious; b) intended to modify behavior; and c) administered with an opened hand to the extremities or buttocks" (Friedman & Schonberg, 1996, p. 853). Clearly, no one can be in favor of child abuse: striking a child with a fist or an object so as to cause bleeding, bruising, scarring, broken bones, and the like. What about spanking? Does it work? As you might imagine, we have to be very careful here, but yes, spanking does work in the sense that it can be an effective means to get a child to stop engaging in a given behavior (Gershoff, 2002; Kazdin & Benjet, 2003).

Are there negative consequences of using spanking as a disciplinary measure? Yes, there are several. Spanking diminishes the quality of parent-child relationships, may result (in the long term) in poorer mental health, and may lead to an increase in criminal or antisocial behaviors (Gershoff, 2002). It seems to convey the message that hitting when frustrated is an acceptable response, and that can lead to bullying—particularly of smaller children.

The problem with almost all the research on the effects of spanking is that it is largely correlational research. Researchers look for differences in parental spanking behaviors and correlate those differences with targeted outcome behaviors. The problem, of course, is that correlational data are just that; they tell us about relationships, but not about cause and effect (See Chapter One, pages 9–11). Just because spanking may be correlated with certain outcomes, we should not presume that those outcomes were *caused* by the spanking. Might there be other, uncontrolled factors that caused the outcomes under study?

So what is a parent to do? A reasonable strategy would be to search for other—non-physical—means of providing discipline. Psychologists have no problem with the idea that some behaviors (for example, dangerous ones) are worthy of punishment. If, from time to time, a parent loses control and spanks a child, well, so be it; it happened. There seems to be little reason to agonize over such an action—so long as it remains isolated. When problems develop, they seem to be most related to the habitual, nearly continuous use of physical hitting or spanking as a means of behavioral control.

And although it almost seems too simple to be true, if one adequately reinforces appropriate behaviors, they will increase in rate, and there will be less opportunity for inappropriate, punishable behaviors to occur.

✓ **STUDY CHECK**

How do psychologists define punishment, and under what circumstances is it an effective means of behavior control?

CYBER PSYCH

(a) An article on spanking is http://www.apa.org/releases/spanking.html It is from the American Psychological Association.

(b) Here are two websites on spanking as punishment. Neither is very even-handed, but both provide some good links. http://www.stopspanking.com and http://www.neverhitachild.org.

Cognitive Approaches to Learning

Cognitive approaches to learning focus on changes that occur within an organism's system of cognitions—its mental representations of itself and its world. Cognitive learning involves acquiring knowledge or understanding that may or may not be reflected in actual behavior. I first alerted you to this issue when we discussed the definition of learning. We agreed that learning is demonstrated by, or inferred from, changes in behavior. The implication is that there may be less than a perfect correspondence between what one has learned and how one performs. In this section, we'll briefly review the work of two theorists who stressed cognitive approaches to learning: Edward Tolman and Albert Bandura.

LATENT LEARNING AND COGNITIVE MAPS

The brain of a rat isn't very large, and its cerebral cortex is small indeed. Can a rat use that brain to "think"—to form and manipulate cognitions? Can it figure things out? Rats can form simple associations. They can learn to associate a light with a shock and a lever-press response with a food pellet, and they can modify their behaviors on the basis of these associations. Can they do more?

Consider a classic experiment performed nearly 85 years ago by Tolman and Honzik (1930). Even then, it was well established that a rat could learn to run through a complicated maze of alleyways and dead ends to get to a goal box, where it would find a food reward. Tolman and Honzik wanted to understand just what the rats were learning when they negotiated such a maze. They used three groups of rats with the same maze.

One group of hungry rats was given a series of exposures to the maze (trials). Each time the rats ran from the starting point to the goal box, they were given a food reward for their efforts. Over the course of 16 days, the rats in this group demonstrated a steady improvement in maze-running. Their rate of errors dropped from about nine per trial to just two. A second group of rats was also given an opportunity to explore the maze for 16 days. However, they were not given a food reward for making it to the end of the maze. When they got to the goal box, they were simply removed from the maze. The average number of errors made by the rats in this group also dropped over the course of the experiment (from about nine errors per trial to about six). The fact that the rats in this group did improve their maze-running skills suggests that simply being removed from the maze provided some measure of reinforcement. Even so, after 16 days, this group was having much more difficulty in their maze-running than was the group receiving a food reinforcer.

Now for the critical group. A third group of rats was allowed to explore the maze on their own for ten days. The rats were not given a food reward upon reaching the goal box, but were simply removed from the maze, as were the rats in the second group. But, beginning on day 11, a food reinforcer was introduced when they reached the goal box; the food was provided on days 11 through 16. Introducing the food reward had a very significant effect on the rats' behaviors. Throughout the first ten days in the maze—without food—the rats showed only a slight improvement. Soon after the food was introduced, however, the rats' maze-running improved markedly. In fact, on days 13 through 16, they made fewer errors than did the rats that received food all along! Figure 5.4 shows the performance of these three groups.

FIGURE 5.4

The performance of rats in a complicated maze were (A) never rewarded for reaching the end of the maze, (B) rewarded every time they reached the end of the maze, and (C) rewarded for reaching the end of the maze only on days 11-16 (Tolman & Honzik, 1930).

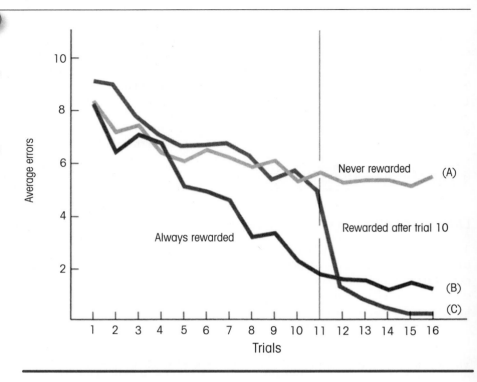

latent learning learning that is, in a sense, hidden and not shown in behavior until it is reinforced

cognitive map a mental picture, or representation, of the physical environment, noting significant landmarks

What do you make of this experiment? Why did the third group of rats do so much better after the food reward was introduced? Did they learn something about the pattern of the maze before they received reinforcement for getting to the goal box? Did they "figure out" the maze early on but fail to rush to the goal box until there was a good reason to do so? Tolman thought they did. He argued that the food rewarded a change in the rats' performance, but that the actual learning had taken place earlier. This sort of learning is called **latent learning** because it is, in a sense, hidden and not shown in behavior until it is reinforced.

During those first ten days in the maze, the rats developed a **cognitive map** of the maze; they formed a mental picture, or representation, of their physical environment, noting significant landmarks when possible. The rats knew about the maze, but until food was provided at the goal box, there was no reason, or purpose, for getting there in a hurry.

What Tolman and Honzik's rats did is impressive. But cognitive maps acquired by small birds that live in the Alps are even more so. These birds spend most of the summer and early fall hiding seeds in the ground (about four or five at a time). During the winter, they find their hidden supplies of seeds with remarkable accuracy. Have they formed cognitive maps of their seed placements? Apparently so. Making their judgments on the basis of nearby landmarks, these Clark's nutcrackers can remember the location of at least 2,500 hiding places (Vander Wall, 1982).

You can find examples from your own experiences that approximate latent learning and the formation of cognitive maps. You may take the same route home from campus every day. If one day an accident blocks your path, won't you be able to use your knowledge of other routes (a cognitive map) to get where you are going? When you park your car in a large parking lot, what do you do as you walk away from your car? Don't you look around, trying to develop a mental image, a cognitive representation, of the parking lot and some of its features? You are to meet a friend in a new classroom building on campus. You arrive early, so you stroll around the building for a few minutes. Isn't it likely that this apparently aimless behavior will be useful if you have to locate a room in that building for class at some later time? If you know that The GAP is on the ground floor, just before the food court, and just after Sears in your neighborhood shopping center, might we not argue that you have formed a cognitive map? Absolutely!

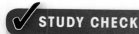 **STUDY CHECK**

Define latent learning and provide an example.

 CYBER PSYCH

(a) http://www.lifecircles-inc.com/tolman.htm is a brief article on Tolman and latent learning.
(b) Here is a 1922 article on the subject from Tolman himself, "A New Formula for Behaviorism," http://psychclassics.yorku.ca/Tolman/formula.htm.

SOCIAL LEARNING THEORY

Albert Bandura's approach to learning is cognitive, and it adds a decidedly social flavor and, for that reason, is referred to as **social learning theory** (Bandura, 2001a, 2001b). The central idea is that learning often takes place through the observation and imitation of models. What makes social learning theory social is that we often learn from others. What makes it cognitive is that what is learned by observation, or modeling, are changes in cognition that may never be expressed as behavior nor be directly reinforced.

social learning theory
learning that takes place through the observation and imitation of models

The classic study of observational learning was reported in 1963 by Bandura, Ross, and Ross. Ninety-six preschoolers were randomly assigned to one of four experimental conditions. One group of children observed an adult model act aggressively toward a large inflated plastic "Bobo" doll. The adult model vigorously attacked the doll. Children in the second group saw the same aggressive behaviors directed toward the doll, but in a movie. The third group watched a cartoon version of the same aggressive behaviors, this time performed by a cat. Children in the fourth group constituted the control group and did not watch anyone or anything interact with Bobo dolls, either live or on film.

Then each child, tested individually, was given new and interesting toys to play with for a brief time. The child was soon led to another room containing fewer, older, and less-interesting toys, including a small version of the Bobo doll. Each child was left alone in the room while researchers, hidden from view, watched the child's behavior.

The children who had seen the aggressive behaviors of the model, live, on film, or in a cartoon, were much more aggressive in their play than were the children who did not have the observational experience. Children in the first three experimental conditions even attacked the Bobo doll the very same way the model had.

According to social learning theory, the children had learned simply by observing. As with latent learning, the learning was separated from performance. The children had no opportunity to imitate (to perform) what they had learned until

It often seems that a great deal of what children learn comes from imitating what they see adults around them doing.

they had a Bobo doll of their own. The learning that took place during observation was internal, or cognitive. As Bandura puts it, "Observational learning is primarily concerned with processes whereby observers organize response elements into new patterns of behavior at a symbolic level on the basis of information conveyed by modeling stimuli" (Bandura, 1976).

Later studies have shown that reinforcement and punishment can play a major role in observational learning. For example, a twist was added to an experiment that replicated the one just described. The difference was that after attacking the doll, the adult models were either rewarded or punished for their behavior. Children who observed the model being punished after attacking the doll engaged in very little aggressive behavior toward their own dolls. Those who saw the model receive reinforcement for attacking the doll acted aggressively, imitating the model's behaviors in considerable detail.

The application of this data can be very straightforward. For example, Bandura's research shows that children learn many potential behaviors just by watching TV. Subsequent research confirms the idea that children learn aggressive behavior from watching violent television programs (Anderson & Bushman, 2002; Bushman & Anderson, 2001; Donnerstein, 2005). There is a consistent relationship between the amount of violent television a child watches and the level of aggressive behavior displayed. Six professional associations, including the American Psychological Association and the American Medical Association, have released a joint statement saying, "at this time, well over 1,000 studies . . . point overwhelmingly to a causal connection between media violence and aggressive behavior in some children" (Joint Statement, 2000, p. 1).

A major concern is for those occasions in which inappropriate behaviors are left unpunished (Donnerstein, 2005). The logic of social learning theory suggests that it would be most unfortunate for one of a child's TV heroes to get away with murder, much less be rewarded for doing so. As it happens, reinforced behaviors of valued models are more likely to be imitated than punished behaviors of less-valued models.

Learning through observation and imitation is a common form of human learning. Television on any Saturday provides many examples, particularly if you watch PBS or HGTV. All day long there are people (role models) trying to teach us how to paint landscapes, build desks and cabinets, do aerobic exercises, improve our golf games, remodel the basement, replace a carburetor, or prepare a low-calorie meal. The basic message is, "Watch me; see how I do it. Then try it yourself."

✓ STUDY CHECK

What is the essence of "social learning theory"?

CYBER PSYCH

(a) A website that provides a nice summary of Bandura's theories, a biography, and more is http://tip.psychology.org/bandura.html.

(b) A very nice website on Bandura and his work on social learning theory is at http://www.muskingum.edu/~psych/psycweb/history/bandura.htm.

(c) http://psychclassics.yorku.ca/Bandura/bobo.htm reports the 1961 "Bobo doll" study by Bandura, Ross, and Ross.

Chapter Summary

How do psychologists define learning?

Learning is demonstrated by a relatively permanent change in behavior that occurs as the result of practice or experience. We can use the same definition for "conditioning" in that it is a simple, basic form of learning.

Describe the steps involved in demonstrating the classical conditioning of the salivation response in dogs to the tone of a bell.

In classical, or Pavlovian, conditioning, a neutral stimulus that originally does not elicit a response of interest is paired with a stimulus that reliably does elicit a given response. As a result, the once-neutral stimulus comes to elicit a response that is similar to the original reflexive response. For example, the unconditioned stimulus, or UCS, of food powder reliably elicits a reflexive, unconditioned response, or UCR, of salivation). The association between the UCS and UCR is unlearned. The conditioned stimulus, or CS (e.g., the tone of a bell), is the previously neutral stimulus, which, after being paired with the UCS, comes to elicit a learned response that resembles the UCR. The learned response is the CR (also salivation).

Briefly describe how Watson and Rayner classically conditioned fear in "Little Albert."

Classical conditioning has its most noticeable effect on emotion or mood. Most of the stimuli to which we respond emotionally have probably been classically conditioned to elicit those responses. In the Watson and Rayner "Little Albert" demonstration, a sudden loud noise (the UCS) was paired with the presentation of the neutral stimulus, a white rat. As a result of such pairings, 11-month-old Albert came to display a learned fear response (a CR) to the originally neutral rat (now the CS). The classically conditioned fear generalized to other, similar stimuli. The demonstration has been used to explain learned emotional reactions to events in our environments.

How can classical conditioning be used in the treatment of phobias?

Phobic disorders are those in which someone experiences an irrational and intense fear of something that is not truly dangerous. Wolpe and others have found that the disorder can be treated using systematic desensitization, which involves training a person to relax and stay relaxed while thinking about a hierarchy of stimuli that are more and more likely to elicit anxiety or fear. If relaxation can be conditioned to thoughts of anxiety-producing stimuli, the sense of calm and relaxation will come to replace the competing response of anxiety.

How does one demonstrate operant conditioning?

Skinner constructed a special apparatus he called an operant chamber. The chamber allowed him to control an organism's environment during learning. A typical chamber for a rat has a bar or a lever and a food cup to deliver reinforcement. A hungry animal is placed in the chamber and is reinforced (with a pellet of food) for the appropriate operant behavior (depressing the bar or lever). Learning occurs as an organism learns to associate a behavior with its consequence. In operant conditioning, it is produced by reinforcing a response so that its rate increases.

Define the concepts of reinforcement and reinforcer, distinguishing between primary and secondary reinforcers and between positive and negative reinforcers.

Reinforcement refers to the *process* of strengthening a response. A reinforcer is any stimulus that increases or maintains the rate of a response, regardless of the nature of the stimulus. A *primary reinforcer* is a stimulus that is in some way biologically important or related to an organism's survival, such as food for a hungry organism or warm shelter for a cold one. No previous learning is required for a primary reinforcer to strengthen or maintain behavior. A *secondary reinforcer* increases or maintains response rates only because of an earlier learning experience. These reinforcers have no direct biological significance for an organism. They take on reinforcing qualities having been previously associated with something else. Examples include praise, money, and letter grades.

A *positive reinforcer* is a stimulus that increases or maintains the rate of the response it follows. Food for hungry organisms, water for thirsty ones, and high grades for well-motivated students are examples. A *negative reinforcer* is an aversive stimulus present before an operant behavior occurs. When that behavior is produced, the aversive stimulus is removed. Behavior occurring before the removal of a negative reinforcer will be strengthened or maintained. Thus, it is the removal of an aversive stimulus that is reinforcing.

How do psychologists define punishment, and under what circumstances is it an effective means of behavior control?

Punishment is the process of decreasing the strength of a behavior by delivering a painful, unpleasant, or aversive stimulus after a behavior has occurred. Punishment can either involve administering a punisher after an undesired behavior has occurred, or withdrawing a stimulus that an organism desires. For example, a child can be spanked for aggressive behavior in the former case, or have television privileges suspended in the latter case. Punishment can be effective in suppressing a response when it is strong enough and is delivered immediately after the response to be punished. Inconsistent use of punishment reduces the effectiveness of punishment for the immediate behavior and desensitizes the organism to the effects of future punishment. The punishment of one response should be paired with the reinforcement of another, more appropriate response. There are several drawbacks to using physical punishment (spanking) with children: It leads only to a temporary suppression of behavior; physical punishment provides children with aggressive role models and a lesson that the way to deal with frustration and anger is through aggression.

Define latent learning and provide an example.

According to E. L. Tolman, latent learning is the acquisition of information (an internal, mental, cognitive process) that may not be demonstrated in performance until later, if at all. Latent learning demonstrates the distinction between learning and performance. Rats can learn their way around a maze, but not demonstrate that they know the pathways of the maze until they are reinforced with food. We cannot say whether Billy can play the piano until we make it worth his while to show us. A cognitive map is a mental picture, or representation, of one's physical environment, noting significant landmarks when possible. The formation of a cognitive map can be viewed as a type of latent learning. When one acquires a cognitive map, one develops a cognitive representation (or picture) of one's surroundings—an appreciation of general location and placement of key objects.

What is the essence of "social learning theory"?

Bandura's social learning theory emphasizes the role of the observation of others (models) and imitation in the acquisition of cognitions and behaviors. We often learn by imitating models. A commonly cited example of social learning is the acquisition of aggressive behaviors based on the viewing of violent television (and other media) programs. Behaviors of a model are most likely to be imitated if the model's behaviors are seen to be reinforced. If a model's behaviors are seen to be punished, they are less likely to be imitated.

Student Study Guide

STUDY TIP #5 "What Should I Study?"

You know my first reaction to this question, don't you? *Everything.* And that's not just *my* initial reaction. You can expect it from all of your professors. We really do like what we're teaching. We really do think that this is just the most wonderful stuff in the world, and we want everybody to know everything.

We often hear academics talking about "empowering students to think critically" about this or that. And this is a fine goal. Indeed, we would like all of our students to be able to think critically about psychological issues, make judgments about psychological claims, and see how psychological concepts are personally relevant. It seems to me, however, that we should back off a little. Let's make sure that we know what we are talking about. Let's get the facts straight before we get involved in deep philosophical discussions about psychology.

It was Ivan Pavlov we associate with classical conditioning, not B. F. Skinner. There are similarities and there are differences between classical conditioning and operant conditioning. Once you are comfortable with these ideas we can move on to discuss *how* Pavlovian or Skinnerian conditioning can be used in advertising or politics. But such a discussion will be rather pointless if the basic concepts are not well understood.

My point? First things first. There is an advantage to learning the terminology, the vocabulary, first. To help with that task, we have placed most important terms and their definitions in the textbook's margins. Then you can look for the major ideas or main points of each section. It is somewhat simplistic, but we have tried to reflect these main points in the "Before You Go On" questions throughout each chapter. The logic is clear: Before you go on, pause and consider what you have just read. Does it make sense? Can you answer the question we have asked there? If you can, fine: Forge ahead. If you cannot, then don't just keep going on. Stop. Reflect. Re-read and think about the section you have just finished.

KEY TERMS AND CONCEPTS

learning _____

_____

reflex _____

_____

classical conditioning _____

_____

orienting reflex _____

_____

phobic disorder _____

_____

systematic desensitization _____

_____

operant conditioning _____

_____

reinforcement _____

_____

reinforcer _____

_____

primary reinforcer _____

_____

secondary reinforcer _____

_____

positive reinforcer _____

_____

negative reinforcer _____

_____

avoidance conditioning _____

_____

punishment _____

_____

spanking _____

_____

latent learning _____

_____

cognitive map _____

_____

social learning theory _____

_____

Practice Test Questions

MULTIPLE CHOICE

1. To say that learning is "demonstrated" by changes in behavior is to suggest that

   _____ a. if we cannot remember something, we did not learn it in the first place.

   _____ b. some changes in behavior do not last very long, or are cyclical.

   _____ c. the only way we can be sure if people have learned anything is to ask them if they have.

   ✓ d. learning is an internal process inferred from performance.

2. As Pavlov noted, when a dog is first brought to the laboratory and stood on a table, and a bell is sounded, the first thing that we will notice is

   _____ a. an orienting reflex.

   _____ b. an unconditioned stimulus.

   _____ c. habituation or acclimation

   _____ d. no response from the dog.

3. In the Pavlovian example of classical conditioning, the UCR was _____ and the CR was _____.

   _____ a. a bell; salivation   _____ c. a bell; food powder

   _____ b. food powder; salivation   _____ d. salivation; salivation

4. We say that systematic desensitization is an application of classical conditioning. If this is so, what serves as the UCR at the beginning of treatment?

   _____ a. an irrational fear

   _____ b. an object or event that causes fear

   _____ c. a state of calm or relaxation

   _____ d. an object or event that causes calm or relaxation

5. The basic thrust, or premise, of operant conditioning is that

   _____ a. under the proper circumstances, any organism can learn to make any response.

   _____ b. organisms learn only responses that are in their own best interest.

   _____ c. behaviors are shaped or controlled by their consequences.

   _____ d. people learn only if they really want to.

6. If operant conditioning is successful, what is most likely to be changed?

   _____ a. the rate or probability of a response

   _____ b. cognitive representations within the organism

   _____ c. the stimuli that produced the learned response

   _____ d. the strength or nature of a response

7. Primary reinforcers are

_____ a. learned.   _____ c. acquired.

_____ b. conditioned.   _____ d. biologically based.

8. The major difference between positive and negative reinforcement is whether

_____ a. something is given or taken away.

_____ b. rates of responses go up or down.

_____ c. responses are rewarded or punished.

_____ d. reinforcers are innate or learned.

9. Which of the following is the best example of negative reinforcement?

_____ a. paying Billy a dollar for each A or B on his report card

_____ b. having a root canal procedure to ease the pain of a toothache

_____ c. spanking Amy for playing with the water in the toilet bowl

_____ d. using poker chips to modify the behaviors of a retarded child

10. Which statement concerning punishment is most justified?

_____ a. Because it creates anxiety, it should never be used with children.

_____ b. Physical punishment is more effective than psychological punishment.

_____ c. Punishment is really only effective if it has been threatened repeatedly.

_____ d. Punishment decreases the rate of the responses that it follows.

11. In general, cognitive approaches to learning tend to emphasize

_____ a. the interaction of genetics and experience.

_____ b. knowing ahead of time what will serve as a reinforcer.

_____ c. changes inside the organism that may not be reflected in behavior.

_____ d. the role of learning in the acquisition of emotions.

12. If learning is "latent," it is, by definition,

_____ a. of no real value to the organism.

_____ b. not (yet) reflected in behavior.

_____ c. learned, but not remembered.

_____ d. displayed only in social situations.

13. When birds bury seeds for use in the winter months,

_____ a. they generally have no idea where to find them when the need arises.

_____ b. they hide so many seeds that they cannot fail to find at least a few to get by on.

_____ c. they form a cognitive map and actually remember where the seeds are hidden.

_____ d. they leave little "markers" on the ground to guide their search in winter.

14. Which of the following does your text offer as an example of social learning theory at work?

_____ a. "how-to-do-it" programs on television

_____ b. Head Start preschool programs

_____ c. college programs for returning adult students

_____ d. software programs for word processing

15. Of the following, what is it that makes Bandura's social learning theory social?

_____ a. the fact that it is a very cognitive approach to learning

_____ b. the concepts of vicarious reinforcement or punishment

_____ c. the requirement that learning be the result of practice or experience

_____ d. the fact that it can only be found in humans and not in non-humans

TRUE/FALSE

1. _____ True _____ False Ivan Pavlov won a Nobel Prize for psychology in 1902.

2. _____ True _____ False In a demonstration of classical conditioning, the first response a subject is likely to make is an orienting reflex.

3. _____ True _____ False You may be punishing responses even though you are intending to reinforce them.

4. _____ True _____ False Because it requires a certain amount of intelligence, only humans are capable of forming cognitive maps.

5. _____ True _____ False Children are more likely to imitate the behaviors of persons who are reinforced for their behaviors than they are to imitate the behaviors of persons who are punished for their behaviors.

Memory

Preview

Memory is so central to our everyday existence that it is nearly impossible to imagine life without it. As students of psychology, we care about memory in an academic, study-learn-test sense, but the importance of memory goes well beyond classroom exams. All of those things that define us as individuals—our feelings, beliefs, attitudes, and experiences—are stored in our memories.

As usual, we'll begin by formulating a working definition of memory. It will soon become clear that human memory is complex, multi-faceted, creative, and elusive. We will consider how information and personal experiences get into memory and how they are stored there. We will explore the possibility that there are several types of memory and see what these varieties of memory might be.

Once we have our foundation set, we turn to the practical matter of accounting for why we forget things. Our focus will be on factors that affect the retrieval of information from memory. Whether we are talking about a simple well-learned habit, a precise definition, a personal experience, or a telephone number, if retrieval fails at a critical time, that information will be of no use to us. What can be done to increase the likelihood that memory retrieval will succeed? In truth, the list is not a very long one. Indeed, we will see that most of the important means of improving memory have to do with how information gets placed into memory in the first place. Throughout this discussion, we will assume that the to-be-remembered information is actually stored in memory. That is, we focus on problems of *retrieval,* not *retention*.

How Can We Best Describe Human Memory?

One approach to human memory is to think about it as a final step in a series of psychological activities that process information. The processing of information begins when sensory receptors are stimulated above threshold levels. The process of perception then selects and organizes the information provided by the senses. With memory, a record of that information is formed.

Although we often give a single label to what we commonly refer to as memory, it is not a single structure or process. Instead, memory is a set of systems involved in the acquisition, storage, and retrieval of information. Memory consists of systems that can hold information for periods of time ranging from fractions of a second to a lifetime. These systems have storage capacities that range from the very limited, like a few simple sounds, to the vast—complex events, the details of an entire human life.

Using memory is a cognitive activity that involves three inter-related processes. The first step is **encoding**, the process of putting information into memory, or forming cognitive representations of information. Encoding is an active process involving a decision (perhaps unconscious) as to which details of an experience to place into memory. Once the representations are in memory, they must be kept there. This process is called **storage**. In order to use stored information, it must be gotten out again—a process called **retrieval**. So if memory involves the

encoding the process of putting information into memory, or forming cognitive representations of information

storage the process of keeping encoded representations in memory

retrieval the process of locating stored information in memory and getting it out in a useful fashion

For most college students, the notion of memory "encoding" is virtually synonymous with "studying."

inter-related processes of encoding, storing, and retrieving information, how shall we describe those "systems" in which these processes operate?

There is some disagreement among psychologists as to how to best characterize the different levels or storehouses that constitute human memory. Most, however, accept the notion of a sensory memory, a short-term memory, and a long-term memory. Let's look at each in turn.

SENSORY MEMORY

Sensory memory stores large amounts of information for very short periods (only a few seconds, or less). The concept of such a very brief memory is a strange one (we usually don't think about remembering something for only a few seconds), but it has a place in the processing of information.

Remember: Information that gets stored in our memories must first have entered through our senses. Simply put, before you can recall what a lecturer says, you must first hear the lecture. To remember a drawing from this book, the image of the drawing must first stimulate your visual system. You can't remember the aroma of fried onions if you've never smelled them.

The basic idea of a sensory memory is that information does not pass immediately through our sensory systems; instead, it is held there for a brief time. Even after a stimulus has left our environment and is no longer present, it has left its imprint, having formed a sensory memory.

sensory memory that aspect of memory that stores large amounts of information for very short periods (only a few seconds or less)

The capacity of sensory memory seems, at least in theory, to be very large. At one time it was believed that we are able to keep as much in our sensory memory as our sense receptors can respond to. Everything above our sensory thresholds gets stored in our sensory memory. Such claims may give sensory memory more credit than it is due. Sensory memory can hold much more information than we can attend to, but there are limits on its capacity.

Sensory memory is typically viewed as being a rather mechanical or physical type of storage. Information is not encoded in sensory memory; you have to take it pretty much as your receptors deliver it. It's as if stimuli from the environment make an impression on our sensory systems, reverberate momentarily, and then rapidly fade or are replaced by new stimuli.

Here are two demonstrations of sensory memory. In a reasonably dark area, stand about 20 feet from a friend who is pointing a flashlight at you. Have your friend swing the flashlight around in a small circle, making about one revolution per second. What do you see? Your *experience* is that of a circle of light. At any one instant, you are seeing where the light is, and you are experiencing from your sensory memory where the light has just been. If your friend moves the light slowly, you may see a "tail" of light following it, but you will no longer see a full circle because the image of the light's position will have fallen from sensory memory.

Has this ever happened to you? Someone asks you a simple question, to which you reply something like "Huh? What'd you say?" Then, before the person even gets a chance to repeat the question, you answer it (which, in turn, may provoke a response like "Why didn't you answer me in the first place?"). Perhaps you did not hear the entire question you were asked, but while it was still echoing in your sensory memory, you listened to it again and formed your answer.

✓ STUDY CHECK

What do psychologists mean by "sensory memory"?

CYBER PSYCH

(a) http://chiron.valdosta.edu/whuitt/col/cogsys/infoproc.html is an excellent interactive essay on the information-processing approach to memory.
(b) A very nice short piece on sensory memory is at: http://psychcentral.com/psypsych/wiki/Sensory_memory.
(c) The Exploratorium is an online version of a hands-on science museum, and there's a section on memory. It may take a minute to find what you're looking for. Go to: http://www.exploratorium.edu/memory/.

SHORT-TERM MEMORY (STM)

short-term memory (STM)
a level, or storage place, in human memory with a limited capacity and, without the benefit of rehearsal, a brief duration

Information can get into sensory memory with relative ease. Once it gets there, where does it go next? Most of it fades rapidly or is quickly replaced with new stimuli. But with a little effort, we can process material from our sensory memories more fully by moving it to short-term memory. **Short-term memory (STM)** is a level, or store, in human memory with a limited capacity and, without the benefit of rehearsal, a brief duration.

FIGURE 6.1

A simplified model of
human memory.

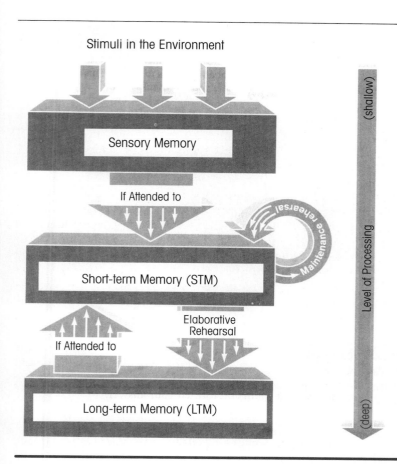

Stimuli in the Environment

Sensory Memory

If Attended to

Maintenance rehearsal

Short-term Memory (STM)

If Attended to

Elaborative
Rehearsal

Long-term Memory (LTM)

Level of Processing
(shallow)
(deep)

Short-term memory is referred to as *working memory* by researcher Alan D. Baddeley (1998, 2001), who sees this memory as something like a workbench or desktop on which we pull together and use the information to which we pay attention. Thus, short-term memory holds information in our consciousness, or awareness, ever so briefly while we "work with it."

Figure 6.1 is a diagram of the model of memory we are building. At the top are stimuli from the environment activating our senses and moving directly to our sensory memory. In the middle is short-term memory. We see that information from sensory memory or from long-term memory can be moved into STM. To get material into short-term memory requires that we attend to it.

Once attended to, information will remain accessible in short-term memory for about 20–30 seconds. That doesn't sound very long, but in many cases, 20–30 seconds is all we need. Consider this scenario. Having studied for hours, you decide to reward yourself with a pizza. Never having called Pizza City before, you turn to the yellow pages to find the number: 555-5897. You repeat the number to yourself: 555-5897. You close the phone book and dial the number without error. Buzzz-buzzz-buzzz-buzzz. Darn, the line's busy! Well, you'll call back in a minute.

Just as you hang up, the doorbell rings. It's the paper carrier. You owe $13.60 for the past two weeks' deliveries. Discovering that you don't have enough cash on hand to pay for the paper and a pizza, you write a check. "Let's see, what is today's

Short-term memory capacity can handle a seven-digit, even a ten-digit, telephone number until we get it dialed.

date? Oh yeah, September 9th. How much did you say I owed you? Oh yes, $13.60, and a dollar and a half for a tip, comes to $15.10. This is check number 1079; I'd better write that down. There you go. Thanks a lot."

The paper carrier leaves, and you return to your studying. Then you recall that you were going to order a pizza. Only five or six minutes have passed since you got a busy signal from Pizza City. As you go to dial, you cannot remember the telephone number. The number, once attended to, was active in your short-term memory. When you were kept from rehearsing it, and particularly when other numbers entered as interfering information, that original telephone number was soon inaccessible.

We can increase the duration of short-term memory by rehearsing the information stored there. The rehearsal we use to keep material active in our short-term memory is **maintenance rehearsal** (or rote rehearsal); it amounts to little more than the simple repetition of the information already in our STM. To get material into STM (encoding), we have to attend to it. By repeating that material (as we might if we wanted to remember a telephone number until we could dial it), we are re-attending to it with each repetition.

The duration of STM is long enough for us to use it in many everyday activities. Usually all we want to do with a telephone number is remember it long enough to dial it. Few people feel the need to make a permanent record of every telephone number they dial. Another example of STM in action is in the processing of language. As you read one of my longer sentences, such as this one, it is

maintenance rehearsal (or rote rehearsal) the simple repetition of information already stored in STM in an effort to keep it accessible

useful to have a short-term storage place to keep the beginning of the sentence in mind until you finally get to the end of the sentence, so that you can figure out the basic idea of the sentence before deciding whether anything in the sentence is worth remembering.

Here's our next question: Just how much information can we hold in STM for that 15 to 20 seconds duration? The answer is "not much"—about five to nine "chunks" of information. A **chunk** is defined as the representation in memory of a meaningful unit of information. Thus, the claim is that we can store about six meaningful pieces of information in STM.

chunk the representation in memory of a meaningful unit of information

We can easily attend to, encode, and store five or six letters in STM. Holding the letters YRDWIAADEFDNSYE in short-term memory would be a challenge. Fifteen randomly presented letters exceed the capacity of STM for most of us. What if you were asked to remember the words Friday and Wednesday? Keeping these two simple words in STM is easy, even though they contain (the same) 15 letters. Here you are storing just two chunks of meaningful information, not 15. In fact, you can easily store 50 letters in short-term memory if you recode them into the one meaningful chunk: "days of the week."

At best, short-term memory works rather like a leaky bucket. From the vast storehouse of information available in sensory memory, we scoop up some (not much, at that) by paying attention to it and holding it for a while until we either use it, hang onto it with maintenance rehearsal, move it along to long-term storage, or lose it.

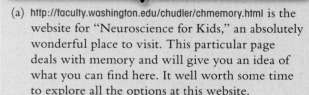

✓ STUDY CHECK

Describe the basic features of short-term, or working memory.

CYBER PSYCH

(a) http://faculty.washington.edu/chudler/chmemory.html is the website for "Neuroscience for Kids," an absolutely wonderful place to visit. This particular page deals with memory and will give you an idea of what you can find here. It well worth some time to explore all the options at this website.
(b) The original paper on the capacity of short-term memory by George Miller is at http://psychclassics.yorku.ca/Miller.
(c) And more: http://www.bbsonline.org/documents/a/00/00/04/46/bbs00000446-00/bbs.cowan.html.

LONG-TERM MEMORY

Long-term memory (LTM) is memory as we usually think of it: memory for large amounts of information that is held for long periods of time. Our own experience tells us that the capacity of long-term memory is huge—virtually limitless. At times we even impress ourselves with the amount of material we have stashed away in LTM. How much can be stored in human memory may never be measured, but we can rest assured that there is no way we will ever learn so much there won't be room for more. (Getting that information out again when we want it is another matter, which we'll get to shortly.)

long-term memory (LTM) memory for large amounts of information that is held for long periods of time

Memories of early birthdays are probably stored in your long-term memory, but can you really retrieve all the details of any of them — or are you just making up events that seem reasonable?

On an experiential basis, we can again impress ourselves with the duration of some of our memories. Assuming you remain free from disease or injury, you're likely never to forget some information, such as your own name or the words to the "Happy Birthday" song. As an adult, you probably can recall several events from your childhood. You can remember many experiences from high school. Perhaps you have some fond memories from grade school. How about memories for pre-school events? Is there an age before which lasting memories are not possible, or, as some argue, do we carry memories of our own births or prenatal experiences? "The earliest scientifically documented childhood memories recalled by adults happened to them when they were around 2 years of age" (Howe, 2003, p. 63).

Simple repetition (maintenance rehearsal) is used to keep material active in short-term memory. This type of rehearsal is also one way to move information from STM to LTM. However, simply attending to information—the essence of repetition—is an inefficient means of encoding information into long-term memory.

elaborative rehearsal to think about information, organize it, form images of it, make it meaningful, or relate it to something already in long-term memories

To encode information into long-term memory, we need to use **elaborative rehearsal**; we need to think about it, organize it, form images of it, make it meaningful, or relate it to something already in our long-term memories. Elaborative rehearsal is not an either/or process. Information can be elaborated to greater or lesser degrees. When we do no more than attend to an item, as in maintenance rehearsal, our processing is fairly minimal, or shallow, and that item is likely to remain in memory for a relatively short time. The more we rehearse an item elaboratively, the easier it will be to remember.

What are the capacity and the duration of long-term memory (LTM)?

How does information get encoded into long-term memory?

How Accurate Are Long-Term Memories?

When we try to remember a fact we learned in school many years ago, it is often easy to determine the accuracy of our recall. As on classroom tests, we are either right or wrong. Determining the accuracy of our memories for past experiences is difficult at best and is sometimes impossible. Do we *really* remember all the details of that family vacation when we were six years old, or are we recalling bits and pieces of what happened along with fragments of what we've been told happened and then adding other details to reconstruct a likely story? Most of the time, the accuracy of one's recall of experiences from the distant past is of little or no consequence. In some situations, such determinations of accuracy can be of critical importance.

A popular misconception is that memory works like a camcorder. That is, when placing something into memory, the record button is pressed (encoding), and that information is recorded exactly as experienced on tape (storage). That experience is gotten out of storage by pressing the rewind button, followed by the play button (retrieval). Although this common view of memory is elegant in its simplicity, it is not how memory works. In reality we store features of what is experienced, and then those features are retrieved, and a likely memory is reconstructed.

Retrieval from memory involves an active construction process, and memories based on such a process may be inaccurate because information is either left out or is added. The view emerging from research in this area is that the construction process involves—as Frederick Bartlett suggested more than 70 years ago—storing patterns of features in which each feature represents a different aspect of what is experienced. Furthermore, the features stored are widely scattered over different parts of the brain. That is, no single part of the brain houses a complete memory. Retrieval of information is rather like putting together a jigsaw puzzle. Features stored in various parts of the brain are reactivated, and they, in turn, reactivate other features. This reactivation process continues until a memory is reconstructed (Schacter et al., 1998).

And sometimes the reconstruction process results in inaccurate reports of what truly did happen. The important point is that memories are not fixed, nor are they necessarily accurate representations of what was experienced. As one memory researcher put it, "We make up new memories every day" (Loftus, 2003).

One example of the importance of accuracy in the retrieval of information from long-term storage involves what is called *repressed memory*. Repression is said to have occurred when extremely unpleasant or traumatic events are pushed deep into the unconscious corners of memory, from which retrieval is, at best, very difficult. A repressed memory is one that is so disturbing to a person that it is pushed deep into the unconscious and is no longer readily available for retrieval.

In recent years the idea of repression, or "motivated forgetting," has created quite a stir. Repressed memories have been linked to psychological symptoms,

The accuracy of long-term memory retrieval is a particularly important issue when witnesses are asked to testify in courts of law about what they remember about a given event.

including eating disorders, anxiety, and depression. One theory is that a repressed memory of childhood sexual abuse (CSA) is at the root of these disorders, and the only way to deal with an individual's symptoms is to recover the repressed memory (or memories) and deal with it.

The central controversy is whether memories recovered in therapy are actual memories or false memories—which may result from leading suggestions made during the course of therapy. Thousands of persons have come forth with accounts of being sexually abused as children—often by a close relative. Based on memories recovered during therapy, individuals have been tried and convicted. And some of these convictions have been overturned as well. In May 1994, for example, a jury in California awarded Gary Ramona $500,000 from a therapist who had "uncovered repressed memories" of childhood sexual abuse from his daughter, Holly. Holly had entered therapy for an eating disorder and had become convinced that her disorder was related to CSA. The jury agreed that the therapist had planted the ideas of abuse in Holly's memory and awarded damages to the girl's father.

Without questioning the enormity of the problem of child abuse or challenging reports of its prevalence, Elizabeth Loftus (1993a, 1993b, 2003) has challenged the authenticity of the repressed memories of some adults who "remember" events that may never have happened in the first place. Loftus has never said that child abuse is not a real phenomenon. It may be, however, that some people genuinely come to believe that they were abused as children in order to help make sense of the difficulties they are now having as adults (Goodman et al., 2003; McNally, 2003a, 2003b). It is possible that repressed memories recovered during therapy may have been implanted by a therapist who (purposefully or not) used suggestive therapy techniques. Imagine a patient who is told that the therapist has "seen dozens of cases" like the patient's, and that in most cases, symptoms are related to repressed memories of childhood sexual abuse. The therapist encourages the patient to work at uncovering and elaborating on the repressed memory. To make matters worse, the therapist may encourage the patient to let his or her imagination run wild. Some therapists even have patients imagine that they were sexually abused (Loftus, 1997).

What is the bottom line on repressed and recovered memories? There is research showing that memories can be implanted. However, this does not mean that all recovered memories are false memories. The problem lies in the ability to distinguish between those recovered memories that are actual memories of real events and those that are false memories resulting from suggestive techniques. The problem of repressed memory recovery presents a challenge not only to psychology, but also to the legal system, which must deal with cases relying on recovered memories.

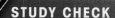

✓ STUDY CHECK

What does research on repressed memories tell us about the accuracy of long-term memories?

CYBER PSYCH

(a) An excellent summary of memory issues in general can be found at this website, but click on "3.1 Constructive Remembering" if nothing else. http://plato.stanford.edu/entries/memory.
(b) http://www.fmsfonline.org is the website for the False Memory Syndrome Foundation. These folks do have an agenda. Please click on the link "About the FMS Foundation."
(c) http://www.jimhopper.com/memory is a website with the opposite point of view of the previous one. Remember: A skeptical mind is a good thing in science.
(d) You really cannot get into the issue of repressed memories without stopping at http://faculty.washington.edu/eloftus.

Improving Memory Retrieval

Encoding, storage, and retrieval are inter-related memory processes. The issue is simple: If you do not encode information properly, you will have difficulty retrieving it. You may not recall a stranger's name simply because you never knew it in the first place. You have had countless encounters with pennies. Can you draw a picture of a penny, locating all its features? Can you recognize an accurate drawing of a penny (Figure 6.2)? In fact, few of us can, and even fewer can recall all its essential features. Nearly 90 percent fail to note that the word Liberty appears right behind Lincoln's shoulder (Nickerson & Adams, 1979). These retrieval failures do not result from a lack of experience but from a lack of proper encoding. Few of us have ever sat down to study (encode) exactly what a penny looks like.

Here's an example to which nearly all students can relate—the difference between recall and recognition. **Recall** occurs when someone produces information to which he or she has been previously exposed. For example, if you were presented with a list of 15 words to learn and were then asked to write down as many of the

recall the process that occurs when someone produces information to which he or she has been previously exposed

FIGURE 6.2

Fifteen drawings of the head of a penny. The fact that we cannot easily identify the correct rendition emphasizes that simple exposure to a stimulus does not guarantee it will be adequately encoded in long-term memory (Nickerson & Adams, 1979).

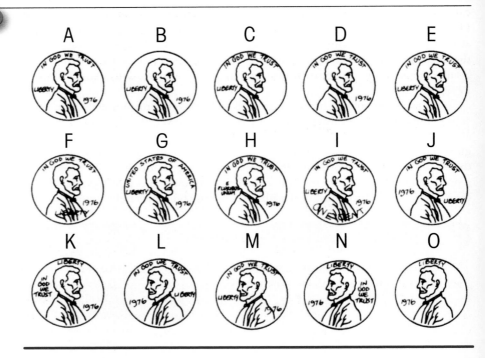

recognition the retrieval process of identifying material that has been previously experienced

words as possible, in any order, you would be using recall. We merely specify the information wanted and say, "Go into your long-term memory, locate that information, get it out, and write it down." For **recognition**, we ask someone to identify material previously experienced. A good example of a recognition task occurs when an eyewitness must try to pick a suspect out of a lineup. The witness was exposed to the perpetrator at the scene of the crime. An image of the perpetrator's face was encoded into memory. During a lineup, the witness is asked if he or she recognizes anyone in the lineup.

When recall and recognition memory are compared, recognition turns out to be a more sensitive measure of memory than recall. In other words, we can often recognize things we cannot recall. For example, have you ever seen someone you know walking toward you, and you recognize the person (perhaps an acquaintance from high school), but you just cannot recall the person's name? In virtually every case, retrieval by recognition is superior to retrieval by recall. Most students would rather take a multiple-choice exam, in which they only have to *recognize* the correct response from among a few alternatives, than a fill-in-the-blank test (or essay test), which requires *recall*.

Consider these questions, each of which is after the same information.

(1) The physiologist best associated with the discovery of classical conditioning was _____.

(2) The physiologist best associated with the discovery of classical conditioning was a) Thorndike b) Helmholtz c) Pavlov d) Skinner.

For the first question, recall was required; the second only required that you recognize Pavlov's name. Reinforcing the notion that encoding and retrieval are related are the data that tell us that students who expect and study for a fill-in-the-blank test of recall will do better on that test than will students who expect and study for a test of recognition. Test scores are best when the measure of retrieval matches the strategy of encoding. There are other ways in which we can see the relationship among encoding, storage, and retrieval, which is where we go next.

HOW INFORMATION GETS IN AFFECTS GETTING IT OUT

Retrieval is most successful when the situation, or *context,* in which retrieval occurs matches the context that was present at encoding. When cues present at encoding are also present at retrieval, retrieval is enhanced. Not only do we encode and store particular items of information, we also note and store the context in which those items occur.

Here's a hypothetical experiment that demonstrates this point (based on Tulving & Thompson, 1973). Students learn a list of 24 common words. Half the students are given cue words to help them remember each item on the list. For the stimulus word "wood," the cue word is "tree"; for cheese, the cue is "green," and so on for each of the 24 words. The other students receive no such cues during their learning (i.e., encoding). Later, students are asked to recall as many words as they can. What happens is that presenting the cue at recall helps those students who had seen it during learning but *decreases* the recall for those who had not seen it during learning. If learning takes place without a cue, recall will be better without it.

A psychology professor has a hypothesis. She believes she can determine the learning ability of students by noting where they sit in the classroom. The best, brightest students choose seats farthest from the door. Poorer students sit by the door, apparently interested in getting easily into and out of the room. (There may be some truth to this, but I am not serious: This is just an example of a hypothesis.) To make her point, she does an experiment. Students seated away from the door are asked to learn a list of words. They can listen to the list, read aloud, only once. A second list of words is needed for the students seated by the door—they've already heard the first list. The list the "smart students" hear contains words such as *university, registrar, automobile, environmental,* and *psychology.* As predicted, they have little problem recalling this list even after just one presentation. The students huddled by the door get the second list: *insidious, tachistoscope, sophistry, flotsam,* and *episcotister,* and the like. Needless to say, the professor's hypothesis will be confirmed.

This obviously is not a fair experiment. Those students sitting by the door will yell foul. The second list of words is clearly more difficult to learn and recall than the first list. The words on the first list are more familiar, and they are easier to pronounce. However, the major difference between these lists is the **meaningfulness** of the items, or the extent to which they elicit existing associations in memory. The *university, registrar, automobile* list is easy to remember because each word in it is meaningful. Each word makes us think of many other things or produces many associations. These items are easy to elaborate. Words like "episcotister" are more difficult because they evoke few, if any, associations.

An important observation: Meaningfulness is not a characteristic or feature built into materials to be learned. Meaningfulness resides in the learner. "Episcotister" may be a meaningless collection of letters for many, but for others it is a word rich in meaning, a word with which they can readily form many associations. What

meaningfulness the extent to which a given stimulus elicits existing associations already stored in memory

Classroom exams really measure what a student can retrieve from memory at a given point in time—not "what they have learned."

is or is not meaningful is a function of one's individual experiences. (An episcotister, by the way, is a type of apparatus used in psychology. To make this word truly meaningful for you, you might want to do some research on episcotisters.)

It follows, then, that one of your tasks as a learner is to do whatever you can to make the material you are learning as meaningful as possible. You need to seek out and form associations between what you are learning and what you already know. You need to elaboratively rehearse what you are encoding so that you can retrieve it later. You need to ask questions about what you are studying. What does this mean? What does it make me think of? Does this remind me of something I already know? How can I make this more meaningful? Perhaps you now see the reason for including "Before You Go On" questions within each chapter.

So retrieval is enhanced when we elaborate on the material we are learning—when we organize it and make it meaningful during the encoding process. Now we'll look at a few encoding techniques, called **mnemonic devices**, that aid retrieval by helping us to organize and add meaningfulness to new material.

Research by Bower and Clark (1969), for example, shows us that we can improve retrieval of otherwise unorganized material if we weave that material into a meaningful story—a technique called *narrative chaining*. A group of college students learned a list of ten simple nouns in a specific order. This is not a terribly difficult task, and the students had little trouble with it. Then they were given another list of ten nouns to learn, and then another, and another until they had learned 12 lists. These students were given no instructions other than to remember each list of words in order.

A second group of students learned the same 12 lists. But they were asked to make up stories that used each of the words on the list in order. After each list was presented, both groups were asked to recall the list of words they had just heard. At this point, there was no difference in the recall scores for the two groups. Then came a surprise. After all 12 lists had been recalled, the students were tested again on their recall for each of the lists. Students were given a word

mnemonic devices techniques that aid retrieval by helping us to organize and add meaningfulness to new material

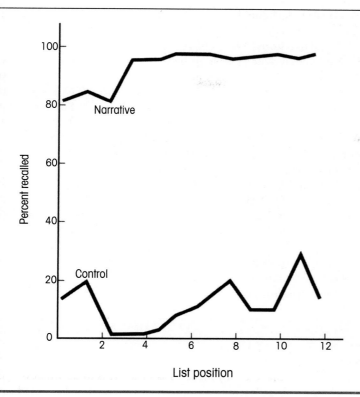

FIGURE 6.3

Percent correct recall for words from 12 lists learned under two study conditions. In the narrative condition, students made up short stories to relate the words meaningfully, whereas in the control condition, simple memorization without any mention of a specific mnemonic device was used (after Bower & Clark, 1969).

from one of the 12 lists and were asked to recall the other nine words from that list. Now the difference in recall between the two groups of students was striking (see Figure 6.3). Students who used a narrative-chaining technique recalled 93 percent of the words (on average), whereas those who did not organize the words recalled only 13 percent. The message is clear and consistent with what we've learned so far: Organizing unrelated words into sensible stories helps us remember them.

Forming mental images can also improve memory. It is the contention of psychologist Allan Paivio that visual images provide a unique way of encoding meaningful information; that is, we are at an advantage if we can encode not only what a stimulus means, but also what it looks like (Paivio, 1971, 1986). Imagery helps us retrieve words such as "horse," "rainbow," and "computer" more readily than words such as "treason," "session," and "effort"—even when the frequency and meaningfulness of the words are equated.

Gordon Bower (1972) asked students to learn lists of pairs of English words. Some students were instructed to form mental images that showed an interaction between the two words. One pair, for instance, was "piano-cigar." Recall for word pairs was much better for those students who formed mental images than for those who did not.

Another imagery-related mnemonic device may be the oldest. It is attributed to the Greek poet Simonides and is called the *method of loci*. The idea here is to get in your mind a well-known location (*loci* are locations)—say, the floor plan of your house or apartment. Visually place the material you are trying to recall in various places throughout your house in a sensible order. When the time comes for you to retrieve the material, mentally walk through your chosen locations, recalling the information you have stored at each place.

Mnemonic devices don't have to be formal techniques with special names, nor do they have to involve imagery. You used a mnemonic trick to learn how many days are in each month when you learned the ditty, "Thirty days hath September, April, June, and November. All the rest have...". Some students originally learned the colors of the rainbow in order (that's red, orange, yellow, green, blue, indigo, and violet) by remembering the name "ROY G. BIV," which I grant you is not terribly meaningful, but it does help. Nursing and medical school students have long used a similar device for learning the 12 pairs of cranial nerves in order (that would be the olfactory, optic, oculomotor, trochlear, trigeminal, abducens, facial, acoustic, glossopharyngeal, spinal accessory, and the hypoglossal). What all those students remember (even after they can no longer associate the correct name with the letter) is, "On Old Olympian Towering Tops, a Finn and German Viewed Some Hops." No doubt you have used several mnemonic devices to organize and make material meaningful. In each case, the message is that retrieval will be enhanced whenever we can organize otherwise-unrelated material in a meaningful way.

✓ STUDY CHECK

Discuss how encoding processes can be used to improve retrieval.

CYBER PSYCH

(a) http://www.mindtools.com/memory.html is a "commercial" site with ads for all sorts of things—some related to memory, some not. "Tools for Improving Your Memory" will get you to a rather long piece in PDF for easy downloading and printing.

(b) Here are several articles on memory that are well worth a look. http://www.cdl.org/resource-library/library_browse.php? type=subject&id=26.

SCHEDULING PRACTICE

Retrieval, no matter how it is measured, depends on how one goes about encoding, rehearsing, or practicing information in the first place. Retrieval also is a function of the amount of practice and how that practice is spaced or distributed. One of the reasons some students do not do as well on exams as they would like is that they simply do not have (or make) enough time to study the material covered on exams. Another reason is that some students do not schedule wisely what time they do have.

Once we decide to learn something, we read, practice, and study the material until we know it. We study until we are satisfied that we have encoded and stored the information in our memories, and then we quit. In other words, we often fail to engage in **overlearning**, the process of practicing or rehearsing material over and above what is needed to learn it. Consider this example, and see if you can extend this evidence to your own study habits.

overlearning the process of practicing or rehearsing material over and above what is needed to learn it

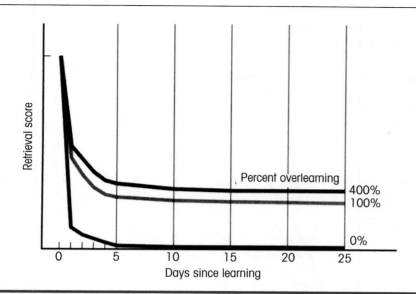

FIGURE 6.4

Idealized data showing the short-term and long-term advantages of overlearning. Note the "diminished returns" with additional overlearning (Krueger, 1929).

A student comes to the laboratory to learn a list of nonsense syllables such as dax, wuj, pib, lep, and zuw. There are 15 such items on the list, and they have to be presented repeatedly before the student can recall all of the items correctly. Having correctly recalled the items, the student is dismissed with instructions to return two weeks later for a test of his recall of the same syllables. Not surprisingly, he does not fare very well on this retrieval task.

What do you think would have happened if we had continued to present the list of syllables at the time of learning, well beyond the point at which it was first learned? Let's say the list was learned in 12 trials. We may have the student practice the list for six additional presentations (50 percent overlearning—practice that is 50 percent more than it took to learning in the first place). What if we required an additional 12 trials of practice (100 percent overlearning), or even an additional 48 trials of practice (400 percent overlearning)?

The effects of overlearning are well documented and very predictable. The recall data for this imaginary experiment might look like those in Figure 6.4. Note three things about these data:

1. If we measure retrieval at various times after learning, forgetting is rather impressive and quite sudden.
2. Overlearning improves retrieval and has its greatest effects with longer retention intervals.
3. There is a "diminishing returns" effect present here; that is, 50 percent overlearning is much more useful than no overlearning; 100 percent overlearning is somewhat better than 50 percent; and 400 percent overlearning is better than 100 percent, but not by very much. For any learning task, or individual, there is probably an optimal amount of overlearning.

The scheduling of learning time is also an important factor in determining the likelihood of retrieval, and it is to this issue we turn next.

FIGURE 6.5

Improvement in performance as a function of the distribution of practice time. The task involved was printing the letters of the alphabet upside-down and backward with 20 one–minute trials separated by rest intervals of various lengths (Kientzle, 1946).

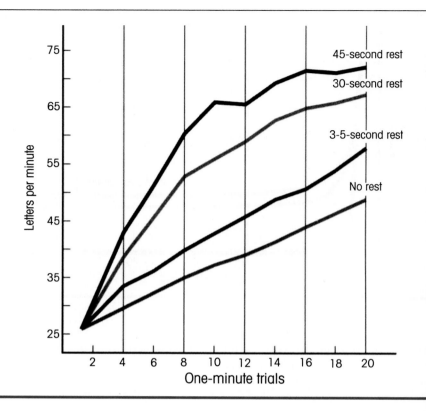

Some of the oldest data in psychology tell us that retrieval will be improved if practice (encoding) is spread out over time with rest intervals spaced in between. The data in Figure 6.5 are fairly standard. In fact, this experiment, first performed in 1946, provides such reliable results that it is commonly used as a student project in psychology classes. The task is to write the letters of the alphabet, upside down and from right to left. (If you think that sounds easy, give it a try.)

Participants are given the opportunity to practice the task under four different conditions. The *massed-practice group* works with no break at all between trials. The three *distributed-practice groups* receive the same amount of practice but get rest intervals interspersed between each one-minute trial. One group gets a three- to five-second rest between trials, a second group receives a 30-second rest, and a third group gets a 45-second rest between trials.

As can be seen in Figure 6.5, participants in all four groups begin at about the same (poor) level of performance. After 20 minutes of practice, the performance of all groups shows improvement, but by far, the massed practice (no rest) group does the poorest, and the 45-second rest group does the best.

The conclusion from years of research is that, almost without exception, distributed practice is superior to massed practice. There are exceptions, however. Some tasks may suffer from having rest intervals inserted in practice time. In general, whenever you must keep track of many things at the same time, you should mass your practice until you have finished what you are working on. If, for example, you are working on a complex math problem, you should work it through until you find a solution, whether it's time for a break or not. And, of course, you should not break up your practice in such a way as to disrupt the meaningfulness of the material you are studying. Meaningfulness is a powerful factor in memory retrieval.

What we're talking about here surely applies to the scheduling of study time. The message is always the same: Short (and meaningful) study periods with rest periods interspersed are more efficient than study periods massed together. There may be times when cramming is better than not studying at all, but as a general strategy, cramming is simply inefficient.

✓ STUDY CHECK

How do overlearning and practice (study) schedules affect retrieval?

CYBER PSYCH

(a) http://www.thememorypage.net is, after all, called "The Memory Page," and you will find it useful.

(b) This is a truly "fun" website on mnemonics and memory improvement. Do explore the link named simply "PI" http://www.memoryelixir.com/mnemonics.html.

(c) There may be a website in cyberspace that lists more mnemonic techniques than http://eudesign.com/mnems, but I doubt it.

Chapter Summary

What do psychologists mean by "sensory memory"?

Memory is a set of systems involved in the acquisition, storage, and retrieval of information. Sensory memory is a memory storage system that stores large amounts of information for very short periods of time.

Describe the basic features of short-term, or working, memory.

Short-term memory is a storage system in which information can be held for several seconds before it fades or is replaced. Encoding information into this memory requires that we attend to it. Information may enter short-term storage from sensory memory or be retrieved from long-term memory. We keep material in STM by re-attending to it, a process called *maintenance rehearsal*. The capacity of short-term memory is approximately five to nine "chunks of information," where a *chunk* is an imprecise measure of a unit of meaningful material. Organizing information into meaningful clusters, units, or chunks can expand the apparent capacity of STM.

What are the capacity and the duration of long-term memory?

Long-term memory (LTM) is a storage system that houses large amounts of information for long, virtually limitless, periods of time. Barring illness or injury, memories of a lifetime are stored in long-term memory. There seems to be no end to the amount of information that can be stored in long-term memory.

How does information get encoded into long-term memory?

Although rote (maintenance) rehearsal can move information into LTM, elaborative rehearsal is much more efficient. This type of rehearsal requires one to think about what is being encoded to organize it, make it meaningful, and relate it to something already stored in long-term memory.

What does the research on repressed memories of childhood trauma and on eyewitness testimony add to the discussion of the accuracy of long-term memories?

Unlike the popular view of memory working like a camcorder, recording information exactly for later playback, memory is a *constructive process*. Features of information are stored, and recall involves a reconstruction of those features. According to this view, stored features are scattered in different areas of the brain. When we want to remember something, a feature is activated that sets off a chain reaction in other related features. Recall can be influenced by several events other than the to-be-recalled event itself.

Repressed memories are events presumed to be in one's long-term memory (retained) but that cannot be retrieved because doing so would be anxiety-producing. Some psychologists have challenged the reality of some repressed memories, as when adults remember incidents of sexual abuse from when they were children.

Some critics of repressed memories maintain that influential suggestions from thera-pists may cause a person to believe that his or her psychological problems stem from repressed memories of events that may, in fact, never have taken place. It may be that our recall of events long past has been influenced by events that have occurred since.

Discuss how encoding processes can be used to improve retrieval.

The ability to retrieve information stored in LTM is partially determined by how one is asked to do so. Recall involves asking someone to produce information to which he or she has been previously exposed. Recognition is a measure of memory in which the information to be retrieved is presented and a person is asked if it can be identified as familiar. Retrieval measured by recognition is generally superior to retrieval measured by recall. We can often recognize things that we cannot recall. Retrieval is maximized when encoding expectations match the means of measur-ing retrieval.

Indeed, retrieval depends heavily on encoding. For example, the greater the extent to which the cues or context available at retrieval match the cues or context available at encoding, the better retrieval will be.

Meaningfulness reflects the extent to which material is associated with infor-mation already stored in memory. In general, the more meaningful the material, the easier it will be to learn and to retrieve. Meaningfulness resides in the individual and not in the material to be learned.

Narrative chaining involves making up a story that meaningfully weaves together otherwise unorganized words or information. Forming mental images, or pictures in one's mind, of information to be remembered is also helpful. The method of loci is an imagery method in which one "places" pieces of information at various locations (loci) in a familiar setting and then retrieves those pieces of infor-mation while mentally traveling through the setting.

How do overlearning and practice (study) schedules affect retrieval?

Overlearning is the rehearsal or practice of material above and beyond that neces-sary for immediate recall. Within limits, the more one engages in overlearning, the greater the likelihood of accurate retrieval. Retrieval also is affected by how one schedules study (or encoding) sessions. In massed practice, study or rehearsal con-tinues without any intervening rest intervals. Distributed practice uses shorter seg-ments of rehearsal interspersed with rest intervals. In nearly every case, distributed practice is found to be superior to massed practice.

Student Study Guide

STUDY TIP #6 "How Should I Study?"

The whole idea of studying—indeed, the whole idea of going to college in the first place—is to learn and remember something that you did not know or remember before. Studying is the active process of placing information into memory in such a way that it can be located and retrieved later. The information that is placed in memory during study is not restricted to simple facts, but also includes knowledge of new ways of discovering information, thinking about information, and evaluating information. Simply: Studying is a process in which stuff "out there" gets put into memory in a usable way.

The first thing to realize is that studying is **an active process.** It is one in which you have to become actively involved. Sorry, but no matter how long you sit there with a book on your lap, nothing is going to happen until you start getting involved with what you are reading. If you are sitting in class daydreaming about last weekend's date, nothing is going to get learned, no matter how brilliant the lecture.

The essence of study is what psychologists call *elaborative rehearsal*. To study effectively is to take to-be-learned material and elaborate on it, to think about it. Make it meaningful. Relate it to something you already know, to something you have learned elsewhere. For example, I use several stories and examples in the text in an effort to make the material meaningful. But these are my stories; they are *my* examples, and it is much more useful to generate your own.

One thing that makes psychology an easier course to study than some others is that (usually) it is fairly easy to relate what you are studying to your personal experience. When the text talks about the value of reinforcement, think about which reinforcers you are working for. When your instructor lectures about Piaget's theory of developmental stages in children, think about a younger brother, sister, niece or nephew, or perhaps your own child or children. The more you can relate what you are learning to what you already know, the better will be your learning, and the better will be your retention.

KEY TERMS AND CONCEPTS

encoding _____

_____

storage_____

_____

retrieval _____

_____

sensory memory _____

_____

short-term memory (STM)_____

_____

maintenance rehearsal _____

_____

chunk _____

_____

long-term memory _____

_____

elaborative rehearsal _____

_____

recall _____

_____

recognition _____

_____

meaningfulness _____

_____

mnemonic devices _____

_____

overlearning_____

_____

Practice Test Questions

MULTIPLE CHOICE

1. Psychologists talk about passing information through three levels or
   compartments of memory called, in order,

   _____ a. encoding, storage, and retrieval.

   _____ b. primary, secondary, and tertiary.

   _____ c. central, peripheral, and somatic.

   _____ d. sensory, short-term, and long-term.

2. For approximately what length of time is information typically held in one's sensory memory?

_____ a. a second or two

_____ b. a minute or two

_____ c. a day or two

_____ d. At least some information is held there permanently.

3. The minimal requirement for keeping information in short-term memory with maintenance rehearsal is that we

_____ a. elaborate it in some way.   _____ c. organize it.

_____ b. make it meaningful.   _____ d. re-attend to it.

4. The amount of information held in STM (i.e., its capacity) can be extended (at least a little bit) if we can _____ that information.

_____ a. rehearse   _____ c. chunk

_____ b. attend to   _____ d. elaborate

5. The best way to encode information into long-term memory is

_____ a. rote repetition.   _____ c. maintenance rehearsal.

_____ b. taking extensive notes.   _____ d. by elaborating it.

6. Elaboratively rehearsing information is largely a matter of organizing it and

_____ a. making it meaningful.   _____ c. retrieving it.

_____ b. re-attending to it.   _____ d. repeating it.

7. If any sort of memory is to be repressed, what sort of memory is it likely to be?

_____ a. nearly anything in STM

_____ b. anxiety-producing events stored in LTM

_____ c. facts stored in LTM

_____ d. habits stored in STM

8. When psychologists talk about "retrieval failure," what assumption do they make?

_____ a. We are dealing with short-term memory.

_____ b. Information is available, even if it is not accessible.

_____ c. There must be some sort of brain damage involved.

_____ d. The material was never stored in the first place.

9. Most people cannot remember all of the features on a one-dollar bill. Which of the following phrases best describes the basic problem in such instances?

_____ a. lack of availability   _____ c. improper encoding

_____ b. poorly worded questions   _____ d. proactive interference

10. Mnemonic techniques enhance or improve retrieval because they

_____ a. involve the continued repetition of information.

_____ b. make material more meaningful.

_____ c. involve the right side of the brain as well as the left.

_____ d. lengthen the storage of LTM.

11. Making up a story that contains all of the words on a list to be learned is a mnemonic device called

　　_____ a. the peg word method.　　　　_____ c. mental imagery.

　　_____ b. the method of loci.　　　　　_____ d. narrative chaining.

12. After we have presented a list of words to Bob eight times, we have evidence that he has learned the list. If we want Bob to engage in 200% overlearning of this list, how many additional presentations would be required?

　　_____ a. 0　　　　　　　　　　　　_____ c. 16

　　_____ b. 8　　　　　　　　　　　　_____ d. 20

TRUE/FALSE

1. _____ True _____ False　For information to be processed into memory, the very first thing that we do to or with that information is to learn it.

2. _____ True _____ False　Of the three levels or types of memory, perceptual attention influences short-term memory the most.

3. _____ True _____ False　The most efficient strategy for encoding information in semantic long-term memory is to use elaborative rehearsal.

4. _____ True _____ False　At least on classroom exams, retrieval measured by recall is superior to retrieval measured by recognition.

5. _____ True _____ False　Retrieval is a skill that can be enhanced with practice.

Motivation and Emotion

Preview

In this chapter, we'll address some important theoretical and practical issues. For the first time, our focus will be on questions that begin with **why**. "Why did she *do* that (as opposed to her doing nothing)?" "Why did she do *that* (as opposed to her doing something else)?" "Why does she *keep doing* that (as opposed to her stopping)?" As you can see, the study of motivation gets us involved with attempts to explain the causes of certain behaviors.

We begin with a definition of motivation and then explore several different approaches to understanding motivation—different "theories of motivation," if you will. As is so often the case, you will see that no one approach tells us all we would like to know about motivation, but each adds something to our appreciation of motivated behavior. This section will summarize instincts, needs and drives, incentives, homeostasis, arousal, and cognitive dissonance as concepts that can explain why we do what we do and keep on doing it. Then we'll look at some motives that have no clear biological basis. They are called "psychologically based motives," and include the needs for achievement, power, and affiliation.

Since its emergence in the late 1800s, psychology has included the study of emotions as part of its subject matter. Psychologists have learned a great deal about emotional reactions, but answers to some very fundamental questions have remained elusive. We wish that psychologists could tell us just what emotions are and where they come from. We want to know how to increase the number and intensity of pleasant emotions and decrease our experience of unpleasant ones. Some emotional reactions do seem quite unpleasant: fear, shame, jealousy, and rage. Just the same, we would not want to give up our ability to experience emotions. To do so would be to surrender the likes of love, joy, satisfaction, and ecstasy. Life without the color of emotion would be flat and drab.

We'll begin this discussion as we have begun many others, by trying to generate an acceptable working definition of the subject at hand. You ought to give that a try yourself before you go on. How would you define emotion? With a definition in hand, we'll look at some attempts to organize or classify the various emotions. This exercise will bring up the notion of basic emotions, what they might be, and if they even exist. We then turn to the physiological bases of emotions. Emotional reactions require the central nervous system, to be sure, but it is the autonomic nervous systems that are most intimately involved. Finally, we'll discuss the outward display of emotion. This will take us first to a consideration of how internal emotional states are communicated from one organism to another.

What Motivates Us?

Motivation involves two sub-processes. The first is arousal—an organism's level of activation or excitement. Here we are using the word "motivation" to describe a force that initiates behaviors, gets an organism going, energized enough to do something and keep doing it. The second sub-process provides direction, or focus, to the organism's behaviors. More than being aroused and active, a motivated organism's behavior is in some way purposeful or goal-directed. Thus, **motivation** is the process that arouses, directs, and maintains behavior.

motivation the process that arouses, directs, and maintains behavior

From its earliest days, psychology has tried to find some systematic theory to summarize and organize what various motivational states have in common. Psychologists have struggled to find one general theory that could be used to account for why organisms tend to do what they do. Here we will review some of these theories in a somewhat chronological order.

INSTINCTS

During the 1880s, psychologists often explained behaviors in terms of **instincts**—unlearned, complex patterns of behavior that occur in the presence of certain stimuli. Why do birds build nests? A nest-building instinct. When conditions are right, birds build nests. It's what birds do. Why do salmon swim upstream to mate? Instinct. Swimming upstream at mating season is part of what it means to be a salmon. These behaviors can be modified by experience, but the force behind them is unlearned or instinctive. It is simply part of their nature to engage in these behaviors.

Instincts may be useful for explaining the behaviors of birds and salmon, but what about people? William James (1890) reasoned that because they are more complex, humans had to have more instincts than do "lower" animals. William McDougall championed the instinctual explanation of human behaviors (McDougall, 1908). He said that human behaviors were motivated by 11 basic instincts: repulsion, curiosity, flight, reproduction, gregariousness, acquisitiveness, parenting, construction, self-assertion, self-abasement, and pugnacity. Soon, McDougall had to extend his list to include 18 instincts. As different behaviors required explanation, new instincts were devised to explain them.

As lists of human instincts got longer and longer, trying to account for more and more behaviors, the problem with this approach became obvious. Particularly for humans, explaining behavior patterns by alluding to instinct only re-labeled

instincts unlearned, complex patterns of behavior that occur in the presence of certain stimuli

Explaining why salmon swim upstream—against incredible odds—in order to spawn can be handled rather easily by attributing the behavior to instinct.

them and did not explain anything at all. Still, those psychologists who argued for instincts did introduce, and draw attention to, an idea very much with us today: We may engage in some behaviors for reasons that are basically biological, or physiological, and more inherited than learned.

NEEDS AND DRIVES

An approach that provided an alternative to explaining behavior in terms of instincts was one that attempted to explain the whys of behavior in terms of needs and drives. We will look at two such theories.

Clark Hull's ideas about motivation were dominant in the 1940s and 1950s (Hull, 1943). In Hull's system, a **need** is defined as a lack or shortage of some biological essential that is required for survival. A need arises from deprivation. When an organism is kept from food, it develops a need for food. Needs give rise to drives. A **drive** is a state of tension, arousal, or activation. If an organism is in a drive state, it is aroused and directed to engage in some behavior to satisfy the drive by reducing the underlying need. Needs produce tensions (drives) that the organism seeks to reduce; hence, this approach is referred to in terms of drive reduction.

need a lack or shortage of some biological essential that is required for survival

drive a state of tension, arousal, or activation

Whereas instincts are tied to specific patterns of behavior, needs and drives are not. They can be used to explain why we do what we do and still allow for the influence of experience and the environment. Going without food may give rise to a need, which in turn gives rise to a drive, but how that drive is expressed in behavior is influenced by an organism's experiences and learning history.

A problem with a drive-reduction approach centers on the biological nature of needs. To claim that needs result only from biological deprivations seems overly restrictive. It may be that not all of the drives that activate a person's behavior are based on biological needs. Humans often engage in behaviors to satisfy learned drives. Drives derived from an organism's learning experience are called **secondary drives**, as opposed to primary drives, which are based on unlearned, physiological needs. In fact, most of the drives that arouse and direct your behavior have little to do with biology. You may feel you need a new car this year. Your brother may convince himself that he needs a new set of golf clubs, and you'll both work very hard to save the money to buy what you need. You may say you are "driven," but it's difficult to imagine how your new car or your brother's golf clubs could be satisfying some sort of biological need. A lot of advertising is directed at trying to convince people that certain products and services are needed, even though, in fact, they will have very little impact on survival.

secondary drives motivating agents or drives derived from an organism's learning experience

A related complication is that organisms often continue behaving even after their biological needs are met. Drives are states of arousal or tension, and the claim is that we behave as we do in order to reduce tension or arousal. Yet we know that sky divers jump out of airplanes, mountain climbers risk life and limb to scale sheer cliffs of stone, monkeys play with mechanical puzzles even when solving those puzzles leads to no other reward, and children explore the pots and pans in kitchen cabinets even when repeatedly told not to. These actions do not appear to be reducing tension, do they? Perhaps these organisms are trying to satisfy a curiosity drive, or an exploration drive, or a manipulation drive. But then we run the risk of trying to explain why people behave as they do by generating longer and longer lists of drives—the same problem that comes up when we try to explain behavior in terms of instinct.

It is difficult to argue for a "need to put one's life in danger by climbing vertical rock formations." The behavior hardly seems to be one that reduces tension.

So what do these complications mean? It seems that people often *do* behave in ways that reduce drives and thereby satisfy needs. How drives are satisfied, or needs are reduced, may reflect each organism's learning history. The concept of drive reduction is a useful one and is still very much with us in psychology, but it cannot be accepted as a complete explanation for motivated behaviors.

Abraham Maslow believed that the needs that motivate human action are few and are arranged hierarchically (Maslow, 1943, 1970). Figure 7.1 summarizes this hierarchy of needs.

Maslow's approach is basically a stage theory. It proposes that what motivates us first are *physiological needs,* including the basic needs related to survival—food, water, and shelter. Until these needs are met, there is no reason to suspect that an individual will be concerned with anything else. Once physiological needs are under control, a person is still motivated, but now by *safety needs*—the need to feel secure, protected from dangers that might arise in the future. We are now motivated to see to it that the cupboard has food for later, we won't freeze this winter, and there's enough money saved to protect against sudden calamity. The hierarchical nature of this theory is already clear. We are not going to worry about what we'll be eating tomorrow if there's not enough to eat today, but if today's needs are taken care of, we can then focus on the future.

Once safety needs are met, concern shifts to *love and belongingness,* a need for someone else to care about us. If these needs are satisfied, then our concern shifts to

Maslow's hierarchy of needs.

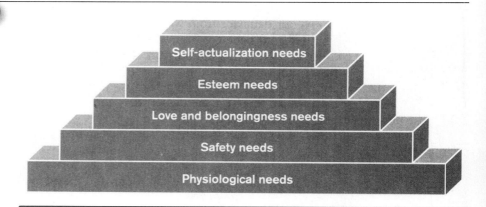

esteem. Our aim is to be recognized for our achievements and efforts. These needs are not physiological, but social. Our behaviors are motivated by our awareness of others and a concern for their approval. A person moves on to higher stages in the hierarchy only if needs at lower stages are met. Ultimately, we may reach the highest stage in Maslow's hierarchy: the need for *self-actualization.* We self-actualize when we become the best we can be, taking the fullest advantage of our potential. We are self-actualizing when we try to be as creative or productive as possible.

In many ways, Maslow's arrangement of needs in a hierarchical fashion reflects the values of Western culture, particularly those that focus on the notion of the individual working hard to overcome obstacles and to achieve. One can hardly expect people to be motivated to grow and achieve success if they are concerned about their very survival on a day-to-day basis. When people's needs for safety, belonging, and esteem are fulfilled, they don't just die, unmotivated to do anything else.

It should be clear to you, as it was to Maslow, that many people never make it to the self-actualization stage in the hierarchy of needs. There are millions of people in this world who have great difficulty dealing with the very lowest stages and who never have the time, energy, or opportunity to be concerned with such issues as self-esteem or belongingness, much less self-actualization.

As a comprehensive theory of human motivation, Maslow's hierarchy has some problems. The truth of the matter is that there is little research support for Maslow's approach to ranking needs in a hierarchy. Perhaps the biggest stumbling block is the idea that anyone can assign ranks to needs and put them in a neat order, regardless of what that order may be. Some people are motivated in ways that violate the ordered-stage approach. Individuals will, for example, freely give up satisfying basic survival needs for the sake of "higher" principles (as in hunger strikes). For the sake of love, people may abandon their own needs for safety and security.

✓ STUDY CHECK

How do psychologists define *motivation,* and how have they used the concepts of instinct, needs, and drives to account for motivated behaviors?

INCENTIVES

One alternative to a drive-reduction approach to motivation focuses on the end state, or goal, of behavior, not needs or drives within the organism. In this view, external stimuli serve as motivating agents, or **incentives**, for behavior. Incentives are external events that are said to pull our behavior from without, as opposed to drives, which are internal events that push our behavior from within. We are pushed by drives, pulled by incentives.

incentives external stimuli that serve as motivating agents

When a mountain climber says she climbs a mountain "because it is there," she is indicating that she is being motivated by an incentive. After enjoying a large meal, we may order a piece of cherry cheesecake, surely not because we need it in any physiological sense, but because it's there on the dessert cart and looks so good (and because previous experience tells us that it is likely to taste good as well).

Some parents want to know how to motivate their children to clean up their rooms. We can interpret this case in terms of establishing goals or incentives. What the parents really want is a clean room, and they would like to have the child do the cleaning. What those parents want to know is how they can get their child to value, work for, and be reinforced by a clean room. If they want the child to be motivated to clean the room, the child needs to learn the value or incentive of having a clean room. How to teach a child that a clean room is a thing to be valued is another story, involving other incentives the child does value. For now, let's just acknowledge that establishing a clean room as a valued goal is the major task at hand and that having a clean room is not an innate, inborn need.

If you think this sounds like our discussion of operant conditioning, you're right. Remember, the basic tenet of operant conditioning is that behaviors are controlled by their consequences. We tend to do (are motivated to do) what leads to reinforcement (positive incentives), and we tend not to do what leads to punishment or failure of reinforcement (negative incentives).

BALANCE OR EQUILIBRIUM

A concept that has proven useful in understanding motivation is balance or equilibrium. The idea is that we are motivated to reach and maintain a state of balance. But what are we motivated to balance? Sometimes maintaining balance involves physiological processes that need to be kept at some level, or within a restricted range, of activity. Sometimes equilibrium is required among our thoughts or cognitions. There are three approaches to motivation that emphasize maintaining a state of equilibrium, or optimal level of functioning: homeostasis, arousal, and cognitive dissonance.

One of the first references to a need for equilibrium can be found in the work of Walter Cannon (1932). Cannon referred to **homeostasis**—a state of balance within our internal physiological reactions. The idea is that each of our physiological processes has a balanced set point of operation. An organism's set point is a level of activity that is "normal or most suitable." When anything upsets this balance, we become motivated, driven to do whatever we can to return to our set point, that optimal homeostatic level of activity. If we drift only slightly from our set point, our physiological mechanisms return us to homeostasis without our intention or

homeostasis a state of balance within our internal physiological reactions

awareness. If automatic processes are unsuccessful, we may have to take action, motivated by the drive to maintain homeostasis.

Everyone has normal, set levels for body temperature, blood pressure, heart rate, basal metabolism (the rate at which energy is used by bodily functions), and so on. If any of these processes deviate from their set point, or homeostatic level, we become motivated to do something that will return us to our state of balance. Cannon's concept of homeostasis was devised to explain physiological processes, but the ideas of balance and optimal level of operation have been applied to psychological processes as well.

arousal an overall level of activation or excitement

Arousal is defined as an overall level of activation or excitement. A person's level of arousal may change from day to day and within the same day. After a good night's sleep and a brisk morning shower, your arousal level may be high. (It also may be high as your instructor moves through class handing out exams.) Late at night, after a busy day at school, your level of arousal may be quite low. Your arousal level is at its lowest when you are in the deepest stages of sleep.

Arousal theories of motivation claim that there is an optimal level of arousal (an "arousal set point") that organisms are motivated to maintain. Drive-reduction theories, remember, argue that we are motivated to reduce tension or arousal by satisfying the needs that give rise to drives. Arousal theories argue that sometimes we seek out ways to increase arousal in order to maintain our optimal arousal level. If you find yourself bored and in a rut, the idea of going to an action-adventure movie may seem like a good one. On the other hand, if you've had a very busy, hectic day, just staying at home doing nothing may sound appealing.

This approach is like Cannon's idea of homeostasis but in slightly more general terms. It suggests that for any situation there is a "best," or most efficient, level of arousal. To do well on an exam, for example, requires that a student have a certain level of arousal. If a student is tired, bored, or just doesn't care, we can expect a poor performance. If, on the other hand, a student is so worried, so uptight and anxious that she or he can barely function, we also can expect a poor exam score. The relation between arousal and the efficiency of performance is depicted in Figure 7.2.

An interesting twist on the theory of arousal is that, for some reason, optimal levels of arousal vary widely from person to person. Some people seem to need and seek particularly high levels of arousal and excitement in their lives. Psychologists call such people "sensation seekers" (Zuckerman et al., 1978, 1980). They enjoy sky diving or mountain climbing and look forward to the challenge of driving in heavy city traffic. Some evidence suggests that there may be a genetic basis for individual differences in sensation-seeking, or risk-taking (Ebstein et al., 1996).

Now let's consider the point of view that we are motivated to maintain a state of balance among ideas or beliefs (our cognitions), as well as among our physiological processes and levels of arousal. That is, we are motivated to maintain what Leon Festinger (1957) calls a state of consonance among our cognitions.

You believe yourself to be a pretty good student. You study hard for an exam in biology and think you're prepared. You judge the exam to be a fairly easy one. But when you get your exam paper back, you discover you failed the test! Now that's hard to accept. You believe that you studied adequately and that the test wasn't difficult. But now you also know you failed the test. Here

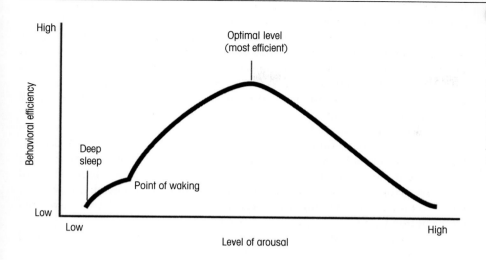

FIGURE 7.2

For each task we attempt, there is an optimal level of arousal. What that level is depends on several factors, including the difficulty of the task. In other words, it is possible to be too aroused (motivated), just as it is possible to be underaroused (Hebb, 1955).

are cognitions that do not fit together. They are not consonant; they are not balanced. You are experiencing **cognitive dissonance**—a state of tension or discomfort that exists when we hold and are aware of inconsistent cognitions. When this occurs, Festinger argues, we are motivated to bring about a change in our system of cognitions. You may come to believe you're not such a good student after all. You may come to believe that your paper was unfairly graded. Or you may come to believe you are a poor judge of an exam's difficulty. This theory doesn't predict *what* will happen, but it does predict that cognitive dissonance will produce motivation to return to a balanced state of cognitive consonance.

These days, almost all smokers experience cognitive dissonance. They know that smoking is a very dangerous habit, yet they continue to smoke. Some reduce their dissonance by convincing themselves that, although smoking is bad for a person's health in general, it really isn't that bad for them in particular, at least not when compared to perceived "benefits."

cognitive dissonance a state of tension or discomfort that exists when we hold and are aware of inconsistent cognitions

SUMMING UP: APPLYING MOTIVATIONAL CONCEPTS

You had a great time. You and your friends spent the day backpacking in the mountains. The signs of spring were everywhere, and you enjoyed every minute. After a full day in the fresh mountain air, no one was terribly choosy about what to have for dinner. Everyone enjoyed large servings of beef stew and baked beans from the can. You even found room for dessert: toasted marshmallows and a piece of chocolate squeezed between two graham crackers.

As your friends settle around the campfire and darkness just begins to overtake the campsite, you excuse yourself. You need to walk off some of that dinner, so you head off to stroll down a narrow trail. As you meander down the trail, you feel totally relaxed, at peace with the world. When you are about 200 yards from the campsite, you think you hear a strange noise in the woods off to your left. Looking back down the trail, you notice that you can barely see the campfire's glow through the trees and underbrush, even though the leaves are not yet fully formed. Well, maybe you'd better not venture too much farther, perhaps just over that ridge, and then—suddenly—from behind a dense thicket, a large growling black bear appears! It takes one look at you, bares its teeth, and lets out a mighty roar! What will you do now?

In this situation, and in many similar, but less dramatic ones, we can be sure of one thing: Your reaction will involve both motivational and emotional states. You will certainly become emotional. Encountering a bear in the woods is not something that one does with reason and intellect alone. You will be motivated to do something; getting away from that bear seems reasonable. (We'll return to this meeting-a-bear-in-the-woods story shortly, when we discuss emotion.)

For now, and granting that this example is somewhat far-fetched and we'll have to oversimplify a bit, let's apply the approaches we have been discussing to explain your behavior. Let's say that, upon seeing the bear, you throw your arms straight up in the air, scream at the top of your lungs, and race back to camp as fast as you can. Your friends, still sitting around the campfire, can see and hear you coming. How might they explain your behaviors?

1. "Clearly, it's a matter of instinct. Humans have a powerful and useful instinct for avoiding large animals in the wild. In this instance, running away is just an unlearned, natural, instinctive reaction to a specific stimulus."

2. "No, I think the fear that arose upon seeing the bear created a tension—a drive—that needed to be relieved. There were several options available, but in your need to reduce your fear, you chose to run away."

3. "Why do you folks keep relying on all this internal instinct-need-drive nonsense? Previous learning experience, even if it was secondhand, taught you that bears in the wild are incentives to be avoided. They are negative goals. You ran back here simply to reach the goal of safety with us, your friends."

4. "I see your reaction as an attempt to maintain a state of equilibrium or balance. Seeing that bear certainly was an emotional experience that increased many physiological functions. Your running away was just one way to try to return those physiological functions to their normal, homeostatic levels."

5. "Why get so complicated with physiological functions? Why not just say that your overall arousal level was much higher than normal—higher than you wanted it to be—so you ran away from the bear simply to lower your level of arousal?"

6. "The same argument can be made for your cognitions—and cognitive dissonance reduction. You know that you like being safe and free of pain. You believe that bears in the woods can be very hurtful, and there's one in front of you. These two ideas are in conflict. You will do something. In this case, you chose to run away. If you believed that a bear in the woods would be afraid of you and of no potential harm, then there wouldn't have been any dissonance, and you wouldn't have run away."

STUDY CHECK

How can incentives, homeostasis, arousal, and cognitive dissonance be useful in explaining motivated behaviors?

CYBER PSYCH

(a) http://allpsych.com/psychology101/motivation.html The AllPsych Online websites are not terribly dramatic, and they are a bit wordy, but they provide good summaries of important issues—and that can be said for this site on motivation.

(b) The list of approaches to motivation above is not an exhaustive list. This website reviews some of those above and adds others. http://changingminds.org/explanations/theories/a_motivation.htm Before moving to the various theories listed here, click on the link to the "ChangingMinds.org" homepage to understand the discrepancies between their list and ours.

Psychologically Based Motives

As much as we might like to think otherwise, those early theorists who directed psychology's attention toward biological or physiological processes were on the right track. A good deal of our behavior *is* motivated by internal, physiological mechanisms. What you are wearing today is at least in part a reflection of your physiological need to maintain your body temperature within certain set limits. We are motivated to drink liquids because of a basic need for water. We are driven to eat because of a hunger drive, based on a need for food. Without attention to these basic, physiological needs—and the drives they give rise to—we could die.

Indeed, you may be able to analyze many of your own behaviors in terms of physiologically based needs and drives. That you had breakfast this morning soon after you got up may have reflected your response to a hunger drive. That you got dressed may have been your attempt to do what you could to control your body temperature, which also may have influenced your choice of clothes. Some (biologically based) sexual motivation may also have affected what you chose to wear today. On the other hand, many of our behaviors are aroused, maintained, and directed (which is to say motivated) by forces that are not clearly biological in origin.

The hypothesis that people are motivated to varying degrees by a need to achieve was introduced to psychology in 1938 by Henry Murray. The **need to achieve (nAch)** is the acquired need to meet or exceed a standard of excellence in one's behaviors. Finding ways to measure this need to achieve and determining its implications has been the focus of David McClelland and his associates (McClelland, 1985; McClelland et al., 1953).

There are short paper-and-pencil tests for the purpose, but nAch is usually assessed by means of the Thematic Apperception Test (TAT). This is a test in which people are asked to tell short stories about a series of rather ambiguous pictures depicting people in various settings. The stories are interpreted and scored according to a series of objective criteria that note references to attempting difficult tasks, succeeding, being rewarded for one's efforts, setting short- and long-term goals, and so

need to achieve (nAch)
the acquired need to meet or exceed a standard of excellence in one's behaviors

on. There are no right or wrong responses. Judgments are made about the references to achievement a person projects into the pictures.

One of the first things McClelland and his colleagues found was that there are consistent differences in measured levels of the need to achieve. A reliable finding about people with high needs for achievement is that, when given a choice, they attempt tasks in which success is not guaranteed (otherwise, there is no challenge) but in which there still is a reasonable chance of success. Both young children and college students who were high in nAch were observed playing a ring-toss game in which the object was to score points by tossing a small ring over a peg from a distance. The farther away from the peg one stood, the more points one could score if successful. In both studies, students with high nAch scores stood at a moderate distance from the peg. They didn't stand so close as to guarantee success, but they didn't choose to stand so far away that they would almost certainly fail. People with low achievement motivation scores tended to go to either extreme—very close, earning few points for their successes or so far away that they rarely succeeded.

People with high achievement needs are not always interested in their own success or in achievement at the expense of others. Particularly in collectivist societies, people may work very hard to achieve goals that are available only to the group of which they are a part.

McClelland would argue that you are reading this text at this moment because you are motivated by a need to achieve. You want to do well on your next exam. You want to get a good grade in this course, and you have decided that to do so you need to study the assigned text material. Some students, however, may read assignments not because they are motivated by a need to achieve, but because they are motivated by a fear of failure. In such a case, the incentive is negative (avoid an F) rather than positive (earn an A). Individuals motivated by a fear of failure tend to take few risks. They choose either tasks in which they are bound to do well or those that are virtually impossible (if the task is impossible they don't have to take responsibility and blame themselves for failures).

It seems that the need to achieve is learned, usually in early childhood. Children who show high levels of achievement motivation are those who have been encouraged in a positive way to excel ("Leslie, that grade of B is very good. You must feel proud!" versus "What! Only a B?"). Children with high needs to achieve are generally encouraged to work things out for themselves, perhaps with parental support and encouragement ("Here, Eli, see if you can do this" as opposed to "Here, dummy, let me do it; you'll never get it right!"). McClelland is convinced that achievement motivation can be acquired by almost anyone of any age, and he has developed training programs to increase achievement motivation levels.

Some people are motivated not only to excel, but also to be in control, to be in charge of both the situation and other people. In such cases, psychologists speak of a **need for power**. Power needs are also measured by the interpretation of stories generated with the Thematic Apperception Test. Please note that a high need for power is, in itself, neither good nor bad. What matters, in an evaluative sense, is the end to which one uses power.

People with high power needs like to be admired. They prefer situations in which they can control the fates of others, usually by manipulating access to information. They present an attitude of "If you want to get this job done, you'll have to come to me to find out how to do it." People with low power needs tend to avoid situations in which others would have to depend on them and tend to be somewhat submissive in interpersonal relationships. Although the situation is changing slowly,

need for power the need to be in control, to be in charge of both the situation and other people

men are more commonly found in positions of power than are women. At the same time, there are no reliable differences between men and women in measured needs for power.

Another psychologically based motivator is the **need for affiliation**—a need to be with others, to work with others toward some end, and to form friendships and associations. Individuals with a high affiliation need express a stronger desire to be with friends than those with a low need for affiliation. For example, college men with a high need for affiliation tend to pick living arrangements that enhance the likelihood of meeting others. As a result, men with high affiliation needs have more housemates and are more willing to share a room than those with low affiliation needs. There are some gender differences in the need for affiliation. Teenage girls, for example, express a greater desire to spend time with girlfriends than do teenage boys to spend time with their peers.

One interesting implication of having a high need for affiliation is that it is often at odds with a need for power. Logic suggests that, if you are simultaneously motivated to be in control and to be with others in a truly supportive way, conflicts may arise. It is more difficult to exercise power over people whose friendship you value than it is to exercise power or control over people whose friendship is of little concern to you. It remains the case, however, that there are circumstances in which we find people who are high on both power and affiliation needs. These are often politicians who enjoy the exercise of power but who also value being public figures and being surrounded by aides and advisors. Affiliation and achievement needs are also somewhat independent. Success can be earned either with others (high affiliation) or on one's own (low affiliation).

Although psychologists are quite confident that achievement and power motives are learned and culturally determined, they are less confident about the sources of affiliation motivation. There is a reasonable argument that the need to affiliate and be with others is at least partly biologically based. We are social animals for whom social isolation is difficult, especially when we are young. On the other hand, some of the degree to which we value affiliation can be attributed to our learning experiences.

Merely affiliating with others does not always satisfy our social needs. Individuals also may have a **need for intimacy**, or a need to form and maintain close affectionate relationships. Intimacy in a relationship involves sharing and disclosing personal information, also known as self-disclosure. Individuals with a high need for intimacy tend to be warm and affectionate, and to express concern for others. There is evidence that women are more likely to show a higher need for intimacy than men (McAdams, 1989).

What happens when our needs for affiliation and intimacy are not met? In this situation, a psychological state called loneliness results. Note that **loneliness** is a subjective, psychological state that arises when there is a discrepancy between relationships we would like to have and those we actually have (Peplau & Perlman, 1982). Being alone does not constitute loneliness. There are people who prefer to be alone and are probably low on the needs for affiliation and intimacy. For some people, loneliness is only temporary. For others, loneliness is a chronic way of life, with few, if any, close relationships. In many cases, lonely individuals lack the social skills necessary to form intimate relationships. A lonely person may have negative expectations for social interactions. They enter social settings (for example, a party) apprehensive and expecting failure. They then act in ways that fulfill this expectation.

need for affiliation the need to be with others, to work with others toward some end, and to form friendships and associations

need for intimacy the need to form and maintain close affectionate relationships

loneliness a subjective, psychological state that arises when there is a discrepancy between relationships we would like to have and those we actually have

STUDY CHECK

Describe the needs for achievement, power, affiliation, and intimacy.

CYBER PSYCH

(a) The notion of a need to achieve has found application in many settings. See http://www.accel-team.com/human_relations/hrels_06_mcclelland.html for a discussion from industrial-organizational psychology.

(b) From a different perspective, http://mentalhelp.net/psyhelp/chap4/chap4j.htm focuses on achievement motivation and mental health.

(c) The site at http://www.businessballs.com/davidmcclelland.htm goes into needs for affiliation and for power.

Defining and Classifying Emotions

In this section, we consider two inter-related issues: defining emotion and classifying primary emotions. The simple goal for this section is to describe human emotions as best we can. Try to recall the last time you experienced an emotion of some significance—perhaps the fear of going to the dentist, the joy of receiving an A on a classroom exam, the sadness at the death of a friend, or the anger at being unable to register for a class you wanted to take. You should be able to identify four components to your emotional reaction:

1. You experience a subjective feeling, or affect, which you may label fear, joy, sadness, anger, or the like.
2. You have a cognitive reaction; you recognize, or "know," what has happened.
3. You have an internal, physiological reaction, involving glands, hormones, and internal organs.
4. You engage in an overt behavioral reaction. You tremble as you approach the dentist's office. You run down the hallway, a broad smile on your face, waving your exam over your head. You cry at the news of your friend's death. You shake your fist and yell at the registrar when you find you can't enroll in the class of your choice.

Note that when an overt behavioral component is added to emotions, we can see how emotions and motivation are related. Emotions are motivators. To be motivated is to be aroused to action. Emotional experiences also arouse behaviors. Theorist Richard Lazarus put it this way: "Without some version of a motivational principle, emotion makes little sense, inasmuch as what is important or unimportant to us determines what we define as harmful or beneficial, hence emotional" (1991a, p. 352).

There has been considerable debate in psychology (and beyond) concerning how best to define emotion. As one researcher puts it, "Despite the obvious importance of emotion to human existence, scientists concerned with human nature have not been able to reach a consensus about what emotion is and what place emotion should have in a theory of mind and behavior" (LeDoux, 1995, p. 209). For now,

Frustration is a commonly experienced emotional state. But is it in any way a "basic" or "primary" emotion?

however, we need a working definition, and we'll say that an **emotion** is an experience that includes a subjective feeling, a cognitive interpretation, a physiological reaction, and a behavioral expression. With this definition in mind, we turn to the related issue of how to classify emotions.

Although cognitions, physiology, and overt behavior are involved in an emotion, there is little doubt that what makes emotion special, if not unique, is the "subjective feeling" component of emotionality. Perhaps it would help if we had a scheme or plan that described and classified various emotional reactions or feelings in a systematic way.

As it turns out, there are several ways to classify emotional responses. Carroll Izard (1993) has proposed a classification scheme calling for nine primary emotions. Izard's nine primary emotions are fear, anger, shame, contempt, disgust, distress, interest, surprise, and joy. Izard calls these nine emotions "primary" because he believes that they cannot be dissected into simpler, more basic emotions and because each is thought to have its own underlying physiological basis. Other emotions are some combination of any two or more of these nine.

Robert Plutchik (1980) argues for eight basic emotions. What makes these emotions primary, Plutchik claims, is that each is directly tied to some adaptive pattern of behavior—these emotions relate to survival. Plutchik's eight primary emotions, and their adaptive significance, are listed in Figure 7.3. Plutchik believes that emotions in addition to these eight are variants of the primary emotions. Rage, for example, may be an extreme emotion, but it is viewed as being essentially the same as anger. Anger in a weaker form is annoyance.

Richard Lazarus (1993) has proposed a theory of emotion that stresses the motivational role of emotionality. He claims that emotion is the result of specific relationships or interactions between people and their environments. Some relations are perceived as (potentially) harmful to one's sense of well-being and yield

emotion an experience that includes a subjective feeling, a cognitive interpretation, a physiological reaction, and a behavioral expression

Plutchik's Eight Primary
Emotions and How They
Relate to Adaptive Behavior

Emotion or feeling	Common stimulus	Typical behavior
1. Anger	Blocking of goal-directed behavior	Destruction of obstacle
2. Fear	A threat or danger	Protection
3. Sadness	Loss of something valued	Search for help and comfort
4. Disgust	Something gruesome or loathsome	Rejection; pushing away
5. Surprise	A sudden, novel stimulus	Orientation; turning toward
6. Curiosity	A new place or environment	Explore and search
7. Acceptance	A member of own group; something of value	Sharing; taking in; incorporating
8. Joy	Potential mate	Reproduction; courting; mating

negative emotions, such as anger, anxiety, fear, shame, or guilt. These are emotions we are motivated to avoid. Some relations are (potentially) beneficial, give rise to positive emotions (such as joy, pride, gratitude, and love), and are emotions we are motivated to seek or approach. Lazarus's list of basic emotions and their relational themes is presented in Figure 7.4.

You will not be surprised to learn that none of the approaches for classifying emotions listed has proven completely satisfactory. Psychologists continue to propose theories to account for the nature of an emotional reaction (Russell, 2003). Whether there are eight or nine primary emotions (or more or fewer) and how they might be combined to form other emotions depends on one's theoretical perspective. One review by Ortony and Turner (1990) listed more than a dozen theoretical

Basic Emotions and Their
Relational Themes

Emotion	Relational theme
Anger	A demeaning offense against me and mine
Anxiety	Facing an uncertain, existential threat
Fright	An immediate, concrete, and overwhelming physical danger
Guilt	Having transgressed a moral imperative
Shame	Failing to live up to an ego ideal
Sadness	Having experienced an irrevocable loss
Envy	Wanting what someone else has
Jealousy	Resenting a third party for the loss of, or a threat to, another's affection or favor
Disgust	Taking in or being too close to an indigestible (metaphorically speaking) object or idea
Happiness	Making reasonable progress toward the realization of a goal
Pride	Enhancement of one's ego-identity by taking credit for a valued object or achievement, either one's own or that of some group with which one identifies
Relief	A distressing goal-incongruent condition that has changed for the better or gone away
Hope	Fearing the worst but wanting better
Love	Desiring or participating in affection, usually but not necessarily reciprocated
Compassion	Being moved by another's suffering and wanting to help

From Lazarus, 1993. Reproduced, with permission, from the Annual Review of Psychology, Volume 44, ©1993 by Annual Reviews, Inc.

versions of primary emotions. A review by Plutchik (1994) lists 16, and none is in complete agreement with any other.

The only issue on which there appears to be a consensus is that emotions represent a *valenced state,* meaning that emotions can be classified as being either positive (relief or happiness, and the like) or negative (fear, anger, or shame, and the like) (Russell, Bachorowski, & Fernández-Dols, 2003). Unfortunately, there isn't even complete agreement on how best to distinguish between positive and negative emotions. Fear, for example, seems like a reasonable candidate for a list of negative emotions. Yet it is clear that fear can be useful and can serve to guide a person's behavior in positive or adaptive ways. After all, to be without fear in the real world can be very dangerous.

So where does this leave us? As sensible as it may sound to try to construct a system of basic, primary, emotions—particularly if such a system had a physiological or evolutionary foundation—such an attempt will prove difficult at best. One problem is that there is less than total agreement on just what basic or primary means when we are talking about emotions. "Thus, the question 'Which are the basic emotions?' is not only one that probably cannot be answered, it is a misdirected question, as though we asked, 'Which are the basic people?' and hoped to get a reply that would explain human diversity" (Ortony & Tumer, 1990, p. 329).

If there is one conclusion regarding emotion with which all theorists agree, it is that part of being emotional is a physiological, visceral response. To put it plainly, being emotional is a gut-level reaction. To be emotional involves more than our thinking, reasoning cerebral cortex. We turn next to a discussion of the physiological aspects of emotion.

✓ STUDY CHECK

What do psychologists mean when they talk about emotion?

What has become of attempts to identify and classify basic emotions?

CYBER PSYCH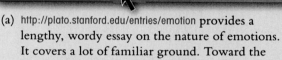

(a) http://plato.stanford.edu/entries/emotion provides a lengthy, wordy essay on the nature of emotions. It covers a lot of familiar ground. Toward the bottom is a link to "Other Internet Resources" and "Links to Emotion." What comes up is nearly overwhelming.

(b) "The Emotion Home Page" is at http://emotion.bme.duke.edu/emotion.html and what a glorious find it is!

(c) http://changingminds.org/expanations/emotions/emotions.htm seems simple at first, but this website has many good links, taking up such issues as "basic emotions," "purpose of emotions," and "the seven deadly sins and seven virtues"—all of which are emotions!

The Physiology of Emotion

Do you remember our story about meeting a bear while walking in the woods? It suggested that after backpacking in the mountains and enjoying a large meal, you took a quiet stroll down a path, only to have a huge bear appear from behind some bushes.

One question we asked was, "What will you do now?" We agreed that, if nothing else, your reaction would be an emotional one. You will experience affect (call it fear, if not panic). You will have a cognitive reaction (realizing you've just encountered a bear and that you'd rather you hadn't). You will engage in some overt behavior (either freezing in your tracks or racing back to the campfire). A significant part of your reaction in this situation (or one like it) will be physiological, or "gut-level." Responding to a bear in the wild is not something people would do in a purely intellectual sort of way. When we are emotional, we respond with our viscera.

Our biological reaction to emotional situations takes place at several levels. Of primary interest is the autonomic nervous system, or ANS. The brain has a role to play in emotion, but first we'll consider the autonomic response.

The autonomic nervous system (ANS) consists of two parts that serve the same organs but have nearly opposite effects. The *parasympathetic division* is actively involved in maintaining a relaxed, calm, and unemotional state. As you strolled down the path into the woods, the parasympathetic division of your ANS actively directed your digestive processes to do the best they could with the meal you'd just eaten. Blood was diverted from the extremities to the stomach and intestines. Saliva flowed freely. With your stomach full, and with blood diverted to it, you felt somewhat drowsy as your brain responded to the lower levels of blood supply. Your breathing was slow, deep, and steady, as was your heart rate. Again, all of these activities were under the control of the parasympathetic division of your autonomic nervous system.

Suddenly, there's that bear! As with any emotional response, the *sympathetic division* of your ANS now takes over. Automatically, many physiological changes take place—changes that are usually quite adaptive.

1. The pupils of your eyes dilate, letting in as much of what light is available, increasing your visual sensitivity.
2. Your heart rate and blood pressure are elevated (energy needs to be mobilized as fast as possible).
3. Blood is diverted away from the digestive tract toward the limbs and brain, and digestion stops. You've got a bear to deal with; digestion can wait until later. Let's get the blood supply out there to the arms and legs where it can do some good (with what is called the fight-or-flight response).
4. Respiration increases, becoming deeper and more rapid; you'll need all the oxygen you can get.
5. Moisture is brought to the surface of the skin in the form of perspiration; as it evaporates, the body is cooled, thus conserving energy.
6. Blood sugar levels increase, making more energy readily available.
7. Blood will clot more readily than usual—for obvious, but it is hoped, unnecessary reasons.

The sympathetic system makes some of these changes directly (for example, stopping salivation and stimulating the cardiac muscle). Others are made indirectly through the release of hormones into the bloodstream, mostly from the adrenal glands. Because part of the physiological aspect of emotion is hormonal, it takes a few seconds for the effect to be experienced. If you were, in fact, confronted by a bear in the woods, you would probably not have the presence of mind to notice, but the reactions of sweaty palms, gasping breaths, and "butterflies in your stomach" take a few seconds to develop.

Is the autonomic and endocrine system reaction the same for every emotion that we experience? That's a very difficult question. There may be slight differences. There appears to be a small difference in the hormones produced during rage and fear reactions. There may be differences in the biological bases of emotions that prepare us for defense or for retreat—fight or flight. Consistent differences in physiological reactions for the various emotional states are, at best, very slight. This issue has been controversial in psychology for many years and is likely to remain so.

When we become emotional, our sympathetic nervous system does not just spring into action on its own. Autonomic nervous system activity is related to, and coordinated by, central nervous system activity.

The brain structure most intimately involved in emotionality is the limbic system. The limbic system is a "lower" center in the brain, consisting of a number of small structures (the amygdala may be the most important for emotionality). These centers are "lower" in the sense of being well below the cerebral cortex and in the sense of being present (and important) in the brains of "lower" animals, such as rats and cats.

The limbic system is most involved in emotional responses that call for defensive or attacking responses—those emotions stimulated by threat. Electrical stimulation or destruction of portions of the limbic system reliably produces a variety of changes in emotional reaction.

The role of the cerebral cortex in emotionality is poorly understood. It seems to be largely inhibitory. That is, the limbic system seems to act as the sources for extreme and rather poorly directed emotional reactions. The cortex interprets impulses from these lower centers and other information available to it and modifies and directs the emotional reaction accordingly. This is another way of saying that the involvement of the cerebral cortex in emotionality is in the cognitive aspect of an emotion. It is the cerebral cortex that is involved in the interpretation and memory of emotional events. When you get back to camp, having just been frightened by a bear, you will use your cortex to tell the emotional details of your story. Emotional reactions tend to be processed in the right hemisphere of the brain; the left hemisphere is usually unemotional.

To review: Along with the autonomic nervous system, the limbic system and the hypothalamus are centers of emotion. These centers are coordinated by higher centers in the cerebral cortex, which, among other things, provides the cognitive interpretation of emotional responses.

✓ STUDY CHECK

Describe the role of the autonomic nervous system and the brain in emotional reactions.

CYBER PSYCH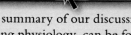

(a) A nice summary of our discussion so far, including physiology, can be found at http://en.wikipedia.org/wiki/Emotion.

(b) The site "Neuroscience for Kids" is *not* just for kids. It is a marvelous place to spend a rainy afternoon. This link is to their section on the autonomic nervous system: http://faculty.washington.edu/chudler/auto.html.

(c) This is a British site on the ANS: http://www.nda.ox.ac.uk/wfsa/html/u05/u05_010.htm. It's from Oxford University, actually.

Expressing Emotion

An aspect of emotion that has long intrigued psychologists is how inner emotional states are communicated to others. Charles Darwin was one of the first to popularize the idea that facial expressions provide indicators of an organism's emotional state. More than a hundred years later, psychologists are discovering evidence that suggests that Darwin might have been correct, but only in restricted ways. For example, it is not likely that emotional expressions are "broadcast" for the benefit of anyone who sees them. At least some are directed at specific observers. Nor is it likely that receivers of emotional expressions can interpret ("decode") such messages simply and reflexively (Russell, Bachorowski, & Fernández-Dols, 2003, p. 343).

In many circumstances, it is very useful for one organism to let another know how it is feeling. As one wild animal approaches a second, the second had better have a good idea about the emotional state of the first. Is it angry? Does it come in peace? Is it just curious, or is it looking for dinner? Is it sad, looking for comfort, or is it sexually aroused, looking for a mate? An inability to make such determinations quickly can be disastrous. Animals need to know the emotional state of others if they are to survive for long.

Non-human animals have many instinctive and ritualistic patterns of behavior they can use to communicate aggressiveness, interest in courtship, submission, and other emotional states. Humans also express their emotional states in a variety of ways, including verbal communication. Surely, if you are happy, sad, angry, or jealous, you can try to tell us how you feel. In fact, the ability to communicate with language often puts humans at an advantage in this regard. Research tells us that emotional states can be reflected in how we speak, even if our message is not related to emotion at all (Bachorowski & Owren, 1995). Even without verbal language, there is a school of thought that suggests that the human animal uses body language to communicate its emotional condition. Someone sitting quietly, slumped slightly forward with head down, may be viewed as feeling sad, even from a distance. We similarly interpret postural cues and gestures as being associated with fear, anger, happiness, and so on. Such expressions often result from learning and may be modified by cultural influences.

Darwin recognized facial expression as a cue to emotion in animals, especially mammals. Might facial expression provide the key to underlying emotions in humans, too? Are there facial expressions of emotional states that are universal among the human species, just as there appear to be among non-humans? A growing body of evidence supports the hypothesis that facial expressions of emotional states are innate responses, only slightly sensitive to cultural influence, but the relation between facial expression and underlying emotion is far from simple.

Paul Ekman and his colleagues have conducted several studies trying to find a reliable relationship between emotional state and facial expression across cultures (Ekman, 1992, 1993). In one large study (Ekman, 1973) college students were shown six pictures of people's faces. In each picture, a different emotion was displayed: happiness, disgust, surprise, sadness, anger, or fear When students from the United States, Argentina, Japan, Brazil, and Chile were asked to identify the emotion experienced by the people in the photographs, their agreement was remarkable. One problem with this study is that all of the participants did have many shared experiences, even though they were from basically different cultures. They were

Given their behaviors, we might infer the emotional state of these zebras. What is most important, however, is that zebras can correctly infer the emotional states of other zebras!

all college students and had many experiences in common (perhaps they had seen the same movies or watched the same TV shows). Even though Ekman's subjects came from different countries, their agreement could be explained in terms of the similarities of their experiences rather than some innate tendency to express emotions through facial expression. A conservative conclusion at this time is that some facial expressions—e.g., for happiness—can be readily identified across cultures, but others—e.g., disgust—are difficult to interpret cross-culturally (Elfenbein & Ambady, 2002)

Another study of facial expression (Ekman et al., 1983) has shown that simply moving one's facial muscles into the positions associated with emotional expression can cause distinctive physiological changes associated with an emotional state. As bizarre as it sounds, the idea is that if you raise your eyebrows, open your eyes widely, and raise the corners of your mouth, you will produce an internal physiological change not unlike that which occurs when you are happy, and you will smile as a result.

✓ STUDY CHECK

What are some of the factors involved in the communication of an emotional state from one organism to another?

CYBER PSYCH

(a) When it comes to psychology of emotional expression, the expert is Paul Ekman. He has a website: http://www.paulekman.com.

(b) Here is a classic piece (at a website we've been to before) on the relation between frustration and aggression: http://psychclassics.yorku.ca/FrustAgg/.

Chapter Summary

How do psychologists define motivation, and how have they used the concepts of instincts, needs, and drives to account for motivated behavior?

Motivation is the process that arouses, directs, and maintains an organism's behaviors. Instincts are complex patterns of unlearned behavior that occur in the presence of certain stimuli. The concept of instinct theories has not been a satisfactory approach for explaining human behaviors. Needs are shortages of some biological necessity. Deprivation leads to a need, which gives rise to a drive, which arouses and directs an organism's behavior. Many drives are more learned than biological and are called secondary drives. Maslow devised a system that places needs in a hierarchy, from physiological survival needs to a need to self-actualize.

How can incentives, homeostasis, arousal, and cognitive dissonance be useful in explaining motivated behaviors?

Focusing on incentives explains behaviors in terms of goals and outcomes rather than internal driving forces. Incentives may be thought of as goals—external stimuli that attract (positive goals) or repel (negative goals). The thrust of balance or equilibrium theories is that organisms are motivated to reach and maintain a state of balance—a set point level of activity. Homeostasis, for example, is a drive to maintain a state of equilibrium among internal physiological conditions, such as blood pressure, metabolism, and heart rate. Other theorists argue for a general drive to maintain a balanced state of arousal, with an optimal level of arousal being best suited for any given task or situation. Leon Festinger claims that we are motivated to maintain consonance, or balance, among cognitive states, thereby reducing, if not eliminating, cognitive dissonance.

Describe the needs for achievement, power, affiliation, and intimacy.

Achievement motivation, or need to achieve (nAch), is a need to attempt and succeed at tasks so as to meet or exceed a standard of excellence. These needs are usually assessed through the interpretation of stories generated in response to the Thematic Apperception Test, or TAT, in which one looks for themes of striving and achievement. The need for power is the need to be in charge, to be in control of a situation, often by controlling the flow of information. Affiliation needs involve being motivated to be with others, to form friendships and interpersonal relationships. The need for intimacy is the need for close, affectionate relationships. Individuals with a high need for intimacy tend to be warm and affectionate and to express concern for others. Although psychologists believe that achievement and power needs are learned and socially influenced, they are not so sure about affiliation and intimacy needs. There may be a biological basis for these latter two needs.

What do psychologists mean when they talk about emotions?

There are four possible components of an emotional reaction: a) the experience of a subjective feeling, or affective component; b) a cognitive appraisal or interpretation; c) an internal, visceral, physiological reaction; and d) an overt behavioral response.

What has become of attempts to identify and classify basic emotions?

Several attempts have been made to categorize emotional reactions. Izard calls for nine primary emotions: fear, anger, shame, contempt, disgust, distress, interest, surprise, and joy. Each of the primary emotions is believed to have its own underlying physiological basis. All other emotions would be combinations of the nine primary emotions. Plutchik argues that there are eight basic emotions and many combinations and degrees of them. Other theorists have proposed as few as two or as many as dozens of primary emotions. Richard Lazarus proposed a theory of emotion that highlights the motivational aspects of emotion. According to this view, we learn that there are certain emotions that we are motivated to avoid (fear, anger, guilt, for example), and others we are motivated to seek out (joy, pride, and love, for example). There does appear to be some consensus that emotions represent valenced states, being either positive or negative, but even then it is not clear just what positive and negative means in regard to emotion. Inconsistencies among theories lead some psychologists to wonder if the attempt to classify basic emotions is misguided. It is difficult to determine how many primary or basic emotions exist.

Describe the role of the autonomic nervous system and the brain in emotional reactions.

Among the changes that take place when we become emotional are those produced by the sympathetic division of the autonomic nervous system. Occurring to varying degrees, these reactions include dilation of the pupils, increased heart rate and blood pressure, cessation of digestive processes, deeper and more rapid breathing, increased perspiration, and elevated blood sugar levels. Most of these reactions require a few seconds to take effect.

Two brain structures closely involved in emotional reactions are the limbic system and the cerebral cortex. The limbic system is most involved in defensive or attacking responses. The role of the cerebral cortex in emotion is not well understood. However, the cerebral cortex appears to play mainly an inhibitory role in emotionality. The cerebral cortex interprets impulses from the limbic system and then modifies and directs the emotional reaction. Thus, the most prominent role of the cortex in emotion is cognitive in nature, giving meaning to emotional experiences.

What are some of the factors involved in the communication of an emotional state from one organism to another?

From the time of Charles Darwin, who theorized that facial expressions provide information about internal states, a great deal of attention has focused on the role of facial expressions in the communication of emotions. Expressing emotions via facial expressions has adaptive value. It allows one to communicate a wide range of emotions that can be interpreted by others. Recent research has made it clear that communicating emotion by facial expression is more complex than Darwin realized, and it involves a specific sender and receiver of such messages. Paul Ekman and his colleagues claim to have identified facial expressions that appear to be universal. They include: happiness, disgust, surprise, sadness, anger, and fear. Subjects from five countries were able to identify the emotion that went with each face shown in a photograph with remarkable accuracy. Again, further research indicates that some emotional states (happiness, for example) are more easily interpreted from facial expression than are others (such as fear and disgust). In addition to facial expressions, organisms—especially humans—communicate how they feel through postural cues and, of course, can verbally express their emotions should they so choose.

Student Study Guide

STUDY TIP #7 Tend To Your Own Stress Levels

Let's take a break from tips about studying *per se* to talk about something very common among college students: **stress.** Stress is an unpleasant, arousing, and disruptive reaction to frustrations, conflicts, and life events. To be alive in the world and paying attention is to experience stress. We may try to structure our lives in ways to reduce our experienced stress, but stress is unavoidable. Relevant to our current discussions, stress interferes with one's study. To study efficiently requires focused attention, concentration, and all the mental energy you can muster. If you are distracted and distressed by stress, anxiety, anger, and confusion, quality study time will be one of the first victims.

The very best way to deal with stress in your life is to deal with (if not eliminate) those events that caused it. In the meantime, however, there are several steps you can take that will help you feel better and work more effectively. It is important, for example, to get enough rest. Being sleep-deprived is in itself stressful. It is important to do whatever you can to stay physically healthy. Engaging in physical exercise can be helpful. Learning techniques of relaxation can be very effective.

And here's a point that is particularly important for college students who are experiencing stress: Social support has enormous advantages. Do not suffer stress alone. If you do not have an adequate circle of friends on campus with whom to share your troubles, seek help elsewhere. Check with your campus counseling center or the office of student services. See your psychology instructor. He or she may not be in a position to help, but I'll bet that your instructor knows of places you can go to get help dealing with any excessive levels of stress in your life. If you are too "stressed out" to use them, none of my "Study Tips" will be of much use.

KEY TERMS AND CONCEPTS

motivation _____

_____

instincts _____

_____

needs _____

_____

drives _____

_____

secondary drives _____

_____

incentives _____

_____

homeostasis _____

_____

arousal _____

_____

cognitive dissonance_____

_____

need to achieve (nAch) _____

_____

need for power _____

_____

need for affiliation _____

_____

need for intimacy_____

_____

loneliness _____

_____

emotion _____

_____

Practice Test Questions

MULTIPLE CHOICE

1. Which of these is *least* involved in motivational states?

    _____ a the arousal of behavior

    _____ b. the memory of behavior

    _____ c. the directing of behavior

    _____ d. the maintenance of behavior

2. Of these, which psychological process is *least* affected by one's motivations?

    _____ a. memory   _____ c. perception

    _____ b. learning   _____ d. sensation

3. What is the major problem with using the concept of instinct to explain human behavior?

_____ a. There are too many human instincts to keep track of.

_____ b. There are too few human behaviors that have a biological basis.

_____ c. Referring to instincts may describe behaviors, but it doesn't explain them.

_____ d. Too many human instincts have opposites, such as needs to socialize and needs to be alone.

4. In Hull's theory (as an example) what gives rise to a drive?

_____ a. a need   _____ c. a behavior

_____ b. a motive   _____ d. a goal or incentive

5. Approaches to motivation that focus on stimuli outside the organism are approaches that focus on

_____ a. incentives.   _____ c. arousal.

_____ b. drives.   _____ d. homeostasis.

6. Which of these terms is most like Cannon's concept of homeostasis?

_____ a. drive   _____ c. fulfillment

_____ b. sensation-seeking   _____ d. balance

7. If given a choice, a person with a high need to achieve (nAch) would probably chose a job in which he or she

_____ a. could succeed with very little effort.

_____ b. would be in a position to control the fate of others.

_____ c. would be working with as many people as possible.

_____ d. could do well, but only with effort and hard work.

8. Of the following, which question reflects a current debate concerning the nature of emotions?

_____ a. Do facial expressions express emotions?

_____ b. Are cognitions required for an emotional experience?

_____ c. Does becoming emotional involve the ANS?

_____ d. Do emotions serve any useful adaptive functions?

9. Which change is *least* likely during an emotional reaction?

_____ a. Heart rate decreases.

_____ b. Digestion stops.

_____ c. Blood flow is diverted to the limbs.

_____ d. Pupils dilate.

10. According to the characterization presented in the text, which of these is *not* included in our conceptualization of an emotional reaction?

_____ a. a subjective feeling, or affect

_____ b. a cognitive awareness of what is happening

_____ c. a judgment of whether the emotion is adaptive

_____ d. an overt behavioral reaction

11. How many basic emotions are there?

      _____ a. 4   _____ c. 9

      _____ b. 8   _____ d. It depends.

12. Which aspect of the brain is most directly involved in emotion?

      _____ a. the thalamus   _____ c. the brain stem

      _____ b. the limbic system   _____ d. the basal ganglia

13. In emotional states, the major role of the cerebral cortex seems to be to

      _____ a. trigger reactions in lower centers, like the limbic system.

      _____ b. increase heart rate and blood pressure.

      _____ c. cognitively interpret the situation at hand.

      _____ d. cause the organism to engage in fight or flight.

14. Which expression of emotion is uniquely human?

      _____ a. verbal description   _____ c. body language

      _____ b. facial expression   _____ d. posture and gestures

TRUE/FALSE

1. _____ True _____ False The concepts of balance, equilibrium, and set-point refer only to physiological conditions or physiological processes.

2. _____ True _____ False Arousal theory tells us that one's performance on a task will continue to improve as one's level of arousal continues to increase.

3. _____ True _____ False Whereas men are motivated by a need to achieve, women are motivated by a fear of failure.

4. _____ True _____ False Emotions that we classify as "negative" seldom have any survival value.

5. _____ True _____ False Most psychologists agree that there are four basic, or primary, emotions.

6. _____ True _____ False The only emotions that appear to be universal are joy and fear.

Personality

Preview

Personality is a term that we use regularly but without giving much thought to exactly what we mean when we use it. Personality often appears to exist in greater or lesser degrees, as in, "She is so bubbly and outgoing! She's just Miss Personality." It also seems that someone's personality can be evaluated as being great or awful or somewhere in between, as in, "True, he doesn't look like much, but he sure has a great personality." We like to think that we are reasonably accurate in our assessments of the personalities of others—and the truth is, we probably are.

The major task of this chapter is to describe some of the theories of personality. First we'll focus on a working definition for both "theory" and "personality." We will organize our discussion of personality theories into five sections, each summarizing a major approach to the study of personality.

Because it is the oldest and arguably the most elegant of the theories of personality, we begin with that of Sigmund Freud. One reflection of the value of Freud's theory is that it attracted the attention and the interest of so many others. Some of them developed smaller, but no less elegant, theories of their own. We then consider how behavioral psychologists and learning theorists have dealt with the notion of human personality. The contrast with Freud's approach is immediately clear. Some psychologists have claimed that if we want to understand human personality, our first focus should be cognitive. We consider these approaches next.

Of the five approaches discussed in this section, students often find the humanistic theories of Rogers and Maslow most to their liking—partly because they allow for the possibility that people can take charge of their own lives and that they are not ruled by inner drives or rewards from the environment. Whereas most theoretical approaches to personality at least address the issue of explaining why people think, act, and feel as they do, the so-called trait theories have no such interest. Their goal is description: How shall we best describe the human personality?

Not all psychologists who claim personality as one of their areas of interest are actively involved in trying to devise a grand theory to describe or explain human nature. Many are involved in research on intriguing aspects of the complex concept we call personality. For example, we'll explore the extent to which personality is really a useful concept when trying to explain someone's behavior. The basic question, first raised nearly 40 years ago, is whether a person's behaviors are determined by the situation presented by the environment, or by those internal dispositions called personality traits. Here is a debate that once raged, but that now may be considered resolved. Finally, we address some of the ways in which psychologists measure or assess an individual's personality.

Introducing Personality "Theories"

theory an organized collection of testable ideas used to describe and explain a particular subject matter

A theory is a series of assumptions or beliefs; in our particular topic, these assumptions are about people and their personalities. Theories are designed both to describe and to explain. The beliefs that constitute a theory are based on observations and are logically related to one another. A theory should lead—through reason—to specific, testable hypotheses. In short, a **theory** is an organized collection of testable ideas used to describe and explain a particular subject matter.

What then is personality? Few terms have been as difficult to define. Actually, each of the theoretical approaches we will study in this chapter generates its own definition of personality. But just to get us started, we'll say that **personality** includes those affects, behaviors, and cognitions of people that characterize them in a number of situations over time. (Here again is our ABC mnemonic.) Personality also includes those dimensions we can use to judge people to be different from one another. So with personality theories, we are looking for ways that allow us to describe how people remain the same over time and circumstances and to describe differences that we know exist among people. Note that personality is something a person brings to his or her interactions with the environment. Somehow, personality originates within the individual (Burger, 2000).

Personality psychology faces three inter-related goals or missions. The theoretical mission of psychologists who specialize in understanding personality is "to account for individuals' characteristic patterns of thought, emotion, and behavior together with the psychological mechanisms—hidden or not—behind those patterns" (Funder, 2001, p.198). The empirical mission of personality psychologists is to gather and analyze observations on how personalities, environmental situations, and behaviors are inter-related. The third mission of personality psychology is "institutional"—to bring together the contributions of many of psychology's sub-fields to better understand the whole person.

personality those affects, behaviors, and cognitions of people that characterize them in a number of situations over time

STUDY CHECK

What is meant by "theories of personality"?

THE PSYCHOANALYTIC APPROACH

We begin our discussion of personality with the psychoanalytic approach associated with Sigmund Freud and his students. We begin with Freud because he was the first to present a unified theory of personality. His theory of personality has been one of the most influential and, at the same time, most controversial in all of science. There are many facets to Freud's theory, but two basic premises characterize the **psychoanalytic approach**: a reliance on innate drives as explanatory concepts for human behavior, and an acceptance of the power of unconscious forces to mold and shape behavior. I should also add that—more than anyone else—Freud emphasized the importance of early childhood experiences. He argued that the most important aspects of anyone's personality were pretty well in place by the age of seven.

Central to Freudian personality theory is the notion that information, feelings, wants, drives, desires, and the like can be found at various levels of awareness or consciousness. Mental events of which we are actively aware at the moment are **conscious**. Aspects of our mental life of which we are not conscious at any moment but that can be easily brought to awareness are stored at a **preconscious level**. When you shift your awareness to think about what you might do this evening, those plans were probably already there, in your preconscious mind.

Cognitions, feelings, and motives that are *not* available either at the conscious or preconscious level are said to be in the **unconscious**. Here we keep ideas, memories, and desires of which we are not aware and cannot easily become aware. The

psychoanalytic approach an approach to personality that focuses on a reliance on innate drives as explanatory concepts for human behavior, and an acceptance of the power of unconscious forces to mold and shape behavior

conscious mental events of which we are actively aware at the moment

preconscious aspects of our mental life of which we are not conscious at any moment but that can be easily brought to awareness

unconscious cognitions, feelings, and motives that are not available either at the conscious or preconscious level and are not easily retrieved

FIGURE 8.1

In the theories of Sigmund Freud, the mind is likened to an iceberg where only a small portion of one's mental life is available in normal waking consciousness; more is available, with some effort of retrieval, at a preconscious level; and most is stored away at an unconscious level from which intentional retrieval occurs only with great effort.

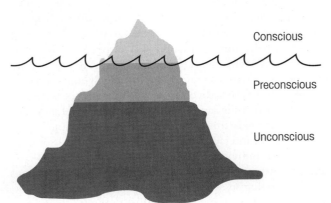

life instincts (eros) impulses for survival, including those that motivate sex, hunger, and thirst

libido the psychic energy through which the sexual instincts operate

death instincts (thanatos) impulses directed toward aggression, death, and destruction

id the totally inborn portion of personality, residing in the unconscious level of the mind, and through which the basic instincts are expressed

pleasure principle the process through which the id functions, indicating a need to find satisfaction for basic pleasurable impulses

significance of this unconscious level of the mind is that even though thoughts and feelings are stored there so that we are completely unaware of them, the contents of the unconscious mind can still influence us. Unconscious content, passing through the preconscious, may show itself in slips of the tongue, humor, anxiety-based symptoms, and dreams. Freud believed that unconscious forces could explain behaviors that otherwise seemed irrational and beyond description. He also maintained that most of our mental life takes place on the unconscious level. Figure 8.1 is a rather standard representation of levels of consciousness as an iceberg—an analogy that Freud used himself.

According to Freudian theory, our behaviors, thoughts, and feelings are largely governed by innate biological drives, referred to as instincts in this context. These are inborn impulses or forces that rule our personalities. There may be many separate drives or instincts, but they can be grouped into two categories.

On the one hand are **life instincts (eros)**, or impulses for survival, including those that motivate sex, hunger, and thirst. Each instinct has its own energy that compels us into action (drives us). Freud called the psychic energy through which the sexual instincts operate **libido**. Opposed to life instincts are **death instincts (thanatos)**. These are largely impulses of destruction. Directed inward, they give rise to feelings of depression or suicide; directed outward, they result in aggression. In large measure, life (according to Freud) is an attempt to resolve conflicts between these two natural but opposed sets of instincts.

Freud believed that the mind operates on three interacting levels of awareness: conscious, preconscious, and unconscious. He also proposed that personality consists of three separate, interacting structures or subsystems: the id, ego, and superego. Each of these structures, or subsystems, has its own job to do and its own principles to follow.

The **id** is the totally inborn portion of personality. It resides in the unconscious level of the mind, and it is through the id that basic instincts are expressed. The driving force of the id is libido, or sexual energy, although it may be more fair to say "sensual" rather than "sexual" so as not to imply that Freud was always talking about adult sexual intercourse. The id operates on the **pleasure principle**, indicating that the major function of the id is to find satisfaction for basic pleasurable impulses. Although the other divisions of personality develop later, our id remains with us always and is the basic energy source in our lives.

Freud's personality structures of id, ego, and superego are not as abstract as many believe at first. A cashier at the end of the day finds an extra $100 in her drawer. The conflict among id ("Go ahead; take it; no one will know") and superego ("No, that's not your money") may put pressure on the ego ("Is this the sort of risk you want to take for $100") may be very real indeed.

The **ego** is the part of the personality that develops through one's experience with reality. In many ways, it is our "self"—at least the self of which we are consciously aware at any time. It is the rational, reasoning part of our personality. The ego operates on the **reality principle**. One of the ego's main jobs is to find satisfaction for the id, but in ways that are reasonable and rational. The ego may delay gratification of some libidinal impulse or find an acceptable outlet for some need. Freud said that "the ego stands for reason and good sense while the id stands for untamed passions" (Freud, 1933).

The last of the structures of personality to develop is the **superego**, which we can liken to one's sense of morality or conscience. It reflects our internalization of society's rules. The superego operates on the **idealistic principle**. One problem with the superego is that it, like the id, has no contact with reality and therefore often places unrealistic demands on the individual. For example, a person's superego may have that person believe that he or she should always be kind and generous and never harbor unpleasant or negative thoughts about someone else, no matter what. The superego demands that we do what it deems right and proper, no matter what the circumstances. Failure to do so may lead to guilt and shame. Again, it falls to the ego to try to maintain a realistic balance between the conscience of the superego and the libido of the id.

Although the dynamic processes underlying personality may appear complicated, the concepts underlying these processes are not as complicated as they sound. Suppose a bank teller discovers an extra $50 in his cash drawer at the end of the day. He certainly could use an extra $50. "Go ahead. Nobody will miss it. The bank can afford a few dollars here and there. Think of the fun you can have with an extra $50," is the basic message from the id. "The odds are that you'll get caught if you take this money. If you are caught, you may lose your job; then you'll have a tough time finding another one," reasons the ego. "You shouldn't even think about taking that money. Shame on you! It's not yours. It belongs to someone else and should

ego the part of the personality that develops through one's experience with reality (in many ways, our "self")

reality principle the process through which the ego functions, seeking to find satisfaction for the id, but in ways that are reasonable and rational

superego the part of personality that can be likened to one's sense of morality or conscience

idealistic principle the process through which the superego operates, seeking adherence to principles of morality and right and wrong

be reported," the superego protests. Clearly, the interaction of the components of personality isn't always this simple and straightforward, but this example illustrates the general idea.

Given that we have reviewed only a few major ideas from a very complex approach to personality, can we make any value judgments about its contribution? Psychologists have debated the relative merits of Freud's works for decades, and the debate continues, with efforts to generate more empirical research. On the positive side, Freud and other theorists with a psychoanalytic orientation must be credited for focusing our attention on the importance of the childhood years and for suggesting that some (even biologically determined) impulses may affect our behaviors even though they are beyond our immediate awareness. Although Freud may have overstated the matter, drawing our attention to the impact of sexuality and sexual impulses as influences on personality and human behavior is also a significant contribution. Freud's concept that the unconscious may influence our pattern of responding to the world has generated considerable research and has found general acceptance (Westen, 1998).

On the other hand, many psychologists have been critical of Freud's theory. Some who followed Freud tended to downplay innate biological drives and take a more social approach to personality development. One of the major criticisms of the psychoanalytic approach is that so many of its insights cannot be tested. Freud thought of himself as a scientist, but he tested none of his ideas about human nature experimentally. Some seem beyond testing. Just what is libidinal energy? How can it be measured? How would we recognize it if we saw it? Concepts such as id, ego, and superego may sound sensible enough, but how can we prove or (more importantly) disprove their existence? A very heavy reliance on instincts, especially with sexual and aggressive overtones, as explanatory concepts, goes beyond where most psychologists are willing to venture.

✔ STUDY CHECK

Briefly summarize some of the features of the Freudian psychoanalytic approach to personality, commenting on references to levels of consciousness, basic instincts, and the structure of personality.

CYBER PSYCH

(a) http://www.psychoanalysis.org is the homepage of the New York Psychoanalytic Institute, and a great site it is. The "About Us" link provides a good summary, and there are good links to resources.
(b) The Freud Museum of London gives us http://www.freud.org.uk with many informative links.
(c) A huge website with scores of relevant links is at: http://mythosandlogos.com/psychoanalysis.html.
(d) "Psychoanalysis: From Theory to Practice, Past and Present" is an article found at: http://www.personalityresearch.org/papers/plaut.html.

THE BEHAVIORAL/LEARNING APPROACH

Many American psychologists in the early twentieth century did not think much of the psychoanalytic approach. Right from the beginning, American psychology was oriented toward the laboratory and theories of learning. Explaining personality in terms of learning and observable behaviors seemed a reasonable course of action.

John B. Watson (1878–1958) and his followers in behaviorism argued that psychology should turn away from the study of consciousness and the mind because the contents of mental life were ultimately unscientific. They argued that psychologists should study observable behavior. Yet here were Freud and the other psychoanalysts arguing that *unconscious* forces are determiners of behavior. "Nonsense," the behaviorist would say. "We don't even know what we mean by consciousness, and here you want to talk about levels of unconscious influence!"

Watson emphasized the role of the environment in shaping behaviors. Behaviorists did not accept the Freudian notion of inborn traits or impulses, whether they were called drives, id, libido, or anything else. What mattered was learning. A personality theory was not needed. An adequate theory of learning would include all the details about personality that one would ever need.

Who we are is determined by our learning experiences, and early experiences do count heavily—on this point Watson and Freud would have agreed. Even our fears are conditioned (remember Watson's "Little Albert" study?). So convinced was Watson that instincts and innate impulses had little to do with the development of behavior that he could write, albeit somewhat tongue in cheek, "Give me a dozen healthy infants, well-formed, and my own specified world to bring them up in, and I'll guarantee to take any one at random and train him to become any type of specialist I might select—doctor, lawyer, artist, merchant, chief, and yes, even beggarman and thief, regardless of his talents, penchants, tendencies, abilities, vocations, and race of his ancestors" (Watson, 1925).

B.F. Skinner (1904–1990) avoided any reference to internal variables to explain behavior, which is the essence of what we normally think of as personality. Skinner believed that psychology should focus on observable stimuli, observable responses, and the relationships among them. He argued—as did Watson—that one should not go meddling about in the mind of the organism. Behavior is shaped by its consequences. Some behaviors result in reinforcement and thus tend to be repeated. Other behaviors are not reinforced and thus tend not to be repeated. Consistency in behavior simply reflects the consistency of the organism's reinforcement history. A pivotal question—from a Skinnerian point of view—is: How will external conditions be manipulated to produce the sorts of consequences that we want?

John Dollard (1900–1980) and Neal Miller (1909–2002) also tried to see if they could use the principles of learning theory to explain personality and how it developed. What matters for a person's personality, they argued, was the system of habits developed in response to cues in the environment. Behavior was motivated by primary drives (upon whose satisfaction survival depended) and learned drives, which developed through experience. For example, pressing an anxiety-producing event into the unconscious is simply a matter of learned forgetfulness; forgetting about some anxiety-producing experience is reinforcing and, consequently, tends to be repeated.

Albert Bandura (b. 1925) is one learning theorist more than willing to consider the internal cognitive processes of the learner. He claims that many aspects of personality are learned, but often through observation and social influence (Bandura, 1999). For Bandura, learning is more than forming connections between stimuli, responses, and resulting reinforcers; it involves a cognitive rearrangement and representation of the world. In simpler terms, this approach argues, for example, that you may learn to behave honestly through the observation of others. If you observe your parents being honest and see their behaviors being reinforced, you may acquire similar responses.

Many critics of the behavioral/learning approach to personality argue that Watson, Skinner, and others dehumanize personality and that even the social learning theory of Bandura is too deterministic. The impression is that everything a person does, thinks, or feels is in some way determined by his or her environment or learning history. This leaves nothing—or very little—for the *person*, for personality, to contribute. Behavioral/learning approaches to personality often are not theories at all, at least not very comprehensive theories. To their credit, learning theorists demand that theoretical terms be carefully defined and that hypotheses be verified experimentally. It is also the case that many ideas reflected in this approach to personality theory have been successfully applied in behavior therapy.

 STUDY CHECK

What is the essence of the behavioral/learning approach to personality, and what are some of its strengths and weaknesses?

CYBER PSYCH

(a) http://psychclassics.yorku.ca/Watson/Battle/watson.htm is a classic paper by John Watson himself, describing his approach to personality.

(b) http://www.personalityresearch.org/papers/naik.html just for balance, is a paper entitled, "Behaviorism as a Theory of Personality: A Critical Look."

(c) http://www.personalityresearch.org/behaviorism.html is an excellent (general) site on behaviorism, with great links to explore.

THE COGNITIVE APPROACH

According to the cognitive approach to human personality, many of the basic cognitive processes humans use (for example, memory and accessing information) intersect with patterns of thought and perception normally thought to be involved in personality.

An early cognitive theory of personality was proposed by George Kelly (1955). According to Kelly, each person has a set of personal constructs that direct his or her thoughts and perceptions. These personal constructs are a part of one's long-term memory, and they exert a directive influence over how information is stored and processed in other memory stores. Unfortunately, Kelly's work was being done just as the "cognitive revolution" in psychology was beginning, and Kelly never really made a connection between his notion of personal constructs and the developing ideas about human cognitive functioning.

Walter Mischel, who was a student of Kelly, provided links between personal constructs and human cognition. Mischel (1973, 1999) proposed a model of personality that included the following four "person variables":

1. Cognitive and behavioral construction competencies: Included in this set of competencies are personal abilities such as intelligence, social skills, and creativity. These competencies would be part of one's procedural memory, or memory involving how to do things.

2. Encoding strategies and personal constructs: Included here are cognitions we use to make sense out of the world. They include beliefs about one's self (for example, "I am a friendly person").

3. Subjective stimulus values: Here a person houses his or her expectations about achieving goals, as well as the weight placed on possible outcomes for goal achievement (for example, rewards).
4. Self-regulatory systems and plans: This dimension includes strategies for self-reinforcement and how those strategies control cognitions.

The cognitive approach to personality fits in well with what is known about human cognition. Kelly and Mischel's approach to personality has withstood the test of time. In fact, during the 20 years since Mischel first proposed his theory, it has undergone only one change: the addition of a fifth, affective, factor. Other cognitive systems have also been proposed that incorporate the time-honored cognitive concepts. There has been a blending of trait and cognitive theories of personality that has provided a rich new area for research into personality.

THE HUMANISTIC APPROACH

To some degree, the humanistic approach to personality contrasts with both the psychoanalytic and behavioral approaches. It claims that people have the ability to shape their own destinies, to chart and follow their own courses of action, and that biological, instinctive, or environmental influences can be overcome or minimized. The humanistic view may be thought of as more optimistic than either the Freudian approach (with its death instincts and innate impulses) or the learning approach (with its emphasis on control exerted by forces of the environment). It tends to focus more on the "here and now" than on early childhood experiences as molders of personality. The humanistic point of view emphasizes the wholeness or completeness of personality, rather than focusing on its structural parts. What matters most is how people perceive themselves and others.

Carl Rogers' (1902–1986) approach to personality is referred to as "person-centered." Like Freud, Rogers developed his views of human nature through the observation of clients in a clinical setting. (Rogers preferred the term *client* to *patient* and the term *person-centered* to *client-centered* to describe his approach.) Rogers believed that the most powerful of human drives is the one to become fully functioning.

To be **fully functioning** implies that the person is striving to become all that he or she can be. To be fully functioning is to experience "optimal psychological adjustment, optimal psychological maturity, complete congruence, complete openness to experience..." (Rogers, 1959, p. 235). People who realize this drive are described as living in the present, getting the most from each experience, not moping around over opportunities lost or anticipating events to come. As long as we act only to please others, we are not fully functioning. To be fully functioning involves openness to one's own feelings and desires, awareness of one's inner self, and a positive self-regard.

Helping children become fully functioning requires that we offer what Rogers calls *unconditional positive regard*. Some of the things children do bring rewards, but other things do not. How we (or children) behave can influence how we are regarded by those we care about. If we behave in an appropriate manner, others regard us positively. If we behave inappropriately, others may regard us negatively. Thus, we tend to receive only conditional positive regard. If we do what is expected or desired, then we get rewarded. As a result, we try to act in ways that bring rewards and avoid punishment; we try to act in ways that please others. Feelings of

fully functioning for humanistic psychology, a goal of personality implying that the person is striving to become all that he or she can be

self-worth are thus dependent on the actions of others who then either reward us, do not reward us, or even punish us. Rogers also argued that we should separate the child's behaviors from the child's self. That means that we may punish a child for doing a bad thing, but never for being a bad child (for example, "I love you very much, but what you have done is dangerous, and I told you not to, and therefore you will be punished"). Helping people achieve positive self-regard is one of the major goals of Carl Rogers' person-centered therapy.

Note that what matters here is not so much what *is*, but what is *felt* or *perceived*. One's true self (whatever it may be) is less important than one's image of oneself. How the world is experienced is what matters. You may be an excellent piano player, but if you feel you are a poor piano player, that perception or self-regard is what matters most.

Abraham Maslow's (1908–1970) basic criticism of the psychology he had studied was that it was altogether too pessimistic and negative. A person was seen as battered about by either a hostile environment or by depraved instincts, many of which propelled the person on a course of self-destruction.

There must be more to living than this, thought Maslow. He preferred to attend to the positive side of human nature. Maslow felt that people's needs are not low and negative but are positive or, at worst, neutral. Our major goal in life is to realize those needs and put them into practice—or to self-actualize.

Let's look, Maslow argued, at the very best among us. Let's focus our attention on characteristics of those who have realized their fullest positive potential and have become self-actualized (see Figure 8.2). Compare this point of view with Freud's, who drew many of his ideas about personality from interactions with his patients, people who hardly could be categorized as self-actualizers. In his search for

---

FIGURE 8.2

Some of the Characteristics or Attributes of Self-Actualizers

1. They tend to be realistic in their orientation.
2. They accept themselves, others, and the world for what they are, not for what they should be.
3. They have a great deal of spontaneity.
4. They tend to be problem-centered rather than self-centered.
5. They have a need for privacy and a sense of detachment.
6. They are autonomous, independent, and self-sufficient.
7. Their appreciation of others (and of things of the world) is fresh, free, and not stereotyped.
8. Many have spiritual or mystical (although not necessarily religious) experiences.
9. They can identify with mankind as a whole and share a concern for humanity.
10. They have a number of interpersonal relationships, some of them very deep and profound.
11. They tend to have democratic views in the sense that all are created equal and should be treated equally.
12. They have a sense of humor that tends more to the philosophical than the hostile.
13. They tend to be creative in their approaches.
14. They are hard-working.
15. They resist pressures to conform to society.

such individuals, Maslow could not find many. Most were historical figures, such as Thomas Jefferson and Eleanor Roosevelt.

Like the others, the humanistic approach has a number of strengths. For one, it reminds us of the wholeness of personality and of the danger in analyzing something as complex as personality in small, artificial segments. The humanistic approach is more positive and optimistic, stressing personal growth and development. As we will see in our discussion of psychotherapy, the humanistic approach has had a significant impact on many therapists and counselors.

Humanistic theories also have drawbacks. A major problem with this approach is much like the basic problem with Freud's theory: It seems to make sense, but how does one go about testing any of the observations and statements made by proponents of the approach? Many of the key terms are defined in general, fuzzy ways. What *is* self-image? How do we really know when someone is *growing?* How can anyone really document the advantages of unconditional positive regard? In many ways, what we have here is a blueprint for living, a vision for the nature of personality, not a scientific theory. There also are critics who claim that the notions of striving to be fully functioning or self-actualized are both naïve and far from universal.

✓ STUDY CHECK

What is the basic thrust of the approaches to personality that are classified as cognitive or humanistic?

CYBER PSYCH

(a) http://www.enquirewithin.co.nz/HINTS/skills2.htm presents an excellent summary of the position of George Kelly.

(b) A list of additional websites that discuss the cognitive approach to personality theory can be found at http://www.psy.pdx.edu/PsiCafe/KeyTheorists/CogApp.htm.

(c) The Association for Humanistic Psychology provides this rich site: http://www.ahpweb.org Do check out the link to "a brief history."

(d) "An Analysis of Carl Rogers' Theory of Personality" is the name of the site at: http://www.wynja.com/personality/rogersff.html.

(e) Maslow's approach is at: http://www.ship.edu/~cgboeree/maslow.html.

THE TRAIT APPROACH

Trait theories of personality have a markedly different flavor than any of the approaches we have looked at thus far. Trait theories have two important aspects. First, the trait approach is an empirical one, relying on research using carefully constructed tests. Second, the trait approach focuses on individual differences in personality and not on measuring which traits are dominant in a given individual. We may define a personality **trait** as "any distinguishable, relatively enduring way in which one individual differs from others" (Guilford, 1959a, p. 5).

Traits are descriptive dimensions. That is, any trait (e.g., friendliness) is not a simple either/or proposition. Friendliness falls on a continuum, and it can range

trait any distinguishable, relatively enduring way in which one individual differs from others

FIGURE 8.3

Sixteen Source Traits as
Identified by Cattell (Each
trait is a dimension.)

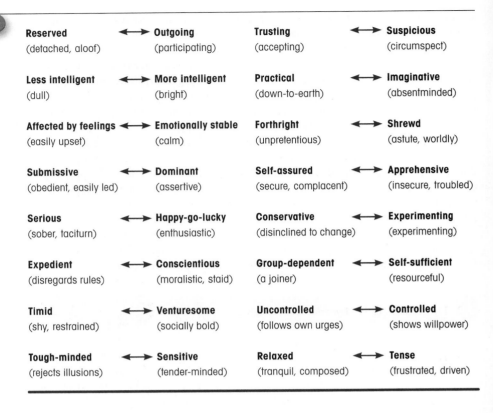

FIGURE 8.3

Sixteen Source Traits as Identified by Cattell (Each trait is a dimension.)

from extremely unfriendly to extremely friendly, with many possibilities in between. Traits need to be measurable so we can assess the extent to which people may differ on those traits. We'll briefly summarize two trait theories: one a classic, the other contemporary.

A classic trait theory is Raymond Cattell's (1905–1998) empirical approach, which relies on psychological tests, questionnaires, and surveys. Talking about personality traits without talking about how they are measured made little sense to him. Cattell used a technique called *factor analysis*—a correlation procedure that identifies groups of highly related variables that may be assumed to measure the same underlying factor (here, a personality trait). The logic is that, if you know that some people are outgoing, you do not need to test them to see if they are sociable or extroverted, because these traits are all highly correlated, and such information would be redundant.

Cattell argued for two major types of personality traits (1973, 1979). *Surface traits* are clusters of behaviors that go together, like those that make up curiosity, trustworthiness, or kindliness. These traits are easily observed and can be found in many settings. More important than surface traits are the fewer number of underlying traits from which surface traits develop. These are called *source traits*. A person's pattern of source traits determines which surface traits get expressed in behavior. Source traits are not as easy to measure as surface traits because they are not directly observable. Cattell's source traits are listed in Figure 8.3.

For many years psychologists have struggled to identify the most reasonable set of personality traits. Cattell found many surface traits and a smaller number of source traits. Other trait theorists have proposed different traits as most descriptive of human personality. Whose theory is correct? Which set of traits is more reasonable? Is there any set of personality traits that is acceptable?

It may surprise you to learn that personality psychologists are coming to a consensus concerning which traits have the most research support as descriptors of personality. This model, or approach, is referred to as the *Five-Factor Model* (McCrae & Costa, 1997, 1999; John & Srivasta, 1999). What are the dimensions of personality that are referred to as the "Big Five"?

Although there is some consensus that five dimensions will suffice to characterize human personality, there is disagreement on how to describe these five. The following is a compilation from several sources (listed above). Please note that there is no particular ranking involved in this list. That is, Dimension I is not to be taken as more important or more common than Dimension IV.

1. Dimension I, called *Extroversion/Introversion,* embodies such things as assurance, talkativeness, openness, self-confidence, and assertiveness, on the one hand, and silence and passivity on the other. The extrovert seeks stimulation, particularly from social situations, and is a generally happy person (Lucas & Fujita, 2000).

2. Dimension II is *Agreeableness* (sometimes *Friendliness*), with altruism, trust, caring, and providing emotional support at one end, and hostility, indifference, selfishness, and distrust on the other.

3. Dimension III is called *Conscientiousness* and amounts to a "will to achieve." It includes self-control, dependability, planning, thoroughness, and persistence, paired with carelessness, impulsivity, negligence, and unreliability. As you might imagine, this dimension correlates well with educational achievement.

4. Dimension IV is an emotionality dimension, usually called *Neuroticism.* In many ways, this is the extent to which one is emotionally stable and able to handle most of the stress that he or she encounters or, at the other extreme, is anxious, depressed, or in some way psychologically disordered. It includes such things as nervousness and moodiness.

5. Dimension V is *Openness to Experience and Culture.* (In this context, "culture" refers to aspects of experience such as art, dance, literature, music, and the like.) This factor includes such characteristics as curiosity, imagination, and creativity. Persons rated low on this dimension are quite focused, with narrow interests and little desire to try different things, such as travel.

The recurrent finding that all personality traits can be reduced to just five, with these names (or names like these), is remarkable. Each of these five traits represents a dimension of possible habits and individual responses that a person may bring to bear in any given situation.

These five traits have emerged from more than 50 years of research in many cultures (McCrae & Costa, 1999). They have emerged regardless of the individuals being assessed, and "the Big Five have appeared now in at least five languages, leading one to suspect that something quite fundamental is involved here" (Digman, 1990, p. 433).

Clearly, trait approaches to personality are different from the others, even in their basic intent. Trait theories do have a few obvious advantages. They provide us not only with descriptive terms, but also with the means of measuring the important dimensions of personality. They give us an idea of how measured traits are related to one another. On the other hand, debate continues concerning the number of traits that are important in personality and in predicting behavior. Even with the so-called Big Five traits, which is the most widely accepted trait theory, there continues to be disagreement over whether the five traits are completely independent and whether personality can be reduced down to five traits (Paunonen & Jackson, 2000).

The basic relevance or value of personality traits also varies from one culture to another. The notion of individual personality traits seems to be relevant and sensible to people in individualistic societies, such as ours and most other Western cultures. In these cultures, people are viewed as individuals, and knowing about the characteristics of those individuals is viewed as helpful. If people are viewed in terms of their membership in a group or a collective (as in collectivistic cultures, such as are found in Asia and South America), then their individual traits will be of less interest than their roles, duties, group loyalties, and social responsibilities (Kitayama et al., 1997).

So, as might have been predicted, when we try to evaluate approaches or theories of personality, there are no real winners or losers. Each approach has its shortcomings, but each adds something to our appreciation of the complex concept of human personality.

✔ STUDY CHECK

What are trait theories of personality?

Briefly describe the trait theory known as "the Big Five."

CYBER PSYCH

(a) http://www.psy.pdx.edu/PsiCafe/KeyTheorists/Cattell.htm or Professor Cattell visits the Psi Café.

(b) A very nice website on the Big Five Factor Model of Personality, with a set of very worthwhile links is at: http://www.personalityresearch.org/bigfive.html.

(c) If you would like to take a real, live Internet test on the Big Five personality traits, just visit http://test.personality-project.org.

Is There a Personality?

Each approach to personality has its own perspective, its own particular point of view. There is one theme, however, that they have in common: They all address the consistency of personality. Someone with an "overdeveloped superego" should be consistently conscientious and feel guilty whenever established standards are not met. Someone who has learned to behave in an aggressive way should behave aggressively in a range of settings. Someone trying to "grow personally and self-actualize" should be consistently open to a variety of new opinions and ideas. Someone with a trait of extroversion should appear outgoing and extroverted most of the time.

Nearly 40 years ago, this very basic assumption about personality was challenged by Walter Mischel (1968). One problem with arguing for the consistency of personality is that personality just may not be consistent at all (Council, 1993). Think carefully about your own behavior and your own personality. Assume for the moment you think of yourself as easygoing. Are you *always* easygoing, easy to get along with? Are there some situations in which you would be easygoing, but others

One's personality dispositions and the situation can interact to turn an otherwise friendly game of racquetball into a fiercely competitive match.

in which you might fight to have your way? Are there some situations in which you tend to be outgoing and social, yet different situations in which your preference is to be alone and not mix in? Such was the thrust of Mischel's challenge: Personality appears to be consistent only when it is viewed in similar or consistent situations.

We may observe consistency in the personality of others for two reasons: First, it is convenient. We like to think that we can quickly and accurately categorize people. If we see someone do something dishonest—say, pick up change left as a tip for a waiter—it is convenient to label that person as basically dishonest. It's easy to assume that the mean, aggressive football player will probably be mean and aggressive off the field as well. Such assumptions may not be true, but they make it easy to form judgments about others. Secondly, we tend to see others only in a restricted range of situations, where their behaviors and attitudes may very well be consistent. The real test would be to see those people in varied situations on many occasions (Mischel, Shoda, & Mendoza-Denton, 2002).

As you might suspect, arguments challenging the very definition of personality created quite a stir. Since Mischel raised the challenge, there has been an exciting barrage of research and debate on this issue. We now see that things may not be as unstable and situation-bound as Mischel suggested. One analysis, using methods borrowed from the field of behavior genetics, argues that most of the variability we see in behaviors reflects individual differences, even more than the pressures of the situation (Vansteelandt & Van Mechelen, 1998).

In fact, most personality theorists today agree that the debate about personality traits versus the situation as determinants of behavior "can at last be declared about 98% over" (Funder, 2001, p. 199). Depending on how you look at it, neither side won or both sides won. Indeed, research supports the position that there are some person-related characteristics or traits that show remarkable stability over a wide range of time and situations. The research also supports the notion that it is folly not to take into account the situation in which behaviors occur.

One result of the debate triggered by Mischel is a view of personality and situational variables known as **interactionism**, which claims that how an individual

interactionism in the context of personality, the claim that how an individual behaves is a function of an interaction of stable personality characteristics and the individual's perception of the situation

behaves is a function of an interaction of stable personality characteristics and the individual's perception of the situation. Neither personality characteristics (inside the person) nor the situation (external environment) can be fully relied on to explain an individual's reaction.

Let's say that Robin agrees to a friendly racquetball game, just for the exercise. At first all goes well, and Robin, a superior player, takes it easy on her opponent. After all, they are just playing for the exercise. In the second game, Robin's opponent makes a few good shots and moves ahead in the score. Then Robin notices a small group of spectators watching them play. As the situation changes, so does Robin's perception of it. "This is no longer fun and games," she thinks to herself as she starts smashing low drives off the front wall. Within just a few minutes, Robin's behavior is considerably different. The situation has been altered, and her behavior becomes forceful and aggressive. As the situation changed, it brought about a change in Robin's behavior: A perceived challenge to her ability brought out competitive reactions. Robin's personality also brought about a change in the situation; to some degree, her competitiveness turned a friendly game into an athletic contest. With interactionism we have an approach that acknowledges the impact of the environment but also allows for the influence of stable, internal personality traits.

✔ STUDY CHECK

How would you characterize the person-situation debate, and how has it been resolved?

CYBER PSYCH

(a) An article on the person-situation "debate" with examples and activities is at: http://faculty.concord.edu/rockc/articles/persit.html.

(b) An interesting approach: Personality and the person-situation debate presented as a series of quotations from the experts in the field can be found at: http://cycad.com/cgi-bin/Brand/quotes/q01.html.

(c) A wonderful essay in PDF on the presence/absence of a "personality" is found at: http://www.princeton.edu/~harman/Papers/Character.pdf.

Personality Assessment or Measurement

As we know, personality is a difficult concept to define. Common to most definitions is the idea that there are characteristics of an individual (called "dispositions" or "traits") that remain fairly consistent over time and over many (if not all) situations. It would be useful to be able to reliably and validly measure those personal characteristics. Let's consider a few of the assessment techniques used to discover the nature of someone's personality.

behavioral observation a personality assessment that involves drawing conclusions about someone's personality on the basis of observations of his or her behaviors

BEHAVIORAL OBSERVATIONS

As we form impressions of the personalities of friends and acquaintances, we usually do so by relying on **behavioral observation**, which, as its name suggests, involves drawing conclusions about someone's personality on the basis of observations of

To learn about the personality characteristics of preschoolers, behavioral observation may be a good place to start. But observations need to be structured and objective, perhaps with the aid of a rating scale.

his or her behaviors. We judge Dan to be bright because he was the only one who knew the answer to a question in class. We feel that Heather is submissive because she seems to do whatever her husband demands.

As helpful as our observations may be, there might be problems with the casual, unstructured observations you and I normally make. Because we have observed only a small number of behaviors in a limited range of settings, we may be over-generalizing when we assume that those same behaviors will show up in new or different situations. Dan may never again know the answer to a question in class. Heather could have given in to her husband only because we were there. That is, the behaviors that we observe may not be typical at all.

Nonetheless, behavioral observation can be an excellent source of information, particularly when the observations being made are purposeful, careful, and structured and when steps are taken to make the observations reliable and valid and to ensure our sample is representative. Among other things, the accuracy of observations is related to the degree of acquaintance between the observer and the person being observed.

Consider an example: A child is reportedly having trouble at school, behaving aggressively and being disruptive. One thing a psychologist may do is visit the school and observe the child's behaviors in the natural setting of the classroom. It could be that the child does behave aggressively and engage in fighting behavior, but only when the teacher is in the room. In other circumstances, the child is pleasant and passive. It may be that the child's aggressive behaviors reflect a ploy to get the teacher's attention.

Observational techniques can be supplemented with a rating scale (such as the one in Figure 8.4). Rating scales provide many advantages over casual observation.

FIGURE 8.4

A graphic rating scale such as this might be used by an employer evaluating current or potential employees.

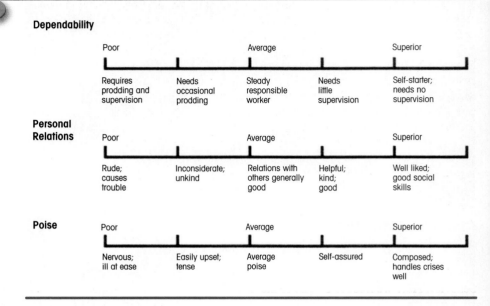

For one thing, they focus the attention of the observer on a set of specified behaviors to be observed. Rating scales also yield a more objective measure of behavior. Using rating scales, behaviors can be observed by several raters. If several raters are involved in the observation of the same behaviors (say, children at play in a nursery school), you can check on the reliability of the observations. If all five of your observers agree that Timothy engaged in hitting behavior on the average of six times per hour, the consistency of that assessment adds to its usefulness.

STUDY CHECK

To what extent is behavioral observation a useful technique for assessing personality?

INTERVIEWS

We can learn some things about people just by watching them. We also can learn about aspects of personality by simply asking people about themselves. The interview is "one of the oldest and most widely used, although not always the most accurate, of the methods of personality assessment" (Aiken, 1984, p. 296). Its popularity is largely due to its simplicity and flexibility.

interview a technique of personality assessment that involves what people say about themselves, rather than what they do

The data of the **interview** are what people say about themselves, rather than what they do. Interview results are usually impressionistic and not easily quantifiable (although some interview techniques are clearly more structured and objective than others). The interview is more a technique of discovering generalities than uncovering specifics.

A major advantage of the interview is its flexibility. The interviewer may decide to drop a certain line of questioning if it is producing no useful information in order to pursue some other area of interest. Studies conducted more than 20 years ago demonstrated very clearly that interviews had very little reliability and even less validity (Tenopyr, 1981). The technique was nearly abandoned as a means of assessing personality. It turned out, however, that the low marks that interviewing received only held for free-form, rambling, unstructured interviews. Structured interviews, on the other hand, involve a specific set of questions to be asked in a prescribed order. The structured interview, then, becomes more like a psychological test to the extent that it is objective and standardized and asks about a particular sample of behavior. Analyses of structured interviews show that their reliability and validity can be very high (Campion, Palmer, & Campion, 1997, 1998).

PSYCHOLOGICAL TESTS

Observational and interview techniques barely qualify as psychological tests. A **psychological test** is defined as an objective, standardized measure of a sample of behavior. Here we'll focus on one of the most-often-used paper-and-pencil personality tests, the **Minnesota Multiphasic Personality Inventory**, or **MMPI-2** for short. The test is called multiphasic because it measures several personality dimensions with the same set of items.

The MMPI-2 (the "2" indicating a 1990 second edition of the test) was designed to aid in the diagnosis of persons with mental disorders and, hence, is not a personality test in the sense of identifying personality traits. The test is a popular test largely because it repeatedly has been shown to be a reliable and valid measure of a set of personality characteristics (Wood et al., 2002).

The MMPI-2 consists of 567 true/false items that ask about feelings, attitudes, physical symptoms, and past experiences. It is a *criterion-referenced test,* which means that items on the test are referenced to one of the criterion groups—either normal persons or patients with a diagnosis of a particular mental disorder. Some of the items appear sensible. "I feel like people are plotting against me" seems like the sort of item someone with paranoia would call "true," whereas normal persons would tend to respond "false." Many items, however, are not as obvious. "I like to visit zoos" is not an MMPI-2 item, but it might have been if individuals of one diagnostic group responded to the item differently from other people. What the item appears to be measuring is irrelevant. What matters is whether people of different groups respond differently to the item. I also need to mention that no one would make even a tentative diagnosis of a psychological disorder on the basis of a person's response to just a few items. What matters is not just the simple scores or even the pattern of scores on any set of items, but the interpretation of those scores by a trained, experienced psychologist.

Finally, many personality tests are designed to measure just one trait and, thus, are not multiphasic. One example is the Taylor Manifest Anxiety Scale. Taylor began with a large pool of items—many of them from the MMPI—and then asked psychologists to choose those items they thought would best measure anxiety. The 50 items most commonly chosen as signs of anxiety make up this test, which has gained wide acceptance. A more recent test, the Endler Multidimensional Anxiety Scale, not only assesses anxiety levels, but also claims to distinguish between anxiety and depression (Endler et al., 1992).

psychological test an objective, standardized measure of a sample of behavior

Minnesota Multiphasic Personality Inventory (MMPI-2) a multiphasic instrument that measures several personality dimensions with the same set of items

FIGURE 8.5

A sample Rorschach-like inkblot. The subject is asked what the inkblot represents and what she or he sees in it.

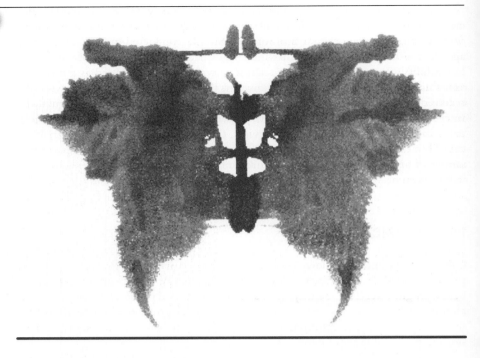

projective technique a method that asks a person to respond to ambiguous stimuli

A **projective technique** asks a person to respond to ambiguous stimuli. The stimuli can be any number of things, and there are no clearly right or wrong answers. Projective procedures are unstructured and open-ended. Because there is, in fact, so little content in the stimulus being presented, the idea is that the person will *project* some of his or her own self (or personality) into the response. In many ways, projective techniques are more like aids to interviewing than they are psychological tests.

Some projective techniques are very simple. The *word association technique,* introduced by Galton in 1879, is a projective procedure. "I will say a word, and I want you to say the first thing that pops into your head. Do not think about your response; just say the first thing that comes to mind." There are no right answers. The hope is that the psychologist can gain some insight into the problems of a patient by using this technique.

Of the projective techniques, none is as well known as the Rorschach inkblot test. This technique was introduced in 1921 by Hermann Rorschach, (see Figure 8.5). There are ten cards in the Rorschach test: Five are black on white, two are red and gray, and three are multicolored. People are asked to tell what they see in the cards or what the inkblot represents.

Scoring Rorschach test responses has been controversial. Standard scoring procedures require attending to many factors: what the person says (content), where the person focuses attention (location), mention of detail versus global features, reacting to color or open spaces, and the total number of distinct responses. Many psychologists have questioned the use of the Rorschach as a diagnostic instrument. Much of what it suggests to an examiner may be gained more directly. For example, Rorschach responses that include many references to sadness, death, and dying are indicative of a depressed person. One wonders if inkblots are really needed to discover such depression. As a psychological test, the Rorschach seems neither reliable nor valid (Wood et al., 2002). Once a very popular instrument, there is evidence that its use is on the decline (Piotrowski, Belter, & Keller, 1998). It is used primarily as an aid to assessment.

The Thematic Apperception Test, or *TAT,* was devised in 1938. This test is a series of ambiguous pictures about which a person is asked to tell a story. The person is asked to describe what is going on, what led up to the situation, and what the outcome is likely to be. It is designed to provide a mechanism to discover a person's hidden needs, desires, and emotions—which will be projected into his or her stories. The test is called a "thematic" test because scoring depends on the interpretation of the themes of the stories. Although scoring schemes are available, scoring and interpretation are usually subjective and impressionistic. It is likely the TAT is popular for the same reason that the Rorschach is: Psychologists are used to it, are comfortable with the insights it provides, and are willing to accept any source of information in order to make a reasonable assessment or diagnosis.

 STUDY CHECK

How might interviews be helpful in assessing personality?

Describe the MMPI-2 and projective tests as measures of personality.

CYBER PSYCH

(a) http://www.guidetopsychology.com/testing.htm is not a particularly pretty website, but it provides a good summary of two important concepts in personality assessment: reliability and validity.

(b) This website is from Dr. James Butcher, the expert on the MMPI http://www1.umn.edu/mmpi.

(c) http://serendip.brynmawr.edu/sci_cult/mentalhealth is a site that addresses all sorts of mental health issues you might find interesting. For the present purpose, scroll down the page to "Projective Techniques," which you will find under "Web Resource List."

Chapter Summary

What is meant by "theories of personality"?

A *theory* is an organized collection of testable ideas used to explain a given subject matter, such as personality. *Personality* includes affects, behaviors, and cognitions that characterize an individual in a number of situations over time. Personality also includes those dimensions that we can use to judge people to be different from one another. Personality resides within a person and includes characteristics that he or she brings to interactions with the environment.

Briefly summarize some of the features of the Freudian psychoanalytic approach to personality, commenting on references to levels of consciousness, basic instincts, and the structure of personality.

Freud's theory of personality has been one of the most influential and most controversial. There are two basic premises to Freud's theory: a reliance on innate drives to explain human behavior and an acceptance of the role of the unconscious in motivating behavior. Freud proposed that at any given time we are aware, or conscious, of only a few things. With a little effort, some ideas or memories can be accessed from our preconscious, whereas others—those in our unconscious mind—may be accessed only with great difficulty. Freud believed that unconscious motives could explain behaviors that seem irrational and that most of our mental lives take place on the level of the unconscious. Freud believed that human behavior was guided by innate biological drives called instincts. The life instincts, or eros, are related to survival and include motives for hunger, thirst, and sex. The death instincts, or thanatos, are related to destruction, such as depression and aggression. The libido is the psychic energy through which the instincts operate.

 The structures of personality, according to Freud, are the instinctive id, operating on the pleasure principle and seeking immediate gratification; the ego, or sense of self that operates on the reality principle, mediating needs in the context of the real world; and the superego, or sense of morality or conscience, which operates on the idealistic principle, attempting to direct one to do what is right and proper.

What is the essence of the behavioral/learning approach to personality, and what are some of its strengths and weaknesses?

Many psychologists have argued that personality can be explained using learning principles and observable behavior. Watson emphasized behavior and argued that psychology should abandon mental concepts. Skinner emphasized the notion of operant conditioning and how one's behaviors are shaped by their consequences. Dollard and Miller tried to explain personality development in terms of learning and habit formation. Bandura stressed the role of observation and social learning in the formation of personality. This approach has been criticized for dehumanizing personality and being too deterministic. Also, the various learning approaches to personality are not comprehensive theories. On the positive side, the approach demands that terms be carefully defined and verified experimentally.

What is the basic thrust of approaches to personality that are classified as cognitive or humanistic?

According to the cognitive approach, basic information-processing strategies such as memory and attention intersect with patterns of thought and perception normally thought to be involved in personality. An early cognitive theory proposed by Kelly suggested that personal constructs, which are a part of long-term memory, direct an individual's thoughts and perceptions. Mischel's approach to personality more clearly links personality constructs with cognitive psychology. According to Mischel, there are four "person variables" that make up personality: cognitive and behavioral competencies, encoding strategies and personal constructs, subjective stimulus values, and self-regulatory systems and plans.

　　The humanistic theories of Rogers and Maslow are alike in many ways, emphasizing the integrity of the self and the power of personal development. Both theorists challenge the negativity and biological bias of psychoanalytic theory, as well as the determinism of behaviorism. On the positive side, this approach reminds us of the wholeness of personality and the inherent dangers in trying to break down a complex concept like personality into artificial segments. Another strength of the approach is its focus on personal growth and striving. The approach has had a positive impact on psychotherapy techniques. On the negative side, the central concepts of the approach are difficult to test in any scientific way.

What are trait theories of personality?

A personality trait is a characteristic and distinctive way in which an individual may differ from others. Trait theories are attempts to discover and organize that set of traits that could be used to describe the characteristics of an individual and also to characterize ways in which any individual may differ from others.

Briefly describe the trait theory known as "the Big Five."

Recent research in personality trait theory suggests that, from all of those traits that have been proposed, five emerge most regularly, although there is as yet no agreement on what to call these dimensions. One version calls them 1) Extroversion-Introversion, 2) Agreeableness or Friendliness, 3) Conscientiousness or Will, 4) Neuroticism, or Stability-Instability, and 5) Openness to Experience and Culture. The trait approach has provided a powerful way of describing and measuring personality dimensions. There is still debate over the number of traits that are involved in personality and whether the so-called "Big Five" traits are independent of one another and can adequately represent personality.

How would you characterize the person-situation debate, and how has it been resolved?

An issue of interest among psychologists who study personality is the extent to which there are internal, individual traits that are consistent over time and over situations. Personality characteristics should be observable within a range of situations. The debate over the consistency of personality variables that began in the late 1960s is essentially over. "Interactionism" has emerged as a compromise, claiming that how a person responds in a certain situation will be determined by the interaction of personality characteristics and that person's perception of the situation.

Chapter 8

To what extent is behavioral observation a useful technique for assessing personality?

Behavioral observation involves drawing inferences about an individual's personality based on observations of his or her overt behaviors. Behavioral observation can be an important tool for assessing personality, particularly when the observations are made in a purposeful, careful, and structured way; if steps are taken to ensure reliability and validity of observations; and if the sample of individuals observed is representative.

How might interviews be helpful in assessing personality?

Interviews simply ask people about their own behaviors and personality traits. The major advantages of the interview are its ease and flexibility of administration. The procedure allows the interviewer to pursue avenues of interest and abandon lines of questioning that are not useful. Unfortunately, unstructured interviews lack validity. Structured interviews (which give up flexibility) show as much reliability and validity as any psychological test.

Describe the MMPI-2 and projective tests as measures of personality.

Multiphasic instruments attempt to measure several characteristics or traits using one set of items. The Minnesota Multiphasic Personality Inventory, or MMPI (revised as the MMPI-2), was developed as an aid to diagnosis. It includes 567 true-false items that discriminate among persons of differing diagnostic categories.

With a projective technique, the assumption is that, in responding to an ambiguous stimulus, a person will project aspects of his or her personality into test responses. Projective techniques include word association tests, the Rorschach test, and the TAT. The Rorschach test includes ten cards showing inkblot patterns. A person is asked what he or she sees on the card or what the inkblot represents. Scoring the test involves attending to what the person says, where the person focuses attention, mentions of detail, and how many direct responses are made. The TAT is a projective technique introduced by Henry Murray in 1938. The test consists of a series of ambiguous pictures. The individual taking the test is required to tell a story to go with each picture, describing what is going on in the picture and the likely outcome. Scoring centers on the themes of the stories told by the examinee. Although the projective techniques continue to be used in clinical practice, there is scant evidence that any of them have any useful degree of reliability or validity.

Student Study Guide

STUDY TIP #8 A Word About Motivation and Goals

Effective study habits are developed, not for their own sake, but to make learning more efficient. You don't go to college to study; rather, you go to learn. A good college student is one who knows how to maximize opportunities to learn. A successful college student is also one who is motivated to learn.

We can learn some things "by accident," without really intending to do so. We may not set out to learn the numbers on the uniforms of the players on our favorite team, but after watching several games, we discover that we can identify the players without a scorecard. Our most efficient learning, however, occurs when we intend to learn, when we make a conscious effort to acquire new information.

Anyone who has a firm goal in mind, who knows what he or she is striving for and why, can be said to be well motivated. Difficulties in learning in college can arise when students have no clear-cut goals, do not really know why they are there, and are not motivated to do well. "Doing well in college" is a very general goal. To be most effective, goals and motives should be as concrete and specific as possible. "Doing well" must therefore be broken down into manageable pieces. First think about this year, then this term. Take each course in turn. What grade do you hope to earn? Then break down each course, perhaps in terms of assignments or exams. What is your goal for your next exam? To prepare for that exam, how many pages of text will you study over the weekend? How many practice problems will you try? Make sure your goals are realistic. It might be noble to strive for an A+ on every quiz, exam, and assignment, but is such a goal realistic? You might have to be ready to accept some compromises. Any student (or any other type of organism) that consistently falls short of goals (even self-established goals) eventually will become frustrated, lose interest, and suffer reduced motivation.

Your goals should not be too stringent, nor should they be too long-range. It's fine to dream of becoming a doctor, but you might be better off concentrating on next week's midterm exam. Short-term goals are usually more effective motivators than are long-term goals.

KEY TERMS AND CONCEPTS

theory_____

_____

personality _____

_____

psychoanalytic approach _____

_____

conscious level _____

_____

preconscious level _____

_____

unconscious level _____

_____

life instincts _____

_____

libido _____

_____

death instincts _____

_____

id _____

_____

pleasure principle _____

_____

ego_____

_____

reality principle _____

_____

superego _____

_____

idealistic principle _____

_____

fully functioning_____

_____

trait_____

_____

interactionism _____

_____

behavioral observation _____

_____

interview _____

_____

psychological test _____

_____

Minnesota Multiphasic Personality Inventory (MMPI-2) _____

_____

projective technique_____

_____

Practice Test Questions

MULTIPLE CHOICE

1. Ideas, thoughts, or memories of which we are not immediately aware, but which we can think about with reasonably little effort, are said by Freudians to be stored in our _____ level of awareness.

   _____ a. immediate   _____ c. preconscious

   _____ b. unconscious   _____ d. subconscious

2. Freud might "explain" war and man's inhumanity toward man in terms of

   _____ a. thanatos.   _____ c. wish-fulfillment.

   _____ b. libido.   _____ d. eros.

3. The aspect or structure of one's personality that is most responsible for feelings of guilt or blame is the

   _____ a. id.   _____ c. libido.

   _____ b. superego.   _____ d. ego.

4. More so than any other theorists discussed, psychologists such as Watson, Dollard, Miller, and Skinner tended to talk about personality in terms of

   _____ a. conscious choices made by individuals faced with difficult decisions to make.

   _____ b. explaining a person's behaviors by referring to environmental factors.

   _____ c. personality traits that remain relatively stable once they are formed.

   _____ d. cognitive representations of the world that guide one's behaviors.

5. Which of these is the most valid criticism of the behavioral approach to personality?

_____ a. It emphasizes the environment so much, that there is little left for the inner, individual person.

_____ b. It relies too heavily on concepts borrowed from biology and physiology.

_____ c. Focusing on only one level of consciousness, it leaves out much of the rich fabric of unconscious processes.

_____ d. Most of the terminology of this approach is very loosely defined.

6. In the context of personality theories, what makes the Big Five so remarkable?

_____ a. The five theorists involved have agreed on what personality is.

_____ b. We now can determine when the environment is most important and when personality is most important.

_____ c. There may be a consensus on how best to describe personality.

_____ d. There are actually five levels of consciousness, not just the three that Freud described.

7. Which concept can best describe how the so-called "person-situation" debate has been resolved?

_____ a. a no-win situation   _____ c. evolutionary

_____ b. useless or pointless   _____ d. interactionism

8. To say that a test, such as the MMPI-2, is "criterion referenced" implies that

_____ a. questions do not have right or wrong answers.

_____ b. people from different known groups respond to items differently.

_____ c. the test is designed to predict who might become mentally ill in the future.

_____ d. test scores have been factor analyzed.

9. The test in which one is assumed to project his or her personality into descriptions of ambiguous inkblots is the

_____ a. Thematic Apperception Test.

_____ b. Minnesota Multiphasic Personality Inventory.

_____ c. Rotter Incomplete Sentences Test.

_____ d. Rorschach Test.

TRUE/FALSE

1. _____ True _____ False Freud based his approach to personality on his experiences as a therapist.

2. _____ True _____ False B. F. Skinner never had a theory of personality, claiming that learning theory would do just fine.

3. _____ True _____ False Unlike Freud, Carl Rogers never engaged in psychotherapy.

4. _____ True _____ False Most trait theories, including the so-called "Big Five" theory, do not include intelligence as a personality trait.

5. _____ True _____ False Both the Rorschach and the TAT are projective tests.

Stress and How to Cope

Preview

Stress is a consequence of living. No college student (or faculty member) is unfamiliar with stress. This chapter covers what psychologists have learned about stress, both its causes and our reactions to it. Our study of stress is divided into two main sections. First we'll see just what psychologists mean when they talk about stress and where stress comes from. What are the common sources of stress in our lives? You realize, of course, that the complete answer to such a question is a complex one. I will try to simplify the issues and will focus on three major categories of events that tend to produce stress: frustration, conflict, and life events. Second, we'll examine the complex patterns of responses we make when we experience stress. We shall see that some reactions to stress can be positive and healthy, while others are maladaptive.

A Few Examples to Work With

Stress is such a common phenomenon that one could argue it is unavoidable. Being "stressed out" seems to be a universal condition—particularly among college students. In that spirit, a list of potentially stressful events could be endless. To guide our study, here is a list of a few (fictitious) examples to which we shall refer throughout this chapter.

- It's Friday, and you have a chance to get away for the weekend. Unfortunately, you have two big exams scheduled for Monday and need the weekend to study.
- Lindsay is almost done typing a term paper on her computer when suddenly the power goes out. Having failed to save her work as she went along, she'll have to redo it all.
- Cindy and Jerry have known each other since grade school. They dated throughout high school and college. Next week, family and friends will join in the celebration of their marriage.
- Doug wants to make the basketball team, but the coach informs him that despite his best efforts, he is just too short to make the team.
- Marian is excited about going to Germany in a student-exchange program, but she's also very nervous about getting along in a new country.
- After 11 years on the road as a salesman, Wayne is being promoted to district sales manager—an office job with a substantial raise in pay.
- Jake cut back his smoking to one pack a day and was considering starting an exercise program. Now he is in a coronary intensive care unit, having just suffered a heart attack.
- Three-year-old Trudy keeps asking her mother for a cookie. Mother steadfastly refuses because it's almost dinnertime. Trudy returns to her room and promptly pulls an arm off her favorite doll.
- You are late for class, driving down a two-lane road, when someone pulls out in front of you and drives ten miles per hour below the speed limit.
- Shirley wants to be a concert pianist, but her music teacher tells her she does not have the talent or discipline to reach that goal.

Life is filled with stress, frustration, and conflict. This list provides a very small sample of the types of stressful events people encounter every day. We'll return to each of these examples and provide others throughout this chapter.

Stressors: The Causes of Stress

Although each of us is familiar with stress and how it feels, psychologists have struggled with how to characterize stress for nearly 60 years (Rice, 1999). A generally acceptable definition is to say that **stress** is a complex set of reactions made by an individual under pressure to adapt. In other words, stress is a *response* that people make to real or perceived threats to their sense of well-being. Stress is something that happens inside people. There are physiological reactions and unpleasant feelings (for example, distress and anxiety) associated with stress. A curious aspect of this response that we call stress is that it often involves such unpleasant affect (emotion or feeling, remember) that it, in turn, acts as a motivating stimulus. If nothing else, when we experience stress we are motivated to do something to reduce it, if not get rid of it altogether.

stress a complex set of reactions made by an individual under pressure to adapt

There are many circumstances or events that can produce stress. The sources of stress are called **stressors**. We'll consider three types of stressors: frustration, conflict, and life events. As we go along, I'll provide examples as a reminder that stress is not necessarily a reaction to an overwhelming or catastrophic event, such as the death of a loved one or a natural disaster. Once we understand where stress comes from, we can consider techniques people use to cope with it.

stressors the sources of stress

FRUSTRATION-INDUCED STRESS

Motivated behaviors are goal-directed. Whether by internal processes or drives or external incentives, we are pushed or pulled toward positive goals and away from negative goals. Now here is an assumption: Organisms do not always reach all of their goals. Have you always gotten everything you've ever wanted? Have you always been able to avoid unpleasantness, pain, or sorrow? Do you know anyone who has?

frustration the blocking or thwarting of goal-directed behavior—blocking that may be total and permanent or partial and temporary

Sometimes we are prohibited from ever reaching a particular goal. At other times our progress may be slower or more difficult than we would like. In either case, we are frustrated. **Frustration** is the blocking or thwarting of goal-directed behavior—blocking that may be total and permanent or partial and temporary (see Figure 9.1).

Stress that results from frustration is a normal, commonplace reaction. Frustration is a stressor, and the stress it produces is part of life. In no way does it imply weakness, pathology, or illness. What matters is how people react to the stressors in their lives.

FIGURE 9.1

A depiction of frustration, the blocking or thwarting of goal-directed behavior.

To someone who is frustrated, the source of the resulting stress may be of little consequence. However, in order to respond adaptively to stress brought on by frustration, it may be helpful to recognize the source of the blocking—the particular stressor—keeping us from our goals. There are two basic types of frustration: environmental and personal.

By definition, frustration is the blocking or thwarting of goal-directed behaviors.

Environmental frustration implies that the blocking or thwarting of one's goal-directed behavior is caused by something or somebody in the environment. (Note that we talk about the source of frustration, not whose fault it is or who is to blame.) Remember our example of Lindsay, who lost her term paper when the power went out? This would be environmental frustration. Lindsay wanted to finish her paper. Her goal-directed behavior led her to use her computer. Something in her environment—a momentary power outage—kept her from reaching her goal. And remember Trudy? She wanted a cookie, but her mother said, "No, it's dinner time." Trudy was also being frustrated by her environment, but in a slightly different way. She wanted a cookie, and her mother blocked that motivated behavior. This type of environmental frustration, in which the source of the blocking is another person, is sometimes called "social frustration."

Occasionally we become frustrated not because something in our environment blocks our progress, but because of an internal or personal reason. This is *personal frustration.* Doug fails to make the basketball team simply because he is too short. Shirley, who wants to be a concert pianist, may be frustrated in her attempt to do so simply because she doesn't have sufficient talent. Shirley's frustration and resulting stress are not her fault (fault and blame are just not relevant, remember), but if she persists in this goal-directed behavior, she will be frustrated. Some of us are learning that simply getting older can be stressful. When someone now has difficulty doing things that at one time were easy to do, the result may be stress. That stress is frustration-induced, and this type of frustration is personal.

✓ STUDY CHECK

Define the terms "stress" and "stressor."

What is "frustration," and in what way can it act as a stressor?

CYBER PSYCH

For this chapter, let's try something a little different. I will provide only two Cyber Psych entries, one after we are through with this discussion of the nature of stress and stressors, the other when we have covered possible reactions to stress.

CONFLICT-INDUCED STRESS

Sometimes we are unable to satisfy a particular drive or motive because it is in conflict with other motives that are influencing us at the same time. That is, stress may result from conflicts within our motivational system. With motivational conflicts, there is the implication of a decision or choice to be made. Sometimes the choice is relatively easy, and the resulting stress will be slight; sometimes decision-making is difficult, and the resulting stress will be greater. When discussing conflicts, we talk about positive goals or incentives that one wishes to approach and negative goals or incentives one wishes to avoid. There are four major types of stress-inducing motivational conflicts.

Conflicts are necessarily unpleasant, stress-producing situations, even when the goals involved are positive. In an **approach-approach conflict**, an organism is caught between two (or more) alternatives, and each of them is positive, or potentially reinforcing (Figure 9.2). If alternative A is chosen, a desired goal will be reached. If B is chosen, a different desirable goal will be attained. This *is* a conflict because both goals/alternatives are not available at the same time. It has to be one or the other.

Once an approach-approach conflict is resolved, the person does end up with something positive, no matter which alternative is chosen. If Carla enters an ice cream shop with only enough money to buy one scoop of ice cream, she may experience a conflict when faced with all the flavors from which she can choose. Typical of conflict, we'll probably see some swaying back and forth among alternatives. We

FIGURE 9.2

A diagram of an approach-approach conflict. In such a conflict, a person is faced with two (or more) attractive, positive goals and must choose between or among them.

approach-approach conflict a motivational conflict in which an organism is caught between two (or more) alternatives, and each of them is positive, or potentially reinforcing

Sometimes motivational conflicts arise when we are forced to make choices from among very positive or attractive alternatives.

A diagram of an avoidance-avoidance conflict. In such a conflict, a person is faced with two (or more) unattractive, negative goals, and must choose between or among them. This is sometimes referred to as a "no-win" situation.

avoidance-avoidance conflict a motivational conflict in which an organism is faced with several alternatives, and each of them is negative or in some way punishing

approach-avoidance conflict a motivational conflict in which an organism is in the position of considering only one goal, and the organism would very much like to reach that goal, but at the same time would very much like not to

multiple approach-avoidance conflict a motivational conflict that arises when an organism is faced with a number of alternatives, each one of which is in some way both positive and negative

can assume that this conflict will be resolved with a choice and that Carla will at least walk out of the store with an ice cream cone of some flavor she likes. Her life might have been easier (at least less stressful) if the store had just one flavor and she didn't have to make a choice.

Sometimes the choices we have to make are much more serious than those involving ice cream flavors. What will be your college major? On the one hand, you'd like to go to medical school and be a surgeon (that's a positive incentive or goal). On the other hand, you would like to study composition and conducting at a school of music (also a clearly positive goal). At the moment, you can't do both. The courses you would take as a pre-med student are different from those you'd take if you were to follow music as a career path. Both are constructive, desirable alternatives, but at registration you have to make a choice, one that may have long-lasting repercussions. The consequences of such a conflict qualify it as a stressor.

Perhaps the most stress-inducing of all motivational conflicts are the **avoidance-avoidance conflicts** (Figure 9.3). In this type of conflict, a person is faced with several alternatives, and each of them is negative or in some way punishing. To be in an avoidance-avoidance conflict is, in a way, to be boxed in so that, no matter what you do, the result will be punishing or unpleasant.

This sort of conflict is not at all unusual in the workplace. Imagine that you are a supervisor in charge of a reasonably large department. Your department has been doing well and is making a profit, but management directs you to cut your operating budget 20 percent by next month. There are ways you can reduce expenses—limit travel, cut down on supplies, reduce pay, eliminate expense accounts—but each involves an action you'd rather not take. If you do nothing at all, you may lose your job. The result may be stress, and the stressor is an avoidance-avoidance conflict.

With **approach-avoidance conflicts**, a person is in the position of considering only one goal (Figure 9.4). What makes this situation a conflict is that the person would very much like to reach that goal, but at the same time would very much like not to. It's a matter of "Yes, I'd love to...Well, I'd rather not...Maybe I would...No, I wouldn't...yes...no." Consider the possibility of entering into a relationship with someone you think of as special. On the one hand, such a relationship might turn out to be wonderful and rewarding. On the other hand, it might put you in the position of being rejected.

Typical of conflict, we will find vacillation between alternatives—motivated to approach and, at the same time, motivated to avoid. Like Marian in our opening examples, you might find yourself in an approach-avoidance conflict if you want to interact with people who are culturally different, perhaps to show that you are open-minded. At the same time, you may be reluctant to initiate such an interaction for fear that your behaviors will be inappropriate or misinterpreted.

Multiple approach-avoidance conflicts may be the most common of the conflicts experienced by adults (see Figure 9.5). This type of conflict arises when an individual is faced with a number of alternatives, each one of which is in some way both positive and negative.

Perhaps you and some friends are out shopping. You realize that it's getting late, and that you all are hungry. Where will you go to lunch? You may have a multiple approach-avoidance conflict here. "We could go to Bob's Diner, where the food is cheap and the service is fast, but the food is terrible. We could go to Cafe Olé, where the food is better, but service is a little slower, and the food is more expensive. Or we could go to The Grille, where the service is elegant and the food is superb, but the price is very high." Granted this is not an earth-shaking dilemma, but in each case, there is a plus and a minus to be considered in making the choice. The more difficult the choice, the greater the induced stress.

Think of your own decision-making processes when you decided to go to college. First, there was the multiple approach-avoidance conflict of whether to go at all. "I could forget about it, just stay here, get a good job, kick back and be happy, but all my friends are going, and college graduates do make more money than high school graduates." The conflicts continue when one considers all of the pluses and minuses of where to go to college. The choices, with their strong and weak points, can be maddening. Stay at home and go to school nearby? Stay in state for lower tuition, but move away from home? Get away from it all to some place you have always wanted to live?

Life is filled with such conflicts, and some of them can cause extreme stress. They may encompass questions of the "What will I do with the rest of my life?" sort. "Should I stay at home with the children (+ and –), or should I have a career (+ and –)?" "Should I get married or stay single, or is there another way (+ and – in each case)?" "Should I work for company A (+ and –), or should I work for company B (+ and –)?" Clearly, such lists could go on and on. Reflect back on the conflicts you have faced just during the past few weeks. You should be able to categorize each of them into one of the four types listed here.

✓ **STUDY CHECK**

What are "motivational conflicts," and in what ways can they act as stressors?

LIFE EVENTS

Frustration and conflict are potent sources of stress and often are simply unavoidable consequences of being a motivated organism. Psychologists have also considered sources of stress that do not fit our descriptions of either conflict or frustration. One useful approach is to look at events and changes that occur in one's life as potential sources of stress.

In 1967, Thomas Holmes and Richard Rahe published the first version of their *Social Readjustment Rating Scale,* or *SRRS* (Holmes & Holmes, 1970). The basic idea behind this scale is that stress results whenever life situations change. The scale provides a list of life events that might be potentially stressful. The original list of such events was drawn from the reports of patients suffering from moderate to high levels of stress in their lives. Marriage was arbitrarily assigned a value of 50 stress points, or life-change units. With "marriage = 50" as their guide, the patients rated a number of other life changes in terms of the amount of stress they might provide. The death of a spouse got the highest rating (100 units), followed by divorce (73 units). Pregnancy (40 units), trouble with the boss (23 units), changing to a new school (20 units), and minor violations of the law (11 units) are some other stress-inducing life-change events on the scale. In a rather direct way, the SRRS gives us a way to measure the stress in our lives.

There is a positive correlation between scores on the SRRS and the incidence of physical illness and disease (Rahe & Arthur, 1978). People with SRRS scores between 200 and 299 have a 50-50 chance of developing symptoms of physical illness

FIGURE 9.4

A diagram of an approach-avoidance conflict. Here, a person is faced with only one goal. What makes this a conflict is that the goal has both positive and negative aspects or features.

FIGURE 9.5

A diagram of multiple approach-avoidance conflict. In such a conflict, a person is faced with two (or more) alternatives, each of which has both positive and negative aspects or features, and a choice must be made between or among the alternatives.

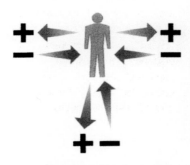

Even life events that appear to positive in nearly all regards (e.g., planning a wedding and picking out a wedding dress) can be very stressful.

within the subsequent two years, whereas 80 percent of those with scores above 300 develop symptoms within the same time period. Several studies that have looked at correlations between SRRS scores and health problems have found the correlations to be positive. The logic is that stress predisposes one to physical illness. But correlations do not tell us about cause and effect, as you recall. And some of the SRRS items are worded to include mention of a physical illness or are health-related. It is not much of a surprise, then, to find that scores on this scale are related to levels of physical illness.

socioeconomic status (SES) a measure that reflects income, educational level, and occupation

Socioeconomic status, or **SES**, is a measure that reflects income, educational level, and occupation. Sensibly, there is a negative correlation between socioeconomic level and experienced stress (Bradley & Corwyn, 2002). SES is related to stress in at least two ways: a) Persons of higher socioeconomic status are less likely than are persons of low SES to encounter negative life events, such as unemployment, poor housing, frequent household moves, and less access to quality health care, and b) Persons of low SES necessarily have fewer resources to deal with stressful life events when they do occur.

It doesn't take a lot of imagination to think of other life situations that are likely to be stress-inducing. For example, being a working mother is a stressor, and to a much greater extent than being a working father (Light, 1997; Matthews et al., 1997). Isn't it logical that being a single parent or being a college student with children can be stressful? Certainly, being diagnosed with a serious, life-threatening disease is a stress-producing life event (Anderson, 1997).

Richard Lazarus (1981, 2000) has argued that psychologists ought to focus more attention on those causes of stress that are less dramatic than major life changes such as the death of a family member, moving, or marriage. What often matters most are life's little hassles—the traffic that goes too slowly, the toothpaste tube that splits, ants at a picnic, the cost of a pizza compared to what it was just a few years ago. This argument claims that big crises or major life-change events are too large to have a direct impact on us. What causes us to feel stressed are the ways in which

FIGURE 9.6

For Middle-aged Adults:	For College Students:
1. Concerns about weight	1. Troubling thoughts about the future
2. Health of a family member	2. Not getting enough sleep
3. Rising prices of common goods	3. Wasting time
4. Home maintenance (interior)	4. Inconsiderate smokers
5. Too many things to do	5. Physical appearance
6. Misplacing or losing things	6. Too many things to do
7. Yard work or outside home maintenance	7. Misplacing or losing things
8. Property, investments, or taxes	8. Not enough time to do the things you need to do
9. Crime	9. Concerns about meeting high standards
10. Physical appearance	10. Being lonely

From Kanner, Coyne, Schaefer, & Lazaarus, 1981.

Ten Common Stressors in the Lives of Middle-aged Adults and College Students

big events produce little, irritating changes—hassles in our lives. Being retired may mean a lack of access to friendly conversation at coffee-break time. A spouse who returns to work may make life more difficult; the other spouse may have to cook dinner on a regular basis for the first time. Thus, stress is not so much a reaction to an event itself but to the hassles it creates.

Lazarus and his colleagues created a scale to assess the extent to which hassles enter people's lives. Respondents to the *Hassles Scale,* as it is called, indicate which hassles have happened to them and rate the severity of the experienced stress. The ten most-commonly cited daily hassles for college students and for middle-aged adults are listed in Figure 9.6. The Hassles Scale turns out to be a better predictor of problems with physical health and a better predictor of symptoms such as anxiety and depression than the *Social Readjustment Rating Scale* (DeLongis et al., 1988).

Other scales have been designed to assess the stressors people encounter in their daily lives. One, the *Comprehensive Scale of Stress Assessment* has been revised for use with teenagers (Sheridan & Perkins, 1992). Significant stressors for teens include such things as "having thoughts of losing your parents or someone else dear to you," "being bombarded by questions and requests," "experiencing high-level noise at school or home," "being around angry people," and "having someone call something you have said or done 'stupid'."

One final note about life-induced stressors: The events in our lives that we characterize as stressors do not have to be negative or unpleasant. Many events that we look forward to and consider changes for the better can bring with them the hassles associated with stress (Folkinan & Moskowitz, 2000; Somerfield & Mc-Crae, 2000). For example, everybody is happy about Cindy and Jerry getting married—no doubt a pleasant, positive life event. At the same time—as anyone who has ever gone through the process will attest—weddings and the preparations for them are stressors. They may produce new conflicts. If Aunt Sarah is invited, does that mean that Aunt Louise must be invited as well? Cindy and Jerry are planning an outdoor reception. What if it rains? And there's Wayne, the experienced salesman, now a sales manager. Wayne may have become used to being on the road and setting his own hours. Now that he has a promotion ("good news"), his daily routine may be drastically altered by his being confined to an office, which may produce new stress.

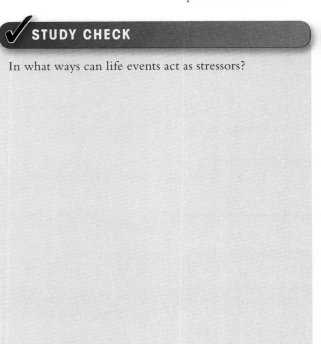

✔ STUDY CHECK

In what ways can life events act as stressors?

CYBER PSYCH

There are hundreds (yes, thousands) of websites in cyberspace that refer to stress in some way. These sites are more in keeping with the science of psychology and stress:

(a) The Science Museum of London maintains this full (and fun) website. One part of the site is called "Naked Science" and covers those scientific issues related to everyday life—such as stress. http://www.sciencemuseum.org.uk/nakedscience/stress/stressors.asp.

(b) http://www.markhenri.com/health/stress.html is a very focused website where you will find the Holmes Rahe Social Readjustment Scale in adults and young people.

(c) There actually is an organization called the American Institute of Stress, and their website is: http://www.stress.org.

(d) The expert on stress—and the person who brought the concept to the attention of his scientific colleagues—was Hans Selye. Here is an extensive essay on Selye. It fills in details that you just don't find in an introductory textbook. http://www.brainconnection.com/topics/?main=fa/selye.

Responses to Stressors

As with so many other things, there are large individual differences in how people respond to stressors. What constitutes a stressor and what someone may do when he or she experiences stress can vary considerably from person to person. Some people fall apart at weddings; others find them only mildly stressful. For some people, simple choices are difficult to make; for others, choices are not enough, and they seek challenges. The variability in stress we see among different people can usually be found within any one person at different times. For example, on one day, being caught in slow-moving traffic might drive you up the wall. In the very same situation a few days later, you find you couldn't care less. So we need to remember that reactions to stressors vary from time to time and from person to person.

Some researchers argue that the amount of stress one experiences and the means of coping with stress are not different for men and women (Baum & Grunberg, 1991; Lazarus, 1993). Others (Taylor et al., 2000), however, argue that there are significant differences between how males and females deal with stress. Whereas males are more likely to display the so-called "fight-or-flight" response to stress, females (and not just human females at that) are more likely to respond with what Taylor and her colleagues call a "tend-and-befriend" response. A father at home alone with a sick and crying child is likely to scurry around to find someone else to look after the baby. A mother in the same situation is more likely to simply call her older sister or her mother, seeking advice.

Some people seem so generally resistant to the negative aspects of stress that they have been said to have *hardy personalities* (Ford-Gilboe & Cohen, 2000; Kobasa, 1979, 1987; Neubauer, 1992). Hardiness in this context is related to three things: a) challenge (being able to see difficulties as opportunity for change and growth, not as a threat to status); b) control (being in charge of what is happening and believing that a person is the master of his or her fate); and c) commitment (being engaged and involved with life and its circumstances, not just watching life go by from the sidelines).

Here's another observation about how people deal with stress: Some responses are more effective or adaptive than others. Stress often follows as a natural consequence of being alive and motivated in the real world. What is unfortunate is that people occasionally develop ineffective or maladaptive strategies for dealing with stressors, meaning that, in the long run, they will not be successful in reducing stress. Let's now consider those strategies for dealing with stress.

STUDY CHECK

Comment on how people may differ in their reactions to stress.

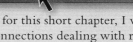

CYBER PSYCH

As I did earlier for this short chapter, I will save our Internet connections dealing with reactions to stress—both effective and ineffective—until the end of the chapter.

Effective Strategies for Dealing with Stress

In the long run, the most effective way to deal with stress is to make relatively permanent changes in our behaviors as a result of the experience of stress. Learning is defined as a relatively permanent change in behavior that occurs as the result of practice or experience. Responding to a stressor with learning makes particularly good sense for frustration-induced stress. In a frustrating situation, the pathway to our goal is being blocked. An adaptive way to handle such a stressor is to learn a new way to reach our goal or to learn to modify our goal (see Figure 9.7).

In fact, much of our everyday learning is motivated by frustration-induced stress. You've had to learn many new responses as a way of coping with frustration. Having been frustrated once (or twice) by locking yourself out of your house or car, you learn to hide another set of keys in a location where you can easily find them. Having been caught at home in a blizzard (or a tropical storm) with no cookies in the house, you have learned to bake them yourself. You may have learned as a child to get what you wanted from your parents by smiling sweetly and asking politely. In each of these cases, what motivated the learning of new responses or the establishment of new goals was the stress resulting from frustration.

FIGURE 9.7

Reacting to frustration
with learning is the most
effective long-term reaction
to stressors. That is,
when one's goal-directed
behaviors are continually
blocked or thwarted, one
should consider bringing
about a relatively permanent
change in those behaviors,
or consider changing
one's goals altogether.

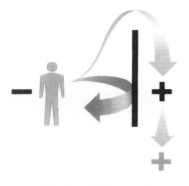

emotion-focused strategies
for coping with stress that deal
with how one feels and with
finding ways to feel different

problem-focused strategies
for coping with stress that
look beyond how one feels
at the moment to search for
and deal with the underlying
situation, or stressor

Learning that is motivated by stress can also teach us the value of escape and avoidance. You now know how to avoid getting into many motivational conflicts. You may have learned that a sensible thing to do once you are in a conflict is to escape from the situation altogether or to make major changes in what is motivating you. This is one way in which stress can be seen as a positive force in our lives. If we were never challenged, if we never set difficult goals, if we never faced stressful situations, we would miss out on many opportunities for personal growth. The stress that we experience surely is unpleasant at the time, but it may produce positive consequences (Carver & Scheier, 1999; Cramer, 2000; Folkman & Moskowitz, 2000).

To say that we should respond to stressful situations by learning new, effective behaviors is sensible enough, but are there any *specific* measures that we can take to help alleviate the unpleasantness of stress in our lives? Indeed, there are many. Here we'll review eight such strategies.

KNOW THE STRESSOR

Remember that stress is a reaction to any one of several types of stressors. If you are experiencing stress in your life, the first thing to do is ask, "Where is this stress coming from?" Are you having difficulty resolving a motivational conflict? What positive or negative goals are involved? Is your goal-directed behavior being blocked? If so, what is the source of your frustration? What recent changes or events in your life are unusually upsetting or problematic? Successful strategy for coping with stress will require change and effort on your part, and the first thing to do is to make sure your efforts are well directed.

Efforts for coping with stress can be categorized as either emotion-focused or problem-focused (Lazarus & Folkman, 1984). The difference is self-evident. Strategies that are **emotion-focused** deal with how you feel and with finding ways to feel different. This is often the first reaction to stressors. "I feel miserable and stressed out; how can I feel better?" Real progress, however, usually requires that you look beyond how you feel at the moment to find the underlying situation causing your present feelings—a **problem-focused** strategy. "Where did this stress come from, and how can I make it go away?"

MINIMIZE THE STRESSOR

Once a stressor has been identified, the next logical question is, "Can I do anything about it? Do I have to stay in this situation, or can I bring about a change?" If an interpersonal relationship has become a constant, nagging source of stress, might this be the time to think about breaking it off? If the stress you experience at work has become overwhelming, might this be a good time to consider a different job? The issue is one of taking control, of trying to turn a challenge into an opportunity.

Granted, all of this sounds very cut and dried, even easy. What makes the process difficult is that usually there is affect involved, often very strong emotional reactions. What I am describing here is largely a cognitive, "problem-solving" approach. If it is going to be at all successful, negative emotions are going to have to be set aside—at least for the time being. Remember: A tendency to take control of potentially stressful situations is one of the characteristics of people with the so-called hardy personality, who usually manage to avoid many of the negative consequences of stress. Even people with terminal illnesses fare much better if they take control, find out everything there is to know about their illness, seek second or third opinions, and make the most of what time they have left (van der Pompe, Antoni, & Heijnen, 1998).

REAPPRAISE THE SITUATION

We should assess whether the stressors in our lives are real or (even partially) imagined threats to our well-being. Making this determination is part of what is called a *cognitive reappraisal* of one's situation (Folkman & Moskowitz, 2000). In the context of stress management, cognitive reappraisal means rethinking a situation to put it in the best possible light.

Is that co-worker really trying to do you out of a promotion? Do you really care if you are invited to the party? Must you earn an A on the next test in order to pass the course? Are things really as bad as they seem? Lazarus (1993, p. 9) sees this as realizing that "people should try to change the noxious things that can be changed, accept those that cannot, and have the wisdom to know the difference"—a paraphrase of an ancient Hebrew prayer.

Meichenbaum (1977) argues that we can deal with a lot of stress simply by talking to ourselves, replacing negative statements (such as, "Oh boy, I'm really in trouble now. I'm sure to be called on, and I'll embarrass myself in front of the whole class") with coping statements (such as, "I'll just do the best I can. I'm as prepared as anybody in here, and in a little while, this will all be over"). This cognitive approach does take a bit of practice, but it can be very effective.

INOCULATE AGAINST FUTURE STRESSORS

Among other things, this strategy involves accepting and internalizing much of what we have been saying about the universality of stress and stressors. It's a matter of convincing yourself that stress has occurred before, will occur again, and that this, too, will pass. It is a matter of anticipation and preparation—truly coming to accept the reality that "worrying about this won't make it any better," or "no matter how bad things look, I'll be able to figure out some plan to deal with it." We know that surgery patients recover faster and with fewer post-surgical complications if they are fully informed before their surgery of what they can expect, how they are likely to feel, and what they can do to aid in their own recovery. People in high-stress jobs (emergency-room personnel, for example) can be trained to anticipate the occurrence of stressors and develop skills to deal with these stressors even before they occur. This "stress-exposure training," or SET, as it is called, can both reduce the perception of stress and increase performance on the job (Salas & Cannon-Bowers, 2001).

Inoculating yourself against future stressors often amounts to trying to develop a sense of optimism in the belief that generally good things, as opposed to bad things, will happen to you. People with this sort of optimistic outlook "routinely maintain higher levels of subjective well-being during times of stress than do people who are less optimistic" (Scheier & Carver, 1993, p. 27).

TAKE YOUR TIME WITH IMPORTANT DECISIONS

Stress often accompanies the process of making tough decisions. You are frustrated. A goal-directed behavior is being blocked. You have to decide if you will pursue a different course of action. Which course of action? Would it be wiser to change your goal? Do you want to do this (+ and -) or do you want to do that (+ and -)? We can make matters worse by rushing a decision "just to have it over with," even granting that occasionally we are faced with deadlines by which final decisions must be made. We can add to an already-stressful situation by racing to conclusions before we have all the facts or before we have explored all the costs and benefits associated with the alternatives we are contemplating. For example, if you can't make up your mind about a new car you're thinking about buying, why not rent one for a few days to see if you'd be happy with it in the long run?

The strategies listed above are suggestions for dealing with the stressor that has caused stress in one's life. As noted above, as problem-focused strategies, these are the only effective, long-term ways to deal with stressors. In the short-term, however, there are some things you can do to combat the unpleasant feelings or effects that accompany stress (that is, emotion-focused strategies). We'll look at three.

LEARN TECHNIQUES OF RELAXATION

Learning effective ways to relax may not be as easy as it sounds, but the logic is simple: Feeling stressed and being relaxed are not compatible. If you can become relaxed, the experience (feelings) of stress will be diminished. Hypnosis may help. Meditation may help. So may relaxation training.

biofeedback the process of providing information to an individual about bodily processes in some form so that the person might be able to use the information to modify those processes

A variety of operant conditioning called biofeedback can provide relief from the tension associated with stress. **Biofeedback** is "the process of providing information to an individual about his [her] bodily processes in some form which he [she] might be able to use to modify those processes" (Hill, 1985, p. 201). A person's heart rate, let's say, is constantly monitored, and the rate is fed back to the person, perhaps in the form of an audible tone. As heart rate increases, the pitch of the tone becomes higher. As heart rate decreases, the tone gets lower. Once the learner knows what his or her heart rate (or blood pressure, or muscle tension, and so on) is doing, a certain degree of control over that response is possible. The reinforcement involved here is simply the newly gained knowledge that a desired change is being made. As a result of being reinforced, the stress-fighting responses increase in their frequency.

ENGAGE IN PHYSICAL EXERCISE

There is a good deal of evidence that physical exercise (aerobic exercise in particular) is a useful agent in the battle against stress (Anshel, 1996; Hays, 1995). Physical exercise is helpful once stress is experienced, but it is difficult to say if exercise combats stress directly or does so indirectly by improving physical health, stamina, self-esteem, and self-confidence. In that regard, exercise can be part of a program to inoculate against stress in the first place. And of course, one must be careful. Deciding that tomorrow you'll start running five miles a day, rain or shine, may be a decision that in itself will

Yes, engaging in regular exercise can be a very effective emotion-focused strategy for dealing with stress. Over-doing it, however, may lead to more stress rather than less.

create more stress than it will reduce. Exercise should not be overly strenuous, should be enjoyable, and should help you feel better about yourself.

SEEK SOCIAL SUPPORT

Finally, there is the advantage of social support for persons who are experiencing stress. Stress is a common phenomenon. Perhaps no one else knows precisely how you feel or has experienced exactly the same situation in which you find yourself, but all of us have known stress, and we are all aware of the types of situations that give rise to it. Social support from friends and relatives or from others, such as physicians, clergy, therapists, or counselors, can be very helpful (Adler & Matthews, 1994; Coyne & Downey, 1991). If at all possible, one should not face stress alone.

Now that we've reviewed some of the steps that can be taken to help alleviate the unpleasantness of stress, let's consider some reactions stress can produce that are not as adaptive.

STUDY CHECK

Briefly summarize both problem-focused and emotion-focused strategies that can be effective in coping with stress.

Ineffective Strategies for Coping with Stress

Coping effectively with stress is a matter of bringing about change. If you do not change, you fixate and accept the same stress from the same stressor. Fixation is seldom an adequate reaction to stress. The adage, "If at first you don't succeed, try, try again" is sound advice. But again and again and again? At some point, we must give up a particular course of action to try something else.

In a way, procrastination is a form of fixation, isn't it? A term paper is due in two weeks, and you can't seem to start, deciding to "put if off until this weekend." The weekend brings no progress either, and the stress of dealing with the paper is momentarily postponed. The catch is that you are going to pay a price. Eventually, you have to do the paper. Then, with very little time before the deadline, you will probably experience stress more than ever before. A long-term study of procrastination in college students found that procrastinators experienced less stress and less illness early in the term, but as the term progressed, they reported greater stress, more illness, and more serious illnesses. Moreover, procrastinators earned significantly lower grades. As the authors of this study put it, "Procrastination thus appears to be a self-defeating behavior pattern marked by short-term benefits and long-term costs" (Tice & Baumeister, 1997, p. 457). In addition to not changing one's behavior or one's goals or simply not doing anything at all, there are two other reactions to stressors that are clearly maladaptive: aggression and anxiety.

There are many causes of aggression, and one source of aggressive behaviors is stress—in particular, the stress that results from frustration. A student expecting a grade of A on a paper receives a grade of C-, returns to her room, and throws her hairbrush at the mirror, shattering it. A driver in a hurry to get to campus rams the rear bumper of the car ahead, judging it to be going far too slowly. Remember Trudy, who was frustrated because she couldn't have a cookie and then tore the arm off her doll? At one time, it was proposed that frustration was the *only* cause of aggression, the so-called **frustration–aggression hypothesis** (Dollard et al., 1939). This point of view claimed that frustration could produce a number of reactions, including aggression, but that aggression was always caused by frustration. We now recognize that there are other sources of aggression (it may be an innate or instinctive response, or it may be a response learned through reinforcement or modeling). It is true, however, that frustration remains a prime candidate as the cause of aggression. Although it usually doesn't do much good in the long run, a flash of aggressive behavior often follows stress.

You are in the parking lot trying to get home from class, and your car won't start. Over and over you crank the ignition. Continuing to turn the key without success is a good example of fixation—it's not doing you any good, but you keep at it, perhaps until you run down the battery. Still frustrated, you swing open the door, get out, kick the front left fender, throw up the hood, and glower at the engine. You're mad! Now, having released a bit of tension, you might feel better for a few seconds, but being angry and kicking at the car, or yelling at someone who offers to assist, won't help you solve your problem.

Another negative consequence of stress is **anxiety**—a general feeling of tension, apprehension, and dread that involves predictable physiological changes. Anxiety is a very difficult concept to define precisely, but everyone seems to know what you are talking about when you refer to anxiety. Like stress, anxiety is a reaction we all have experienced. Often it is a reaction that accompanies stress. We can think

frustration-aggression hypothesis the point of view that frustration is common, and the only cause of aggression

anxiety a general feeling of tension, apprehension, and dread that involves predictable physiological changes

of anxiety as an unpleasant emotional component of the stress response. As much as anything else, we want to rid ourselves of stress in order to minimize our anxiety.

Sometimes the amount of stress and anxiety in a person's life become more than he or she can cope with effectively. Feelings of anxiety start to interfere with normal adaptations to the environment and other people. Such feelings may become the focus of one's attention. More anxiety follows, and then more distress, and more discomfort, and more pain. For many people—tens of millions of people in the United States and Canada—the anxiety that accompanies stress is so discomforting and so maladaptive that we say they are suffering from a psychological disorder.

✓ STUDY CHECK

Describe three inappropriate, ineffective reactions to stress.

CYBER PSYCH

(a) "Mindtools" has several intriguing websites. This one is particularly relevant: http://www.mindtools.com/smpage.html.

(b) There are many websites dealing with "stress management." Please remember the caveat included with this one: "Inclusion of a website link on this page does not necessarily imply endorsement of that site's health related content." It's at: http://www.imt.net/~randolfi/StressLinks.html.

(c) The website of the "International Stress Management Association is http://www.isma.org.uk. The link on the homepage called "Links" is a good place to go.

(d) And here is a website from Australia. What I like about it is that it is a simple, no-nonsense site. The homepage, for example, has a link to "200 stress tips" that is worth a visit. http://www.stresstips.com.

Chapter Summary

Define the terms "stress" and "stressor."

Stress is defined as a complex set of reactions made by a person under pressure to adapt. Stress is a response that an individual makes to real or perceived threats to his or her well-being that give rise to physiological reactions and unpleasant feelings like distress and anxiety. Feelings of stress are aroused when an individual is exposed to a stressor. There are three types of stressors: frustration, conflict, and life events. Although in some cases stress is aroused because of some major event (for example, the death of a loved one), it need not be. In some cases consistent but relatively minor events can arouse stress.

What is "frustration," and in what way can it act as a stressor?

Frustration is the blocking or thwarting of goal-directed behaviors. If someone or something in one's environment blocks goal-directed behaviors, environmental frustration is the result. If the source of the frustration is a personal characteristic, we have personal frustration.

What are "motivational conflicts," and in what ways can they act as stressors?

Motivational conflicts are stressors. They are situations in which we find ourselves faced with difficult choices to make with regard to our motivated behaviors. In an approach-approach conflict, one is faced with two or more attractive (positive) goals and must choose between or among them. In an avoidance-avoidance conflict, a choice must be made between or among unpleasant (negative) alternatives. In an approach-avoidance conflict, there is one goal under consideration; in some ways that goal is positive, in others it is negative (it attracts and repels at the same time). In a multiple approach-avoidance conflict, a person faces a number of alternatives, each of which has its strengths and its weaknesses, and a choice must be made between or among them.

In what ways can life events act as stressors?

Many psychologists argue that life events, particularly changes in one's life situation, can act as stressors. The Social Readjustment Rating Scale (SRRS) is one example of an instrument that measures the amount of stress by having a person indicate recent life-change events. High scores on such scales are associated with an above-average incidence of physical illness. Some psychologists claim that the little hassles of life can be more stressful than large-scale life events. Life-change events do not have to be negative or unpleasant events to act as stressors. Socioeconomic status (SES) relates to stress in at least two ways. First, individuals in higher SES brackets are less likely than lower SES individuals to encounter negative life events that can arouse stress. Second, low SES individuals have fewer resources to deal with life events that arouse stress.

Comment on how people differ in their reactions to stress.

People may respond differently to the same stressor. What some find merely challenging, others may find overwhelmingly stressful. Reaction to stressors varies over time: Events that do not seem stressful today may be very stressful tomorrow. Some people are particularly resistant to stressors and have been called "hardy personalities." Such people tend to see difficulties as opportunities, have a sense of being in control of their lives, and are fully engaged in and committed to life.

Briefly summarize both problem-focused and emotion-focused strategies that can be effective in coping with stress.

In general, the most effective means of dealing with stress is to deal with the stressors that caused it by learning new behaviors that help cope with those stressors. There are two approaches to dealing with stress. One is problem-focused and includes such things as identifying the specific stressor causing stress, removing or minimizing the stressor, reappraising the situation, inoculating against future stressors, and taking one's time in making difficult decisions. Battling the feelings associated with stress—with what are called emotion-focused approaches—includes learning relaxation techniques, engaging in physical exercise, and seeking social support.

Describe three inappropriate, ineffective reactions to stress.

Maladaptive reactions to stressors are those that interfere with attempts to change behaviors as a result of experiencing stress. Fixation describes a pattern of behaviors in which a person tries repeatedly to deal with stressors, is unsuccessful, but does not try anything new or different. Aggression often results from stress, particularly frustration. Although aggression may yield a momentary release of tension, it usually does not remove the original stressor. Anxiety is yet another maladaptive response to stress. This general feeling of apprehension and dread is often the aspect of experienced stress that motivates us to do something about it.

Student Study Guide

STUDY TIP #9 The Key to Effective Listening in Class

"But I never missed a class!" is a claim that instructors often hear from students who have not done well on an exam and who have not yet learned the difference between attending a class and taking an active part in that class. This difference has a significant impact on how well students learn. The real key is preparation.

It is always easier to listen to and understand information with which you are familiar than it is to try to listen to and understand totally unfamiliar information. To be sure, few lectures or class activities are designed to be about something you knew very well before you took the class. The material will have to be somewhat new; that's what you're paying for. But if you prepare carefully, lectures and class discussions will not seem totally alien. Once a semester is under way, preparing for class will be relatively easy. You will have had time to develop some sense of what will be happening in class.

At the very least you should review recent lecture notes and preview the text for each class meeting. Perhaps the most important thing to do is to familiarize yourself with the vocabulary terms that might come up in class. If you're familiar with the vocabulary before you go to class, listening for ideas, unifying themes, and over-arching concepts will be easier because you won't have to struggle with the definitions of new terms. You will then have more time to concentrate, select, organize, and summarize your thoughts in coherent notes.

Good listening is a matter of attitude. To be an effective listener, you must be in the proper frame of mind. As you take your seat, you have to rid your mind of thoughts of the activities of the day. You cannot do a good job of listening to a lecture if you're thinking about last night's date or this afternoon's lunch. You'll have difficulty attending to what is going on in class if you're still focused on a disagreement with a loved one. You can't contribute to a class discussion if all you're prepared to talk about is last weekend's game. Get your mind warmed up: What's the professor going to be talking about today? What contributions will you be expected to make? How will today's class fit in with what you already know? When you find yourself totally surprised at what is being said in class you have not prepared adequately.

KEY TERMS AND CONCEPTS

stress _____

_____

stressors_____

_____

frustration_____

_____

approach-approach conflict _____

_____

avoidance-avoidance conflict _____

_____

approach-avoidance conflict _____

_____

multiple approach-avoidance conflict _____

_____

socioeconomic status (SES) _____

_____

emotion-focused strategies _____

_____

problem-focused strategies _____

_____

biofeedback_____

_____

frustration-aggression hypothesis _____

_____

anxiety_____

_____

Practice Test Questions

MULTIPLE CHOICE

1. In what way can we say that stress is like a motivator?

_____ a. It has a physiological component.

_____ b. It feels bad.

_____ c. It arouses and directs behavior.

_____ d. It occurs without awareness.

2. A real or perceived threat to one's sense of well-being defines

_____ a. stress.   _____ c. a psychological disorder.

_____ b. anxiety.   _____ d. a stressor.

3. The concept of frustration is based on which fundamental assumption?

_____ a. People are basically good and mean well.

_____ b. Motivation and emotion both involve a visceral reaction.

_____ c. Behavior is motivated, or goal-directed.

_____ d. Stress results from negative, unfortunate experiences.

4. Which of these provides the best example of frustration?

_____ a. You get a flat tire on the way to an important meeting.

_____ b. You can't decide what courses to take next semester.

_____ c. Your best friend is going to get married.

_____ d. You win the lottery and now everyone wants to be your friend.

5. As adults, which conflict situation do we tend to experience the LEAST?

_____ a. approach-approach

_____ b. avoidance-avoidance

_____ c. approach-avoidance

_____ d. multiple approach-avoidance

6. Scott is going to get a new car and cannot decide if he wants the white one or the red one. Scott is in a(n) _____ conflict.

_____ a. approach-approach   _____ c. approach-avoidance

_____ b. avoidance-avoidance   _____d. multiple approach-
                                                      avoidance

7. Josh used to be able to play 36 holes of golf in a day without much effort, Now, given his age and general physical condition, he finds it too tiring to play that much, and this—in turn—he finds stressful. We would best describe Josh's stress as induced by

_____ a. environmental frustration.

_____ b. personal frustration.

_____ c. an approach-approach conflict.

_____ d. a frustration-aggression hypothesis.

8. The most adaptive reaction to the stressors in one's life is

_____ a learning.   _____ c. aggression.

_____ b. frustration.   _____d. fixation.

9. Of these mechanisms for coping with stress and stressors, which is the most ineffective or inefficient?

_____ a. engaging in cognitive reappraisal

_____ b. gathering social support

_____ c. fixating

_____ d. taking relaxation training

10. What, essentially, is conflicted when we are in a conflict?

_____ a. perceptions   _____ c. motives

_____ b. emotions   _____d. cognitions

11. Which of the following seems to be describing something other than an avoidance–avoidance conflict?

    _____ a. out of the frying pan, into the fire

    _____ b. all dressed up and no place to go

    _____ c. damned if you do and damned if you don't

    _____ d. stuck between a rock and a hard place

12. When adults rate the most stress-inducing life event they can imagine, which event gets scored as the most stressful?

    _____ a. the death of a spouse

    _____ b. an exam just before the holidays

    _____ c. a divorce

    _____ d. an illness while pregnant

13. Persons with "hardy personalities" demonstrate each of the following EXCEPT a tendency to

    _____ a. see difficulties as challenges and opportunities.

    _____ b. try to get more and do more than most others.

    _____ c. believe that one is in control of one's fate.

    _____ d. be actively involved in what is going on in one's life.

14. Which of the following strategies is classified as "problem-focused" rather than "emotion-focused"?

    _____ a. engaging in cognitive reappraisal

    _____ b. learning techniques of relaxation

    _____ c. seeking social support

    _____ d. engaging in physical exercise

TRUE/FALSE

1. _____ True _____ False Stress is so unpleasant, so negative a reaction, that we can say that the only way to be truly happy in life is to avoid stress altogether.

2. _____ True _____ False The "frustration-aggression hypothesis" claims that all aggression results from frustration.

3. _____ True _____ False When goal-directed behaviors are blocked or thwarted, the result is frustration.

4. _____ True _____ False Avoidance-avoidance conflicts cannot be resolved, which is why they are so stressful.

5. _____ True _____ False Something that is a stressor for one person may not be for another person.

6. _____ True _____ False Because making difficult decisions can be stress-inducing, psychologists recommend that tough decisions be made quickly to get them over with, so that one may deal with the resulting stress and then "move on."

7. _____ True _____ False Learning techniques of relaxation, as in biofeedback, is an example of a so-called "problem-focused strategy" for dealing with stress and stressors.

Psychological Disorders and Therapy

CHAPTER TEN

Preview

Mental illness is something that most folks simply do not want to talk about. Many would rather not even think about the commonality of psychological disorders. Few of us like hearing that in a given year about 30 percent of the adult population will experience a diagnosable mental illness. People who will share the gory details of their abdominal surgery at the dinner table may hesitate to mention that stress in their lives is growing to unbearable levels.

Psychological disorders are common. Some are very dramatic; a few may be devastating. But most can be treated successfully, even cured, if we talk openly about our psychological problems and seek help for them. This chapter provides an overview, a sketch of the psychological disorders.

Let's begin, as we have in previous chapters, with the definitions of a few basic terms. Then we'll review some of the anxiety disorders. These all-too-common disorders share one characteristic: anxiety. They include such disorders as generalized anxiety disorder, panic disorder, phobia, obsessive-compulsive disorder, and post-traumatic stress disorder.

In most cases, the mood of concern when psychologists talk about the "mood disorders" is depression. Sad to say, depression is an emotional reaction familiar to all of us. Clearly, one can be depressed without having a disorder of any sort. Sometimes the border between normal depression and abnormal depression is very unclear and difficult to diagnose. In many cases, however, there is no doubt.

We'll end our brief exposure to psychological disorders with a few words about schizophrenia, arguably the most devastating disorder of all. Schizophrenia is an attack on all that makes us human; it has an impact on affect, cognitions, and behavior. It is a disorder that involves a gross impairment of functioning (difficulty dealing with the demands of everyday life), and a gross impairment in reality testing (a loss of contact with the real world as the rest of us know it).

This chapter ends with a discussion of psychotherapy. No matter what the specifics, the major goal of psychotherapy is to help a person to think, feel, or act more effectively. We'll focus on three varieties of psychotherapy and see that each approaches therapeutic interactions a bit differently. We'll begin by considering psychoanalytic approaches and then go on to humanistic and behavioral techniques.

What *Is* Abnormal?

We all have a basic idea of what is meant by such terms as abnormal, mental illness, or psychological disorder. The more we think about psychological abnormality, however, the more difficult it becomes to define. The concept of abnormality as it is used in psychology is not a simple one. We'll use this definition: **Abnormal** refers to maladaptive cognitions, affects, and/or behaviors that are at odds with social expectations and result in distress or discomfort. That is lengthy, but to be complete, our definition must include all these aspects. Let's consider each in turn.

abnormal in psychology, maladaptive cognitions, affects, and/or behaviors that are at odds with social expectations and result in distress or discomfort

In psychology, the term "abnormal" requires being sensitive to cultural differences. What may be abnormal in middle America may very well not be in Tibet, for instance.

The reactions of people with psychological disorders are maladaptive. This is a critical part of our definition. Thoughts, feelings, and behaviors are such that the person does not function as well as he or she could without the disorder. To be "different" or "strange" does not mean that someone has a psychological disorder. There must be some impairment, breakdown, or self-defeating interference with one's growth and functioning.

Another observation reflected in our definition is that abnormality may show itself in a number of ways. A person with a disorder may experience abnormal affect, engage in abnormal behaviors, have abnormal cognitions, or any combination of these. Here again is our ABCs mnemonic.

Any definition of psychological abnormality should acknowledge social and/or cultural expectations. What may be abnormal and disordered in one culture may be viewed as quite normal or commonplace in another. In some cultures, loud crying and wailing at the funeral of a total stranger is considered strange or deviant; in others, it is common and expected. In some cultures, to claim you have been communicating with dead ancestors would be taken as a sign of mental disturbance; in others, it would be treated as a great gift. Even within any one culture, behaviors that are appropriate, or at least tolerated, in one situation, say a party, may be judged as inappropriate in another context, say, a religious service.

A final point: Psychological disorders involve distress or discomfort. People we consider abnormal are suffering or are the source of suffering in others. Psychological disorders cause emotional distress, and individuals with such disorders are often the source of distress and discomfort to others—friends and family who care and worry about them. The behaviors, thoughts, or feelings associated with a psychological disorder are not what the individual wants to experience. They are beyond the individual's control, and that in itself is distressing (Widiger & Sankis, 2000).

Complex as it is, I hope you see that there is a reason for each point in our definition of abnormal: maladaptive behaviors or mental processes, at odds with social expectations, and that result in distress or discomfort.

CLASSIFYING PSYCHOLOGICAL DISORDERS

diagnosis the act of recognizing a disorder on the basis of specified symptoms

One way of dealing with the broad concept of psychological abnormality is to consider each psychological disorder separately in terms of how that disorder is diagnosed, where **diagnosis** is the act of recognizing a disorder on the basis of specified symptoms. Once individual disorders are identified, it is helpful to organize them in a systematic way.

In 1952, the American Psychiatric Association published a system for classifying psychological disorders, the *Diagnostic and Statistical Manual of Mental Disorders,* which became known as the *DSM.* Reflecting significant changes with each edition, the fourth edition, the *DSM-IV,* was published in 1994 and revised once again in the summer of 2000 as the *DSM-IV-TR* (or Text Revision).

The *DSM-IV-TR* is the system of classification most widely used in all mental health fields today. Indeed, I've used the *DSM-IV-TR* as a major source of information for this chapter. The *DSM-IV-TR* lists 297 different diagnostic categories(!), compared to only 106 in the original *Manual.*

It makes good sense to have a classification system for psychological disorders. The major advantage, of course, is communication. People cannot hold a reasonable conversation about a patient's problem if they disagree on the definition of the diagnosis appropriate for that patient. If everyone agrees on the *DSM-IV-TR*'s definition, then at least they're using the same terms in the same way. Still, classification schemes can cause difficulties.

Assigning labels to people may be useful, but it also can be dehumanizing. It may be difficult to remember that Sally is a complex and complicated human being with a range of feelings, thoughts, and behaviors, not just a "paranoid schizophrenic." In response to this concern, the *DSM-IV* refers only to disordered behaviors, not to disordered people. That is, it refers to paranoid reactions, not to individuals who are paranoid—to persons with anxiety, not anxious persons.

A second problem inherent in classification and labeling is falling into the habit of believing that labels explain behavior. Diagnosing and labeling a pattern of behaviors does not explain those behaviors. It does not tell us why such a pattern of behaviors developed or what we can or should do about them now. How do you know that Bruce has paranoid schizophrenia? He has strange, bizarre, unfounded beliefs about himself and his world, that's why. Why does he have these strange beliefs? Well, because he is a paranoid schizophrenic, of course. Rather circular, isn't it? Moreover, labels can create unfortunate, lasting stigmas and negative attitudes about people. Learning that someone is "psychologically disordered" or is "mentally ill" may cause a wide range of negative reactions, and the label often sticks long after the disorder has been treated and the symptoms are gone.

In this chapter, we'll consider a variety of psychological disorders. As we do so, there are a few important points I would like you to keep in mind.

1. *"Abnormal" and "normal" are not two distinct categories.* They may be thought of as end points on some continuum we can use to describe people, but there is a large gray area between the two in which distinctions get fuzzy.
2. *Abnormal does not mean dangerous.* True, some people diagnosed with mental disorders may cause harm to themselves or to others, but most people with psychological disorders are not dangerous at all. Even among persons who have been in jail for violent crimes, those with psychological disorders have no more subsequent arrests than do persons without disorders. As David

Holmes (2001, p. 546) puts it, "…we do not see headlines such as 'person with no history of mental illness commits murder,' although, in fact, that situation is more prevalent."

3. *Abnormal does not mean bad.* People with psychological disorders are not bad or weak people, in any evaluative sense. They may have done bad things, and bad things may have happened to them, but it is certainly not in the tradition of psychology to make moral judgments about good and bad.

4. *Most depictions of psychological disorders are made in terms of extreme and obvious cases.* Psychological disorders, like physical disorders, may occur in mild or moderate forms. It is well accepted that no two people are exactly alike and that there are individual differences in psychological functioning. No two people, even with the same diagnosis of a psychological disorder, will be alike in all regards.

A WORD ON "INSANITY"

In common practice, the terms psychological disorder, mental disorder, and behavior disorder are used interchangeably. There is one term, however, with which we need to exercise particular care, and that is *insanity.* Insanity is not a psychological term. It is a legal term. It relates to problems with psychological functioning, but in a restricted sense. Definitions of insanity vary from state to state, but to be judged

Insanity is a legal term, not a psychological one.

insanity a legal concept, usually requiring evidence that a person did not know or fully understand the consequences of his or her actions at a given time, could not discern the difference between right and wrong, and was unable to exercise control over his or her actions at the time a crime was committed

insane usually requires evidence that a person did not know or fully understand the consequences of his or her actions at a given time, could not discern the difference between right and wrong, and was unable to exercise control over his or her actions at the time a crime was committed. The American public has long over-estimated the use of an insanity defense in courts of law. The public's perception is that an "insanity plea" is "used too much"—in about 37 percent of all felony cases. In fact, it is used in less than 1 percent of all felony cases and is successful in only 26 percent of those cases (Silver, Cirincione, & Steadman, 1994).

A related issue, known as competence, has to do with a person's mental state at the time of trial. The central issues are whether a person is in enough control of his or her mental and intellectual functions to understand courtroom procedures and aid in his or her own defense. If not, a person may be ruled "not competent" to stand trial for his or her actions, whatever those actions may be. Most likely, a person who is judged incompetent will be placed into a mental institution until he or she becomes competent to stand trial.

✔ STUDY CHECK

How do psychologists define the concept of "abnormality"?

How are psychological disorders classified?

Compare and contrast "psychological disorders" and "insanity."

CYBER PSYCH

(a) "Internet Mental Health" is a monster site with many useful links. From the homepage at http://www.mentalhealth.com click on the link "Disorders." For each disorder on the list you get both an American and a European description, articles on treatment, and further links to recent research, booklets, magazine articles, and additional Internet website links.

(b) For a sense of what the *DSM-IV* is all about, a very accessible website is at http://allpsych.com/disorders/disorders_dsmIVcodes.html.

(c) In Q&A format, The American Psychiatric Association addresses "inanity" at http://www.psych.org/public_info/insanity.cfm.

The Anxiety Disorders

anxiety a feeling of general apprehension or dread accompanied by predictable physiological changes

Anxiety is a feeling of general apprehension or dread accompanied by predictable physiological changes: increased muscle tension; shallow, rapid breathing; cessation of digestion; increased perspiration; and drying of the mouth. Thus, anxiety involves two levels of reaction: subjective feelings (e.g., fear or dread) and physiological responses (e.g., rapid breathing). The major symptom of anxiety disorders is felt anxiety, often coupled with "avoidance behavior" or attempts to resist or avoid any situation that seems to produce anxiety.

Anxiety disorders are the most common of all the psychological disorders, affecting 19.1 million (13.3 percent) of the adult U. S. population (ADAA, 2003). International data suggest that at any point in time between 8 and 20 percent of children and adolescents have the disorder. Anxiety disorders are two to three times more likely to be diagnosed in women than in men. Percentages of this sort do not convey the enormity of the problem. We're talking about millions of real people here—people like you and me. In this section, we will consider five anxiety disorders: generalized anxiety disorder, panic disorder, phobic disorder, obsessive-compulsive disorder, and post-traumatic stress disorder.

The major symptom of **generalized anxiety disorder (GAD)** is distressing, felt anxiety. With this disorder we find unrealistic, excessive, persistent worry. People with generalized anxiety disorder report that the anxiety they experience causes substantial interference with their lives and that they need a significant dosage of medications to control their symptoms. The *DSM-IV* adds the criterion that people with this disorder find it difficult to control worry or anxiety.

The experienced anxiety of this disorder may be very intense, but it is not brought on by anything specific in the environment; it just seems to come and go (or come and stay) without reason or warning. People with GAD are usually in a state of uneasiness and seldom have any clear insight or ideas about what is causing their anxiety. Those of us without any sort of anxiety disorder will (or can) be anxious from time to time, but when we are, we know why. The self-reports of persons with GAD show that their major concerns are an inability to relax, tension, difficulty concentrating, feeling frightened, and being afraid of losing control.

In the generalized anxiety disorder, the experience of anxiety may be characterized as chronic, implying that the anxiety is nearly always present, albeit sometimes more so than at other times. For a person suffering from **panic disorder**, the major symptom is more acute—an unpredictable, unprovoked onset of sudden, intense anxiety, or a "panic attack." These attacks may last for a few seconds or for hours. Attacks are associated with many physical symptoms—a pounding heart, labored breathing, sweating, trembling, chest pains, nausea, dizziness, and/or numbness and trembling in the hands and feet. There is no one particular stimulus to bring it on. The panic attack is unexpected. It just happens. Early in the disorder, nearly 85 percent of patients with panic attacks make visits to hospital emergency rooms, convinced that they are suffering some life-threatening emergency (Katerndahl & Realini, 1995). With panic disorder, there is a recurrent pattern of attacks and a building worry about future attacks.

Initial panic attacks are often associated with stress, particularly from the loss of an important relationship. A complication of panic disorder is that it can be accompanied by feelings of depression (Kessler et al., 1998). This may be why the rate of suicide and suicide attempts is so high for persons with a diagnosis of panic disorder (20 percent), which is higher than that for persons diagnosed with depression alone (15 percent).

The essential feature of **phobic disorders** (or phobias) is a persistent and excessive fear of some object, activity, or situation that leads a person to avoid that object, activity, or situation. Implied in this definition is the notion that the fear is intense enough to be disruptive. Also implied is the fact that there is no real or significant threat involved in the stimulus that gives rise to a phobia; that is, the fear is unreasonable, exaggerated, or inappropriate. Did you notice that with this disorder I used the term fear, not anxiety? What is the difference? In nearly every regard, the two are exactly alike. The difference is that fear requires an object. One is not just "afraid." One is afraid of something. We may say that you are afraid *of* the dark, but we probably would not say that you are anxious of the dark.

Many things in this world are life-threatening or frightening. For example, if you drive your car down a steep hill and suddenly realize the brakes aren't working, you will probably feel an intense reaction of fear. Such a reaction is not phobic

generalized anxiety disorder (GAD) a disorder characterized by chronic, distressing, felt anxiety

panic disorder a disorder characterized by acute, unpredictable, unprovoked onset of sudden, intense anxiety, or a "panic attack."

phobic disorders (or phobias) a persistent and excessive fear of some object, activity, or situation that leads a person to avoid that object, activity, or situation

As much fun as these folks seem to be having, you would not want to be part of this group if you had a phobia about being in large crowds.

obsessive-compulsive disorder (OCD) an anxiety disorder characterized by a pattern of recurrent obsessions and compulsions

obsessions ideas or thoughts that involuntarily and constantly intrude into awareness

compulsions constantly intruding, repetitive behaviors

because it is not irrational. Similarly, few of us enjoy the company of bees. That we don't like bees and would prefer they not be around us does not mean we have a phobic disorder. Key to a diagnosis is intensity of response. People who have a phobic reaction to bees (called *mellissaphobia*) may refuse to leave the house in the summer for fear of encountering a bee and may become genuinely anxious at the buzzing sound of any insect, fearing it to be a bee. They may become uncomfortable reading a paragraph, such as this one, about bees. Figure 10.1 presents a very small sample of the varieties of phobic disorder known to psychologists.

The **obsessive–compulsive disorder (OCD)** is an anxiety disorder characterized by a pattern of recurrent obsessions and compulsions. **Obsessions** are ideas or thoughts that involuntarily and constantly intrude into awareness. Generally speaking, obsessions are pointless or groundless thoughts, most commonly about cleanliness, violence, disease, danger, or doubt. Many of us have experienced mild, obsessive-like thoughts—for example, worrying during the first few days of a vacation if you really did turn off the stove. To qualify as part of OCD, obsessions must be disruptive; they must interfere with normal functioning. They are also time-consuming and are the source of anxiety and distress.

Compulsions are constantly intruding, repetitive behaviors. The most commonly reported compulsions are hand-washing, grooming, and counting or checking behaviors, such as checking repeatedly that the door is really locked. (See Figure 10.2.) Have you ever checked an answer sheet to see that you've really answered all the questions on a test and then checked it again, and again, and again? To do so is compulsive. It serves no real purpose, and it provides no real sense of satisfaction, although it is done very conscientiously in an attempt to reduce anxiety or stress. People with OCD recognize that their behaviors serve no useful purpose; they know that they are unreasonable but cannot stop them.

An obsession or compulsion can exert an enormous influence on a person's life. Consider the case of a happily married accountant, the father of three. For reasons he cannot explain, he becomes obsessed with the fear of contracting AIDS. There is no reason for him to be concerned; his sexual activities are entirely

The PHOBIA:	is a fear of:
acrophobia	high places
agoraphobia	open spaces
algophobia	pain
astraphobia	lightning and thunder
autophobia	one's self
claustrophobia	small, closed places
hematophobia	blood
monophobia	being alone
mysophobia	dirt or contamination
nyctophobia	the dark
pathophobia	illness or disease
thanatophobia	death and dying
xenophobia	the unknown
zoophobia	animals, in general

FIGURE 10.1

A sample of phobias, some relatively common (agoraphobia, claustrophobia, pathophobia, nyctophobia, zoophobia), the others quite rare.

monogamous; he has never used drugs; he has never had a blood transfusion. Still, he is overwhelmed with the idea that he will contract this deadly disease. Ritualized, compulsive behaviors are associated with his obsessive thoughts: He washes his hands vigorously at every opportunity and becomes anxious if he cannot change his clothes at least three times a day (all in an effort to avoid the dreaded AIDS virus).

Notice that we are using "compulsive" in an altogether different way when we refer to someone being a compulsive gambler, a compulsive eater, or a compulsive practical joker. What is different about the use of the term in such cases is that although the person engages in habitual patterns of behavior, he or she gains pleasure from doing so. The compulsive gambler enjoys gambling; the compulsive eater loves to eat. Such people may not enjoy the consequences of their actions in the long term, but they feel little discomfort about the behaviors themselves.

Obsessive-compulsive disorder is much more common than once believed. It afflicts nearly one of every 200 teenagers (OCD is commonly diagnosed in childhood or adolescence), and as many as five million Americans.

Common Obsessions:	Common Compulsions:
Contamination fears of germs, dirt, etc.	Washing
Imagining having harmed self or others	Repeating
Imagining losing control of aggressive urges	Checking
Intrusive sexual thoughts or urges	Touching
Excessive religious or moral doubt	Counting
Forbidden thoughts	Ordering/arranging
A need to have things "just so"	Hoarding or saving
A need to tell, ask, confess	Praying

FIGURE 10.2

A few of the more common obsessions and compulsions found in patients with OCD. (From the website of the Obsessive-Compulsive Foundation, www.ocfoundation.org retrieved July, 2003).

PTSD may be a long-term after-effect of experiencing a personal trauma.

post-traumatic stress disorder (PTSD) a disorder involving distressing symptoms that arise some time after the experience of a highly traumatic event

An anxiety disorder that has been the subject of much public discussion over the past decade is **post–traumatic stress disorder (PTSD)**. This disorder involves distressing symptoms that arise some time after the experience of a highly traumatic event, where trauma is defined by the *DSM-IV-TR* as an event that meets two criteria: a) the person has experienced, witnessed, or been confronted with an event that involves actual or threatened death or serious injury, and b) the person's response involves intense fear, helplessness, or horror. The disorder was first recognized with the publication of the *DSM-III* in 1980 and was seen as a reasonable diagnosis for many mental health problem of veterans returning from the war in Vietnam. Ironically, the disorder affected only 1.2 percent of Vietnam veterans (compared to 3.7 percent of Korean War veterans and up to ten percent of World War II veterans (McNally, 2003).

There are three clusters of symptoms that further define PTSD:

1. re-experiencing the traumatic event (e.g., flashbacks or nightmares)
2. avoidance of any possible reminders of the event (including people who were there)
3. increased arousal or "hyper-alertness" (e.g., irritability, insomnia, difficulty concentrating).

The traumatic events that trigger this disorder are many, ranging from natural disasters (e.g., floods or hurricanes), to life-threatening situations (e.g., kidnapping, rape, assault, or combat), to the loss of property (e.g., the house burns down; the car is stolen). First-hand experience with trauma may not be a requirement for the appearance of post-traumatic stress syndrome symptoms. The disorder has been diagnosed in survivors of the destruction of the World Trade Center buildings on September 11, 2001, and also has been found in some of those who witnessed the attacks from the streets of New York City. It even has been diagnosed in some who simply seemed to get "caught up" in the continuous television images of that horrific day and its aftermath.

Nearly 20 percent of women exposed to trauma will experience the symptoms of post-traumatic stress disorder, compared to 8 percent of men. It is important to keep in mind that, in response to traumatic stressors, only a minority of people ever develop PTSD symptoms (McNally, 2003b, p. 237). Interestingly, the course of PTSD does not show a predictable pattern of lessening symptoms. Indeed, over a four-year period following diagnosis, symptoms actually increase in number and severity (Port, Engdahl, & Frazier, 2001).

mood disorders psychological disorders that clearly demonstrate disturbances in emotional reactions or feelings

✔ STUDY CHECK

Briefly describe each of the following: generalized anxiety disorder, panic disorder, phobic disorder, obsessive-compulsive disorder, and post-traumatic stress disorder.

CYBER PSYCH

(a) There is a group called "The Anxiety Disorders Association of America," and their website is at http://www.adaa.org. The group is "dedicated to informing the public, healthcare professionals and legislators that anxiety disorders are real, serious and treatable." There are many great links here, including "About Anxiety Disorders." The "Fast Facts and Media" link is also well worth a visit.

(b) OCD is likely the most difficult of the anxiety disorders to fully appreciate. The website of the "Obsessive Compulsive Foundation can be highly recommended. It is at http://www.ocdfoundation.org. Nearly all of the links listed on the left side of the homepage are informative.

The Mood Disorders

Mood disorders clearly demonstrate disturbances in emotional reactions or feelings. We have to be careful here. Almost all psychological disorders have an impact on mood. With mood disorders, however, the duration and/or intensity or extreme nature of a person's mood is the major symptom.

Listed under the general classification of mood disorder are several specific disorders differentiated in terms of such criteria as length of episode and severity of symptoms. There is mounting evidence that different varieties of depression may involve different underlying brain structures or brain circuitry (Davidson et al., 2002).

Making a diagnosis of **major depressive disorder** can be a challenge. For one thing, a person must have experienced two or more depressive episodes, where such an episode is defined as a period of at least two weeks during which the person experienced five or more of the following symptoms nearly every day: a) depressed or sad mood, b) loss of pleasure or interest in normal activities, c) weight loss or dramatic change in appetite, d) either significantly more or less sleep than normal, e) either physical slowness or agitation, f) unusual fatigue or loss of energy, and g) recurrent thoughts of death or suicide.

major depressive disorder two or more depressive episodes, where such an episode is defined as a period of at least two weeks during which the person experienced five or more of the following symptoms: a) sad mood, b) loss of pleasure or interest in normal activities, c) weight loss or dramatic change in appetite, d) significantly more or less sleep than normal, e) physical slowness or agitation, f) unusual fatigue or loss of energy, and g) recurrent thoughts of death or suicide

This mood disorder is diagnosed about two times more frequently in women than in men; during any six-month period, approximately 6.6 percent of women and 3.5 percent of men will have an episode of major depression (Nolen-Hoeksema, 2001). This ratio of 2:1 holds across nationalities and ethnic groups. Unfortunately, relapse and recurrence are common for those who have had a depressive episode. A recent and large-scale study (Kessler et al., 2003) found that in a 12-month time frame, nearly 7 percent of their sample met the criteria for major depressive disorder, that more than half of this group had symptoms that were rated as severe to very severe, and that nearly 60 percent also had a diagnosable anxiety disorder. Sorry about all these statistics, but think about the results of this last study. It means that in any year, over 13 million Americans will have major depression, millions of them suffering greatly from it.

dysthymia a milder, but chronic, form of depression involving recurrent pessimism, low energy level, and low self-esteem

Dysthymia [diss-thigh´-me-a´] is essentially a milder, but chronic form of depression. The disorder involves recurrent pessimism, low energy level, and low self-esteem. Whereas major depression tends to occur in a series of extremely debilitating episodes, dysthymia is a more continuous sense of being depressed and sad. By definition, the depressed mood must last at least two years—and may last for 20 to 30 years.

For both major depression and dysthymia, there need not be any event or situation that precipitates the person's depressed mood. That is, to feel overwhelmingly depressed upon hearing of the death of a close friend is not, in itself, enough to be regarded as a disorder of any sort. We all may feel periods of mild depression from time to time. With major depressive disorder, the depression is significant and is associated with many additional symptoms. With dysthymia, the depression is particularly long-lasting.

bipolar disorder episodes of depression interspersed with episodes of mania

mania an extraordinarily elevated mood with feelings of euphoria or irritability

In **bipolar disorder**, episodes of depression are interspersed with episodes of mania. (This disorder is still often referred to as "manic depression.") **Mania** is characterized as an elevated mood with feelings of euphoria or irritability. In a manic state, a person shows an increase in activity, is more talkative than usual, and seems to get by with less sleep than usual. Mania is a condition of mood that cannot be maintained for long. It is too tiring to stay manic for an extended time. As is true for depression, mania seldom occurs as an isolated episode. Follow-up studies show that recurrences of manic reactions are common. Relapse is found in nearly 40 percent of those who have been diagnosed as having a manic episode. People are rarely manic without also showing periods of depression. Approximately two million Americans suffer from bipolar disorder.

The answers to the question "What causes depression?" depend largely on how and where one looks. It seems most likely that depression is caused by several different but inter-related causes—both biological and psychological. There are clear indicators that major depressive disorder and bipolar disorder have a genetic basis. In fact, researchers have identified a variation of a certain brain chemistry gene that predicts which people are likely to develop depression following a traumatic or highly stressful life event (Caspi et al., 2003). This point gets us to the following model for the development of psychological disorders.

diathesis-stress model the proposal that individuals inherit multiple genes, which may give rise to the predisposition to express certain behaviors, but these behaviors are expressed only if activated by stress or trauma

We may talk about a genetic basis for depression, but clearly, people do not inherit depression—they inherit genes. What the **diathesis-stress model** proposes is that individuals inherit multiple genes, which may give rise to the tendency or predisposition to express certain behaviors, but these behaviors are expressed only if activated by stress or trauma. "Diathesis" is a term that literally means "a condition which makes someone susceptible to developing a disorder." In our current discussion,

Simply being depressed is not, in and of itself, an indication of a psychological disorder. Depressing things happen to all of us, and feeling depressed in such a circumstance is not to be taken as "abnormal."

then, the proposal would be that some people inherit predispositions to develop a depressive disorder when they encounter stress in their lives. Faced with the same or similar stress, someone else may have a diathesis to develop coronary heart disease or gastrointestinal problems, while someone else might respond to that stress with no disease or disorder at all. This interactive explanation is applicable to all sorts of disorders. A person may have a genetic predisposition to develop sinus infections. But without exposure to the agents that produce such infections, none will occur.

✓ STUDY CHECK

What are the mood disorders?

What is the essence of the "diathesis-stress model"?

CYBER PSYCH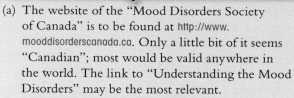

(a) The website of the "Mood Disorders Society of Canada" is to be found at http://www. mooddisorderscanada.ca. Only a little bit of it seems "Canadian"; most would be valid anywhere in the world. The link to "Understanding the Mood Disorders" may be the most relevant.

(b) The site: http://www.nimh.nih.gov/healthinformation/ depressionmenu.cfm is a government-sponsored Internet presence dealing with mood disorders. It is not clear at first, but there are dozens of active links on this page.

(c) A pharmaceutical company sponsors http://www. depression.com, so be careful of possible bias. The link to "Understanding Depression" is a good one.

Schizophrenia

schizophrenia a disorder characterized by a distortion of reality, a retreat from other people, and disturbances in affect, behavior, and cognition

Schizophrenia is a diagnosis for what may be several different disorders, which have in common a distortion of reality, a retreat from other people, and disturbances in affect, behavior, and cognition (our ABCs again). The analogy with cancer is crude, but reasonable. If you hear that a friend has cancer, that is certainly not good news. But how bad the news is depends upon answers to a few questions, such as, "What sort of cancer is it?" "Is it a small spot of skin cancer on the tip of an ear, prostate cancer, breast cancer, pancreatic cancer, brain cancer?" "How aggressive, or fast-spreading, is the cancer?" So it is with schizophrenia, a term so general that it raises many follow-up questions.

Schizophrenia can be found around the world at the same rate: about 1 percent of the population (Buckley et al., 1996). People in developing countries tend to have a more acute (intense, but short-lived) course—and a better outcome—of the disorder than do people in industrialized nations. In the United States, schizophrenia accounts for 75 percent of all mental health expenditures. Schizophrenia occurs slightly more frequently in men than in women, and males are more likely to be disabled by the disorder and have a higher relapse rate (Aleman, Kahn, & Selten, 2003).

The prognosis for schizophrenia is not very encouraging. About 25 percent do recover fully from their first episode of the disorder and have no recurrences; in about 50 percent of the cases, there is a recurrent illness with periods of remission in between, and in the other 25 percent of cases there are no signs of recovery, and there is a long-term deterioration in functioning.

If treatment begins immediately after an initial episode, the prognosis is better, with as many as 83 percent recovering (Lieberman et al., 1993). We see this phenomenon with many physical ailments: The sooner treatment begins, the better the likelihood of recovery.

Only recently has a consensus developed for classifying the disorder into types on the basis of positive and negative symptoms. One dimension of schizophrenia is typified by **negative symptoms**—characterized by a loss of or a decrease in normal functions. These symptoms include emotional and social withdrawal, apathy, and reduced energy, motivation and attention.

negative symptoms those symptoms of schizophrenia characterized by a loss of or a decrease in normal functions

positive symptoms those symptoms of schizophrenia largely characterized by hallucinations and delusions

hallucinations false perceptions—perceiving that which is not there or failing to perceive that which is

delusions false beliefs—ideas that are firmly held regardless of evidence to the contrary

The other dimension of schizophrenia is typified by **positive symptoms**, largely hallucinations and delusions. **Hallucinations** are false perceptions—perceiving that which is not there or failing to perceive that which is. Schizophrenic hallucinations are often auditory, taking the form of "hearing voices inside one's head." **Delusions** are false beliefs, ideas that are firmly held regardless of evidence to the contrary. Delusions of someone with schizophrenia are inconsistent and unorganized. Positive symptoms of schizophrenia also may include disordered thinking and speech, bizarre behaviors, and inappropriate affect. Someone displaying these symptoms may say something like, "When you swallow in your throat like a key it comes out, but not a scissors, a robin too, it means spring" (Marengo & Harrow, 1987, p. 654), or the person may giggle and laugh or sob and cry for no apparent reason, or may stand perfectly still for hours at a time. (See Figure 10.3.)

The usefulness of this negative-positive distinction is that there may be differences in both the causes and the most effective treatment plans for the two types. In brief, we find the correlates of negative symptoms to include enlarged ventricles in the brain, a clearer genetic basis, more severe complications at birth, a lower educa-

FIGURE 10.3

Classifying schizophrenia
on the basis of positive
and negative symptoms.

Schizophrenia with NEGATIVE SYMPTOMS
is characterized by: emotional and social withdrawal, and/or reduced energy and motivation,
and/or apathy, and/or poor attention.

Schizophrenia with POSITIVE SYMPTOMS
is characterized by: hallucinations (false perceptions), and/or delusions (false beliefs), and/
or disordered thinking or speech, and/or bizarre behaviors, and/or inappropriate affect.

tional level, poorer adjustment patterns before onset, and a poorer prognosis given
the relative ineffectiveness of medications. Correlated with positive symptoms are
excesses of the neurotransmitter dopamine, relatively normal brain configuration,
severe disruptions in early family life, over-activity and aggressiveness in adolescence, and a relatively good response to treatment.

I need to make two things clear. First, as unsettling as these symptoms may be,
the average patient with schizophrenia does not present the picture of the crazed,
wild lunatic often depicted in movies and on television. Day in and day out, the
average patient is quite colorless, withdrawn, and of very little danger. Their "dif-
ferentness" may be frightening, but people with schizophrenia are seldom more
dangerous than anyone else. Second, when literally translated, schizophrenia means
"splitting of the mind," where the split of the mind of the patient from the real
world and social relationships as the rest of us experience them. The term has never
been used to describe multiple or split personalities of the Jekyll and Hyde variety.
Such disorders do occur, but they are of a totally different sort.

✓ STUDY CHECK

What is schizophrenia, and what are the differences
between positive and negative symptoms of the
disorder?

CYBER PSYCH

(a) A very complete — if occasionally
"technical" — website on schizophrenia is that of
the National Library of Medicine. It can be found
at http://www.nlm.nih.gov/medlineplus/schizophrenia.html.

(b) The National Alliance for Research on
Schizophrenia and Depression — NARSAD — is
a donor-supported research organization. Their
website is not as "rich" or glossy as many, but
what you will find there is cutting edge research.
It is at http://www.narsad.org.

Psychotherapy Techniques

Thirty years ago, only 13 percent of the population sought psychotherapy at any
time in their lives. Today, more than 30 percent will have experience in psychotherapy during their lifetimes. Americans seek help from mental health professionals twice as often as they visit internists. Let's now consider a few of the types of
techniques or approaches that psychotherapists may employ. Please understand that

Ever since Freud's early days of psychoanalysis, psychotherapy is rightfully thought of as "talk therapy," but listening plays an equally important role.

summarizing a complex psychotherapeutic approach in a few short paragraphs can hardly do justice to the intricacies of these techniques. About all that we can do here is provide some sense or "flavor" of these psychotherapies, while trying not to trivialize them.

PSYCHOANALYTIC APPROACHES

I have included this approach in our short list for two reasons: (a) nearly everyone has heard of Freud and psychoanalysis, and (b) it was the very first attempt to treat psychological disorders without any reliance on medications. In 1881, Sigmund Freud graduated from the University of Vienna Medical School. From the start, he was interested in what were then called nervous disorders. What mattered, Freud believed, was to have the patients talk about everything relevant to their lives in order to get at the underlying conflicts that were causing their symptoms. Freud's method became known as the "talking cure," better known as psychoanalysis.

Psychoanalysis is based on several assumptions, most of them having to do with conflict and the unconscious mind. For Freud, life is often a struggle to resolve conflicts between naturally opposing forces. The biological, sexual, aggressive strivings of the id are often in conflict with the superego, which is associated with being overly cautious and experiencing guilt. The strivings of the id also can be in conflict with the rational, reality-based ego, which may be called upon to mediate between the id and the superego. Anxiety-producing conflicts that go unresolved are **repressed**; that is, they are forced out of awareness into the unconscious mind. Conflicts and anxiety-producing traumas of childhood can be expected to produce symptoms of psychological disturbance later in life.

According to Freud, the way to rid oneself of anxiety is to enter the unconscious, identify the details of the repressed, anxiety-producing conflict, bring it out into the open, and then work to resolve it. The first step is to gain insight into the

repression the process of forcing out of awareness into the unconscious mind those thoughts, beliefs, or motives that cause anxiety

true nature of a patient's problems; only then can problem-solving begin. Thus, the goals of Freudian psychoanalysis are insight and resolution of repressed conflict.

Psychoanalysis with Sigmund Freud was a time-consuming (up to five days per week for as many as ten years!), often tedious process of aided self-examination. The major task for the patient was to talk openly and honestly about all aspects of his or her life, from early childhood memories to the dreams of the present. The main task of the therapist/analyst was to interpret what was being expressed by the patient, always on the lookout for clues to possible repressed conflict. Once identified, the patient and the analyst could work together to resolve the conflicts underlying the symptoms that brought the patient to analysis in the first place.

Sigmund Freud died in 1939, but his approach to psychotherapy did not die with him. It has been modified (as Freud himself modified it over the years), but it remains true to the basic thrust of Freudian psychoanalysis.

Early in the twentieth century, Freudian psychoanalysis was the only form of psychotherapy, and through the 1940s and 1950s, it still was the therapy of choice. In recent years, psychoanalysis has become less common, and strict Freudian psychoanalysis has become rare, but it remains a viable option for many therapists, particularly for those treating patients with "milder disorders" (Gabbard, Gunderson, & Fonagy, 2002, p. 505).

How has the Freudian system of therapy changed? First, note what hasn't changed: To qualify as a psychoanalytic approach, the basic aim of therapy must be the uncovering of deep-seated, unconscious conflict, often caused by childhood experiences, and the removal of defenses so that such conflicts can be resolved.

Probably the most significant change since Freud's practice is the concern for shortening the length of analysis. Now psychotherapists talk about time-limited, or short-form, psychoanalytic therapy. Today's analysts take a more active role than did Freud, using interviews and discussions. Modern psychoanalysts, although not insensitive to the impact of childhood experience, tend to spend more time exploring the present. For example, a patient may come for analysis complaining about feelings of depression and anger to the point that the analyst believes there is a real and present danger that the patient might harm himself or herself or even commit suicide. The thrust of therapy is in the here and now, dealing with the patient's current anger and depression until the analyst is convinced the danger of self-harm has abated.

✔ STUDY CHECK

What is the essence of Freudian psychoanalysis, and how is the process different today from when it was practiced by Freud?

CYBER PSYCH

(a) A website hosted by the American Psychiatric Association provides a very good summary of the varieties of psychotherapy and psychotherapists at http://www.psych.org/public_info/psythera.cfm.

(b) There are several good websites that give guidance to those who wonder how to go about choosing the "right" psychotherapist. A particularly straightforward site is http://www.psychotherapyguild.com/choosing.html.

(c) Check out the links at http://users.rcn.com/brill/freudarc.html. It is a HUGE site with many details about Freud and psychoanalysis.

HUMANISTIC APPROACHES

There are many different types of humanistic psychotherapies. What they all have in common is a concern for self-examination, personal growth, and development. The goal of these therapies is not to uncover deep-seated conflicts, but to foster psychological growth and help a person take full advantage of life's opportunities. Based on the premise that people can take charge of themselves and their futures, that they can grow and change, therapy is directed at assisting with these processes. In many regards, this approach, which was very popular in the 1960s and 1970s, is well suited for someone who does not have a psychological disorder but is simply seeking to be a better person.

Client-centered therapy, also called Rogerian therapy after its founder, Carl Rogers, best typifies the humanistic approach. As its name suggests, the client is the center of the therapeutic interaction. Given his medical training, Freud called the people he dealt with patients. Rogers never used the term *patient,* and before his death in 1987 began using the term *person-centered* rather than *client-centered* to describe his approach to therapy.

In Rogers' view, therapy provides a special opportunity for a person to engage in self-discovery. Another way to express this is to say that a goal of client-centered therapy is to help the individual self-actualize—to grow and develop to the best of his or her potential.

What are the characteristics of client-centered therapy? Again, there are variants, but the following ideas characterize a client-centered approach: The focus is on the present, not the past or childhood. The focus is on affect or feelings, not beliefs or cognitions; that is, you are more likely to hear, "How do you feel about that?" than "What do you think about that?" The therapist will attempt to reflect, or mirror—not interpret—how a client is feeling (using statements such as "You seem angry" or "Does that make you feel sad?"). This so-called *reflective listening,* assessing and reflecting the true nature of a client's feelings, is not easy to do. It requires that the therapist be an active listener and be empathic, or be able to understand and share the essence of another's feelings.

Throughout each session, the therapist tries to express **unconditional positive regard**. This is the expression of being accepting and non-critical. "I will not be critical. If that is the way you feel, then that is the way you feel. Anything you say in here is okay, so long as you are being honest—not honest with me; that doesn't matter. Are you being honest with yourself?" Most of the positive regard that we get in this world is conditional: If, then. If you behave as you should, then you will be well thought of. If you do what I ask, then I will give you a reward.

unconditional positive regard the expression of being accepting and non-critical

---

✔ **STUDY CHECK**

What are the major features of client-centered therapy?

CYBER PSYCH

(a) The links and the resources available at http://www.allanturner.co.uk are very impressive—and worth a look.

(b) You can find a classic article by Carl Rogers himself ("Significant aspects of client-centered therapy") at http://psychclassics.yorku.ca/Rogers/therapy.htm.

Behavioral Approaches

There is no one behavior therapy; it is a collection of several techniques. What unites these techniques is that they are "methods of psychotherapeutic change founded on principles of learning established in the psychological laboratory" (Wolpe, 1981, p. 159). The main assumption of behavior therapy is that maladaptive behaviors are learned, and thus they can be unlearned. There are many principles of learning and many psychological disorders to which such methods and principles can be applied. In this section, I will list a few types of learning theory that have become part of behavior therapy.

Systematic desensitization, the application of classical conditioning to alleviate feelings of anxiety, particularly those associated with phobic disorders, is one of the first applications of learning theory to meet with success. It was introduced by Joseph Wolpe in the late 1950s, although others had used similar procedures earlier. Systematic desensitization is basically a matter of teaching a person first to relax totally and then to remain relaxed as he or she thinks about or is exposed to ever-increasing levels of stimuli that produce anxiety. If the person can remain calm and relaxed, that response can be conditioned to replace the anxious or fearful response previously associated with a particular stimulus.

A relatively new form of behavior therapy, *exposure and response prevention,* has shown promise as a treatment for obsessive-compulsive disorder (OCD), a disorder that is usually resistant to psychotherapy. In one clinic, patients are exposed for two hours, five days a week, for three weeks to whatever stimulus situation elicits obsessive thinking or compulsions. They are asked to vividly imagine the consequences they fear without engaging in their usual compulsive or obsessive routine; the procedure is also repeated in homework assignments. This is followed by a maintenance program of phone calls and clinic visits. For example, a patient who is obsessed with dirt and germs is told to sit on the floor and imagine that she has become ill because of insufficient washing and cleaning. For the first two weeks, she must not wash her hands (at all) and can take a shower for only ten minutes every other day. In the third week, she can wash her hands for 30 seconds, five times a day. This program claims that 75 to 83 percent of the patients who complete the regimen show significant and lasting improvement (Foa, 1995).

Aversion therapy is another example of learning applied to solving psychological problems. In aversion therapy, a stimulus that may be harmful but that produces a "pleasant" response is paired with an aversive, painful stimulus until the original stimulus is avoided. For example, every time you put a cigarette in your mouth, a painful shock is delivered to your lip. Every time you take a drink of alcohol, you get violently sick to your stomach from a nausea-producing drug. Every time a child molester is shown a picture of a young child, he gets an electric shock.

Techniques of aversion therapy do not sound like the sort of things anyone would agree to voluntarily. Many people do, however, volunteer for such treatments, for two reasons: First, aversion therapy is very effective at suppressing a specific behavior—at least for a while—and second, it is seen as the lesser of two evils. (Shocks and nausea-producing drugs are not much fun, but people see continuing their inappropriate, often self-destructive, behaviors as even more dangerous in the long run.) Aversion therapy, in any form, is not commonly practiced, and when it is, it usually tends to suppress behaviors for only a relatively short time. During that time, other techniques may be used in an attempt to bring about a more lasting

systematic desensitization
the application of classical conditioning to alleviate feelings of anxiety, particularly those associated with phobic disorders

change in behavior. In other words, aversion therapy is seldom effective when used alone; it is usually used in conjunction with other therapy.

Contingency management and contingency contracting borrow from the learning principles of operant conditioning. The idea is to have a person appreciate the consequences of his or her behaviors. Appropriate behaviors lead to rewards and the chance to do valued things, whereas inappropriate behaviors do not lead to reinforcement and provide fewer opportunities.

In many cases, these procedures work well. As operant conditioning would predict, their effectiveness is a function of the extent to which the therapist has control over the situation. If the therapist can manage the control of rewards and punishments (called *contingency management*), he or she stands a good chance of modifying the client's behavior. For example, in an institutional setting, if a patient (e.g., a severely disturbed person with schizophrenia) engages in the appropriate response (leaving her room to go to dinner), then the patient gets something she really wants (a chance to watch TV for an extra hour). In an outpatient setting, the therapist tries to arrange the situation so that the client learns to reinforce his or her own behaviors when they are appropriate.

Contingency contracting amounts to establishing a contract with a client so that exhibiting certain behaviors (preparing dinner) results in certain rewards (watching TV). In many cases, contingency contracting involves establishing a token economy. What this means is that the person is first taught that some token—a checker, a poker chip, or just a check mark on a pad—can be saved. When enough tokens are accumulated, they are cashed in for something of value to the person. With contracting, the value of a token for a specific behavior is spelled out ahead of time. Because control over the environment of the learner is most complete in such circumstances, this technique is particularly effective in institutions and with young children.

✓ STUDY CHECK

What are some of the techniques that qualify as behavior therapies?

CYBER PSYCH

(a) The site http://www.aabt.org is the homepage for the Association for the Advancement of Behavior Therapy. It greatly expands upon our brief discussion.

(b) http://www.guidetopsychology.com/sysden.htm is a rich website devoted exclusively to systematic desensitization.

Chapter Summary

How do psychologists define the concept of "abnormal"?

Within the context of psychological disorders, "abnormal" refers to maladaptive behaviors, cognitions, and/or affect at odds with social expectations that result in distress or discomfort.

How are psychological disorders classified?

The *DSM-IV-TR* is the text revision of the fourth edition of the *Diagnostic and Statistical Manual of Mental Disorders,* published by the American Psychological Association. It is the most widely used classification system for psychological disorders. The *DSM-IV-TR* spells out criteria for diagnosing disorders on the basis of observable symptoms. The major advantage of classifying psychological disorders is that it provides one standard label and cluster of symptoms for each disorder that all mental health practitioners can use; as such, it is a basis for improved communication. It does have its limitations, however. Schemes of classification can confuse description with explanation; classifying and labeling persons as having psychological disorders may overlook the larger group or society of which that individual is a part.

Compare and contrast "psychological disorders" and "insanity."

Psychological disorder, mental disorder, and behavior disorder are concepts used to label abnormal mental and behavioral conditions. Insanity is a legal term. It relates to psychological problems but refers to an individual's state of mind at the time of a crime. The question of insanity centers on whether a person knew or fully understood the consequences of his or her actions, knew the difference between right and wrong, and could exercise control over his or her actions at the time of a crime.

Briefly describe each of the following: generalized anxiety disorder, panic disorder, phobic disorder, obsessive-compulsive disorder, and post-traumatic stress disorder.

Anxiety disorders are the most common variety of psychological disorder. They are characterized by experienced, felt anxiety, usually coupled with attempts to avoid or escape from situations likely to bring on additional anxiety. The defining characteristic of *generalized anxiety disorder* is a high level of anxiety that cannot be attributed to any particular source. The anxiety is diffuse and chronic. The defining symptom of a *panic disorder* is a sudden, often unpredictable, attack of intense anxiety, called a panic attack. Such attacks may last for seconds or for hours. There is no particular stimulus that prompts the attack. A *phobic disorder* is typified by an intense, persistent fear of some object, activity, or situation that is no real threat to the individual's well-being—in brief, an intense, irrational fear. Phobias imply attempts to avoid the phobic object. Obsessions are thoughts or ideas that involuntarily and constantly intrude into awareness. They often are pointless or groundless thoughts about cleanliness, violence, disease, danger, or doubt. Compulsions are constantly intruding repetitive behaviors. The most common are hand washing, grooming, and counting or checking behavior. Obsessions and compulsions are the main symptoms of *obsessive-compulsive disorder,* or *OCD. Post-traumatic stress disorder,* or *PTSD,* is a disorder in which the symptoms of anxiety, recurrent and disruptive dreams, and recollections of a highly traumatic event (e.g., rape, combat, or natural disaster) occur well after the danger of the event has passed.

What are the mood disorders?

In the mood disorders, a disturbance in affect or feeling is the prime, and perhaps only, symptom. Most commonly the disorder involves depression; less commonly we find mania and depression occurring in cycles *(bipolar mood disorder).* Whether the major symptom is depression or mania, there is no reason for the observed mood. *Major depression* affects about twice as many women as men. It involves two or more episodes in which a person experiences sad mood, loss of pleasure, weight loss or change of appetite, physical slowness or agitation, either significantly more or less sleep than usual, unusual fatigue, and/or thoughts of death or suicide. *Dysthymia* involves depression that may be a bit less devastating or debilitating, but which is chronic (lasting for at least two years), involves recurrent feelings of pessimism, low energy levels, and low self-esteem.

What is the essence of the "diathesis–stress model"?

The diathesis-stress model is an attempt to account for the source of a disorder (such as mood disorders) as an interaction of inherited, genetic predispositions and environmental stressors. The point is that neither, by themselves, will result in a particular disorder.

What is schizophrenia, and what are the differences between positive and negative symptoms of the disorder?

Schizophrenia is a label applied to disorders that involve varying degrees of impairment. It occurs in about 1 percent of the population worldwide and, in general, is characterized by a distortion of reality, a retreat from others, and disturbances in affect, behavior, and cognition. About 25 percent of those diagnosed with the disorder recover fully from their first episode, while in 50 percent of cases, symptoms are recurrent with periods of remission. In 25 percent of cases, there is no recovery and a deterioration of functioning.

There may be a difference between schizophrenia with positive symptoms and schizophrenia with negative symptoms. Negative symptoms involve a loss of normal functioning, social and emotional withdrawal, reduced energy and motivation, apathy, and poor attention. Positive symptoms are hallucinations (false perceptions) and delusions (false beliefs). Positive symptoms also include disordered thinking, bizarre behavior, and inappropriate affect.

What is the essence of Freudian psychoanalysis, and how is the process different today from when it was practiced by Freud?

Freudian psychoanalysis is aimed at uncovering repressed conflicts (often developed in childhood) so that they can be resolved. Although the basic principles of psychoanalysis have remained unchanged since Freud's day, some changes have evolved. There is now more effort to shorten the time frame of analysis; there is less emphasis on childhood experiences and more concern with the here and now. Present-day analysis is also more involved with current feelings and interpersonal relationships than when it was practiced by Freud.

What are the major features of person-centered therapy?

Although there are different humanistic approaches, they share a focus on self-examination, personal growth, and development. These therapies focus on factors that foster psychological growth rather than uncovering deep-seated conflicts. A major premise is that the individual can take charge of himself or herself and grow and develop. Client-centered or person-centered therapy, associated with Carl Rogers, is based on the belief that people can control their lives and solve their own problems if they can be helped to understand the true nature of their feelings. It promotes self-discovery and personal growth. The therapist reflects the client's feelings, focuses on the here and now, and tries to be empathic, actively listening to and relating to the person's feelings. Throughout therapy, the therapist provides unconditional positive regard for the client.

What are some of the techniques that qualify as behavior therapies?

Behavior therapy is a collection of several techniques that have grown out of laboratory research on principles of learning. The main premise of behavior therapy is that maladaptive behaviors are learned, so they can be unlearned. Systematic desensitization applies principles of classical conditioning to the treatment of anxiety. In systematic desensitization, a person is taught to relax totally and then to remain relaxed as he or she thinks about or is exposed to anxiety-producing stimuli. The new relaxation response becomes classically conditioned to the stimulus, replacing the anxiety reaction. Exposure and response prevention is a treatment used for obsessive-compulsive disorder. Patients are exposed to the stimulus that evokes obsessive thinking and are then told to imagine the consequences of what they fear without engaging in their usual obsessive or compulsive routine. The procedure is repeated in homework assignments followed by a maintenance program of phone calls and clinic visits. During aversion therapy, one stimulus is paired with another aversive, painful stimulus until the original stimulus is avoided. Although aversion therapy is unpleasant, individuals still opt for it because it is very effective in suppressing behavior, and it is seen as better than the original behavior.

Contingency management involves a health professional gaining control over the rewards and punishments that control a patient's behavior. Patients can be rewarded for productive behaviors and/or punished for unproductive behaviors. In contingency contracting, a contract is established with a patient, specifying those behaviors that will be rewarded and those that will be punished. When enough rewards are accumulated, they may be traded for something the patient wants.

Student Study Guide

STUDY TIP #10 On Taking Useful Notes in Class

Attending class and listening carefully are important because lectures are presented to you only once. This is also why you'll need some written record of the information presented orally in class. Good lecture notes, written in your own style, are valuable tools for learning. There is a large body of research devoted to note-taking. Here I'll just touch on two principles that will help you learn psychology—or any other discipline.

1. **Select and organize what you hear.** It is probably already apparent to you that there is no way you can write down everything that is said in class. This can be an advantage. Note-taking should be an active process of selecting and organizing information. Although it is generally better to take too many notes than too few, it is important to be an active listener who participates in class, not a passive, mechanical writer. The notes you take will be yours, so put them in a form that you can use. Except for technical terms and new vocabulary, use your own words. Copying information is not learning it. Develop shortcuts. Feel free to abbreviate, but only if you will able to understand your symbols and notes when you go back to study them. From time to time, taking no notes at all may be best. Thinking about what is being said or participating in a class discussion may be more meaningful.

2. **Edit and review your notes.** Classroom notes are always "works in progress." Immediately after class, while material is still fresh, review your notes, fill in gaps, underline for emphasis, note unclear sections that need further work, and use the margins to jot down information you did not have time to record during class. Several times a week, as part of your study, continue the editing process. Use your textbook or other notes or outside readings, or consult with your instructor for correct spellings, missing details, clarification, and the like. After each quiz or exam in the course, go back and critically evaluate your own notes. To what extent did they help? How can they be improved? Did you write too much? Too little? Was the format you used the best possible for you?

KEY TERMS AND CONCEPTS

abnormal _____

_____

diagnosis _____

_____

insanity _____

_____

anxiety _____

_____

generalized anxiety disorder _____

_____

panic disorder _____

_____

phobic disorders _____

_____

obsessive-compulsive disorder _____

_____

obsession _____

_____

compulsion _____

_____

post-traumatic stress disorder _____

_____

mood disorders _____

_____

major depressive disorder _____

_____

dysthymia _____

_____

bipolar disorder _____

_____

mania _____

_____

diathesis-stress model _____

_____

schizophrenia _____

_____

negative symptoms _____

_____

positive symptoms_____

_____

hallucinations _____

_____

delusions _____

_____

unconditional positive regard _____

_____

systematic desensitization _____

_____

Practice Test Questions

MULTIPLE CHOICE

1. As you read this item, which provides the best estimate of the percentage of North Americans suffering from a psychological disorder?

   _____ a. 10 percent

   _____ b. 20 percent

   _____ c. 40 percent

   _____ d. There is no way to make such an estimate.

2. Which words, terms, or concepts are NOT included in your textbook's definition of abnormality?

   _____ a. maladaptive

   _____ b. bizarre or strange

   _____ c. distress or discomfort

   _____ d. affect, behavior, and/or cognition

3. Which of the following is TRUE concerning people with psychological disorders?

   _____ a. They tend to be more dangerous than others.

   _____ b. They usually realize that they have some sort of problem.

   _____ c. They are distinctly different from persons who are normal.

   _____ d. They are people who have poor self-control or will power.

4. Classification schemes and labels for psychological disorders, such as those found in the DSM-IV-TR, have some potential problems. Which of these is NOT one of those problems?

    _____ a. Labels tend to dehumanize real human suffering.

    _____ b. There is no logical or sensible rationale behind such schemes.

    _____ c. They usually focus on the individual and not the larger group to which the person belongs.

    _____ d. Schemes and labels may define and describe, but they do not explain.

5. Tracy reports feeling anxious, nervous, and "on edge" all day long. She is tired but cannot seem to sleep well. Sometimes she feels like crying for no reason at all. If Tracy has a disorder, the best diagnosis is probably that Tracy is experiencing a _____ disorder.

    _____ a. psychogenic fugue   _____ c. generalized anxiety

    _____ b. obsessive-compulsive   _____ d. panic

6. What two words best differentiate between panic disorder and generalized anxiety disorder?

    _____ a. acute and chronic   _____ c. rational and irrational

    _____ b. stimulus and response   _____ d. distress and discomfort

7. More than anything else, what is the difference between fear and anxiety?

    _____ a. Fear is more commonly irrational; anxiety is rational.

    _____ b. Fear involves the autonomic nervous system, anxiety does not.

    _____ c. Fear is the symptom of a disorder; anxiety is not.

    _____ d. Fear requires an object; anxiety does not.

8. Constantly checking and rechecking to confirm that the front door is really locked may be a sign of

    _____ a. a fugue state.

    _____ b. a phobia.

    _____ c. a conversion disorder.

    _____ d. an obsessive-compulsive disorder.

9. Which of these is most likely to result from experiencing some real, life-threatening event?

    _____ a. psychogenic fugue   _____ c. post-traumatic stress disorder

    _____ c. child abuse   _____ d. panic attacks

10. The collection of disorders called "mood disorders" has as its major symptom

    _____ a. disorganized thinking and confusion.

    _____ b. the experience of strange, unexplainable behaviors.

    _____ c. disturbances of affect.

    _____ d. cognitive disorientation.

11. By far, the most common form of mood disorder is

_____ a. depression.   _____ c. paranoia.

_____ b. bipolar.   _____ d. mania.

12. Concerning mood disorders, which of the following is FALSE?

_____ a. Depression is more common in women than in men.

_____ b. It is more common to find depression alone than mania alone.

_____ c. Depression generally occurs in a series of episodes.

_____ d. The symptoms of mania rarely recur or relapse.

13. Which of these symptoms tends NOT to be associated with schizophrenia?

_____ a. high levels of felt anxiety

_____ b. social withdrawal and retreat from others

_____ c. flattened affect

_____ d. disturbed cognitions, including delusions

14. Which of these would be considered to be a positive symptom of schizophrenia?

_____ a. a good prognosis   _____ c. hallucinations

_____ b. loss of affect   _____ d. social withdrawal

15. What makes a psychiatrist different from a psychologist is that the psychiatrist

_____ a. practices psychotherapy.

_____ b. is more knowledgeable in matters of testing and diagnostics.

_____ c. went to medical school.

_____ d. is more likely to be Freudian in orientation and practice psychoanalysis.

16. What do all of the psychotherapies have in common?

_____ a. They all involve talking and listening.

_____ b. They all are used to assist with medical treatments.

_____ c. They all seek to discover repressed conflicts.

_____ d. They all require a long-term (two- to three-year) commitment.

17. Freudian psychoanalysis is based on many assumptions, including each of the following EXCEPT that

_____ a. the patient may be truly unable to tell the analyst why he or she is experiencing anxiety.

_____ b. early childhood experiences can have an impact on the way that one feels as an adult.

_____ c. once the analyst gets the patient to act better, he or she will think and feel better.

_____ d. the true nature of the patient's problem may be revealed in the content of his or her dreams.

18. A basic premise of psychoanalysis after Freud is

    _____ a. there is no good reason for anxiety to feel so negative and unpleasant.

    _____ b. hypnosis can be a useful way of developing transference.

    _____ c. anxiety stems from some sort of repressed conflict.

    _____ d. analysis is meant to be a time-consuming process, usually lasting for years.

19. To be an active listener and to be able to share and understand the feelings of others is to

    _____ a. offer unconditional positive regard.

    _____ b. be existential.

    _____ c. self-actualize.

    _____ d. be empathic.

20. Most of the techniques of behavior therapy come from

    _____ a. suggestions made by previous patients.

    _____ b. Freud's theories.

    _____ c. the learning laboratory.

    _____ d. research in education.

TRUE/FALSE

1. _____ True _____ False Insanity is a term that comes from the legal profession, not from psychology or psychiatry.

2. _____ True _____ False By definition, psychological disorders must involve one's affect, behaviors, or cognitions.

3. _____ True _____ False Although it is classified as an anxiety disorder, there is increasing evidence that OCD has a strong biological basis.

4. _____ True _____ False Dysthymia is another (technical) term for major depressive disorder.

5. _____ True _____ False Schizophrenia means "split mind" — literally, splitting of the mind into two (or more) different, yet distinct, personalities.

6. _____ True _____ False About one-quarter of those diagnosed with schizophrenia will simply never get better.

7. _____ True _____ False Anybody can be a psychotherapist, but only a person with an MD can be certified as a psychoanalyst.

8. _____ True _____ False All psychotherapies are designed to ultimately bring about a change in a person's affect, behavior, and/or cognition.

9. _____ True _____ False By definition, contingency contracting is essentially the opposite of unconditional positive regard.

Roles, Rules, and Relationships

Preview

social psychology the field of psychology concerned with how others influence the thoughts, feelings, and behaviors of the individual

In this chapter we consider the psychology of people as they really live, interacting with others as social organisms in a social world. **Social psychology** is the field of psychology concerned with how others influence the thoughts, feelings, and behaviors of the individual. Social psychologists focus on the person or the individual in a group setting and not on the group *per se*, which is more likely to be the focus of sociologists. Because we are social organisms, we are familiar, each in our own way, with many of the concerns of social psychology.

To claim that we are familiar with the concerns of social psychology has certain implications. On the one hand, it means that social psychology is perceived as relevant because it deals with everyday situations that affect us all. On the other hand, it means that we are often willing to accept common sense and our personal experiences as the basis for our explanations of social behavior. Although common sense and personal experience may sometimes be valid, they are not acceptable for a scientific approach to understanding social behavior. Social psychology relies on experimentation and other scientific methods as sources of knowledge about social behavior.

Over the last 50 years, much of social psychology has taken on a cognitive flavor. That is, social psychologists are attempting to understand social behavior by examining mental structures and processes (cognitions) reflected in such behavior. A premise of this approach is that we do not view our social environment solely on the basis of the stimulus information it presents us. Instead, the argument goes, we have developed cognitions (for example, social norms or expectations and attitudes) that influence our interpretation of the world around us. Social cognition is largely about how we come to make sense of the social world in which we live and how that information influences our judgments, choices, attractions, and behaviors (Bordens & Horowitz, 2002). Specifically, this chapter covers a) social roles and norms, b) forming and maintaining small groups, c) attitudes, d) conformity e) obedience, f) social attributions, and g) forming and keeping interpersonal relationships.

Social Roles and Norms

Most of us have come to believe that we have a pretty good sense of who we are. By and large, we are "in touch with our feelings," have a reasonable idea of what we know and don't know, and can predict how we are likely to behave in most situations. A psychologist might say that we have developed a fairly accurate "sense of self." Social psychologists would argue that to fully understand who we are in the world, we need a "sense of selves"—that we are, in fact many different individuals in a social world.

social roles expectations about how we are to feel, think, and act associated with each of the positions we fulfill

Each of us, the argument goes, fills several *social positions*. We may be son or daughter, brother or sister, father or mother, perhaps grandfather or grandmother. We may be a college student or a college professor. We may be a salesperson or a consumer. In fact, during the day we find ourselves filling many different positions in our society. The significance of this point of view is that associated with each of the positions we take, there are **social roles**—expectations about how we are to feel, think, and act while in those positions.

Even within the same family there are several social positions, several social roles—and the possibility of role conflict.

As infants become children and then adolescents and eventually adults in their social world, they come to appreciate the subtle expectations associated with the positions they occupy. That is to say, as we develop, we become *socialized*—we learn what those in our environments expect of us. And we change our behaviors, even our affects and cognitions accordingly. It's simple, really. You don't act the same way in class as you do at home at the dinner table with family or at a party with friends. In ways subtle and not so subtle, you adjust to become a somewhat different person depending upon the social situation in which you find yourself. That is, you take on different social roles. I can hear the differences in my voice when I am on the phone. If I am in my office talking to a student, I sound rather "professorial." My entire demeanor and tone change when I'm chatting with a friend. I even pick up a bit of a Southern drawl when I am talking to my daughter, who lives in West Tennessee. We hold a variety of positions in our society. We assume different social roles, and thus change our "self" depending upon the situation in which we find ourselves.

One consequence of holding several positions and thus accepting several social roles is that conflict becomes a real possibility. **Role conflict** occurs when a person is faced with two or more sets of expectations and cannot meet one without some sacrifice of the other(s). It should not take you long to generate examples from your own experience. A young father wants to go to his daughter's important Sunday-afternoon soccer game, but also feels a need to visit his mother in a nursing home. Father roles and son roles are in conflict. Many role conflicts originate when there is tension between what one is expected to do as an employee and expectations that are associated with being a family member—"Do I finish my project this weekend or go to the family reunion?"

In this context, there is another concept from social psychology that we can consider here. In some instances, the expectations associated with social roles carry with them a strong sense of right and wrong. **Social norms** are unwritten but generally accepted "rules" that govern the appropriateness of behaviors in social

role conflict difficulties that arise when a person is faced with two or more sets of expectations and cannot meet one without some sacrifice of the other(s)

social norms unwritten but generally accepted "rules" that govern the appropriateness of behaviors in social situations

Part of becoming socialized in our culture is learning all of the expectations that accompany being a patient and going to the doctor's office for an examination (including the expectation that you will have to wear a silly robe).

situations. Every society, every culture, has quite a list of "do's and don'ts" that most people come to appreciate. One simply does not sit at a lunch counter and pick up and read someone else's newspaper—at least not without asking. In American society, on a crowded sidewalk, the rule is usually "stay to the right."

Social norms are often no more than social custom or what can be seen as ordinary politeness. Sometimes, however, what develop as social norms become viewed as important enough to be codified in the official laws of the land. When there was very little vehicular traffic, it was the norm to drive your wagon on the right side of the road. With increased traffic, it became necessary to make it a law that in the United States, one drives on the right side of the road. Spitting on the sidewalk probably has always violated social norms. But, with increased population, and concern about public heath issues, in most communities, spitting in public has become prohibited by law.

Social norms imply that individuals learn to appreciate and then conform to certain expectations. This is no more important a social task than when one is in a small group setting. It is to this subject that we turn next.

 STUDY CHECK

Define and give examples of social positions, social roles, and social norms.

CYBER PSYCH

It is a very long URL, but a good, simple summary essay on role conflict is at http://www.bc.edu/bc_org/avp/wfnetwork/rft/wfpedia/wfpWFRCent.html.

How We Live: In Small Groups

So far, we have talked about social *positions,* social *roles,* and social *norms* in a large, societal sort of way. These concepts of positions, roles, and norms are even more relevant in the context of small groups. In truth, we spend a good bit of time every day functioning in small groups—groups made up of family, friends, co-workers, fellow students, and so on. We have certain positions within these groups, and we behave in accordance with norms that are clear to all members of the group.

In social psychology, a **group** is defined as two or more individuals who interact with and influence each other (Bordens & Horowitz, 2002, p. 289; Worchel et al., 2000, p. 414). Simply having a collection of people who happen to be together at the same time and place does not constitute a group. Implied in the definition of "group" are notions such as cooperation, coordination, understood procedures, accepted norms, and mutual support.

Membership in some groups is quite involuntary. You cannot, after all, choose to be a member of any family. If you are in the military (which, in itself, may be voluntary) and are assigned to a patrol for a dangerous task, choosing to opt for another assignment is not likely. Membership in many groups is totally voluntary, including choices such as church, social club, sorority, fraternity, or gang. At least deciding to join may be voluntary; being accepted for membership can be a different matter,

Groups also can be differentiated in terms of their major functions (Burns, 2004). For example, one type of group is the **instrumental (or task-oriented) group**, which exists in order to perform some task or reach some specific goal. A group of students charged with completing an eight-week research project is an example of an instrumental group. So is a jury. The sole purpose of a jury is to find the truth of claims made in a courtroom and to reach a verdict. Once that is accomplished, the group is disbanded. The other major type of group is **affiliative (or social-oriented) groups**, which exist for more general, and often more social, interpersonal reasons. Here is where joining a sorority would fit in. The purpose of such groups (as the name suggests) is to *affiliate* with others whose company you value. These may very well be people with whom you share values, backgrounds, and ideals. Membership is meant to yield pleasure, enhanced self-esteem, support, and perhaps even a bit of prestige.

It is easy to see that we are dealing with endpoints of a continuum here, isn't it? There may be clear-cut examples in our experiences of both instrumental and affiliative groups, but many of the groups to which we belong seem to involve the characteristics of both. Sometimes we are lucky and can work within a task-oriented group that is made up (mostly) of good friends or people we enjoy being with. Sometimes groups that were formed exclusively for social, affiliative purposes take on projects that require working together to reach specified goals. Groups formed for the purpose of psychotherapy often reflect both task and social orientations. Yes, there is a primary, instrumental goal of providing insight and assistance for persons with psychological problems, but it also is often the case that such groups function best when feelings of genuine warmth and support develop. (Once again, we see that there are few clear-cut distinctions in psychology.)

How do groups—task-oriented, instrumental groups in particular—get formed or develop as working entities in the first place? They don't "just happen." They evolve. According to psychologist Bruce Tuckman, groups develop through several identifiable stages (Tuckman, 1965). He gave these stages the catchy names

group two or more individuals who interact with and influence each other

instrumental (or task-oriented) group a group that exists in order to perform some task or reach some specific goal

affiliative (or social-oriented) groups a group that exists for more general, and often more social, interpersonal reasons

of "forming, storming, norming, and performing," only later adding a final "ad-journing" stage to his list (Tuckman & Jensen, 1977). Let's look at each stage in turn. As you read through this list, see if you can think of groups in your own experience that formed this way.

Stage I—Forming: The group first comes together. Everyone is very polite, largely driven by a desire to be accepted by the others. Everyone makes every effort to avoid conflict or controversy. Everyone is guarded in his or her opinions and is generally reserved. Not much actual progress is made. This is largely a stage of gathering information—about how the group is likely to function, about the strengths and weaknesses of others, about who might emerge as the real leader.

Stage II—Storming: Politely deferring to others can last only so long. In this stage it becomes time to start talking about serious issues, the task at hand, and how the group is going to move forward. Tuckman viewed this storming phase as one of competition and conflict—often about issues of personal relationships within the group. Generalities no longer suffice. The group needs to know who is going to be responsible for what, what the time frame for progress is going to be, and how the individuals in the group are going to be evaluated. Given the nature of these conflicts, some members may retire to obscurity while others tend to "take over" and dominate.

Stage III—Norming: As Stage II winds down, the group becomes established, with its scope, goals, and responsibilities made clear and agreed upon. Having been through a stage of conflict (all of which need not be resolved), everyone has better appreciation of the strengths and weaknesses of the others. Individuals are prepared to give up (at least some of) their own private views and work as a cohesive, effective group. Perhaps for the first time, it is in this stage that members begin to genuinely listen to one another. Feedback becomes important. Morale and creativity increase. The group begins to become self-defensive, afraid of pressures from outside the group that might bring about change. At the same time, a concern (fear) can develop that group will break up after having reached its goals.

Stage IV—Performing: Tuckman was clear in pointing out that not all groups reach this stage. It is one of high productivity, cohesiveness, and loyalty to the group. By now everyone knows everyone else and what can be expected from each member. The focus of the group becomes both task oriented ("Let's get this job done.") and socially oriented ("Let's help each other out here.").

It was some years later that Tuckman decided that he should add a fifth stage to his list, a *Stage V—Adjourning.* For every group, there is a time of "completion," of disengagement and letting go. For groups that have reached Stage IV, this can be a difficult, sad time. Still, the work has been done, friendships have been formed, a worthwhile experience has been enjoyed ... and now it is time to move on.

A final note: Because group effectiveness is such an important issue, social psychologists have long studied what they call **group cohesiveness**. Group cohesiveness refers to the strength of the relationships that link the members of a group (Forsythe, 1990). Essentially, it is the force that keeps a group together, and it is influenced by several factors. Among the most important are:

group cohesiveness the strength of the relationships that link the members of a group

- *Mutual attraction.* Groups may stay together for the very simple reason that the members find each other attractive or friendly. The more attracted to one another the members of a group are, the more cohesive it is (Levine & Moreland, 1990).
- *Physical closeness.* This is a simple matter, but the greater the physical distance between members of a group, the less cohesive that group will be. There are times when people simply come together in the same physical space and demonstrate little of the defining nature of group activity (interaction and influence, remember), but because of their closeness they come to think of themselves as a real group. An example would be most college classrooms—particularly lecture classes.
- *Adherence to norms.* When members live up to group norms without resistance, the group is more cohesive. Deviance from norms, even by a minority of members, erodes cohesion.
- *Success at moving toward goals.* Groups that succeed are more satisfying and hence more cohesive than groups that fail. Note that success is not necessarily defined as goal attainment as much as it is defined in terms of noticeable progress toward goal attainment. Also note that this is true regardless of what the goal may be. For some task-oriented groups it may be finishing a job. For more socially oriented groups, goals may be defined in terms having fun, or "getting along."

✓ STUDY CHECK

How do social psychologists define groups, how are they formed, and what keeps them together?

CYBER PSYCH

(a) http://www.mapnp.org/library/grp_skll/theory/theory.htm is a very nice website on the "basic nature of groups and how they develop."
(b) A series of articles about group dynamics in the workplace can be found at: http://www.accel-team.com/work_groups/.
(c) Two websites on Tuckman are http://www.chimaeraconsulting.com/tuckman.htm and even more at: http://www.infed.org/thinkers/tuckman.htm.

Social Influence

As we have noted, to be a social animal in a social world implies interaction and influence. In many circumstances, the ways in which we are influenced by others is subtle, hardly noticeable. In other circumstances, we are influenced by others in direct and significant ways.

CONFORMITY

One of the most direct forms of social influence occurs when we modify our behavior, under perceived pressure to do so, to make it consistent with the behavior of others, a process referred to as **conformity**. Although we often think of

conformity the modification of behavior, under perceived pressure to do so, to make it consistent with the behavior of others

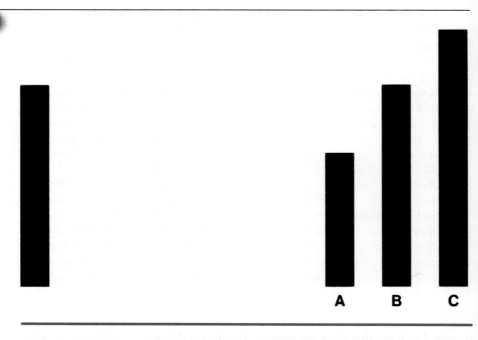

FIGURE 11.1

The type of stimuli used in Asch's conformity experiments. Subjects are to say which of the three lines on the right (A, B, or C) equals the line on the left. Associates of the experimenter will occasionally make incorrect choices, even though the correct choice is always as obvious as this one.

conformity in a negative way, it is a natural and often desirable reaction. Conformity helps make social behaviors efficient and, at least to some degree, predictable.

When he began his research on conformity, Solomon Asch believed that people are not terribly susceptible to social pressure when the situation in which they find themselves is clear-cut and unambiguous. Asch thought an individual would behave independently of group pressure when there was little doubt that the individual's own judgments were accurate. He developed an interesting technique for testing his hypothesis (Asch, 1951, 1956).

A participant in Asch's experiment joined a group seated around a table. In his original study, the group consisted of seven people. Without the knowledge of the participant, six of the people in the group were confederates of the experimenter; they were "in" on what was happening. The real participant was told that the study dealt with the ability to make perceptual judgments. The participant had to do nothing more than decide which of three lines was the same length as a standard line (Figure 11.1). The experimenter showed each set of lines to the group and collected responses, one by one, from each member of the group. There were 18 sets of lines to judge, and the real participant was always the last one to respond.

Each judgment involved unambiguous stimuli: The correct answer was obvious. On 12 of the 18 trials, however, the confederates gave a unanimous but *incorrect* answer. What would the "real" participants do? How would they resolve this conflict? Their eyes were telling them what the right answer was, but the group was saying something else.

The results of his study surprised Asch, because they did not support his hypothesis. When confederates gave "wrong" answers, conformity occurred 37 percent of the time. Participants responded with an incorrect answer that agreed with the majority on more than one-third of the trials. Moreover, three-quarters of Asch's participants conformed to the group pressure at least once.

In subsequent studies, Asch tried several variations of his original procedure. In one experiment, he varied the size of the unanimous, incorrect majority. As you might expect, the level of conformity increased as the size of the majority increased, leveling off at three or four people. Participants gave incorrect judgments only four percent of the time when just one other incorrect judgment preceded their own. In another study, Asch found that participants gave an erroneous judgment only ten percent of the time when there was but one dissenter among the six confederates who voiced an accurate judgment before the participants gave theirs. In other words, when the participants had any social support for what their eyes had told them, they tended to trust their own judgment. This is known as the true partner effect. If the true partner withdrew support, conformity returned to its previous rate.

Several factors influence the amount of conformity observed. If you believe that the majority facing you is highly competent, you are more likely to conform than if you believe the majority is less competent. Imagine being in this study having been told that all of the participants were draftsmen or engineers and that you were filling in for someone who could not be there that day. The nature of the stimulus task also affects levels of conformity. Remember that Asch used a simple line judgment task, which had a clearly correct answer. As the ambiguity of the stimulus increases, conformity increases as well.

There is a small gender difference, with women conforming slightly more than men, especially when a male conducts the experiment. You should not be surprised to learn that there are predictable cultural differences in the conformity to group pressures. In those cultures characterized as "collectivist," in which the individual normally serves the group rather than self (largely Asian and many Middle-Eastern cultures), conformity scores are much higher than in Western, "individualistic" cultures.

Conformity involves yielding to the perceived pressure of a group. In most cases, it is assumed, group members are peers, or at least similar to the conformer. When someone yields to the pressure of a perceived authority, the result is obedience. It is to this issue we turn next.

✓ STUDY CHECK

What is conformity, and how was it demonstrated by Solomon Asch?

CYBER PSYCH

No one is immune to conformity. We all conform, and we do so nearly every day—most of the time without our conscious awareness. These sites focus on the conformity process:
(a) A very full site on dependency and conformity is http://mentalhelp.net/psyhelp/chap8.
(b) Here is an interesting site on the "need to conform." Check out their links: http://changingminds.org/explanations/needs/conformity.htm.

OBEDIENCE

Adolph Eichmann, arguably the "architect" of the Holocaust during World War II, was captured by Israeli agents in 1961. He was placed on trial for crimes against humanity. In that trial, Eichmann's principal defense was that he was only a mid-level

There are several social situations in which obedience to authority is called for—the military provides a good example.

officer, a simple administrator, who was "just following orders." It was his contention that he organized the trainloads of Jews sent to concentration camps and the gas chambers at the behest of individuals who had the power to inflict punishment if he did not obey them.

Is "just following orders" a legitimate excuse? This question preyed on the mind of social psychologist Stanley Milgram (1933–1984). Milgram had been a student of Solomon Asch and was interested in the conditions that lead to conformity. The participants in Asch's studies took the experimental procedures seriously, but the consequences of conforming or maintaining independence were rather trivial. At worst, they might have experienced some discomfort as a result of voicing independent judgments. There were no external rewards or punishments for their behavior, and there was no one telling them how to respond. Milgram went beyond Asch's procedure. He wanted to see if an ordinary person placed in an extraordinary situation would obey an authority figure and inflict pain on an innocent victim. Milgram's research, conducted in the early 1960s, has become among the most famous and controversial in all of psychology. His experiments pressured participants to comply with the demands of an authority figure. The demand was both unreasonable and troubling (Milgram, 1963, 1965, 1974).

All of Milgram's studies involved the same basic procedure. Participants arrived at the laboratory to find that they would be participating with a second person (a confederate of the experimenter). The experimenter explained that the research dealt with the effects of punishment on learning and that one participant would serve as a "teacher," while the other would act as a "learner." The roles were assigned by a rigged drawing in which the participant was always assigned the role of teacher, while a confederate was always the learner. The participant watched as the learner was taken into a room and wired to electrodes to be used for delivering punishment in the form of electric shocks.

After the teacher received a sample shock of 45 volts, just to see what the shocks felt like, the teacher received his instructions. He was to read to the learner a list of four pairs of words. The teacher was then to read the first word of one of the pairs, and the learner was to supply the second word. The teacher sat in front of a rather imposing electric "shock generator" that had 30 switches. From left to right, the switches increased by increments of 15 volts, ranging from 15 volts to 450 volts. Labels were printed under the switches, ranging from "Slight" to "Moderate" to "Extreme Intensity" to "Danger: Severe Shock." The label at the 450-volt end read "XXX."

As the task proceeded, the learner periodically made errors according to a pre-arranged schedule. The teacher had been instructed to deliver an electric shock for every incorrect answer. With each error, the teacher was to move up the scale of shocks, giving the learner a more potent shock with each new mistake. (The learner, remember, was part of the act, and no one was actually receiving any shocks.)

When the teacher hesitated or questioned whether he should continue, the experimenter was ready with a verbal prod, "Please continue," or "The experiment requires that you continue." If the participant protested, the experimenter became more assertive and offered an alternative prod, such as, "You have no choice; you must go on."

Milgram was astonished by the results of his study, and the results still amaze us. Twenty-six of Milgram's 40 participants—65 percent—obeyed the demands of the experimenter and went all the way to the highest shock and closed all of the switches. In fact, no participant stopped prior to the 300-volt level, the point at which the learner pounded on the wall in protest. A later variation of this study added vocal responses from the learner (voice feedback), who delivered an increasingly stronger series of demands to be let out of the experiment. The level of obedience in this study was still unbelievably high, as 25 of 40 participants—62.5 percent—continued to administer shocks to the 450-volt level. As shown in Figure 11.2, the level of obedience decreased as the distance between the "teacher" and "learner" decreased. Obedience dropped when the teacher and learner were in the same room (proximity). The lowest levels of obedience were observed when the teacher was required to physically force the learner's hand onto a shock plate device (touch proximity).

The behavior of Milgram's participants indicated that they were concerned about the learner. All participants claimed that they experienced genuine and extreme stress in this situation. Some fidgeted, some trembled, many perspired profusely. Several giggled nervously. In short, the people caught up in this situation showed obvious signs of conflict and anxiety. Nonetheless, they continued to obey the orders of the experimenter even though they had good reason to believe they might be harming the learner. A re-analysis of audiotapes made during Milgram's study was completed in 2000 (Rochat, Maggioni, & Modigliana, 2000). This study suggests that participants were much more concerned about the learner than even Milgram may have believed. The researchers heard protests from teachers and defiant resistance to continuing, fairly early in the shock-generation process. Even by the 150-volt level of shock, nearly half of the teachers stopped to check with the experimenter to be reassured that they were doing the right thing.

Milgram's first study was performed with male participants ranging in age from 20 to 50. A later replication with adult women produced precisely the same results: 65 percent obeyed fully. Other variations of the procedure uncovered several factors that could reduce the amount of obedience. Putting the learner and teacher in the same room or having the experimenter deliver orders over the

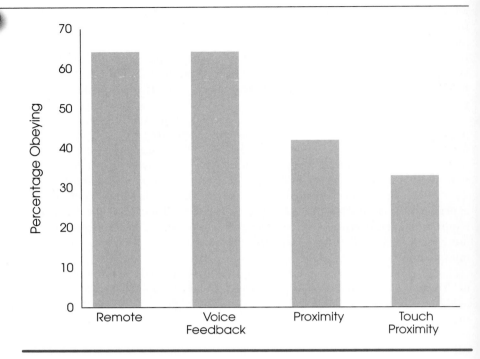

FIGURE 11.2

Results from Milgram's experiments on the distance between the teacher and the learner and the level of shock administered

telephone rather than in person reduced levels of obedience markedly. When the shocks were to be delivered by a team made up of the participant and two confederates who refused to give the shocks, full-scale obedience dropped to only 10 percent. Obedience also was extremely low if there was a conflicting authority figure, one urging the participants to continue and the other urging the participant to stop. When given the choice, participants obeyed the authority figure who said to stop.

Upon hearing about these distressing results, many people tend to think of Milgram's obedient participants as unfeeling, unusual, or even downright cruel and sadistic people (Safer, 1980). Nothing could be further from the truth. The participants were truly troubled by what was happening.

Attributing evil personality characteristics to the "teachers" is particularly understandable in light of the unexpected nature of the results. Commenting on this research, some have suggested that perhaps the most significant aspect of Milgram's findings is that they are so surprising. As part of his research, Milgram asked people, including a group of psychiatrists and a group of ministers, to predict what they would do under these circumstances and asked them to predict how far others would go before refusing the authority. Respondents predicted very little obedience, expecting practically no one to proceed all the way to the final switch on the shock generator.

In reading about Milgram's research, it should have occurred to you that putting people in such a stressful situation could be considered ethically objectionable. Milgram himself was concerned with the welfare of his participants. He took great care to debrief them fully after each session. He told them that they had not really administered any shocks and explained why deception had been used. It is, of course, standard practice to conclude an experimental session by disclosing the true purpose of the study and alleviating any anxiety that might have arisen.

Milgram reported that, after debriefing, the people in his studies were not upset at having been deceived. Their principal reaction was one of relief when they learned that no electric shock had been used. Milgram indicated that a follow-up study performed a year later with some of the same participants showed that no long-term adverse effects had been created by his procedure. Despite his precautions, Milgram was severely criticized for placing people in such an extremely stressful situation. One of the effects of his research was to establish in the scientific community a higher level of awareness of the need to protect the well-being of research participants.

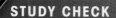

✓ STUDY CHECK

How was obedience demonstrated in Stanley Milgram's laboratory?

CYBER PSYCH

As much as we may not like the idea that we all conform to social pressure, the notion that we may yield to the pressure of an authority figure to do something that is unethical or improper is even more difficult to accept.

(a) http://www.stanleymilgram.com/milgram.html is probably the definitive website on the researcher and his work.

(b) A piece from the American Psychological Association on obeying and resisting malevolent orders is at http://www.psychologymatters.org/milgram.html.

(c) In his own words, this website reviews Milgram's obedience research: http://www.age-of-the-sage.org/psychology/milgram_perils_authority_1974.html.

Interpersonal Attributions

Social cognitions are useful in our attempts to make sense of the social context in which we live. There may be no better example of research in this area than that of social psychologists working with **attribution theory**. Such psychologists are interested in understanding the cognitions we use when we try to explain the causes or sources of our own or others' behavior. The main issue boils down to the question, "Do we tend to attribute behaviors or events we observe in the world around us to internal or external sources, to personal dispositions, or to environmental factors?"

An **internal attribution** explains the source of a person's behavior in terms of a characteristic of the person—a personality trait or disposition (for this reason they are often called dispositional attributions). For example, if you have a friend who is chronically late, you might conclude that this is a personal characteristic. There is something about this friend's personality that tends to make him late for

attribution theory an attempt to understand the cognitions we use when we try to explain the causes or sources of our own or others' behavior

internal attribution explaining the source of a person's behavior in terms of a characteristic of the person—a personality trait or disposition

external attribution explaining the source of a person's behavior in terms of the situation or context outside the individual

nearly everything. You would have made an internal attribution. An **external attribution** explains the source of a person's behavior in terms of the situation or context outside the individual (often called situational attributions). For example, if you have a friend who is hardly ever late, you will probably make an external attribution if he is late once or twice (his alarm clock failed to go off; he got caught in heavy traffic, etc.).

We tend to rely on different types of information when making judgments about the sources of behavior. Imagine, for example, that your friend is late only when he is supposed to be at work. As far as you know, he is not late any other time. That information is useful because of its *distinctiveness* (lateness shows up only when he's dealing with work). As a result, you may take it as a signal of problems in the workplace. A second source of information is *consistency,* or how regular is the behavior pattern you observe. For example, if your friend is always late for work, this is a consistent pattern of behavior. Compare this with someone who is late only occasionally. The final source of information is *consensus,* which is a matter of what other people do in the same situation. If nobody else is consistently late for work, then consensus is low. If almost everyone is also late for work, consensus is high. Compared to the other types of information, consensus information tends to be under-used.

Using information about distinctiveness, consensus, and consistency is important in determining the kinds of attributions we make about our own behaviors and about the behaviors of others (Kelley, 1992). The manner in which the three sources of information mix determines the type of attribution you make. High consensus (everyone else is late for work), high consistency (my friend is always late), and high distinctiveness (my friend is only late for work) lead to an external attribution. That is, it must be something about the job situation causing lateness (perhaps a boss who doesn't care if people are late for work). On the other hand, low consensus (nobody else is late for work), high consistency (my friend is always late for work), and low distinctiveness (my friend is late for just about anything: golf games, dates, etc.) lead to an internal attribution. It must be something about your friend that causes his lateness.

As we gain experience in our social environments, we get rather good at understanding why people do what they do—and why we behave as we do. Nonetheless, it is obvious that we often err in our attributions. In many cases, such errors are of little consequence. Occasionally, misattributing someone's motivation can cause serious difficulties. Social psychologists can tell us quite a bit about attribution errors.

In general terms, we make attribution errors because of pre-existing cognitive biases that influence our judgments of causality. An example of such a bias is the **fundamental attribution error**—the general tendency to favor (over-use) internal, personal attributions for behaviors rather than external, situational explanations. We see a man pick up a wallet that has been dropped on the pavement and race half a block to return it to its owner. We say to ourselves, "Now there's an honest man." (And we predict that he will act honestly in a variety of situations.) The truth is, however, that the fellow returned the wallet only because he knew that we saw him pick it up. If no one else was around, the wallet may not have been returned. Again, the fundamental attribution error is the tendency to disregard, or discount, situational factors in favor of internal, dispositional factors when we make inferences about the causes of behaviors.

fundamental attribution error the general tendency to favor (over-use) internal, personal attributions for behaviors rather than external, situational explanations

We make a fundamental attribution error when we explain someone's behaviors in terms of their dispositional personality, rather than the situation. Given this scene you might imagine this person to be a young mother who is very active and athletic and greatly enjoys being outside. Indeed, it may be that nothing could be further from the truth.

As it happens, the fundamental attribution error can be a powerful bias. Even when we are told of situational factors that determined someone's behaviors, we are likely to stick to our guns that what we saw had to do with the *person* and not the *situation*. We read a brief position paper in favor of gun-control legislation, and jump to all sorts of conclusions about the person who wrote the paper. Curiously, even if we are then told that the paper was written only as an assignment and does not reflect how the writer actually feels about gun control, we will maintain our internal attributions "If she didn't really feel that way, she couldn't have written such a good paper" (McClure, 1998).

Many attribution biases, such as the fundamental attribution error, are more common in Western cultures (Norenzayan & Nisbett, 2000). People from India, for example, make fewer dispositional attributions than do Americans (Miller, 1984). Indians are more likely than Americans to explain behavior in terms of the situation or the environment than in terms of personality traits, abilities, or inabilities. That is, they are more likely to use a situational inference process than do Americans.

There are other biases that lead us to make incorrect attributions about ourselves or others. One is called the **just world hypothesis**, in which people believe that we live in a world where good things happen to good people and bad things happen to bad people. It's a sort of "everybody gets what they deserve" mentality. We see this bias (or fallacy) when we hear people claim that victims of rape often "ask for it by the way they dress and act." In fact, even the victims of rape sometimes engage in self-blame in an attempt to understand the random nature of the crime (Montada & Lerner , 1998).

Another bias that affects our attributions is the **self-serving bias**. It occurs when we attribute successes or positive outcomes to personal, internal sources and failures or negative outcomes to situational, external sources. We tend to think that we do well because we're able, talented, and work hard. Whereas, when we do

just world hypothesis the belief that we live in a world where good things happen to good people and bad things happen to bad people

self-serving bias the tendency to attribute successes or positive outcomes to personal, internal sources and failures or negative outcomes to situational, external sources

poorly, it is the fault of someone or something else. "Boy, I did a great job of painting that room" versus "The room looks so shoddy because the paint was cheap and the brush was old" is an example. Some cognitive theorists argue that depression can be explained as a failure to apply the self-serving bias. That is, some people may get into the habit of blaming themselves for failures or negative outcomes no matter where the real blame resides or regardless of whether there even is any blame to attribute.

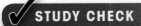

STUDY CHECK

What are "attributions," and what are some attribution errors?

CYBER PSYCH

(a) http://www.as.wvu.edu/~sbb/comm221/chapters/attrib.htm provides an easy-to-read essay on attribution theory.
(b) A summary of attribution theory in outline form is at http://www.usu.edu/psy3510/personatt3.html. It covers quite a bit more than we did above, so proceed carefully.

Interpersonal Attractions

interpersonal attraction a favorable, positive, and powerful attitude toward another person

Finally, let us consider **interpersonal attraction**—a favorable, positive, and powerful attitude toward another person. Interpersonal attraction reflects the extent to which someone has formed positive feelings and beliefs about another person and is prepared to act on those affects and cognitions.

Social psychologists have put forth several theoretical models to account for interpersonal attraction. Let's briefly review three such theories.

The simplest theory is the *reinforcement-affect model.* This approach states that we are attracted to (have positive attitudes toward) people whom we associate with rewarding experiences. It also follows that we tend not to be attracted to those we associate with punishment. One implication of this point of view is that you're going to like your instructor, and seek him or her out for other classes in the future, if you get (or earn) a high grade in his or her class.

Another popular theory of interpersonal attraction is *social exchange theory.* According to this approach, what matters most is a comparison of the costs and benefits of establishing or maintaining a relationship. For example, Leslie may be attracted to John but feels that entering into a relationship with him is not worth the grief that she would get from friends and family, who believe John is lazy and untrustworthy. This point of view takes into account a series of comparative judgments made in social situations. Being attracted to someone else is not just a matter of "Is this a good thing?" It's a matter of "Is the reward I might get from this relationship worth the cost, and what other alternatives exist at the moment?"

A third approach to interpersonal attraction is *equity theory,* which considers the appraisal of rewards and costs for both parties of a social relationship. That is, you may feel a relationship is worth the effort you have been putting into it, but if your partner in that relationship does not feel likewise, the relationship is in danger.

There are many reasons why couples are attracted to each other, and similarity is a very powerful factor.

What matters is that both (or all) members of a relationship feel they are getting a fair deal (equity). The best relationships are those in which members receive an equal ratio of rewards to costs.

Finally, remember a point we first discussed in the context of mate selection: Few people enter into relationships having carefully considered all of the factors these models imply. That is, assessments of reinforcement, exchange, or equity value are seldom made at a conscious level.

Having reviewed four general models of interpersonal attraction, let's now look at some research evidence related to attraction. What determines whom you will be attracted to? What factors tend to provide the rewards, or the positive reward/cost ratios, that serve as the basis for strong relationships? We'll consider four common determinants of attraction.

Reciprocity, our first principle, is perhaps the most obvious: We tend to value and like people who like and value us. The attention of others can be a powerful reinforcer. This is particularly true if the attention is positive, supportive, or affectionate. The value of someone else caring for us is particularly strong when that someone else initially seemed to have neutral or negative attitudes toward us. In other words, we are most attracted to people who like us now, but who didn't originally.

Our second principle, *proximity,* suggests that physical closeness yields attraction. Sociologists, as well as your own experience, will tell you that people tend to establish friendships (and romances) with others with whom they have grown up, worked, or gone to school. Residents of apartments or dormitories, for example, tend to become friends with those other residents living closest to them. Being around others gives us the opportunity to discover just who provides those interpersonal rewards we seek in friendship. Of course, with the advent of the Internet we have to redefine the definition of proximity. Physical closeness is becoming less important. The ability to communicate with someone halfway around the world as if he or she were right next door does bring people close together interpersonally and psychologically, if not physically.

Physical attractiveness is related to interpersonal attraction. The power of physical attractiveness in the context of dating was demonstrated experimentally in a classic study directed by Elaine Walster (Walster et al., 1966). University of Minnesota freshmen completed several psychological tests as part of an orientation program. Students were randomly matched for dates to an orientation dance, during which they took a break and evaluated their assigned partners. The researchers hoped to uncover intricate, complex, and subtle facts about interpersonal attraction, such as which personality traits might mesh in such a way as to produce liking and closeness. As it turned out, none of these psychological factors was important. The impact of physical attractiveness was so powerful that it wiped out all other effects. For men and women, the more physically attractive their date, the more they liked that date and the more they wanted to date her or him again. Numerous studies of physical attractiveness followed this one. Some of these studies gave participants a chance to pick a date from a group of several potential partners (using descriptions or pictures). Not surprisingly, participants almost invariably selected the most attractive persons to be their dates.

We seldom have the luxury of asking for a date without the possibility of being turned down. When experiments added the possibility of rejection, an interesting effect emerged: People no longer chose the most attractive candidates, but selected partners whose level of physical attractiveness was more similar to their own. This behavior is called the *matching phenomenon,* and it occurs for physical attractiveness and social status. Even when we consider relationships between or among friends of the same sex, we find that they tend to be similar when rated for physical attractiveness.

A fourth determinant of interpersonal attraction is *similarity.* There is a large body of research on similarity and attraction, but the findings are consistent, and we can summarize them briefly. Simply put, the more similar another person is to you, the more you will tend to like that person, and the more you are likely to believe that person likes you. We also tend to be repelled, or put off, by persons we believe to be dissimilar to us. Opposites may occasionally attract, but similarity is the glue that holds together romances and friendships over the long term. It is this principle that makes it difficult for people to form significant interpersonal relationships with persons of other cultures or other ethnic groups (Stephan, 1985).

Why is similarity important? Similarity enhances attraction because, through a process of *social comparison,* we can readily have our attitudes and beliefs verified by others. Such verification is immensely rewarding. The rewards we derive from others verifying our attitudes strengthen our attraction to those individuals. Similarity also enhances attraction because we have come to believe that we can predict how a similar person will act in social situations. This predictability is also rewarding, and thus it enhances attraction. Finally, we are likely to believe that individuals similar to us will like us in return. Once again, this is a source of interpersonal reward. Being liked by another person is, for most of us, very rewarding.

STUDY CHECK

Briefly describe three theories of interpersonal attraction and summarize some of the factors known to influence such attractions.

CYBER PSYCH

The how's and why's of interpersonal attraction have intrigued social psychologists for years. Person A and Person B may become life-long friends, while Person C can barely stand to spend time with either A or B. These websites expand on this topic.

(a) a pleasant summary in outline form is at: http://users.ipfw.edu/bordens/social/attract.htm.

(b) It is a somewhat strange piece, but "The psychology of close relationships" is at: http://www.thedoctorwillseeyounow.com/articles/feature/behavior/index.shtml.

Chapter Summary

Define and give examples of social positions, social roles, and social norms.

Social positions are those defined niches that a person can fill within a given social structure. Any one person usually fills several social positions. A male may be a husband, son, father, grandfather, worker, employer, soccer coach, consumer, parishioner, member of the Board, and much, much more. Social roles are the learned expectations of how one is to feel, think, and behave, given the social position being filled at the time. Social norms are important, general expectations about how one should and should not act in social situations. Particularly important social norms form the basis for most laws in a society.

How do social psychologists define groups, how are they formed, and what keeps them together?

According to social psychologists, a group is a collection of two or more persons, characterized by interaction and influence. Groups may be *task-oriented* (or *instrumental*), which is to say directed at working toward some identified goal, or they may be *socially oriented* (or *affiliative*), which is to say that their purpose is for social support and enjoyment. According to Tuckman, group formation proceeds through stages: *forming* (getting together without much trust or guidance), *storming* (being critical, searching for what to do and how), *norming* (characterized by cohesion, creativity, and security), *performing* (get the job done with tight, strong interpersonal relationships,) and *adjourning* (when the group terminates its activities and disengages from relationships). The *cohesion* that keeps groups together is based on mutual attraction, physical closeness, adherence to group norms, and success at making progress toward the group's goals.

What is conformity, and how was it demonstrated by Solomon Asch?

Conformity is a social process in which behavior is modified in response to perceived pressure from others so that the behavior is consistent with that of others. Conformity is often thought of in negative terms, but it helps to make social behavior efficient and predictable. In Asch's studies, people made judgments about unambiguous perceptual stimuli: the length of lines. During some trials, confederates gave judgments that were clearly incorrect before the actual participant had a chance to respond. There were situations in which yielding to perceived group pressure could be lessened, but many of Asch's participants followed suit and conformed.

Conformity increases as the size of the majority increases—up to a point—and then levels off. The more competent the majority is perceived to be, the greater the conformity. If the minority is perceived as competent, conformity decreases. Conformity increases if an ambiguous task is used. There is a small gender difference, with women conforming more than men when a male is the experimenter or if group pressure is involved. There are also cultural and sociopolitical climate relationships with conformity.

How was obedience demonstrated in Stanley Milgram's laboratory?

Obedience means complying with the demands of an authority figure, even if such compliance is against one's better judgment. People in Milgram's experiments were led to believe they were administering more and more potent shocks to another person in a learning task. When they hesitated to deliver shocks, an authority figure, the experimenter, prodded them to continue. All participants obeyed to some degree, and nearly two-thirds delivered what they thought was the most intense shock, even over the protests of the learner. Those who obeyed in Milgram's experiments were neither cruel nor inhumane. Rather, the experimenter created a powerful social situation that made it difficult to refuse the authority figure's orders. As Milgram moved the teacher and learner closer together (in the same room), obedience dropped. The lowest rate of obedience was observed when the teacher actually had to touch the learner to give him a shock. When a group administered the shocks and two group members refused to continue, obedience also was reduced. Having the experimenter leave the room and deliver orders by telephone or adding another authority figure who tells the participant to stop the experiment also reduced obedience.

What are "attributions," and what are some attribution errors?

Attributions are cognitions we use to explain the sources of the behaviors we see in our social worlds. Internal attributions identify the source of behavior as within the person and are also called dispositional attributions. External attributions find the source of behaviors to be outside the person and are also known as situational attributions.

The fundamental attribution error leads persons to overuse internal, or personal, attributions when explaining behaviors. It is most common in Western cultures. Those who hold to the just world hypothesis are likely to believe that good things happen only to good people and that bad things happen only to bad people, who in some way deserve their misfortune. With self-serving bias, we attribute our successes to our own efforts and actions and our failures to other, external factors.

Briefly describe three theories of interpersonal attraction and summarize some of the factors known to influence such attractions.

The *reinforcement model* of interpersonal attraction claims that we are attracted to those persons we associate with rewards or reinforcers. The *social exchange model* adds cost to the equation, claiming that what matters in interpersonal relationships is the ratio of the benefits received to the costs invested in that relationship. The *equity model* suggests that all members of a relationship assess a benefit/cost ratio, and the most stable relationships are those in which the ratio is nearly the same (equitable) for all parties, no matter what the value of the benefits for any one member of the relationship.

The principle of *reciprocity* states that we tend to like people who like us in return. This is the most straightforward example of interpersonal attraction being based on a system of rewards. *Proximity* promotes attraction, in part, by means of the mere exposure effect: Being near another person on a frequent basis gives us the opportunity to see what that other person has to offer. We also tend to be attracted to people we judge physically *attractive*. Finally, the principle of *similarity* suggests that we tend to be attracted to those we believe to be similar to ourselves.

Student Study Guide

STUDY TIP #11 The Essentials of Textbook Study

No matter what the course, there will be more information stored in your textbook than could ever be presented in class. Therefore, learning how to get information from your text is one of the most important skills you can acquire while in college. Here are a few general ideas.

1. **Prepare for textbook study.** Develop expectations about all that you read. Read the chapter preview; skim the summary; glance at the headings, subtitles, and illustrations. Even before you begin reading, you should have a series of questions in mind. "What is this all about?" "How can I make sense of this?" "How will this show up on an exam?"

2. **Read textbooks differently.** Reading a chapter in a textbook is not studying. Studying is a process in which you must get actively and personally involved. It requires a great deal more concentration than does reading for pleasure. It involves you asking and seeking answers to questions. There are times when you should actually stop reading! Stop, pause, and think about what you've just read. Does it make sense? If not, do not go on making matters worse.

3. **Make textbook study an active process.** You must be mentally active and alert while studying so that you can search, question, and think. Underlining or highlighting in textbooks has become a common practice. It is often misused. The purpose of highlighting is to emphasize passages in the text so that essential points can be reviewed economically. When 80 percent of a page is underlined for emphasis, however, it is the remaining 20 percent that usually appears more striking.

4. **Use the textbook's margins.** You can increase the value of your textbook as a study aid by using its margins for your personal notations. Make your text a storehouse of references. Cross-reference textbook material with information in your notes. If it's your book, use it—don't be afraid to write in it.

KEY TERMS AND CONCEPTS

social psychology _____

_____

social roles _____

_____

role conflict _____

_____

social norms _____

_____

group _____

_____

instrumental (task-oriented) group _____

_____

affiliative (social-oriented) group _____

_____

group cohesiveness _____

_____

conformity _____

_____

attribution theory _____

_____

internal attribution _____

_____

external attribution _____

_____

fundamental attribution error _____

_____

just world hypothesis _____

_____

self-serving bias _____

_____

interpersonal attraction _____

_____

Practice Test Questions

MULTIPLE CHOICE

1. The main difference between social positions and social roles is that social roles are

   _____ a. judged by one's society to be right or wrong, good or bad.

   _____ b. pretty much the same for males and females in Western societies.

   _____ c. require study and memorization to be effective.

   __X__ d. are learned and then barely conscious reactions.

2. When Solomon Asch studied conformity, he found each of the following EXCEPT that

   _____ a. even participants' perceptual judgments could be influenced by group pressure.

   _____ b. most of his participants (more than 75%) conformed at least once.

   _____ c. the least amount of social support was sufficient to help a person resist group pressure.

   __X__ d. most of the participants continued to conform even after they knew that the group's members were confederates of the experimenter.

3. In an Asch conformity situation, when will conformity to group pressure be the greatest? When the other participants in the study group are presented as being

   _____ a. friends and classmates.   _____ c. social psychologists.

   __⊖__ b. architects and draftsmen.   __X__ d. apathetic conformists.

4. The major difference between conformity and obedience is

   _____ a. peer pressure.

   __X__ b. the presence of an authority figure.

   _____ c. the nature of the task involved.

   _____ d. the person's perception that there is social pressure.

5. Which result does NOT follow from Milgram's studies of obedience?

   __⊖__ a. Personality characteristics of the subjects allowed Milgram to predict who would obey and who would not.

   ____ b. When told about the experiment, virtually no one believed that he or she would have delivered the shocks.

   _____ c. No participants in the experiment stopped delivering shocks before the 300-volt level, when the "learner" began protesting.

   _____ d. More than half of the participants delivered the highest level of shock to the "learner."

6. Which conclusion from Milgram's research is justified?

_____ a. Persons of some nationalities are more likely to obey than are others.

_____ b. When told to harm others, few people felt guilty about it.

_____ c. The perception of authority is a powerful force in conformity.

_____ d. Women are more likely to conform than are men.

7. What is the major reason why some have criticized Milgram's study of obedience as being unethical?

_____ a. He made a fundamental attribution error.

_____ b. He shocked people without their consent.

_____ c. He allowed participants to believe that they were hurting someone.

_____ d. He failed to adequately debrief his participants.

8. Attributions are typically made in terms of each of the following EXCEPT

_____ a. internal vs. external factors.

_____ b. dispositional vs. situational factors.

_____ c. learned vs. inherited factors.

_____ d. intrinsic vs. extrinsic factors.

9. When we over-emphasize personal reasons in our explanations of another's behaviors and overlook the forces of the environment, we are

_____ a. making a fundamental attribution error.

_____ b. demonstrating a belief in the just world hypothesis.

_____ c. employing a self-serving bias in our judgment.

_____ d. failing to take into account the actor–observer bias.

10. Basically, attribution theory deals with

_____ a. different techniques for changing the attitudes of others.

_____ b. how we tend to explain the behaviors of ourselves and others in social situations.

_____ c. factors and processes that lead to interpersonal attractions.

_____ d. forming expectations about how we should behave in social situations.

11. Which of these is NOT a theory or model used to explain the basis of interpersonal attraction?

_____ a. equity model   _____ c. dissonance model

_____ b. social exchange model   _____ d. reinforcement model

12. With regard to interpersonal attraction, which statement is FALSE?

_____ a. The "mere exposure" phenomenon tells us that familiarity breeds contempt.

_____ b. We tend to like and value those who like and value us.

_____ c. Physical attractiveness is correlated with attraction.

_____ d. People tend to be attracted to those who have similar attitudes.

13. Which is likely to have the LEAST impact on attraction?

_____ a. physical proximity   _____ c. attitudinal similarity

_____ b. physical attractiveness   _____ d. perceived sexuality

TRUE/FALSE

1. _____ True _____ False   Social positions are learned, but social roles are inherited.

2. _____ True _____ False   By definition, people are more likely to obey than to conform.

3. _____ True _____ False   Asch found that some people will conform most of the time, no matter what their perception of the nature of the group applying pressure to conform.

4. _____ True _____ False   Up to a point, the more people who express the same judgment, the more likely an individual will yield or conform to that judgment.

5. _____ True _____ False   Even Milgram was surprised by the results of his experiments.

6. _____ True _____ False   Most people attribute their own successes to dispositional factors and their own failures to situational factors.

7. _____ True _____ False   Even if someone likes us now, if they did NOT like us originally, we probably will not value them as a friend.

Interpersonal Communication

Preview

The focus of this chapter is the essence of social psychology: interpersonal communication. As social animals, we influence others, as they influence us. We let others know how we are feeling, what we believe, and what we intend to do. We communicate our state of affairs to those around us, and they inform us in turn.

As we have in previous chapters, we begin with matters of definition. What is the nature of interpersonal communication? Can anybody do it? Are humans the only organisms that communicate? How do we know when communication has occurred?

We will see that communication can involve a range of messages, transmitted in many forms, by various means, over many communication channels. Verbalizing with the spoken or written word is but one way of sharing with others. We'll see that non-verbal communication involves posture, gestures, facial expressions, and more. In this context, we will also take a look at proxemics: the study of our appreciation and use of space and territory. We will spend a brief section focusing on listening as a part of interpersonal communication.

The chapter ends with a consideration of two real-world applications of interpersonal communication: attempts to change attitudes through the process of persuasion and making decisions as members of a group.

The Communication Process

model a simplified version, outline, or presentation of what is acknowledged to be a very complex process or system

In science, a **model** is a simplified version, outline, or presentation of what is acknowledged to be a very complex process or system. I suspect that you and I are ready to accept the premise that interpersonal communication is a complex process, involving many variables and possible outcomes. It would be helpful, then, to have a simplified model of that process that we could use in order to get a handle on the basics. Then we can add to our model as we go along.

I propose that we develop our own model of communication, one based on several different models that have evolved over the years. (The first model to have an impact on psychology was proposed in 1949 by Claude Shannon and Warren Weaver, engineers who were working for a telephone company. Using this model to account for the full range of all interpersonal communication has proven to be difficult, largely because much of it is over-simplified.)

The first observation that should be reflected in our model is that communication takes two—a *source* and a *destination*. The implication is that at any one time, communication is in one direction, from the source to the destination. The source initiates a *message* through a transmitter, and communication occurs when the destination is influenced by that message through a *receiver*. You can follow this discussion as we go along by referring to Figure 12.1.

As an example, let's say that you are trying to explain to a friend some new device that you have built. You are the source unit, your friend is the destination unit, and the message has to do with your new device. As you can see in Figure 12.1, your message is carried on a *communication channel*.

We'll talk more about communication channels and messages in the next section, but it is clear that humans can use many different channels and messages

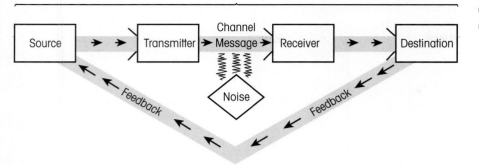

FIGURE 12.1

The Shannon-Weaver Model of Communication with additions discussed in the text.

of many different sorts. You may begin by using what Shannon and Weaver called a "vocal-auditory channel" and simply tell your friend about your invention. You talk (vocal); your friend listens (auditory). Given that Shannon and Weaver were telephone company engineers, we should not be surprised that this talking–listening format was foremost in their model. As one example of another message and channel, you might—frustrated by your inability to describe your device in words—grab a pencil and paper and begin communicating with drawings that represent your ideas. In fact, we are capable of receiving information using any of our senses as receivers. We find out all sorts of things about the world in which we live based on odors, tastes, and the way things feel (using senses of touch and pressure).

We need to add another feature to our model: *noise*. Noise is the term that refers to all the possible difficulties that can arise in getting a message between the source and the destination. In the simple example of a telephone conversation, noise could be static on the line, perhaps caused by a nearby thunderstorm. In a social context, "noise" might arise from other people in the room (being loud or physically coming between a speaker and listener). Anything that disrupts or interferes with a message on a communication channel is **noise**.

Now let's add a bit to our model. Assume for the moment a communication event that is intentional. You really want your friend to appreciate the new device that you've designed. Your message is verbal at first. You try to tell your friend what you have done, and why. The transmitter, then, would be all of your vocal apparatus—your lungs, diaphragm, vocal cords, tongue, teeth, and lips—as you try to articulate your message. Your friend's receiver would be the apparatus of hearing—outer ear, eardrum, cochlea, etc. Here is the important question: Where does that message originate and where is that message going? It comes from your mind, doesn't it? It comes from your memory, where you have stored all your experiences with your new device. The challenge for you is to translate all your experience and memories and thoughts into a message your friend can understand. Where is that message going? It is going to your friend's mind, ultimately to fit into his or her set of existing cognitions and memories.

When you have finished describing your new device, your friend will not have the same mental picture or understanding of it that you do. Our abilities to communicate with each other are never that good. They are never perfect. Perhaps the best you can hope for is a general understanding of the essential nature of your

Noise refers to all possible difficulties that can arise in getting a message between the source and the destination.

Interpersonal communication is not a uniquely human endeavor—but it is a very common one.

project or how you feel about it. Even if your friend comes to fully appreciate all the details of your device, when he thinks about it, the associations formed will be different from those that you have. You can recall when you first got the idea to build such a thing. You remember the excitement you felt as you began putting it together. Your friend will not have any of those associations. Everything your friend (the destination unit) receives will be filtered, and perhaps distorted, by his expectations, values, beliefs, and memory (you may be using terminology your friend does not understand). To some degree, after the communication is over, your cognitions and affects will always be different from those of your friend.

At this point we can introduce an important feature of interpersonal communication: *feedback*. As you talk to your friend, messages come back to you—a nod, a smile, an "oh, I see," or "uh-huh; yup" that let you know that you're having some success. You may get more negative feedback—a frown, a shaking of the head, a "whaaa?" or "I don't get it." Source units (people) can choose to ignore feedback from destination units (other people). For example, you probably have had teachers who ignore negative feedback from the students in class and just keep droning on. But communication is enhanced when feedback is attended to and messages are adjusted accordingly.

Psychologists interested in interpersonal communication do think of sources and destinations as people. That is what "inter" (between) "personal" (people) *means*. But before we go on, reflect for a moment on the units of communication. Must they be people? Can't my dog communicate—often clearly—to the neighbor's cat? If you have a pet, I'll bet it communicates with you, and vice versa, with regularity. My computer can communicate with yours, and the message will not be over a vocal-auditory channel.

In this context, let me mention just one final issue that is important to psychologists: the *purpose* of the interpersonal communication in the first place. Most simple models typically assume that the purpose of interpersonal communication is to inform, and in a great many cases, it is. But let us simply acknowledge that some communication is meant to entertain (e.g., a stand-up comedian), persuade (e.g., a debating politician), inspire (e.g., a sermonizing preacher), frighten (e.g., an aggravated baby-sitter), mislead (e.g., a sleight-of-hand magician), soothe (e.g., a parent singing a lullaby), or simply get attention (e.g., an EMS driver on the way to an accident scene). I know that you easily can add to this list. The notion of purpose or intent of communication is difficult to illustrate in a simple drawing such as Figure 12.1.

That's a start. Now we need to focus a little bit more on the nature of messages and channels of communication. We also have to acknowledge that the best of messages on the clearest of channels will be of little use unless there is a prepared and attentive audience destination unit around.

✔ STUDY CHECK

What are the essential characteristics of interpersonal communication?

CYBER PSYCH

(a) Articles on the importance of providing and interpreting feedback "with grace and dignity" can be found at http://humanresources.about.com/cs/communication/ht/Feedbackimpact.htm and at http://humanresources.about.com/cs/communication/ht/receivefeedback.htm.

(b) A pleasant summary article on the Shannon-Weaver Model and criticisms of it are at: http://www.aber.ac.uk/media/Documents/short/trans.html.

The Message: More than Verbal

We have seen that providing a message on a vocal-auditory channel is a common variety of interpersonal communication, but it surely is not the only one. Let's explore that insight a bit more here. There are four issues to consider: 1) verbal vs. non-verbal messages, 2) intentional vs. unintentional messages, 3) the impact of social context, and 4) the use of space and distance in interpersonal communication.

NON-VERBAL COMMUNICATION

We first discussed verbal and non-verbal communication in Chapter Seven when we were talking about how internal emotional states are shared with others. Surely, I can tell you how I feel, or at least I can try to express my feelings in words. But even without my saying a word (without using a language message on the vocal-auditory channel, to use our current terminology), you may appreciate my emotional state simply from my posture and my facial expression. Have you ever said or thought, "Words just can't express how I feel"? In addition, we use proximity to others, gestures, posture, facial expression, and other such non-verbal cues to convey information about our cognitive state of mind as well as our affect.

In fact, more than half of the meanings that are communicated in a social situation are conveyed non-verbally. Moreover, when our words say one thing, but our body language says another, our non-verbal message is more likely to be believed than is our verbal message. "To be a competent communicator requires mastery of both non-verbal and verbal streams of communication." (Burgoon & Bacue, 2003, p. 180). It is also true that just as there are individual differences in producing an effective communication, with non-verbal cues, the skill of the receiver in understanding or decoding those cues is equally important.

The importance and the very nature of non-verbal communication rules, displays, and customs vary enormously across cultures. There are differences in how people express and how they interpret nonverbal cues, depending on cultural setting. For example, being openly expressive, standing close to someone with whom you are communicating, or making eye contact "are valued and expected in some cultures but considered overly direct, aggressive, or invasive in others" (Burgoon & Bacue, 2003, p. 183).

There are gender differences in non-verbal communication as well. Here (from Burgoon & Bacue, 2003, and Hall, 1978) are a few research findings in which psychologists have confidence. Although the differences tend to disappear in private conversation, in public settings, women are significantly more expressive in their non-verbal cues than are men. They simply produce and are more responsive to non-verbal behaviors. When men do use gestures or body movements, they are more expansive and demonstrative, but they are less likely to use such cues in a public setting.

Women are more accommodating in interpersonal communications. They listen more and interrupt less than do men. They provide better and more non-verbal feedback and position themselves closer together. Women smile significantly more often than men during communication.

Let us now consider *intentionality*. When we think about interpersonal communication, we most often think first of conscious, intentional attempts to share an idea, a belief, a plan of action with others. Our example of telling a friend about something you had designed was certainly one of an intentional communicative act. I want you to learn about psychology, so I schedule a lecture or write a book. I want to buy something and ask a store clerk where to find it. I want to have a group of my friends vote for my favorite candidate in an upcoming election and try to convince them of the wisdom of doing so. I sit with my wife in the evening, reflect on what has happened during the day, and make plans for tomorrow. These are intentional communication events. I enter my mental set of cognitions, my memories and feelings, find those I would like to share, and do my level best to create a message that conveys my intention(s).

As it happens, a great deal of interpersonal communication takes place constantly without any intention whatsoever. Most of these messages are non-verbal, although when we speak, our use (or misuse) of grammar, our vocabularies, even any hint of "accent" can convey many meanings to our listeners. When I first arrived in Tennessee for graduate school, I did not have to tell any natives that I had just arrived from New York. All I had to do was start talking.

The car you drive, the clothes you wear, your hair style, your tattoos and body piercings (or lack thereof) communicate volumes about who you are in a social world. The very way you move down the hall (slowly, sliding, slumping, striding) communicates. Of course, sometimes such non-verbal communication cues are quite intentional indeed. They exist for effect, often shock effect, but they reflect intentional, conscious choices. Very often such messages are not intentional. And the truth is, the Shannon-Weaver model of communication rather assumes an intentional effort to move information from a source unit to a destination—what Michael Reddy (1989) has called a "conduit metaphor."

One final point about messages in interpersonal communication: They must be considered in the *context* in which they occur. Messages do not occur in vacuums.

Simply the way one dresses or wears his or her hair can communicate volumes.

The meaning of a message depends upon its context. This is true even when communication involves a language message. In fact, the main (if not the only) purpose of language is communication. Language helps us share our thoughts, feelings, intentions, and experiences with others. Language use is social behavior. **Pragmatics** is the study of how language is related to the social context in which it occurs. Our understanding of sarcasm (as in "Well, this certainly is a beautiful day!" when in fact it is rainy, cold, and miserable), or simile (as in "Life is like a sewer..."), or metaphor (as in "His slam dunk to start the second half was the knockout blow"), or cliché (as in "It rained cats and dogs") depends on many things, including an appreciation of the context of the utterance and the intention of the speaker.

pragmatics the study of how language is related to the social context in which it occurs

The rules of interpersonal communication (for example, turn-taking) are also part of the pragmatics of speech. We have learned that it is most efficient to listen while others speak and to speak when they listen. We all know what it is like to have a "conversation" with someone who violates this rule.

Pragmatics involves decisions based on the perception of the social situation at the moment. Think how you modify your language use when you talk to your best friend, a preschool child, a professor in her office, or a driver who cuts you off at an intersection. Contemporary concerns about "political correctness" seem relevant here, don't they? In most contexts, words such as *pig, Uncle Tom, boy,* and *girl* are reasonable and proper; in other contexts they can evoke angry responses. In some American Indian cultures, periods of silence—even lengthy periods of silence—during a conversation are common and acceptable. Someone not familiar with this pragmatic reality could become anxious and upset about long pauses

299

in the midst of a conversation (Basso, 1970; Brislin, 1993, pp. 217–221). As you can imagine, translations from one language to another can cause huge changes in meaning as cultural contexts change. Two of my favorites (from Berkowitz, 1994) are the translation of the slogan "Finger Lickin' Good" into Chinese, yielding, "Eat Your Fingers Off" and in Taiwan, the 1980s slogan "Come alive with the Pepsi Generation" becomes "Pepsi will bring your ancestors back from the dead."

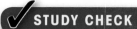

✔ STUDY CHECK

How do non-verbal messages, intentionality, and social context impact interpersonal communication?

CYBER PSYCH

(a) The site http://www.healthteacher.com/teachersupports/skills4.asp provides an excellent summary on effective interpersonal communication and touches on the issues raised in this section.

(b) The same can be said for http://muextension.missouri.edu/explore/comm/cm0109.htm.

(c) http://www.asha.org/public/speech/development/pragmatics.htm is a site devoted specifically to the development of language pragmatics from the American Speech and Hearing Association.

(d) A summary on pragmatics is at http://www.universalteacher.org.uk/lang/pragmatics.htm.

PROXEMICS: SPACE, DISTANCE, AND TERRITORY

Imagine you are seated in the library, studying at a large table. There is no one else at the table. In fact, there is no one else in the room. Then another student enters the room and sits right next to you. Although there are seven other chairs, she chooses to sit in the one just to your left. Or imagine that you are in the process of buying a car. While you are examining a new car, a salesman approaches, stands right in front of you (not more than eight inches away), and begins to tell you about the features of the car you are looking at. Or say that in your psychology class you always sit in the same seat. The term is about over, and you have gotten to know some of the people who sit near you. The next time you go to class, you find there is someone else in "your seat." Or imagine you are a homeowner who has spent years getting the backyard to look just the way you want it to. Then children from down the street discover that going through that rose garden makes a great shortcut on their way to school.

In each of these scenarios, and in hundreds of others, you probably will feel a sense of discomfort. Your personal space, or your territory, has been invaded without your invitation. The study of the appreciation and use of physical space and territory is called **proxemics**, and it has been an active research area for psychologists for many years (Hall, 1966).

Personal space is mobile. It goes with you where you go. It is an imaginary "bubble" of space that surrounds you and into which others may enter comfortably by invitation only. The extent of your personal space depends on the situation, as well as other factors, including your age (Aiello & Aiello, 1974), gender (Evans &

proxemics the study of the appreciation and use of physical space and territory

personal space an imaginary, mobile, "bubble" of space that surrounds you and into which others may enter comfortably only by invitation

Allowing others to be this close—even for the purpose of studying—would give psychologists the impression that these were good friends.

Howard, 1973), cultural background (Pandey, 1990), and who the "intruder" happens to be. You will be more likely to allow an invasion of your personal space by someone you know well, by someone about your age, or by an attractive member of the opposite sex (Hayduk, 1983). Personal space also seems to be slightly smaller for females than for males (Heshka & Nelson, 1972).

The anthropologist Edward Hall (1966) claimed that personal space is also determined in part by one's culture. Westerners, for example, are said to require more personal space than do people of Arab, Japanese, or Latin cultures (Sommer, 1969; Kaya & Weber, 2003). These stereotypes may be over-generalized. Evidence of cultural differences in personal space is not compelling; too many other situational factors are more powerful (Hayduk, 1983).

In a now-classic article, Hall (1966) claimed that personal space can be divided into four different distances, each relevant for different types of social interaction and for Western cultures.

1. *Intimate distance* is defined as being between actual contact and about 18 inches. This space tends to be reserved for very special, intimate communications: displays of affection by lovers, offerings of comfort, and the like. Intimate space is usually reserved only for people you know well and care about, and you will feel uncomfortable if someone else is in it.

2. *Personal distance,* according to Hall, is reserved for day-to-day interactions with acquaintances and friends. It extends from about 18 inches to approximately four feet, or just beyond arm's length. This space can be seen clearly in social gatherings in which clusters of persons gather around to share in conversation. Actual physical contact in this sort of situation is unusual and unwelcome. We typically keep our bubble of personal space adjusted to this size.

3. Hall refers to the distance of four to 12 feet as *social distance*. This distance is used for social interactions with persons we do not know well. It commonly

includes some physical barrier, such as a desk or table, between us and others around us. Within this space, communication can continue, but there is an implied message of lack of intimacy. This is the distance used for conducting routine business or for formal meetings.

4. Finally, there is *public distance,* in which personal contact is minimized, though communication remains possible. This distance is defined as being between 12 and 25 feet. Formal lectures in large classrooms, performances from a stage, and after-dinner talks presented from the head table are examples. Because of the distances involved, communication in these settings tends to flow in only one direction.

We are apt to feel pressured or uncomfortable whenever any of these distances is violated. When that stranger sits next to you in the library, she is violating your personal space. The salesperson with his or her nose almost touching yours is violating your intimate space. When a lecturer leaves the podium and begins to wander through the audience, we feel strange because our defined public space is being invaded.

territoriality the setting-off and marking of a piece of a geographical location as one's own

Territoriality is also related to the use of space. It involves the setting off and marking of a piece of a geographical location as one's own. It is the tendency to declare that "this space is mine; it's my turf, and someone else can enter here only at my request or with my permission." It represents a non-verbal form of interpersonal communication.

Territoriality was first studied extensively in non-humans (e.g., Lorenz, 1969). Many species of animals establish, mark, and defend geographical areas that they use for finding and hunting food, for mating, or for rearing their young. These territories are often defended vigorously — with ritualistic posturing and threats of aggression, but seldom with actual combat (Leger, 1992).

People, too, establish territories as their own, not to be entered without invitation. Altman (1975) noted that, like personal space, territories vary in their size and value. Some are *primary territories,* defined as exclusive — ours and no one else's. "This is my room, and you'd better stay out of it." We often invest heavily in our primary territories. We decorate our homes, yards, dormitory rooms, or apartments to mark our space. Primary territories are well marked, claimed for the long term, and staunchly defended. By controlling primary territory, we maintain a sense of privacy and a sense of identity.

Altman suggests that we are sensitive to two other types of territory: secondary and public. *Secondary territories* are more flexible and less well defined than are primary territories. They are areas set aside for social gatherings, not so much for personal privacy. Members of the faculty may stake out a room in a college building as a faculty lounge and may be unnerved to discover students using it, even if they are using it to study. Secondary territories are not "owned" by those who use them and tend not to be used for expressing personal identity. There may be a sign on the door that says "Faculty Lounge," but the area can be used for other functions, and occasional intrusions by non-faculty may be tolerated.

Public territories are those we occupy for only a short time. They are not ours in any literal sense, and we will not feel much distress if these territories are violated. While waiting for a plane, you sit in a seat in the airport terminal and place your luggage at your feet. You get up for a minute to buy a newspaper, and when you return, you discover that someone has claimed your seat. In such a situation, you may be momentarily annoyed, but you will have less difficulty in finding another seat than in starting a confrontation.

Personal space and the territories we claim as our own serve many functions. They provide a sense of structure and continuity in what otherwise may seem to be a complex and ever-changing environment. They help us claim a sense of identity. They help us set ourselves apart from others. They regulate and reinforce needs for privacy. Although expressed differently from culture to culture, these needs appear to be universal (Kaya & Weber, 2002; Lonner, 1980). When space and territory are violated, the result is likely to be negative outcomes: anxiety, distress, and sometimes even aggressive attempts of reclamation.

✓ STUDY CHECK

What is the psychological significance of personal space and territory?

CYBER PSYCH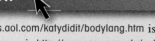

(a) http://members.aol.com/katydidit/bodylang.htm is a website on proxemics as is http://www.cs.unm.edu/~sheppard/proxemics.htm, which is the much shorter of the two.

(b) A website on songbird territoriality is http://www.ornithology.com/lectures/Territoriality.html.

(c) A great site: http://www.ilo.org/ciaris/pages/english/tos/strprinc/territor/tx_princ/princp_1.htm.

(d) A charming article on territoriality among inhabitants of the oceans is at http://ladywildlife.com/animal/oceanterritories.html.

Listening: More than Hearing

In this section let us first acknowledge that interpersonal communication is a two-way street. It requires both a sender and a receiver. Here we focus on "message reception skills in social communication"—how receivers go about comprehending and evaluating what they receive (Wyer & Adaval, 2003). Although I will focus on a form of communication that I trust is relevant to you at the moment—listening in a classroom setting—the basic principles apply to any variety of interpersonal communication.

Really good listeners are difficult to find. Most people assume that anyone who is not hearing-impaired is necessarily a good listener; but, sadly, such is not the case. The problem is that listening well is tough. It takes effort. It takes concentrated, sustained, strained, attention. As we listen to someone else talking, most of us are concentrating more on what our response is going to be than we are on what the other person is saying. In truth, most of us would rather listen to ourselves than to anyone else.

Anyone can be a good, effective, efficient listener. Good listening is a skill that can be learned. It's largely a matter of attitude and practice. Here's a list of tips to make you a better listener in the classroom (based on Gerow & Gerow, 2004).

1. **Sit where you can hear and see what is going on.** Now there's an obvious point. You don't have to sit right in the middle of the very first row, but you do have to sit where you can hear clearly and where you can see what is written on the board or projected on the screen.

2. **Sit where you can avoid distractions.** To get the most out of class, you need to concentrate on what the lecturer is saying, and you need to do whatever you can to minimize stimuli that can compete for your attention. Try to avoid sitting by the windows, for instance. Try not to sit where you can easily watch people passing by in the hall when the door is left open. Sure, you can sit with your friends, but only if your friends are interested in getting the most out of class. You also want to sit where you won't be too comfortable and likely to fall asleep. It is impressive just how much an instructor can notice from the front of the classroom. To test this out, let me suggest that you stand up at the front of the room yourself some day and look around. From the lecturer's perspective, dozing off, passing notes, whispering to others, and so on are obvious.

3. **Be as prepared as possible.** Being prepared for class means that you will walk in with a reasonably good idea of what to expect. You will have thought about this class and what is going to happen in it. The process is not all that mysterious. There are three good sources to guide you: 1) the class syllabus, 2) previous classes, and 3) your textbook. You will be a much better listener to the extent that you can anticipate the topic of each day's lecture and know the technical terms in advance.

4. **Flush your mind.** As you take your seat and open your notebook, try to rid your mind of distracting thoughts, ideas, or problems that can compete for your attention. This is not the place to agonize over the exam you took earlier in the day. It is certainly no place to sit and study for an exam coming up later in the day. This is not the time to plan tonight's menu, nor is it the place or the time to worry about some problem you're having with a friend or family member. This is the time and the place to concentrate (for just 45 minutes or so) on what a lecturer is saying. There will be time to deal with other important issues later.

5. **Listen for highlights.** Try to process what the lecturer is saying. What is the big picture? What are the *main points?* Is there an *organization* or *structure* to this material that matters? What are the key, important *terms?* Does the lecturer seem to have a *personal bias* or point of view about the topic being discussed?

6. **Make the material meaningful.** Even as you listen, can you (quickly, easily) think of any way(s) to relate what is being said to your own experience? Can you relate this material to what you've already learned in this course or in others? Relating what you are learning to what you already know is what meaningfulness is all about. There will be more time to do this later, when you go over your notes, but if ideas occur to you now, you'll want to jot them down. Doing so will keep you actively involved in what is being said.

7. **Take complete and careful notes.** You'll want a written transcription of each lecture's highlights. It's even a good idea to take just a moment at the end of a class to review your notes and fill in information that is still available in memory.

8. **If anything is unclear, ask.** You will have to determine the appropriate time for asking questions about a lecture. Some instructors welcome and invite questions during the lecture itself, others provide opportunities for questions toward the end of each class period, and some allow no class time at all for questions. In this last case, you'll have to follow up with the lecturer (or a graduate student teaching assistant) at some other time, preferably during office hours. Asking for additional explanations or information provides that feedback we discussed earlier that makes interpersonal communication interpersonal—not just one-way.

9. **Attend to your classroom etiquette.** This point is simply a reminder of the benefits of being considerate and respectful. The short of it is that you don't want to engage in the very same behaviors that would aggravate and distract you if they were happening around you. Save conversations with friends until after class. It is simply inappropriate to eat or drink in class. If you cannot stay awake in class, please find someplace other than the classroom for your nap. Wearing hats (or caps, even with the brim turned backward) in class can be viewed as distracting and disrespectful. Raising your hand and being acknowledged should precede speaking up in class.

Finally, let me underscore the point that listening well is a process that requires nurturing. Although we often take it for granted, our listening skills will improve with practice—focused, effortful practice.

✔ STUDY CHECK

List some of the factors that can improve successful listening.

CYBER PSYCH

Hearing is a natural process; listening takes practice.
(a) You may find some useful tips at the website of the International Listening Association: http://www.listen.org.
(b) Click the links under "Various Perspectives" at the site: http://www.mapnp.org/library/commskls//listen/listen.htm.
(c) Empathy and listening from a psychological perspective are covered at http://mentalhelp.net/psyhelp/chap13/chap13c.htm and
(d) a business perspective at http://www.businesslistening.com/listening_skills.php.

Real-World Examples

In this last section we'll explore two examples of the application of our discussion of interpersonal communication: changing attitudes through persuasion and decision-making within a group setting.

CHANGING ATTITUDES BY PERSUASION

Purposively setting out to change someone's attitudes is certainly a process of "social influence," and when it is done through means of persuasion it is a process of interpersonal communication (Dillard & Marshall, 2003). Let us define **persuasion** as the application of rational and/or emotional arguments (communications) to deliberately convince others to change their attitudes or behavior (Bordens & Horowitz, 2002). The most widely accepted model of persuasion is called the Yale communication model (after the university at which the research was done). According to this classic model, the ability to persuade someone depends on three factors: 1) the source of a message (who delivers the message), 2) the characteristics of the message (what is said), and 3) the nature of the audience (to whom the

persuasion the application of rational and/or emotional arguments (communications) to deliberately convince others to change their attitudes or behavior

Even in small groups of business associates, the task at hand may be one of using persuasion to change the attitudes of others.

message is directed). These three factors affect internal processes such as attention to, comprehension of, and acceptance of a persuasive message. In this section, we will explore how the source, message, and audience affect persuasion. Throughout, see how this discussion fits with what we have discovered about the Shannon-Weaver model of communication.

The most important characteristic of the source of a persuasive message is the communicator's credibility. Everything else being equal, a highly credible communicator will be more persuasive than a low-credibility communicator. As it happens, there are two components of **credibility** or believability: expertise and trustworthiness. Expertise refers to the skills, qualifications, training, and credentials of the communicator. For example, former Secretary of State General Colin Powell (also formerly Chairman of the Joint Chiefs of Staff for the U.S. military) has a high level of expertise with regard to military matters. You are likely to be more impressed by a message about defense spending coming from him than a message from, say, a private pulled from the ranks or someone with no military experience.

credibility the believability, expertise, and trustworthiness of a communicator

Trustworthiness refers to the motivations behind the communicator's attempt to persuade you. Trustworthiness goes to the question of "Why is this person trying to convince me?" For example, you might trust an automotive review you read in the magazine *Consumer Reports* because they have no vested interest in convincing you to buy one car or another. On the other hand, you might be less trusting of a review in a magazine that accepts large sums of money from a particular car maker. In this case, you might question the motives of the reviewer. Interestingly, a communicator who is perceived as arguing against what might appear to be his or her own best interests (for example, a senator representing a tobacco-growing state arguing for strict control of cigarettes) is likely to be perceived as trustworthy.

Although credibility is the single most important source characteristic in persuasion, there are others. For example, a pleasant voice and expressive face affect persuasiveness (note the non-verbal aspect of the message here). Additionally, the physical attractiveness of the communicator, the similarity of the communicator to the target of the message (audience), and the rate of speech (moderately fast delivery enhances persuasion) all affect persuasion.

How a message is put together can influence the amount of persuasion that occurs. One important message characteristic is the nature of the appeal made. In what is called a **rational appeal**, one uses facts and figures to persuade an audience. For example, if we wanted people not to drink and drive, we could present statistics concerning the number of alcohol-related traffic accidents and fatalities reported each year. Although rational appeals can be effective, **emotional appeals**—aimed at arousing an emotional state—can be even more effective. This is especially true of fear appeals, which attempt to persuade through the arousal of fear. A fear appeal to persuade people not to drink and drive might depict graphic photographs of accident scenes involving drivers who were drunk.

Generally, fear appeals can be effective. However, there are three conditions that are necessary for a fear appeal to be effective. First, the appeal must arouse a significant amount of fear. Second, the target of the appeal must believe that the dire consequences depicted in the appeal could happen to him or her. Finally, the appeal must include instructions about how to avoid the dire consequences depicted in the appeal (drink only at home; use a designated driver; take a taxi and retrieve your car tomorrow). This third condition is crucial. People have to believe that there is something they can do that will reduce or eliminate the source of the fear.

The audience to whom an appeal is targeted also influences persuasion. For example, the opinions that members of the audience already hold play a part in persuasion. If a message is very different from audience members' pre-existing opinions (known as high discrepancy) there is less persuasion than if the message is only moderately different from the pre-existing opinions (moderate discrepancy). This is because the content of the highly discrepant message is likely to be rejected by audience members. A moderately discrepant message will not be rejected as quickly or as fully as a highly discrepant message, allowing for some persuasion to occur. Similarly, if there is too little discrepancy, you will not get much persuasion. In this case, the persuasive message may be nothing more than a restatement of the audience member's existing opinion, and little or no persuasion will take place.

Audience characteristics and message characteristics often interact to affect persuasion. That is, whether a message is effective sometimes depends on the nature of the audience. For example, rational appeals tend to work best on well-educated audiences who are better able to make sense out of the facts and statistics presented. On the other hand, fear appeals work best with less-educated audiences. In this case then, the extent to which a fear appeal is effective depends in part on the target audience.

rational appeal a communication that uses facts and figures to persuade an audience

emotional appeal a communication that is aimed at using an arousing emotional state to persuade an audience

✓ STUDY CHECK

What are some factors involved in the interpersonal communication process called "persuasion"?

CYBER PSYCH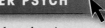

(a) A lengthy piece on coercive persuasion and brainwashing can be found at http://www.rickross.com/reference/brainwashing/brainwashing8.html.

(b) A brief, useful summary, focusing on changing attitudes is found at http://www.as.wvu.edu/~sbb/comm221/chapters/abc.htm.

(c) A pleasant essay is found at: http://www.csudh.edu/dearhabermas/attpersuas03.htm. What makes it particularly pleasant is the use of contemporary examples.

DECISION-MAKING WITHIN GROUPS

Many of the decisions we face in our daily lives are made in group settings (Gouran, 2003). Committees, boards, family groups, and group projects for a class are only a few examples. There is logic in the belief that group efforts to solve problems should be superior to the efforts of individuals. Having more people available should mean having more talent and knowledge available. It also seems logical that the cohesiveness of the group might contribute to a more productive effort, and for some groups and some problems, this is exactly the case. But we know better than to assume that just because a conclusion is logical it is necessarily true.

Decades of research show us that groups can, and often do, outperform individuals. Here is a partial list of what we know about group decision-making:

- Groups outperform the average individual in the group mainly because groups recognize a correct answer to a problem more quickly, reject an incorrect answer, and have better memory systems than the average individual.
- Groups comprising high-quality members perform better than groups with low-quality members.
- As the size of the group increases, the resources available to the group increase as well. However, "process loss" (loss of productivity due to faulty group interaction) also increases. Additionally, in larger groups there is likely to be less member participation than in smaller groups.
- When the problem a group must resolve involves a great deal of interaction, interpersonal cohesiveness (how much members like each other) and task-based cohesiveness (mutual respect for skills and abilities) increase productivity. When a problem does not require much interaction, task-based cohesiveness increases productivity, but interpersonal cohesiveness does not.

Although it is generally true that groups outperform individuals, there are some liabilities attached to using groups to make decisions. Here are two aspects of group decision-making that can lead to low-quality decisions.

When he was an MIT graduate student in industrial management, James Stoner gave participants in his study a series of dilemmas to consider (Stoner, 1961). The result of each decision was to be a statement of how much risk a fictitious character in the dilemma should take. One dilemma, for example, involved a star quarterback choosing a play to call late in an important game with an archrival. One choice—a simple play, likely to succeed—would lead to a tie score, whereas the other choice—a very risky play with only a slim hope of success—would lead to certain victory. Much to his surprise, Stoner found that the decisions made by groups were much riskier than those individual group members made prior to participating in the group decision. He called this move away from conservative solutions a **risky shift**. For example, doctors, if asked individually, might claim that a patient's problem (whatever it might be) could be handled with medication and a change in diet. If these same doctors were to jointly discuss the patient's situation, they might conclude that a new and potentially dangerous (risky) surgical procedure was necessary.

Several hundred experimental studies later, we now know that this effect also occurs in the opposite direction, a cautious shift (Levine & Moreland, 1990). In other words, the risky shift is simply a specific case of a more general **group polarization effect**, which means that group participation will make an individu-

risky shift in group decision-making, a tendency to move away from conservative solutions

group polarization effect the observation that group participation will make an individual's reactions more extreme, or polarized

While meeting in a group, doctors may agree on a course of treatment that is significantly more dangerous than any would have attempted if the decision were a personal one—a "risky shift" in decision-making.

al's reactions more extreme, or polarized. Group discussion usually leads to an enhancement of the beliefs and attitudes of the group members that existed before the discussion began. One explanation for group polarization is that the interpersonal communications involved give group members an opportunity to hear persuasive arguments they have not previously considered, which can lead to a strengthening of their original attitudes. Another possibility is that, after comparing attitudinal positions with one another, some group members feel pressure to catch up with other group members who have more extreme attitudes.

Many years ago, Irving Janis (1972) described a related phenomenon of influence he calls **groupthink**, such an excessive concern for reaching a consensus during group decision-making that critical evaluations are withheld. Janis maintains that this style of thinking emerges when group members are so interested in maintaining harmony within the group that differences of opinion or alternative courses of action are suppressed. Janis maintained that groupthink is most likely to occur in cohesive groups.

groupthink such an excessive concern for reaching a consensus during group decision-making that critical evaluations are withheld

Janis saw some common threads running through bad group decisions that he identified as eight indicators of groupthink:

1. An illusion of invulnerability: The group members believe that nothing can harm them, which leads to excessive optimism.
2. Rationalization: Rather than realistically evaluating information, group members collectively rationalize away damaging information.
3. Unquestioned belief in the groups' inherent morality: The group sees itself on the side of what is right and just. This leads group members to ignore the moral implications and consequences of their actions.
4. Stereotyped views of the enemy: The "enemy" is characterized as too weak or stupid to put up any meaningful resistance to the group's planned course of action,
5. Conformity pressures: Direct pressure is placed on any member of the group who dissents from what the group wants to do.
6. Self-censorship: Because of the conformity pressure, individual members of the group who may want to say something keep silent because of the potential consequences.

7. An illusion of unanimity: Because of self-censorship, the group suffers the illusion that everyone agrees with the course of action planned by the group.
8. Emergence of self-appointed "mindguards": Self-appointed mindguards emerge to protect the group from damaging outside information. These people intercept potentially damaging information and don't pass it along to the group.

By analyzing historical events (such as responding to the bombing of Pearl Harbor, the invasion of the Bay of Pigs, and the explosion of the space shuttle *Challenger*) in terms of groupthink, Janis found that such situations involved a cohesive decision-making group that was relatively isolated from outside judgments, a directive leader who supplied pressure to conform to his position, and an illusion of unanimity.

Generally, Janis's groupthink hypothesis has weathered the test of time. However, some research suggests that group cohesiveness may not be as crucial to the emergence of groupthink as originally believed. Directive leadership and consensus-seeking, which makes groups more concerned with morale and getting members to agree than with the quality of the decision, are important precursors of groupthink. There also is good evidence that time pressure—or the perception of time pressure—increases the likelihood to seek consensus and solution, whether the solution is a good one or not (Kelly, Jackson, & Huston-Comeaux, 1997).

 STUDY CHECK

What are some of the factors known to influence decision-making in groups?

 CYBER PSYCH

Given all the possible practical applications of the issue, it is not surprising that there are so many websites devoted to group decision-making and avoiding the pitfalls thereof.

(a) A simple tutorial on making group decisions effectively is at the University of Arizona website: http://www.union.arizona.edu/csil/leadership/101/groupdecision.php.

(b) http://www.chacocanyon.com/pointlookout/041117.shtml provides a two-part essay on effective group decision-making.

(c) Groupthink summary: http://www.au.af.mil/au/awc/awcgate/army/groupthink.htm.

Chapter Summary

What are the essential characteristics of interpersonal communication?

Interpersonal communication requires two units (people): a source unit and a destination unit. Communication is primarily in one direction, with a message traveling on a communication channel between the two. Each unit has a transmitter for sending messages and a receiver for accepting them. A loop of feedback from the receiver back to the source is seen as essential for reasonable communication. Noise is the term given to any event that interferes with the clear transmission and reception of a communication message. Although interpersonal communication is necessarily intended for humans, communication among non-humans and even machines, such as computers, clearly is possible. There are many factors that together make it very unlikely that any interpersonal communication will be perfect.

How do non-verbal messages, intentionality, and social context impact interpersonal communication?

Although the vocal-auditory may be a commonly used method in interpersonal communication, it is surely not the only one. A great deal of communication occurs non-verbally, through facial expression, posture, and gestures. In fact if your "body language" conveys a message of sadness or depression, even if you say you are happy, the sad/depressed message will prevail. Women tend to be better at using and interpreting non-verbal cues. Communication occurs constantly even without intention. One conveys meaning about oneself through such means as dress, hairstyle, manner of movement, and the like. All interpersonal communication must be evaluated in context. The meaning of a message depends upon the social context in which it occurs. The study of the impact of context on communication is called pragmatics. It accounts for such subtleties as sarcasm, simile, metaphor, and cliché.

What is the psychological significance of personal space and territory?

Personal space is the imaginary bubble of the area around a person into which others enter only by invitation or in specified situations. It is mobile, going wherever the person goes. There are several types of personal space (*intimate, personal, social,* and *formal*) defined for various situations. *Territory,* on the other hand, is a claim to certain areas of the environment. Territories may be defended against intrusions. They can provide a sense of identity and are often used as statements of self-expression. Intrusion into an individual's personal space or territory may lead to tension, anxiety, stress, and/or aggression. The study of issues of personal space and territory is called *proxemics.*

List some factors that improve successful listening.

Although hearing is an automatic reaction to sounds in the environment, listening is a skill that can improve with practice. To listen well requires that a destination unit (the listener) be positioned to be able to hear well in the first place, away from possible distractions. Listening requires concentrated attention, and it benefits from preparation (having a sense of what the message might be makes it easier to understand). All irrelevant thoughts and ideas should be flushed from awareness. The listener is most successful when focusing on highlights and making every effort to make the incoming message meaningful by relating it to what is already stored in memory. Listening also profits from feedback: If a message is not clearly understood, asking follow-up questions is advised.

What are some of the factors involved in the interpersonal communication process called "persuasion"?

Persuasion is the application of rational and/or emotional arguments (via interpersonal communication) to convince others to change their attitudes or behavior. The Yale communication model is the most widely accepted model of persuasion. The three factors outlined by this model are the source of a persuasive message (who delivers the message), the characteristics of the message, and the nature of the audience. A communicator's credibility, or believability, is an important factor in determining attitude change. Credibility consists of expertise (the qualifications of the source) and trustworthiness (the motivation of the source). All other things being equal, a communicator with high credibility is more persuasive than one with low credibility. In addition to credibility, the attractiveness of the communicator and his or her perceived similarity to the audience affect persuasion. Discrepancy refers to the difference between the initial position of the audience and the content of a persuasive message. Too much or too little discrepancy leads to little or no attitude change. A moderate amount of discrepancy leads to the most persuasion. Fear appeals are effective in producing attitude and behavior change when three conditions are met. First, the fear aroused must be quite high. Second, the target of the message must believe that the dire consequences depicted in the appeal could happen. Third, specific instructions must be given on how to avoid the dire consequences. The third factor is crucial. Without it, a fear appeal will not work, even if the first two conditions are met.

What are some of the factors known to influence decision-making in groups?

Groups often outperform the average individual because groups recognize a correct answer and reject an incorrect answer more quickly, and they have better (or at least larger) memory systems than the average person. Groups with high-quality members perform better than groups with low-quality members. Increasing group size increases resources available to the group, but it also increases process loss. In larger groups, member participation is less than in smaller groups. Interpersonal cohesiveness and task-based cohesiveness enhance group performance when a problem requires a great deal of interaction.

Although there are advantages to problem-solving in a group setting, there are also liabilities. Group polarization (originally known as the risky shift) is the tendency for group discussion to solidify and enhance pre-existing attitudes. Groupthink is an excessive concern for reaching a consensus at the expense of carefully considering alternative courses of action. Groupthink has been found to contribute to bad group decisions. Irving Janis identified eight symptoms of groupthink: an illusion of invulnerability, rationalization, an unquestioned belief in the group's morality, stereotyped views of the enemy, conformity pressures, self-censorship, an illusion of unanimity, and the emergence of self-appointed mindguards.

Student Study Guide

STUDY TIP #12 Preparing For Exams: The Difference Between Learning and Performance

Learning is a process that takes place inside an individual. We cannot see learning take place. We cannot plot its course. What we must do is infer that learning has taken place by measuring an individual's *performance*. Simply put, learning involves acquiring new information; performance involves retrieving that information when it is needed. And, justifiably or not, it is your performance that tends to be evaluated. Your performance, not your learning, earns your grades in the classroom and your raise or promotion in the workplace.

So how will this great insight help you study? If you accept my premise, it means that you need to spend time and effort learning new information—here, new information about psychology. But then you also ought to spend some time practicing what is really going to be graded: your retrieval of that information. And how do you do that? In the simplest terms, you test yourself. You test yourself (practice retrieval) before your instructor comes along and tests you for real.

There are a couple of things you might consider. Once you have finished reading a section of the textbook, feel that you understand it quite well, and can adequately answer the "Study Check" questions there, think about how the information in that section might show up on your next classroom exam. If you had to generate three multiple-choice questions over that material, what might they be? Yes, you may "know" the information now, but will you recognize it when it appears on a test? The other thing that you can do, of course, is to work through the "Practice Test Questions" that we have provided for each of the chapters in the text. These questions are not likely to show up on your classroom exams, but at least they give you an idea of what sorts of questions we psychology professors can dream up. A note: Please don't rely on Practice Test Questions as a primary means of studying. They really don't help much in the process of elaborating on new information and forming new memories. They are designed to help in improving your performance, not your original learning.

KEY TERMS AND CONCEPTS

model_____

_____

pragmatics_____

_____

persuasion_____

_____

rational appeals_____

_____

emotional appeals _____

_____

risky shift _____

_____

group polarization effect _____

_____

groupthink _____

_____

Practice Test Questions

MULTIPLE CHOICE

1. Interpersonal communication can be seen as a component of the larger area of study in social psychology known as

  _____ a. sociology.   _____ c. attribution theory.

  _____ b. social influence.   _____ d. social cognition.

2. The Shannon-Weaver Model of Communication was produced by

  _____ a. psychologists.   _____ c. neuroscientists.

  _____ b. engineers.   _____ d. philosophers.

3. Although there are many possible channels of communication, most interpersonal communication is carried on the _____ channel.

  _____ a. electro-chemical   _____ c. source-destination

  _____ b. vocal-auditory   _____ d. neuro-biological

4. In the context of interpersonal communication, "feedback" refers to

  _____ a. something that can interfere with the transmission of a message.

  _____ b. understanding what one is going to say before one says it.

  _____ c. messages flowing from destination units to source units.

  _____ d. non-language messages that manage to get on the vocal-auditory channel.

5. Of the following, which is TRUE concerning non-verbal communication?

  _____ a. Humans use non-verbal communication to a greater degree than members of any other species.

  _____ b. Females are better, more attuned, receivers of non-verbal messages than are males.

  _____ c. The use of non-verbal cues in communication is consistent across all known cultures.

  _____ d. Non-verbal messages are much more likely to be intentional than non-intentional.

6. Pragmatics is the study of how _____ influences the meaning of an interpersonal communication.

_____ a. grammar   _____ c. social context

_____ b. meaning   _____ d. listening skills

7. Psychologists have identified many types of space or territory. That with the smallest area is called

_____ a. intimate space.   _____ c. social space.

_____ b. personal space.   _____ d. public space.

8. What is likely to be the response made to an invasion of personal space?

_____ a. stress   _____ c. anxiety

_____ b. physical aggression   _____ d. withdrawal

9. If you are taking an exam in a classroom, you are occupying

_____ a. someone's social space.   _____ c. a public territory.

_____ b. a primary territory.   _____ d. someone's secondary space.

10. A communicator is trying to persuade others to change their attitudes. Which characteristic of the communicator is LEAST important in predicting whether the communication will be successful?

_____ a. credibility   _____ c. expertise

_____ b. celebrity   _____ d. trustworthiness

11. The main difference between a persuasive communication and any other type of interpersonal communication is that persuasion is an attempt to

_____ a. produce a change in another's way of thinking.

_____ b. provide new and different information.

_____ c. help someone reach a decision on some matter.

_____ d. create an emotional sort of reaction.

12. Stoner's concept of "risky shift" is best viewed as but one aspect of a larger issue called

_____ a. the group polarization effect.

_____ b. the fundamental attribution error.

_____ c. Milgram's obedience effect.

_____ d. the emotional appeal to persuasion.

13. Janis's concept of "groupthink" tells us that

_____ a. groups often strive to reach consensus, right or wrong.

_____ b. individuals are more likely to express divergent opinions in a group setting than they would if they were alone.

_____ c. individual members of a group prefer that others in the group do most of the work.

_____ d. group decisions tend to be conservative and unoriginal.

TRUE/FALSE

1. _____ True _____ False Non-verbal messages occur with intention and without intention.

2. _____ True _____ False The pragmatics of communication takes into account the cultural norms or expectations in which the communication occurs.

3. _____ True _____ False Persuasive arguments can be either rational or emotional or both.

4. _____ True _____ False The most important predictor of whether a persuasive communication will be effective is the extent to which it is true, i.e., based on facts.

5. _____ True _____ False When it comes to making decisions, groups typically outperform individuals.

Psychology in the Workplace

Preview

This chapter looks at industrial/organizational, or I/O, psychology—one of the fastest-growing areas of specialization in psychology. The Society for Industrial-Organizational Psychology (SIOP) reports that in 1945 it had 130 members and now has over 3,000 full members and more than 2,500 student affiliates. **Industrial/organizational (I/O) psychologists** specialize in the scientific study of affect, behavior, and cognition in the workplace. A major focus of industrial/organizational psychology is "a concern for both the effectiveness of the organization and the well-being of individuals" (Ryan, 2003, p. 25). The main goals of industrial/organizational psychology are a) to help employers deal with employees fairly, b) to help make jobs more interesting and satisfying, and c) to help workers be more productive (Harris, 2003).

We'll look at two thrusts of I/O psychology. First we'll discuss how best to fit the right person to a given job. This will get us involved with what is meant by "doing a good job," and a consideration of how employers can select, train, and motivate someone to do that job well. Then we'll examine how best to fit a job to the person, which involves such matters as the quality of work life, job satisfaction, and worker safety. Each of these issues is meaningful to anyone who has ever entered the world of work.

What It Means to Do "Good Work"

It is to everyone's advantage to have the best available person assigned to do any job. Employers benefit from having workers who are well-qualified and motivated to do their work. Employees benefit from being assigned to tasks that they enjoy and that are within the scope of their talents and/or abilities.

What is involved in getting the best person to do a job? The issues from the perspective of the I/O psychologist are personnel selection, training, and motivation. One way to get a person to do good work is to select and hire someone who already has the ability and the motivation to do that work. On the other hand, we may choose to train people to do good work. We may also have to face the task of motivating people with ability to do good work. But before we can select, train, or motivate someone to do a job, we need to understand the nature of the job itself.

Assume you are an industrial/organizational psychologist hired by a company to help select a manager for one of its retail stores in a shopping center. You cannot begin to tell the company what sort of person they are looking for until you have a complete description of the job this manager is to do. You have to understand the duties and responsibilities of a store manager in this company. Then you can translate that job description into the measurable characteristics a successful store manager should have. This is to say that you would begin with a **job analysis**, "a detailed description of the work functions to be performed on the job, the conditions under which the job is to be performed, and the KSAs [knowledge, skills, and abilities] that are needed to perform those tasks" (Salas & Cannon-Bowers, 2001, p. 476).

A job analysis may be written by someone who is presently in the job in question or by a supervisor of that job position. What matters most is that those who are

---

industrial/organizational (I/O) psychologists those who specialize in the scientific study of affect, behavior, and cognition in the workplace

job analysis a detailed description of the work functions to be performed on the job, the conditions under which the job is to be performed, and the KSAs [knowledge, skills, and abilities] that are needed to perform those tasks

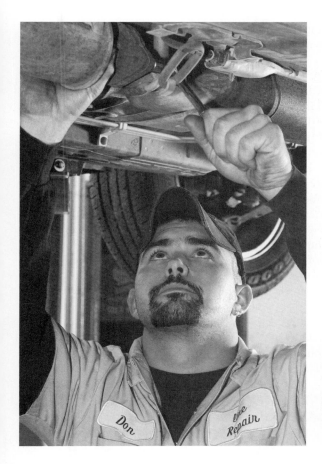

Before a car dealership starts looking for mechanics for their service department, they would be well advised to do a careful job analysis of just what it is they are looking for.

doing the job analysis understand the KSAs involved in the job. Typically, writing a complete job analysis is a two-step process. The first step involves compiling a complete description of what a person in that job is expected to do. These are usually referred to as the job requirements and include the most important duties and responsibilities of the position to be filled. In a way, this list of tasks provides the main reasons why the job exists in the first place.

There are several sources of information that can be used. Most companies have job descriptions for their employees, but these are usually stated in very general terms, such as "supervise workers in the store; prepare payrolls; maintain acceptable levels of sales; monitor inventory; schedule workloads," and the like. To be useful, a job analysis must be specific and describe the actual behaviors engaged in by someone in a given position. Does a store manager have to know how to operate the cash register and inventory control devices? Does the manager deal with the sales staff on a one-to-one basis or in groups? Are interactions with employees informal, or are there scheduled, formal meetings that need to be organized? This list of questions can be a long one. The underlying concern at this level of analysis is, "On a daily basis, just what does a store manager for this company do?"

Once duties and responsibilities are specified, the second step requires that these be translated into terms of measurable personal characteristics. That is, what performance criteria are required to do a job well? What are the characteristics a person in this position needs in order to do that job as well as possible? In fact, these criteria are often referred to as job/worker specifications. In recent years there has been an increasing interest in extending the job analysis to include a cognitive task analysis, which implies that it often is important not only to know what an employee has to *do,* but it also is important to understand what an employee has to *know* (Reynolds & Brannick, 2001). That is, what are the mental abilities and mental processes required to do this job well?

There are several areas that might be explored at this point. Smith (1976), for example, distinguishes between what she calls "hard" (objective) criteria and "soft" (subjective) criteria. The former come from available data—salary, number of units sold, number of days absent, and the like. Soft criteria require a certain degree of judgment—sense of humor, congeniality, creativity, and so on. For example, assume that your psychology department wants to give an award to its "student of the year." Some of the criteria that determine which student has done a good job and is worthy of such an award may be hard data—class standing, a certain grade point average, and a minimum number of psychology classes. Other criteria may be subjective, or soft. The department may want to give this award to a student only if he or she is known to many members of the faculty, has been active in the Psychology Club, or has impressive communication skills. These criteria require the judgment of those who are making the award. Most job analyses involve considering both hard (objective) and soft (subjective) criteria.

✓ STUDY CHECK

What is involved in doing a complete job analysis?

CYBER PSYCH

As important as they are, we should not be surprised that there are so many websites devoted to job analyses.

(a) http://harvey.psyc.vt.edu is an award-winning, private website.

(b) Yes, there is a site devoted just to job analysis: http://www.job-analysis.net.

(c) An almost unbelievably complete site on job analyses is at: http://www.hr-guide.com/data/G000.htm.

Finding People Who Can Do Good Work

Personnel selection involves devising procedures to help one decide which of many applicants to hire, *and* making decisions relating to retention, promotion, and termination. If the job analysis has been done properly and performance criteria are clear, the I/O psychologist has a list of those duties and characteristics in which the employer is interested. The task now is to find the individual who has those characteristics.

Useful information can be taken from a well-constructed application form. A job application form can serve three useful functions. (1) It can be used as a rough screening device. Some applicants may be denied simply because they do not meet some basic requirement for the job, such as a minimal educational level or specific job experience. (2) It can supplement or provide cues for interviewing. Bits of data from application forms can be pursued later, during in-depth interviews. (3) It provides biographical data *("biodata"),* including educational and work history, which may be useful in making predictions about a candidate's potential. Many I/O psychologists list biographical information on application forms as the best source of data for predicting success on the job.

An integral part of personnel selection procedures is the employment interview. There are clear advantages of the process. It gives the employer (or his or her representative) a chance for a face-to-face encounter with a job applicant. It also has the advantage of flexibility; a line of questioning may be dropped if it is not providing useful information. Unfortunately, the data on the quality of information gained from unstructured, open-ended, free-wheeling interviews has not been supportive. For one thing, interviews, by their very nature, involve the interaction of two people: the interviewer and the applicant. Some interviewers are simply more effective than others.

Since the early studies questioning the usefulness of interviews, there has been a significant shift toward the use of highly structured interviews in which a specific set of questions is to be asked in a specified order. These procedures may give up flexibility, but the benefit in terms of reliable and valid data far outweigh any losses.

In addition to the job application form and the interview, personnel selection often involves psychological testing. Many tests are designed to assess only one specific characteristic of the applicant (e.g., finger dexterity, which a job analysis may indicate to be relevant for an assembly-line worker in an electronics plant). Others are more general, assessing several skills and abilities. Tests of intelligence or certain personality traits may be necessary, particularly when evaluating candidates for managerial or supervisory positions. There are literally hundreds of published paper-and-pencil tests designed to measure a wide range of behaviors and characteristics, from typing skills, to mechanical aptitude, to leadership style, to motivation for sales work, to critical thinking skills. Some popular tests of general traits or abilities are being modified to focus more sharply on work-related items.

In general, the most useful of all psychological tests are those that assess some sort of cognitive function, such as ability or achievement tests (Hough & Oswald, 2000). One of the most controversial questions in all of psychology (not just I/O) is whether tests of general intelligence are better predictors of job performance than are tests of specific cognitive ability or aptitude. At this point, the best answer seems to be "it depends." It depends on which tests of which behaviors are used. Although personnel selection usually focuses on measures of cognitive ability, personality inventories, both general and specific, have been very useful in making employment decisions.

From time to time, it may be necessary to construct one's own test to assess some unique or special ability not measured by available instruments. A form of testing found in employment settings is called **situational testing**, in which applicants are given the opportunity to role-play the task they may be hired to do. If you were going to hire someone to work at the counter of your dry-cleaning business, for instance, you might ask an applicant how he or she would respond to an irate customer whose clothes were damaged in cleaning. Role-playing the part of an angry customer while the applicant plays the part of employee might provide very useful information.

situational testing a test setting in which applicants are given the opportunity to role-play the task they may be hired to do

It may not always be practical or possible to find people who have the characteristics, abilities, and motivation for doing the type of work we have in mind. It may be that the major personnel issues involve training and motivating existing workers to do good (or better) work. Let's first look at training.

✓ STUDY CHECK

What are some of the sources of information that can be used when making personnel decisions?

CYBER PSYCH

If you understand the nature of a job and what it will take to do that job well, how do you choose someone from among all those who have applied for that job? This is a classic issue in industrial/organizational psychology.

(a) http://www.hr-guide.com/selection.htm is nearly a definitive website on personnel selection.

(b) The Society for Industrial and Organizational Psychology hosts http://www.siop.org/_Principles/principlesdefault.htm, a site on personnel selection.

Training People to Do Good Work

Training employees is one of the major concerns of business, industry, and government. The cost of such training runs into billions of dollars every year (Bassi & Van Buren, 1999). Training and retraining present employees will become even more critical than it has been in the past. This is because a) the number of persons entering the workforce is decreasing, b) the knowledge and skill level demands of the workplace are rapidly escalating, and c) more businesses operate in a global, worldwide community (Schultz & Schultz, 1998). Training to increase sensitivity and communication skills when dealing with employees and customers from a variety of ethnic and cultural backgrounds is becoming more common—and more necessary (Muchinsky, 2000).

training the systematic acquisition of attitudes, concepts, knowledge, roles, or skills that result in improved performance at work

In the context of industrial/organizational psychology, **training** means "the systematic acquisition of attitudes, concepts, knowledge, roles, or skills that result in improved performance at work." (Goldstein, 1991). Training is a systematic intervention, not a hit-or-miss approach to instruction. Training programs have been successful in many organizational settings, with various types of personnel, and as indicated by a number of productivity criteria, including quantity and quality of work, cost reduction, turnover, accident reduction, and absenteeism. Developing a successful training program is a complex enterprise. Let's review the steps involved in designing and implementing a training program.

Training programs are designed to address some need within the organization. So one of the first things you have to do is an assessment of instructional needs. A complete needs assessment is much like a job analysis and cognitive task analysis in personnel selection. Several questions need to be answered at this stage. What is the problem that training is supposed to solve? Is production falling? Is there a new product that salespeople need to know about? Is the accident rate too

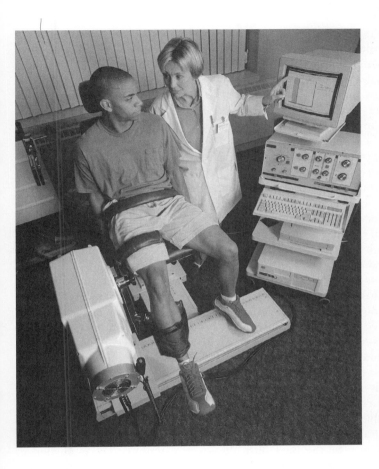

In these days of evolving technology—particularly in the medical field—training employees is a high priority. Training not only keeps practitioners abreast of new techniques, but also helps to keep them motivated and doing the best possible job.

high? Is the company downsizing—reducing the number of employees? At this point, one difficult question to face is whether a training program is really needed at all.

A second step translates general goals into training objectives. At this stage, general statements of outcomes will no longer suffice. Now you need specific statements of what you expect the training program to accomplish. Precisely what do you want trainees to know (or be able to do) at the end of the training session that they do not know (or do not do) now? Your training program will usually be evaluated in terms of these specific objectives. Even before you begin actual training, you will want to specify criteria by which your training can be evaluated when it is over. You might want to design a pre-test procedure to assess your trainees in terms of their present skill or information levels so that you know the level at which training should begin.

After you have determined the criteria for assessing outcomes, you have to decide how you will go about the actual training. Given what you know about your needs, objectives, and employees, what will be the most efficient type of training mechanism you can use to reach your goals?

There are many methods that might be used in a training program, and a significant part of the job of an I/O psychologist is to propose the most cost-effective, valid, easy-to-use, and engaging method available. In some cases, bringing workers together for classroom instruction works well. On the other hand, there are situations in which assembling large numbers of workers would be unrealistic. For example, automobile manufacturers can hardly be expected to have all car salespeople report to the home office for instruction on improvements in the new models of cars they will be selling. At times, training has to go to the worker—in the form of printed material, taped programs, computer- or web-based programs or live presentations by a trainer—rather than having workers go to the training.

A designer of a training program will have many decisions to make about the methods to be used. Should he or she use "live" instructors, or should information be presented in some media format: print, audiotapes, videotapes, videodisks, CD-ROMs, on-line, and the like? Should training be formalized and time-limited, or can trainees work individually, at their own pace? Will there need to be hands-on experience? Will training be held in groups or be individually oriented? Will on-the-job training be efficient or disruptive? Can the job or task be simulated for the purposes of training?

The options are many, and all should be considered, because some are clearly more effective than others for certain types of training. Some trainers fall into the habit of using only one or two techniques for a range of needs and objectives. For example, televised instruction may be useful to point out a few new features of an automobile to a salesperson, but ineffective for describing the details of a new health insurance program. By and large, presenting information is less effective than demonstrating it, and involving one's audience as participants (a hands-on, or simulation, approach) is most effective. In general terms, no particular training technique is superior in all circumstances. What is needed is a "fit" between present training needs and available training techniques.

When a training program is finished, the I/O psychologist is ready to reconsider what may be the most difficult aspect of training: the evaluation of the success of the training. What is required is a measure of the extent to which training transfers to the actual job in the workplace (thus meeting the needs that prompted the training in the first place). There are difficulties involved in doing quality evaluations of training programs. I will make only three observations:

1. Training programs can be evaluated at various levels. You may ask participants to rate how they feel about the program. You may assess the extent to which the training has produced behavioral changes. You may measure how much has been learned, perhaps with formal testing before and after training. (Do you recognize our ABCs here?) You may also go right to the bottom line and ask about increases in productivity or profit.
2. Training programs that do not include ways of evaluating both short-term and long-term effectiveness will generally be of little value. Sadly enough, very few training programs are well evaluated—particularly in terms of long-term benefits. Many seem to be taken simply on faith or face value simply because of their logical appeal.
3. The greater the effort put into the assessment of organizational needs, job analysis, performance criteria, and the establishment of training objectives at the beginning of a training project, the easier it will be to evaluate the program when it is over.

✓ STUDY CHECK

What are some of the factors that need to be considered in the design, implementation, and evaluation of training programs?

CYBER PSYCH

Given the significant ways in which the nature of work changes on an almost-daily basis, training current workers as well as new hires has become a major concern for every business and industry. These sites expand on our discussion.

(a) An excellent article, with useful links is at: http://www.managementhelp.org/trng_dev/basics/reasons. htm.

(b) The site at http://www.workrelationships.com/site/articles/ problememployee.htm provides a most interesting article on training "problem employees."

Motivating People to Do Good Work

Let's review for a moment. Our major concern in this section is fitting a person to a job—that is, finding someone to do good work. The first step in this process involves carefully delineating just what is meant by good work. To this end, one does a job analysis and lists specific performance criteria for the job. An employer can go through the process of selection, trying to find the best person for the job—someone who already has all of the knowledge, skills, and abilities (KSAs) to do the job well. Another possibility is to train a present employee to do good (or better) work. There remains an important consideration. Something may be missing: motivation to do good work. Being able to do a job well and wanting to do a job well are two different matters. Notice, too, that issues of training and motivation are both ongoing concerns. People change and jobs change. Seldom will one training program or one attempt to motivate employees be sufficient over the long term.

As you can imagine, I/O psychologists always have been interested in how to motivate employees to do their best work. When we talk about work motivation, we are referring to three inter-related processes: arousing (getting the worker to do a task), directing (getting the worker to do the task we want done), and sustaining (keeping the worker at the task). As you also can imagine, there is no one answer to questions of how to motivate workers to do a good job and stick with it. I'll briefly review a few of the more popular approaches.

The expectancy theory of work motivation has been around for years and has been modified by many theorists, but it is best associated with Victor Vroom (1964). It is highly cognitive in its orientation. **Expectancy theory** says that workers be-have rationally and logically, making work-related decisions based on their beliefs, judgments, and expectations.

Vroom's expression of his theory is quite complex, but what it amounts to is that we are motivated to do good work if we expect rewards to be contingent on levels of performance, and if we value the rewards that are being offered. Addition-ally, we must believe that rewards are attainable—that we really can do the work to a level of performance that will earn those valued rewards.

expectancy theory the approach that workers behave rationally and logically, making work-related decisions based on their beliefs, judgments, and expectations

There are several implications here for employers concerned about motivating employees. For one thing, employers should see if the outcomes that follow good work are truly valued by the workers. For example, in one company, good work is rewarded by recognition with a plaque and a free trip awarded at the annual company dinner. What if most of the workforce finds company dinners a huge bore, getting plaques an embarrassment, and trips a nuisance (arranging for transportation, babysitters, and so on)? What if the employees would rather have a cash bonus or longer coffee breaks? That is, what if the employees actually believe there is little value in what the company thinks are rewards?

Another implication of expectancy theory is that workers understand the relationship between their behaviors and outcomes. Simply, workers need to know just what to expect if they behave in a certain way. Which behaviors lead to positive outcomes, and which lead to negative outcomes? Why should any employee work very hard, put in overtime, and take work home on the weekend if he or she has little or no reason to believe that such behaviors will lead to valued rewards? In fact, fewer than a third of workers believe their compensation is based on their work performance (Plawin & Suied, 1988).

Another classic approach to work motivation, called equity theory, is associated with J. Stacy Adams (1965). **Equity theory** is also cognitive, claiming that what matters most to workers is their perception of the extent to which they are being treated fairly compared to fellow workers in similar work situations.

In Adams's view, workers make social comparisons (or cognitive judgments) concerning how much they are getting from the organization compared to what they are putting into it. That is, the worker judges the extent to which effort, skill, education, experience, and so on (inputs) are being rewarded by salary, praise, fringe benefits, or awards, (outcomes). Then this ratio of inputs and outcomes is compared with a ratio from some other, similarly placed employee. If the relationship is perceived as being about the same—or equitable—the worker will not be motivated to change. However, if there is a perceived inequity when compared to the inputs and outcomes of a fellow worker, changes can be predicted. The worker may increase or decrease inputs (work longer or shorter hours, take fewer or more breaks) or try to effect a change in outcomes. What matters most is not the actual value of what a worker gains for his or her efforts. What matters is the *perception of equity*. A worker will be more willing to maintain effort (input) and take a cut in pay (outcome) if he or she believes that everyone else in the company is taking a similar pay cut (Eccles & Wigfield, 2002).

How work-related goals are set has been the centerpiece of a number of approaches to worker motivation. This approach assumes that workers are motivated to perform any task for which goals are clearly and specifically detailed. In order for goal-setting to have a positive influence on a worker's behavior, two things are necessary: First, the goal must be clear. The worker must be perfectly aware of just what he or she is working for. Second, the employee must accept the goal as worth the effort.

Goal-setting is the approach to motivating workers that has received the most research interest. Here are some general conclusions.

equity theory the claim that what matters most to workers is their perception of the extent to which they are being treated fairly compared to fellow workers in similar work situations

1. Difficult but achievable goals tend to increase productivity more than easy goals. The issue here seems to hinge on the acceptance of goals as being worthwhile. Goals that are too easy may simply fail to require any change in performance. On the other hand, goals that are perceived as being too difficult and beyond the abilities of workers are not likely to be very useful.

2. Specific, focused, goals are better than general ones. Simply telling workers to "do better" or "do your best" provides little information about what behaviors are expected.

3. Feedback informing workers of their progress toward established goals is important in maintaining motivated behaviors. Feedback delivered soon after an appropriate response is made is more effective than delayed feedback.

4. It may seem reasonable to predict that goals set by employers and employees working together are more effective than goals established by employers alone, but the evidence suggests that this is not necessarily the case. What matters most is that the employee be aware of specific goals and accept those goals as reasonable.

5. The data are a bit murky here, but it seems best to offer rewards for positive performance rather than to threaten punishment for poor performance. That is, a message of "If you do this well, you'll get a raise," is likely to be more effective than "If you mess this up, you'll get demoted."

6. Cultural concerns are also relevant here. The more people are used to working together (as in collectivist cultures), the more important it is to be involved in goal-setting. In Western (individualistic) cultures, involvement in goal-setting is less critical.

There are other useful approaches to work motivation. Some refer to motivational theories and concepts we introduced in Chapter Seven, where we discussed motivation in general. That is to say, some approaches stress the importance of workers' needs (as in Maslow's theory about a hierarchy from basic physiological needs to needs to self-actualize). Some stress the importance of conditioning procedures and attending to the consequences of behavior (an approach called organizational behavior management when applied in work environments).

Here's a brief summary of our discussion. Workers will tend to be motivated to do a good job if:

1. Clear and specific goals are established and accepted.
2. The goals employers set match workers' expectations and needs.
3. Workers see clearly the relationship between their work performance and accepted outcomes.
4. Workers judge the outcomes that follow from their efforts as being in line with those earned by fellow workers making similar efforts.
5. Workers are given feedback about the nature of their work.

Now let's shift our emphasis slightly from a concern about finding and fitting the person to the job to the issue of fitting the job to the person. In large measure, our interest is in what we call job satisfaction. What can be done to make jobs more satisfying? What are the consequences of doing so?

STUDY CHECK

What are some of the factors that affect the motivation of workers to do a good job?

CYBER PSYCH

How to motivate anyone to do anything—much less a worker to do a job well—has intrigued psychologists for decades. These sites are oriented toward motivation in the workplace.

(a) A great site with many useful links is http://www.accel-team.com/motivation/index.html.

(b) http://www.motivation-tools.com/workplace is a very clever site on "Motivation in the Workplace."

Job Satisfaction and Performance

We have considered what employers can do to find the best person for a given task. For the remainder of this chapter, let's change our perspective a bit and focus on some of the issues relevant to the person on the job in the workplace. There are two concerns here. The first has to do with job satisfaction. Let's define the concept and then see how it is related to job performance. The second issue has to do with safety in the workplace. How can jobs be designed to maximize employee safety and health?

job satisfaction the attitude one holds toward one's work: a pleasurable or positive emotional state resulting from the appraisal of one's job or job experiences

Job satisfaction refers to the attitude one holds toward one's work: "a pleasurable or positive emotional state resulting from the appraisal of one's job or job experiences" (Locke, 1976, p. 130). It amounts to an employee's affective or emotional responses toward his or her job. We may refer to job satisfaction in general terms, but an employee's degree of satisfaction can vary considerably for various aspects of the job itself (Riggio, 2002). As you know from your own work experience, you might be reasonably happy with your physical working conditions, unhappy with the base salary, pleased with your fringe benefits, satisfied with the challenge provided by the job, very dissatisfied with relationships with co-workers, and so on. In fact, there may be as many facets of job satisfaction or dissatisfaction as there are aspects to the job.

A great deal of research has looked for relationships between job satisfaction and characteristics of workers. Here is a brief summary of some of that research:

1. There is a positive correlation between global job satisfaction and age. Younger workers tend to be most dissatisfied with their jobs (The Conference Board, 2003), but there also is evidence that older employees develop dissatisfaction with their jobs toward the end of their careers.

2. Data on gender differences in job satisfaction are inconsistent and are virtually nonexistent when pay, tenure, and education are controlled.

3. Racial differences in job satisfaction have consistently been shown to be small in the United States, with Caucasians having more positive attitudes about their jobs than African Americans, and Mexican Americans showing more satisfaction than Caucasians.

4. Satisfaction is positively related to the perceived level or status of one's job or occupation. In other words, jobs of lowest rank tend to be filled by the least satisfied workers.

Job stress is a major contributor to lack of satisfaction and to burnout, two factors that predict absenteeism and turnover.

5. The data are few, but there appear to be some cultural differences in job satisfaction. In one survey of ten countries, Sweden had the largest proportion of satisfied workers (63 percent), whereas Japan had the fewest (20 percent) (de Boer, 1978).

The headline read, "U.S. Job Satisfaction Hits Record Low." The survey, conducted in July 2003, was reported in September (The Conference Board, 2003). Apparently, in the summer of 2003, fewer than half of all American workers were satisfied with their jobs. The sample of 5,000 workers reflected dissatisfaction with nearly every aspect of their jobs, being most unhappy with promotion policies and company programs for education and training. About the only job-related factor receiving a positive reaction from the majority of respondents was the commute to and from work. An important question for industrial/organizational psychologists is whether job satisfaction is related in any lawful way to job performance.

It may seem reasonable to assert that "a happy worker is a productive worker"—that an increase in job satisfaction will be reflected in increased worker productivity. For the last 50 years, many managers and executives have assumed, pretty much without question, a causal relationship between satisfaction and productivity. In many ways, satisfaction and productivity are related, but the relationship is not a simple one. Research often refutes the contention that increased performance necessarily results from increased satisfaction. The only conclusion we can draw about these two variables is that, in some instances, they may be correlated. Cause-and-effect statements are out of the question.

The lack of a consistent relationship between satisfaction and productivity may not be that difficult to explain. Some workers may hate their present jobs but work hard at them so they can be promoted to another position they believe they will prefer. Some workers may be very satisfied with their present positions simply because expectations for productivity are low, and if demands for productivity were to increase, satisfaction might decrease. Indeed, increasing productivity may increase satisfaction, rather than vice versa (Elovaino et al., 2000). Motivated employees, who want to do their best, will be pleased to enter a training program to improve on-the-job efficiency. Doing the job better leads to pride and an overall increase in satisfaction for one worker, while for another, the same training program may be viewed as a ploy on the part of management to make his or her life miserable.

I should not give the impression that job satisfaction is totally unrelated to work behaviors. Job satisfaction measures can be used to aid the prediction of which workers are likely to be absent from work and which are likely to quit. Job satisfaction is not the best predictor of absenteeism (marital status, age, and size of one's work group are better predictors), but the correlations are at least consistent. The relationship between dissatisfaction with one's job and turnover is even stronger, although this relationship may not be direct. That is, dissatisfaction may be an important contributing factor, but it is only one of several variables that can be used to explain why a person leaves a job.

job burnout a prolonged and negative response to stressors in the workplace

Job "burnout" is a concept that is clearly related to absenteeism, intention to leave a job, and actual turnover. It is not just the opposite of job satisfaction; it is more a prolonged response to stressors in the workplace (Maslach, 2003). Job burnout has three dimensions, and the most important of these is exhaustion. Exhaustion reflects a part of job dissatisfaction that is related to stress and "just being sick of coming to work every day." The other two aspects of job burnout are cynicism ("Nobody cares what I do in this job, so why should I give a darn about the job") and inefficiency. As might be predicted, employees going through job burnout often bring considerable, unpleasant "negative spillover" into their lives outside work (Burke & Greenglass, 2001).

We also have to remember that many times people are forced to be absent from work or to quit their jobs for reasons that have nothing at all to do with the job or the employer—illness and family concerns, for example. Still, the logic that persons who are most unhappy with their work are the ones most likely to leave it does have research support.

✔ STUDY CHECK

What is meant by "job satisfaction," and how is it related to job performance?

CYBER PSYCH

The Internet is a good source of information on job satisfaction and its relation to job performance.
(a) One excellent article on the issue is at http://www.mapnp.org/library/prsn_wll/job_stfy.htm.
(b) Another good article can be found at http://www.hrzone.com/articles/mood.html.
(c) http://www.employeesatisfactions.com is yet another good source.

Industrial-organizational psychologists have long been concerned about worker safety.

Safety in the Workplace

In this final section, we review one of the oldest concerns of I/O psychology: safety in the workplace. The statistics are impressive. One survey claims "approximately 6500 job-related deaths from injury, 13.2 million non-fatal injuries, 60,300 deaths from disease, and 862,200 illnesses are estimated to occur annually in the civilian American workforce" (Leigh et al., 1997, p. 1557). The cost of these deaths, injuries, and illnesses is $315 billion each year. This says nothing of the pain and suffering involved. The challenge is clear: Increase the safety of the workplace. But how?

One approach to worker safety is based on the popular notion that some people are simply more "accident prone" than others, or that at least there are a few personality traits consistently related to high incidences of accidents. If this were true, safety could be improved by not hiring those applicants who are prone to accidents. The problem is that there just don't seem to be people who are, in general, more accident-prone than anyone else (which may reflect our inability to adequately assess such a trait.) Still, there is some obvious sense to this approach. The less qualified, the less trained, or the less motivated a person is for a job, the more likely that person will have an accident—particularly if the job is a dangerous one (Cooper, 1998). This is especially true for workers younger than 25 or older than 55, who have more accidents than workers between those ages (Haight, 2003).

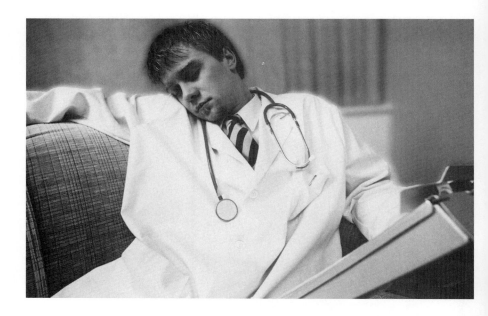

One issue that clearly predicts accidents and errors on the job is fatigue. Particularly in the medical professions, I/O psychologists continue to press for better scheduling of work hours.

There currently is a popular opinion in the field of occupational safety that accidents and injuries could be significantly reduced if only workers were better trained and better motivated to avoid bad worker behaviors. A position consistent with our earlier discussion is that workers often need to be motivated to work safely. At first you might think that anyone in his or her right mind would want to work safely and avoid being in an accident. You might be right. But does the worker know *specifically* what constitutes safe behavior? Does the worker know that the employer values safe work and that safe work will be rewarded? If such is not the case, workers may cut corners, working too quickly—and often too dangerously—if they think that rewards are only for amount of work and output. A long, detailed warning label, for instance, may be so long and so detailed that the worker for whom it was intended won't even bother reading it. In short, employers must see to it that workers are trained in safe ways to do their jobs and that they realize that safe behaviors are valued (Smith, 2003). Workers need to appreciate that a climate of safety is an integral part of the organization for which they work and that the leadership of that organization shares in the vision of establishing safety excellence (Blair, 2003). What matters most, as we have seen before, is clearly establishing safety goals, providing feedback to workers, and reinforcing those behaviors that lead to attaining stated goals.

What Landy (1989) called the *engineering approach* to worker safety attempts to reduce accidents by designing safer equipment and implementing safer procedures. Over the years, this approach has been the most successful in a range of applications. "Even with the growing use of behavior-based processes, the dominant paradigm in safety has been—and continues to be—to design the safest equipment, physical work environments, and protective devices possible" (Sarkus, 2003). Examples abound. When I was in high school, I had a summer job working in a pressroom. There was a huge paper cutter there that could slice through 1000 sheets of paper with ease. Once the paper was positioned, a large steel blade descended across the paper, making two stacks where there had been one. To get that blade to fall, the machine's operator had to manipulate two levers—one was pulled from left to right, while the other was pressed downward. There was no way the operator could lose a finger (or hand or arm) in that paper cutter, because both hands had to be below the deck of the cutter to get the blade to work.

Complex control panels are engineered with safety in mind so that the most important dials, meters, buttons, and switches are in clear view and are easy to read and interpret. Work areas are designed so that there is adequate illumination and sufficient space, and so that scrap materials and trash can be easily removed. Computer screens have shields to protect against glare and radiation, and keyboards are now engineered (and are continually re-engineered) to reduce physical damage to the wrist that may result from spending hours at the keyboard.

Engineering approaches to accident prevention may involve matters such as the scheduling of work time. There is ample evidence of a positive relationship between fatigue and accidents. Scheduling work time (by reducing overtime work, for example) to minimize fatigue seems to improve safety. Clearly, the very best way to improve safety in the workplace is to "engineer" that workplace to be as safe as possible, to have an organization that truly believes in safety and is able to communicate that commitment to its employees, and to train, motivate, and reinforce employees for working safely.

✓ STUDY CHECK

What steps can be taken to improve the safety of workers?

CYBER PSYCH

There is unanimous agreement that all steps should be taken to assure safety in the workplace. This may be easier said than done.

(a) Probably no source is more complete than the website of the Occupational Safety and Health Administration: http://www.osha.gov.

(b) Here's a similar site from the CDC: http://www.cdc.gov/node.do/id/0900f3ec8000ec09.

Chapter Summary

What is involved in doing a complete job analysis?

Doing a proper job analysis involves two stages. First, there is the construction of a complete and specific description of the activities performed by someone in a given position (i.e., a listing of the behaviors required to do the job). Second, there must be a series of steps that indicate the knowledge, skills, and abilities (KSAs) required to do the job (called performance criteria).

What are some of the sources of information that can be used when making personnel decisions?

Personnel selection (and retention) may use several assessment tools, including application forms, interviews (unstructured or structured), psychological tests (already published or created for a specific purpose), and situational tests to measure relevant characteristics of employees and potential employees. Of these, the unstructured interview seems to be of least value.

What are some of the factors that need to be considered in the design, implementation, and evaluation of training programs?

Billions of dollars are spent each year training and retraining employees. Several factors need to be considered in the design and implementation of training programs. These include an assessment of the organization's instructional needs (what training, if any, is required), the development of specific training objectives, the means by which training will be evaluated, and the selection of the media and methods for the actual training. Once training has begun, it should be monitored constantly to see if objectives are being met. After training has been completed, the training program should be evaluated in the short- and long-term, as should the transfer of information and skills from training to actual on-the-job performance.

What are some of the factors that affect the motivation of workers to do a good job?

Even workers with ability may not do a good job unless they are motivated to do so. We reviewed three approaches to worker motivation. Vroom's expectancy theory argues that workers develop expectations about relationships between their work behaviors and the likelihood of certain outcomes. They will be most highly motivated to behave in ways that earn valued rewards. Adams's equity theory says that what matters most is the perception of fairness or equal reward for equal effort when one's work efforts are being compared with those of someone else at the same level in the organization. Locke's goal-setting approach claims that what is critical is that workers be aware of the job goal(s) and that they accept the goal(s) as worth the effort.

What is meant by "job satisfaction," and how is it related to job performance?

Job satisfaction refers to the attitude that one holds toward one's work. It amounts to an employee's affective or emotional responses to his or her job. Satisfaction is relevant to the job overall (global) and to specific aspects of the job. Although job satisfaction and productivity may be related, there is little evidence that the relationship is a strong one or that one causes the other. Interventions designed to improve job satisfaction often result in an increase in productivity, but interventions to increase productivity often increase job satisfaction. Job satisfaction and job burnout are best related to absenteeism and turnover.

What steps can be taken to improve the safety of workers?

I/O psychologists have long been interested in making the workplace as safe as possible. There are two main approaches to increasing safety within organizations. One, an engineering approach, focuses on doing everything possible to design safe equipment and a safe work environment. The other, a psychological or behavior-based approach, focuses on making sure that workers know what constitutes safe behavior and understand that organizational management and leadership value safe behaviors.

Student Study Guide

**STUDY TIP #13 Preparing for Exams:
Some Thoughts on Multiple-Choice Exams**

Multiple-choice exams are the most common for students in their first psychology course. I know that you have taken hundreds of multiple-choice tests over your academic career. I also know that general "rules" have many exceptions. Nonetheless, there are some hints about taking multiple-choice exams that we can review quickly.

1. **There is no substitute for being prepared.** No matter how clever or lucky you are, the best way to prepare for an exam of any type is to study for it.
2. **Relax—be cool.** You're prepared for this exam. This is no time to panic. Take a deep breath, exhale slowly, and relax.
3. **Read the directions and give the test a quick once-over.** Yes, you probably know what to do, but take a minute to make sure that you're following the directions. Scan the whole test. Estimate time needs.
4. **Skip items of which you are unsure.** If you encounter an item for which the answer is not immediately obvious, that's okay. Don't agonize over it. Skip it. Just don't forget to come back to it later.
5. **Be sure you know what the item is asking about.** You know that you know the material. If it's not immediately clear, you've got to find a match between what you know and what this item is asking about.
6. **Eliminate distracting alternatives.** If you don't see the best answer right away, at least mark out those that are clearly wrong, that don't fit grammatically, or that say the same thing as some other alternative.
7. **See if the answer to one item can be found somewhere in another item.** Imagine one question that asks: "In Hemingway's *The Old Man and the Sea*... ." followed later by a question that asks, "who wrote *The Old Man and the Sea*?" Believe me, it happens.
8. **Look out for double negatives.** If something is said to be "not false," then it's true. If someone is "not unintelligent," then he or she is smart.
9. **Avoid absolute statements (most of the time).** Particularly in psychology, very little is always or never, but may be often or seldom.
10. **Do not be afraid to change your answer.** No matter what you may have been told, there is no evidence that students are likely to change from correct answers to incorrect ones. Change your answers if you'd like.

KEY TERMS AND CONCEPTS

industrial/organizational (I/O) psychology _____
_____

job analysis _____

_____

training _____

_____

expectancy theory _____

_____

equity theory _____

_____

job satisfaction _____

_____

job burnout _____

_____

Practice Test Questions

MULTIPLE CHOICE

1. There are several things an employer can do to improve the quality of the workforce. Which of these is LEAST important?

    _____ a. Find good people to start with.

    _____ b. Work to improve employee satisfaction.

    _____ c. Train the present workforce to work well.

    _____ d. Motivate employees to do their best.

2. Typically, an employee selection program begins with

    _____ a. a listing of required or desired characteristics provided by management.

    _____ b. an inventory of available tests and assessment techniques.

    _____ c. an appraisal of current employees.

    _____ d. a complete job analysis.

3. A job analysis may include each of these, but to be useful, it should include performance criteria, or

    _____ a. a full listing of salaries, wages, and benefits.

    _____ b. a listing of situations in which the job is to be performed.

    _____ c. a list of characteristics needed for someone to do the job well.

    _____ d. a listing of input from everyone else regarding what the duties of the job are.

4. In a job analysis, when Smith differentiates between "hard" and "soft" criteria, she is really differentiating between

_____ a. physical labor jobs and mental labor jobs.

_____ b. objective data and subjective judgments.

_____ c. blue-collar and white-collar positions.

_____ d. professionally gathered data and general impressions.

5 Of the following techniques for gathering information about prospective employees, which tends to provide the LEAST useful information?

_____ a. psychological tests   _____ c. assessment centers

_____ b. unstructured interviews   _____ d. application forms

6. In devising a training program for employees, what is the first question that an I/O psychologist should ask?

_____ a. Who is going to receive this training?

_____ b. What techniques will be used to get information across to the trainees?

_____ c. How will the outcome of the training be evaluated?

_____ d. Is this training really necessary?

7. By far, the approach that employers most often use in attempting to increase productivity is

_____ a. employee training.

_____ b. motivational seminars.

_____ c. improving morale.

_____ d. finding new and different employees.

8. In general, training programs are usually evaluated in terms of

_____ a. job analyses.   _____ c. employees' needs.

_____ b. training objectives. _____ d. trainee satisfaction.

9. Although clearly there are exceptions, which approach to employee training in general is the most effective?

_____ a. one that involves hands-on experience

_____ b. one that uses classroom instruction by an expert

_____ c. one that uses as many media as possible

_____ d. one that involves repeated demonstrations

10. Which level of evaluation of a training program is likely to be of LEAST interest to the employer?

_____ a. amount of information acquired

_____ b. extent to which actual behaviors have been changed

_____ c. how participants feel about the training received

_____ d. extent to which profitability has been increased

11. Which of the following is seldom a goal of any program to motivate employees?

_____ a. getting the worker to do any task

_____ b. getting the worker to do the task we want done

_____ c. getting the worker to enjoy the task being done

_____ d. getting the worker to keep at the task

12. Equity theory claims that what matters most to employees is the extent to which

_____ a. they are making more money than employees in similar positions.

_____ b. they understand the goals they are trying to reach.

_____ c. they perceive that they are being treated fairly compared to others.

_____ d. they expect to be rewarded for what they value.

13. Job satisfaction

_____ a. is positively correlated with overall productivity.

_____ b. levels are pretty much the same in all known cultures.

_____ c. is a good predictor of absenteeism and employee turnover.

_____ d. causes increased performance on the job.

TRUE/FALSE

1. _____ True _____ False In the United States and in other industrialized nations, worker safety issues are no longer viewed as a significant problem.

2. _____ True _____ False Psychological testing and other assessment techniques can identify accident-prone individuals.

3. _____ True _____ False Application forms provide a good source of biodata.

4. _____ True _____ False Structured interviews are more valid than unstructured interviews.

5. _____ True _____ False Vroom's 1964 expectancy theory is mostly cognitive in its approach to employee motivation.

Chapter One

MULTIPLE CHOICE

1. **b** If you *feel* anything, you are having, or experiencing affect. Remember: Cognitions are thoughts or ideas. Conflicts often give rise to affect.

2. **c** Psychologists study all of these things, but the only answer that is general enough not to exclude a part of psychology's subject matter is alternative **c**.

3. **c** All you need to do here is recognize the definition of the term "hypothesis."

4. **d** What makes psychologists "scientist-practitioners" is that they spend most of their time trying to apply psychological knowledge to problems in the real world. That is, they "practice" the "science" of psychology.

5. **c** No matter which of the scientific methods one uses in psychology, all of them flow from first making careful observations of one's subject matter.

6. **a** Yes, there are many specific methods, but ultimately they will yield either a correlation or a cause-and-effect statement resulting from experimentation.

7. **a** When doing an experiment, the most important—and often the most difficult—thing is to be sure that one has adequately controlled all extraneous variables.

8. **b** The independent variable is the one that you manipulate; here, the amount or dosage of the drug. Degree of improvement might be your dependent variable, while the type of disorder being treated and other concurrent therapies would be extraneous variables.

9. **b** Some psychologists may have gone to medical school, but doing so is not a requirement; neither is majoring in psychology as an undergraduate. To be called a psychologist may require getting a license but seldom requires an interview with any sort of board.

10. **b**   Alternatives **c** and **d** tell us about psychology's subject matter. When psychology began, the focus was on applying scientific methods to deal with old philosophical questions about the nature of the mind.

TRUE/FALSE

1. **F**   There are many ways of gaining insight into the nature of the world and the organisms that populate it. As it happens, psychology values science above the others, but there are others.

2. **T**   There are lots of different ABCs, but in psychology, our ABCs are indeed affect, behavior, and cognition.

3. **T**   Clinical and counseling psychologists are among those scientist-practitioners who apply psychological information in the real world.

4. **F**   Probably most of what we know in psychology we have learned by doing experiments, but it is not correct to argue that experimentation is the only scientific method that psychologists use.

5. **T**   Actually, in recent years it has been the most popular choice of major.

Chapter Two

MULTIPLE CHOICE

1. **c**   Be careful here. The periods of the embryo and the fetus are parts of the prenatal period. Conception is an event that begins the prenatal period, not a stage or period in itself.

2. **b**   It is when the organism is in the form of an embryo that it is most sensitive to the formation of physical defects.

3. **d**   Alcohol abuse is certainly the most devastating factor leading to birth defects of these listed, and even moderate alcohol consumption is generally discouraged.

4. **d**   The different stages of Piaget's theory are defined in terms of how the child goes about forming or modifying schemas on the basis of his or her interaction with the environment.

5. **d**   The ability to manipulate abstract concepts neatly defines the stage of formal operations.

6. **a**   No matter the truth or falsity of alternatives **b**, **c**, or **d**, it is totally unreasonable to say that it lacks attention to cognitive processing. Cognitive processing is what the theory is all about.

7. **c**   Melanie is probably in Piaget's stage of concrete operations, which would be typical for a 9-year-old. (Did it bother you that this item is "out of order"? This is something for which you need to be alert.)

8. **c**   Kohlberg's is referred to as a theory of moral development.

9. **b**   About 65 percent of children in the United States (and around the world) will form attachments during their first year.

TRUE/FALSE

1. **T**   There are many signs and symptoms associated with fetal alcohol syndrome (retarded physical growth, poor coordination, poor muscle tone, etc.). By definition, one sign is mental retardation.

2. **F**   Hardly! Pregnant women are being advised to abstain from any and all alcoholic beverages.

3. **T**   Yes, this is one of the most common criticisms of Piaget's theory.

4. **T**   Most of Kohlberg's theory of moral development was based on the study of males. Gilligan suggests that females *may* have a different style of morality than do males.

5. **T**   There is simply no doubting that attachment formation is a two-way process.

Chapter Three

MULTIPLE CHOICE

1. **c**   Although some (including G. Stanley Hall and Anna Freud) would claim that alternative **b** is correct, current thinking would make alternative **c** your best choice. Alternatives **a** and **d** are almost silly.

2. **a**   Penile erections and nocturnal emissions typically occur for some time before puberty in boys, which is indicated by the presence of live sperm cells.

3. **b**   Menarche occurs in girls, not boys; it defines the beginning of puberty; it is triggered by estrogens, not androgens, and—for reasons not fully understood—seems to be occurring at a younger age than ever before in history.

4. **a**   At least at the time of their adolescence, early-maturing boys seem to experience an "advantage" over the other named groups.

5. **d**   The first three alternatives are not even associated with Piaget. But did you note how this question goes back to the previous chapter? That will happen from time to time.

6. **a**   Although at first they may appear contradictory, independence and interdependence characterize early adulthood.

7. **c**   Here again, this item hinges on your knowledge of Erikson's stages. Early adulthood is associated with conflicts between intimacy and isolation.

8. **a**   Aren't some of these alternatives funny? What I am getting at here is the observation that mate selection is most often based on similarities, not that "opposites attract."

9. **a**   And the range of concern is very wide from one culture to another.

10. **c**   There is no doubt that the only alternative here that is even close to being true is the third one.

11. **c**   Not everyone "buys" Kübler-Ross' scheme, of course, but her stages are, in order: denial, anger, bargaining, depression, and acceptance.

TRUE/FALSE

1. **F**   To some of us (and to parents of adolescents in particular) this may appear to be true, but it isn't. It reflects more of an incorrect stereotype than reality.

2. **T**   This is about as nice a summary statement about early and late maturation as I can muster.

3. **F**   We often hear this used as an "excuse" for some pretty silly behaviors by middle-aged adults, but there is little hard evidence for a general period or stage of development that we can characterize as a mid-life crisis.

Chapter Four

MULTIPLE CHOICE

1. **d**   Alternative **a** is rather meaningless. Alternatives **b** and **c** are more related to perception than to sensation, but alternative **d**, transduction, is nearly synonymous with sensation.

2. **a**   Perception may involve all of the terms in all of the alternatives, but, by definition, it is a cognitive process involving the selection and organization of incoming sensory information.

3. **d**   You might get this one by elimination. The first alternative is downright silly. The second and third both say virtually the same thing, which makes **d** the best choice.

4. **a**   Attentional factors can be classified in many ways, of course, but of these alternatives, the choice would be the scheme used in your text, referring to them as stimulus or personal factors.

5. **d**   To say that some stimuli are attended to because of an expectation to perceive them is to say that one has developed a mental set.

6. **a**   Speech sounds within a word are perceived and organized together because they are close together, which reflects the Gestalt factor of proximity—which means "nearness" in space or time.

7. **d** Alternatives **a** and **b** are quite absurd. Alternative **c** is a correct statement, but relevant to three-dimensionality. The retina is two-dimensional, making the last statement the best choice.

8. **b** The logic here — extrapolating from research cited in the text — is that persons in environments that are cramped and cluttered are less often required (or able) to view things (such as approaching camel caravans) over great distances.

6. **c** Perceptual constancies allow us to perceive familiar objects as unchanged, even though our sensory experience may change — making alternative c the best choice.

TRUE/FALSE

1. **T** This correctly states the inverse relationship between one's threshold and one's sensitivity — as one increases, the other decreases.

2. **T** This is true by definition. If you're not convinced, maybe you should go back and check.

3. **F** This one is almost tricky. The name is deceiving. In fact, motion parallax has little to do with our perception of motion, real or illusionary. It is a cue to depth and distance.

Chapter Five

MULTIPLE CHOICE

1. **d** Alternative **a** is simply not true. Alternatives **b** and **c** may be true, but are not related to the word "demonstrated," which makes **d** the correct choice.

2. **a** The very first thing that will happen is that a bell will be sounded and, reflexively, the dog will orient toward it.

3. **d** Actually, because the bell and the food powder in the first three alternatives are stimuli and not responses, the only possible answer here is the last alternative.

4. **a** This is a tough one. The person comes to desensitization with a (learned) irrational fear, which now acts as *if it were* a UCR to be replaced with a newly acquired CR of relaxation. All of that means that the first alternative here is the best one.

5. **c** I doubt that many psychologists would even agree with the statements made in alternatives **a**, **b**, and **d**, which makes the third alternative the correct choice here.

6. **a** The relatively permanent change in behavior that occurs as a result of operant conditioning is a change in the rate or probability of a response.

7. **d** Actually, the first three alternatives all say pretty much the same thing, which is a major clue that the answer is the last alternative. "Primary" as a descriptor in psychology often refers to something that is based in evolution, biology, or physiology.

8. **a** Positive reinforcers are given to organisms after an appropriate response, while negative reinforcement involves taking away something (that is usually painful).

9. **b** Because the root canal procedure takes away the pain of the toothache, the end result is very reinforcing (how reinforcing depends on how painful the toothache was to begin with). The reinforcement here is negative reinforcement.

10. **d** Actually, the first three alternatives are each quite false. The only thing that we can say for sure is that punishment decreases response rates—by definition.

11. **c** Cognitive approaches emphasize cognitions, cleverly enough. That means that they focus on changes inside the organism that may or may not be evidenced in overt behavior.

12. **b** "Latent" means "hidden from view," or "not presently observable." Hence, the second alternative is the best choice.

13. **c** This seems strange, but, in fact, birds can (and do) create incredibly elaborate cognitive maps of their territories in which they bury their seeds for future use.

14. **a** Maybe it's just me, but I think that all those DIY television shows that are aimed at teaching us how to do all sorts of things—from tuning car engines to installing a deck to upholstering furniture and making quilts—follow the lead of social learning theory, in a "see how I do it, then try it yourself" sort of way.

15. **b** Vicarious reinforcement and vicarious punishment deal with the consequences of observing someone else being reinforced or punished and are, therefore, social concepts.

TRUE/FALSE

1. **F** I really like this item (and I have used it in several upper-division classes, but not in the beginning course). It is false for two reasons. Pavlov won his prize in 1904, not 1902, but that's pretty picky. There is no Nobel Prize for psychology—Pavlov's was in medicine.

2. **T** Yes, this is the first response, which needs to be habituated before actual conditioning begins.

3. **T** It is important to remember that the intention of the person doing the reinforcing (or the punishing) is quite irrelevant in operant conditioning. What matters is the effect that one's actions have on the behavior of the "learner," which makes this statement true.

4. **F** You didn't fall for this one, did you? Remember, Tolman first demonstrated cognitive maps in rats. As it happens, it is very easy to generate

human examples, but the point is that this phenomenon is not restricted to humans.

5. **T**   They certainly are.

Chapter Six

MULTIPLE CHOICE

1. **d**   The key to this item is that we're talking about "levels" or "compartments"; otherwise, alternative **a** would look pretty good. The best alternative here is the last one.

2. **a**   Of all our different varieties of memory, the duration of sensory memory is by far the shortest. Some folks say less than one second, some say about a second, but even an alternative that says "a few minutes" is way too long.

3. **d**   You have to be careful on this one. The word "minimal" is very important here. Any one of these alternatives will do the job, but the minimum necessary is simply paying attention to it again.

4. **c**   The best term (although arguments could be made for some of the other alternatives) is the technical term "chunk," largely because the others are more related to duration than to capacity.

5. **d**   The best way is to "work with it," using elaborative rehearsal.

6. **a**   We say that elaborative rehearsal gets information into LTM, so "retrieving it" won't do. Alternatives **b** and **d** say the same thing and are related to STM, so the answer is that it involves making the material (more) meaningful.

7. **b**   Long-term memories of traumatic, anxiety-producing experiences are the sorts that are typically repressed.

8. **b**   When we talk about retrieval failure, we are probably going to assume that the information that cannot be remembered is in memory but cannot be gotten out for some reason, which is essentially what the second alternative is saying.

9. **c**   The simple thing to say is that we cannot remember these features because we have never really tried to learn them, which is to say that they have never been properly encoded.

10. **b**   More than anything else they may do, mnemonic devices enhance the meaningfulness of what we are encoding.

11 **d**   This item provides a good description of what is involved in narrative chaining.

12. **c**   If Bob engages in no more trials, overlearning = 0%; 8 trials = 100%; 16 trials = 200%, and 20 trials = 250% overlearning.

TRUE/FALSE

1. **F**   No, actually, before we learn it we must attend to and perceive it, but before that we must sense that information.

2. **T**   Indeed, because paying attention is so central to STM, we find its capacity limited.

3. **T**   This statement is simple in that it does not bother to tell us just what elaborative rehearsal is, but in its simplicity, it is true.

4. **F**   No, in fact, quite the opposite is true.

5. **F**   In fact, practicing the retrieval of learned information is exactly what you are doing right now. I hope it helps. It should.

Chapter Seven

MULTIPLE CHOICE

1. **b**   We say that motivation arouses, directs, and maintains behavior. Now memory is surely involved in motivation—it's involved in nearly everything—but it is less central than the other three.

2. **d**   Actually, the more complex, or "higher" a psychological process, the more likely that motivation will be a significant factor. The best choice here is the nearly physiological process of sensation.

3. **c**   There is value to the notion of instinct, of course, but with regard to human behavior, instinct tends more to name and describe than to explain anything.

4. **a**   Don't get rattled just because I dropped a name in here. In virtually anyone's system—including Hull's—needs give rise to drives.

5. **a**   Drives, arousal, and homeostasis all refer to conditions or states within the organism, whereas incentives are thought of as being "out there" in the environment.

6. **d**   By definition, homeostasis is a condition of balance or equilibrium.

7. **d**   The best alternative here is the last one.

8. **b**   I don't think that any of the others are debatable at all, but there is now quite a discussion centering on the role—or even the necessity—of cognition for emotional experiences.

9. **a**   Heart rate increases, it doesn't decrease—in fact, think of this item in terms of "what would you like to have happen if you were faced with a bear in the woods?"

10. **c**   It is not possible to have an emotional reaction without the processes named in alternatives **a**, **b**, and **d**. If there is ever a judgment made about the adaptive value of an emotion, it would be made later.

11. **d** This one is sort of silly, isn't it? Different theorists have different ideas, and for now the safest thing that we can say is that it depends—mostly on which theorist you'd like to believe.

12. **b** As we've seen, all parts of the brain tend to work together and all of its aspects are involved in all reactions, but having said that, it is the limbic system that is most involved in emotionality.

13. **c** The main role of the cerebral cortex is to bring a cognitive, thoughtful analysis to the situation that is being experienced.

14. **a** This has less to do with emotion than it does with the difference between humans and non-humans. Only humans can talk (verbalize) about how we feel.

TRUE/FALSE

1. **F** At one point in history, we might have been able to say that this statement was true, but now we see that these concepts can be applied well beyond physiological functioning.

2. **F** Well, at first, maybe, but what makes this statement false is that if arousal continues to rise, eventually it will become so high as to be debilitating.

3. **F** With regard to achievement and failure, there is little evidence that there are any sensible gender differences at all.

4. **F** Actually, some of the "negative" emotions—fear, for example—may have more survival value than some of the "positive" emotions.

5. **F** Here's this one again. Previously, it was item #11 in multiple-choice form. Psychologists have come to no general agreement on the number of primary emotions—and are wondering if there even is such a thing as a primary, basic, emotion.

6. **F** The text addresses the universality of facial expressions of emotion and suggests that anger, fear, disgust, sadness, and happiness are all expressed in the same way across cultures. This does not mean that there are not even more emotional expressions in common, as yet not confirmed.

Chapter Eight

MULTIPLE CHOICE

1. **c** The key here is "reasonably little effort." This indicates that the information is stored at the preconscious level.

2. **a** In fact, Freud had quite a bit to say about war and its destructive power. He suggested that humans must have some sort of drive for destruction, which he called *thanatos,* to match their drive for life and survival, which he called *eros.*

3. **b** It is our superego that informs us of moral issues and keeps us in touch with "right and wrong." When forces of the id overwhelm the superego, the result is often guilt.

4. **b** The psychologists listed here would say that forces outside the organism—forces in the environment, not the person—should be used to explain behavior.

5. **a** Although a reasonable criticism of all behavioral approaches, this one is most often leveled at Skinner's.

6. **c** The Big Five are personality traits (or clusters of traits). What makes them remarkable is the extent of consensus about their universality.

7. **d** We've seen this term before in other contexts. Here we are talking about the interaction of situational and dispositional influences on behavior.

8. **b** What makes the MMPI-2, for example, criterion-referenced is that each item tends to be answered differently by people from different known groups.

9. **d** Which is why it is referred to as the Rorschach Inkblot Test.

TRUE/FALSE

1. **T** Actually, Freud was a physician and therapist first and a personality theorist later. He based his theories on many things, including observations of his patients and himself.

2. **T** In fact, we may argue that Skinner never really had much of a learning theory either, but to the extent that learning theories were developed, they would suffice for Skinner.

3. **F** Rogers' form of therapy was quite different from Freud's, of course, but Rogers developed a very popular form of psychotherapy.

4. **F** Virtually all personality theories, including the listing of the "Big Five," include intelligence (or something very much like it) as an important aspect of one's personality.

5. **T** They are projective tests in the sense that they are so ambiguous that the person must project aspects of his or her personality into test responses.

Chapter Nine

MULTIPLE CHOICE

1. **c** Although alternatives **a** and **b** may be true (alternative **d** is meaningless), it is the third statement that best describes the relationship between stress and motivation.

2. **d** This is a good definition of a stressor—not stress, please note. Stress is a reaction or a response.

3. **c** By definition, frustration is the blocking or thwarting of goal-directed behavior and is based on the assumption that, in fact, behaviors are goal-directed.

4. **a** The first example is one of frustration—environmental frustration at that.

5. **c** I suppose that we could argue about this one, because I do not have quality data to support my assertion that as adults we tend to "keep our options open" and are seldom faced with a situation in which there is just one option available, and thus less frequently do we get "trapped" in simple approach-avoidance conflicts.

6. **a** I think that most of us will agree that we're not going to feel too sorry for Scott, momentarily stuck in an approach-approach conflict.

7. **b** This is a long one (and a little self-disclosing), isn't it? What I mean to be getting at here is someone who is experiencing frustration and stress because of some personal reason, hence, personal frustration.

8. **a** Only learning—bringing abut a relatively permanent change—is an adaptive response to the stressors in our lives.

9. **c** Each of the others is at least a little bit helpful, but fixating—just doing the same thing over and over—obviously isn't working and is inefficient.

10. **c** We have to perceive a problem. We have to think about it (a cognition). We are likely to get emotional. But stress-inducing conflicts are called "motivational conflicts" because what is conflicted are our motives, drives, desires, wishes, wants, etc.

11. **b** Isn't this one downright "cute"? Being all dressed up with no place to go might lead to the experience of stress, but I cannot see how it can be classified as an avoidance-avoidance conflict.

12. **a** There seems to be no more stress-producing experience (on average) than the loss of one's spouse.

13. **b** The first, third, and fourth alternatives describe the hardy personality type quite well, whereas the second alternative is unrelated.

14. **a** Cognitive reappraisal is the only technique mentioned here that actually gets to the source and nature of one's stressor, rather than dealing with the feelings that result from stress.

TRUE/FALSE

1. **F** Wouldn't it be sad if this statement were true? It would be sad because it is just not possible to "avoid stress altogether."

2. **T** The frustration-aggression hypothesis is wrong, of course, but this is what it says.

3. **T** This is a pretty good definition of frustration.

4. **F** Avoidance-avoidance conflicts are nasty and unpleasant, and resolving them can be difficult at times, but surely they can be resolved.

5. **T**   Not only can something be a stressor for someone and not for someone else, but that same event may not produce stress at some other time.

6. **F**   Quite the contrary. Rushing through a tough decision just to get it over with may end up causing you even more grief. The advice is to take one's time and be as sure as possible.

7. **F**   Relaxation techniques surely can help one feel better, and there's nothing wrong with that, but relaxation is an emotion-focused strategy because it will not help minimize or eliminate the stressor underlying the stress.

Chapter Ten

MULTIPLE CHOICE

1. **b**   Granted that it's only an estimate, and granted that it's a bit too conservative, but of these choices, the best would be to say that approximately 20 percent of the population has a psychological disorder at any point in time.

2. **b**   Yes, some reactions of persons with psychological disorders may seem strange or bizarre, but these terms are certainly not part of the definition of abnormality.

3. **b**   One of the sad realities of mental disorders is that—in virtually every case—the person with the disorder is (or at one time was) aware of the fact that something is not right. The other alternatives are simply false statements.

4. **b**   There are several problems with schemes for labeling and classifying disorders, but each of those schemes is certainly based on some logical or sensible rationale for doing so.

5. **c**   This is a pretty good description of the symptoms of generalized anxiety disorder.

6. **a**   The anxiety in panic disorder is acute—of short duration, but intense—while the anxiety of generalized anxiety disorder is chronic—of long duration.

7. **d**   Typically, fear requires an object; anxiety does not. We talk of being afraid of something, which implies an object of that fear.

8. **d**   This would be a definitional symptom of obsessive-compulsive disorder.

9. **c**   Real, life-threatening events eventually can result in a wide range of disorders, but the best choice here is post-traumatic stress disorder because it virtually defines the disorder. (Again, you've got to know those definitions!)

10. **c**   The only "catch" here is to recall that "affect" is related to emotion or mood.

11. **a**   This one isn't even close, and the answer is depression. Also note that paranoia isn't even a mood disorder.

12. **d**   As is the case for depression, episodes of mania tend to recur and relapse. In other words, we seldom find just one isolated case of mania.

13. **a**   There may be some anxiety associated with schizophrenia, but it is not likely, and the other symptoms virtually define the disorder.

14. **c**   A good prognosis is surely a good thing, but it is not a symptom. Loss of affect and social withdrawal are indeed losses and, hence, are negative symptoms. The most common positive symptoms of schizophrenia are hallucinations and delusions.

15. **c**   The only possible problem with this item is its simplicity. Both practice psychotherapy. I'd hate to make the statement in alternative b in a room full of psychologists, and psychoanalysts are likely to be Freudian, whether they be psychologists or psychiatrists.

16. **a**   Freud correctly characterized psychotherapy as "talk therapy." The last three alternatives may be true of some forms of therapy but are not true "generally."

17. **c**   Alternative c is a better statement for a goal of behavior therapy than for Freudian analysis.

18. **c**   Psychoanalysis today is significantly changed from the way that Freud practiced it, but what makes it psychoanalysis is the same basic assumption that disordered symptoms reflect repressed conflict of some sort.

19. **d**   Here we have a rather straightforward definition of empathy.

20. **c**   Behavior therapies in general are aimed at bringing about relatively permanent changes in one's behaviors following principles derived from the psychology of learning laboratories.

TRUE/FALSE

1. **T**   Insanity is a term that has been around for a long time in many different contexts. As it is used today, however, it is a legal term, not a psychological one.

2. **T**   Psychological disorders have an impact on one's psychological functioning, and we have agreed that one's psychological functioning involves either affect, behavior, or cognition.

3. **T**   As our understanding of underlying physiological and genetic processes continues to increase, the reality of this statement will, I suspect, generalize much beyond OCD.

4. **F**   No. Dysthymia does involve depression, but it is much less severe and less debilitating than major depression.

5. **F**   Schizophrenia does mean (literally) "splitting of the mind," but not into separate personalities. The split referred to is a split from reality as the rest of us experience it.

6. **T**   And about one-quarter will get better and stay that way, while about half seem to get better for a while and then (for myriad reasons) relapse and have their symptoms return.

7. **F**   This one is false on two counts. Not just anybody can be a psychotherapist, and psychoanalysts can be psychologists as well as psychiatrists.

8. **T**   This is the one thing that all psychotherapies have in common—a goal of bringing about some sort of lasting change. The differences have to do with how to go about making that change.

9. **T**   This one takes some thought. Unconditional positive regard provides reinforcement for virtually everything the client says (or does), whereas contingency management will provide conditional positive regard; one earns reinforcement only for doing what is appropriate. Hence, they are, in this way, opposites.

Chapter Eleven

MULTIPLE CHOICE

1. **d**   There is certainly no doubt that social roles are learned and are barely at a conscious level of awareness. Some positions may involve learning, but many are simply "assigned" to us.

2. **d**   The last alternative is the best choice here because IF Asch's participants knew that the others in the "group" were confederates of Asch, the project would not have worked at all.

3. **b**   Here you are, judging lines, surrounded by people you do not know, believing them to be architects and draftsmen—who work with lines all day long. Isn't it likely that you would defer to their judgment—no matter what your eyes were telling you?

4. **b**   What makes obedience obedience is that it is conformity to the demands or wishes of an authority figure, real or perceived.

5. **a**   The last three statements are quite true, although perhaps a bit picky, but there is no indication that the first is true.

6. **c**   Of these choices, the only truly justified conclusion is that the perception of authority is a strong force in conformity.

7. **c**   None of the other alternatives is at all true, but Milgram did put people through considerable stress when he led them to believe that they were actually delivering a shock to another person.

8. **c**   Actually, alternatives a, b, and d are just different ways of saying exactly the same thing. I cannot imagine how learned vs. inherited factors fit into a discussion of attribution.

9. **a**   These actions provide a good definition of the fundamental attribution error.

10. **b**   Social psychologists are interested in each of these, of course, but attribution theory specifically concerns how one goes about explaining the behaviors of others and oneself.

11. **c** I suppose that it would not be too difficult to imagine a theory of inter-personal attraction based on cognitive dissonance (a very powerful no-tion). But, as far as I know, we'd have to imagine it, whereas each of the others is a well-known model.

12. **a** The first statement is, in fact, quite the opposite of reality. If anything, familiarity breeds attraction. (And please don't forget: As always, we're talking "in general." There are exceptions.)

13. **d** Sexuality is an important component of attraction for some, but com-pared to the others, it would be rated last, or least important.

TRUE/FALSE

1. **F** I suppose that you could argue that this is wrong on both counts.

2. **F** I'm not sure that I even know what this statement means! If anything, we are more likely to conform than to be in situations where obedience is even an issue.

3. **F** Yes, there are individual differences in the likelihood to conform, but group composition issues are significantly more important. As it is stated, this is not an accurate statement.

4. **T** This is precisely what Asch found in his experiments.

5. **T** He surely was.

6. **T** Here is a true piece of social psychology that may not conform to com-mon sense.

7. **F** Actually, we are probably going to like someone who likes us now but didn't originally, even more than we might like someone who has liked us from the start—which is quite a mouthful, but makes sense if you go over it a couple of times.

Chapter Twelve

MULTIPLE CHOICE

1. **b** Although there may be a number of cognitions involved, interpersonal communication is largely a matter of a sender trying in some way to influence a receiver.

2. **b** Claude Shannon and Warren Weaver were engineers employed by the Bell Telephone company.

3. **b** Most of the time "when people communicate" they do so by talking to each other—i.e., by using the vocal-auditory channel.

4. **c** Actually, it means the same thing here as it does in nearly every other context: messages originating in the destination unit, sent back to the source unit.

5. **b** For alternatives **a**, **b**, and **c**, the very opposite is true.

6. **c** Indeed, such is the very definition of pragmatics.

7. **a** These labels for psychological space judgments are listed in order from smallest to largest.

8. **a** How one responds to that stress remains to be seen, but the invasion of one's personal space is a stressor, producing stress.

9. **c** All this space and territory labeling does get confusing, but I believe the only relevant alternative here is the third one.

10. **b** It may be helpful to have a communicator who is a celebrity delivering your message, just to get people's attention, but if that celebrity is not perceived as credible, expert, and trustworthy, it will do little good.

11. **a** Most persuasive communications are aimed at changing attitudes—getting someone to change his or her mind about some issue.

12. **a** It turns out that group membership tends to make decision-making go to extremes—and not necessarily risky ones—which is what group polarization is all about.

13. **a** The problem with groupthink is not that it is pressure to reach a consensus, but that it is pressure to reach a consensus no matter if that consensus is right or wrong.

TRUE/FALSE

1. **T** Only a moment's reflection on your own communications will convince you of the truth of this statement.

2. **T** Actually, this statement provides quite a nice definition of exactly what pragmatics is all about.

3. **T** Often they are both.

4. **F** Finally, a statement in this test that is false. Lying is likely to backfire in the long run, but literal truth is well down the list of important predictors of attitude change.

5. **T** They do so for many reasons, most importantly the ability to bring so many resources to bear on the problem.

Chapter Thirteen

MULTIPLE CHOICE

1. **b** Well-intended employers might take steps to see that their employees are happy or satisfied with their jobs, but the truth is that employee satisfaction is the least important of these factors.

2. **d** Any of the first three statements might describe actions you would like to take, but to get things going, one first does a complete job analysis.

3. **c** Again, if you were an employer looking to hire people, you might be concerned with each of these things, but it would be critical to have decided on performance criteria which, by definition, are those characteristics an employee will need to do the job well.

4. **b** Hard criteria are objective and can be measured, while soft criteria are more subjective and call for opinions or judgments.

5. **b** Unstructured interviews are notoriously poor in terms of validity as an assessment technique (which is not to say that interviews have no place in the process, particularly if they are structured interviews).

6. **d** I think that this is quite insightful. The very first thing that must be asked—and too often is not—is whether any sort of training program is needed in the first place.

7. **a** The data are clear on this one. In terms of money and time invested, employers will most likely go with training to try to increase productivity.

8. **b** Training programs are evaluated in terms of specific behavioral goals that are specified in the program's training objectives.

9. **a** As is the case for virtually all types of training and education, the more the trainee is actively involved in a hands-on experience, the better the training will be.

10. **c** We could probably debate this one, but I think that employers would be least concerned about how the participants felt about their training and most concerned with bottom-line profitability issues. The real answer, of course, will depend on the original goals of the training.

11. **c** Again, I think the best argument is that one would be least interested in whether the employee enjoyed what he or she was doing, so long as he or she did it well.

12. **c** By definition, equity theory deals with the workers' perception of fair treatment compared to other workers at the same level within the organization.

13. **c** Although job satisfaction is not a good predictor of job productivity (and it certainly does not cause increased performance), it is a good predictor of absenteeism and turnover.

TRUE/FALSE

1. **F** Issues of worker safety are very important indeed. Over $100 billion is lost each year in the U.S. to industrial accidents. Did you note how these first two items are "out of order"?

2. **F** Unfortunately, they cannot. There does not seem to be any constellation of personality traits that can lead us to predict whether a person is likely to be accident-prone.

3. **T** Again, this is so simple, it may have given you pause to think. Biodata are types of information about oneself—exactly the sorts of things asked for on application forms.

4. **T**   Definitely. In fact, structured devices of any sort are more valid than unstructured ones.

5. **T**   Vroom believed that workers behaved rationally and logically and, on that basis, constructed a cognitive model of worker motivation.

A

AAHSA (American Association of Homes and Services for the Aging). (2003). Nursing home statistics. From the AAHSA website at www.aahsa.org.

AARP (American Association of Retired Persons). (1993). Census Bureau ups 65+ population estimates. *AARP Bulletin, 34,* 2.

AARP (1995). Negative stereotypes still plague older workers on the job. *AARP Bulletin, 36,* April, p. 3.

ADAA (Anxiety Disorders Association of America). (2003). *Statistics and facts about anxiety disorders.* Silver Spring, MD: Author.

Adams, J. S. (1965). Inequity in social exchange. In L. Berkowitz (Ed.), *Advances in experimental social psychology.* New York: Academic Press.

Adler, N., & Matthews, K. (1994). Health psychology: Why do some people get sick and some stay well? *Annual Review of Psychology, 45,* 229–259.

Aiello, R. R., & Aiello, T. D. (1974). The development of personal space: Proxemic behavior of children 6 through 16. *Human Ecology, 2,* 177–189.

Aiken, L. R. (1984). *Psychological testing and assessment* (4th ed.). Boston: Allyn & Bacon.

Ainsworth, M. D. S. (1989). Attachments beyond infancy. *American Psychologist, 44,* 709–716.

Aleman, A., Kahn, R. S., & Selton, J. (2003). Sex differences in the risk for schizophrenia. *Archives of General Psychiatry, 60,* 565–571.

Altman, I. (1975). *The environment and social behavior.* Monterey, CA: Brooks/Cole.

American Psychiatric Association. (2000). *Diagnostic and statistical manual of mental disorders, Fourth Edition Text Revision (DSM-IV-TR).* Washington: American Psychiatric Association.

Anderson, C. A., & Bushman, B. J. (2002). Human aggression. *Annual Review of Psychology, 53,* 27–51.

Anshel, M. H. (1996). Effect of chronic aerobic exercise and progressive relaxation on motor performance and affect following acute stress. *Behavioral Medicine, 21,* 186–196.

Armas, G. C. (2003). Worldwide population aging. In H. Cox (Ed.). *Annual editions: Aging.* Guilford, CT: McGraw-Hill.

Asch, S. E. (1951). The effects of group pressure upon the modification and distortion of judgment. In H. Guetzkow (Ed.), *Groups, leadership, and men.* Pittsburgh: Carnegie Press.

Asch, S. E. (1956). Studies of independence and conformity: I. A minority of one against a unanimous majority. *Psychological Monographs: General and Applied, 70* (Whole No. 416), 1–7.

B

Bachorowski, J., & Owren, M. J. (1995). Vocal expression of emotion: Acoustic properties of speech are associated with emotional intensity and context. *Psychological Science, 6,* 219–224.

Baddeley, A. (1998). *Human memory: Theory and practice* (Rev. ed.). Boston: Allyn & Bacon.

Baddeley, A. D. (2001). Is working memory still working? *American Psychologist, 56,* 851–864.

Baer, J. S., Sampson, P. D., Barr, H. M., Conner, P. D., & Streissguth, A. P. (2003). A 21-year longitudinal analysis of the effects of prenatal alcohol exposure on young adult drinking. *Archives of General Psychiatry, 60,* 377-385.

Balleyguier, G., & Melhuish, E. C. (1996). The relationship between infant day care and socio-emotional development with French children. *European Journal of Psychology of Education, 11,* 193–199.

Bandura, A. (1976). Modeling theory: Some traditions, trends and disputes. In W. S. Sahakian (Ed.), *Learning: Systems, models, and theories.* Skokie, IL: Rand McNally.

Bandura, A., Ross, D., & Ross, S. A. (1963). Imitation of film-mediated aggressive models. *Journal of Abnormal and Social Psychology, 66,* 3–11.

Bandura, A. (1999). Social cognitive theory of personality. In D. Cervone, & Y. Shoda, (Eds.). *The coherence of personality: Social-cognitive bases of consistency, variability, and organization.* New York: Guilford.

Bandura, A. (2001a). Social cognitive theory: An agentic perspective. *Annual Review of Psychology, 52,* 1–26.

Bandura, A. (2001b). On shaping one's future: The primacy of human agency. Paper presented at the annual meeting of The American Psychological Society, Toronto, June 14, 2001.

Barnett, R. C., & Hyde, J. S. (2001). Women, men, work, and family: An expansionist theory. *American Psychologist, 56,* 781–796.

Bassi, L. J., & Van Buren, M. E. (1999). *The 1999 ASTD state of the industry report.* Alexandria, VA: The American Society for Training and Development.

Basso, K. (1970). To give up words: Silence in Western Apache culture. *Southwestern Journal of Anthropology, 26,* 213–230.

Baum, A., & Grunberg, N. E. (1991). Gender, stress, and health. *Health Psychology, 10,* 80–85.

Bee, H. (1992). *The developing child* (6th. ed.). New York: HarperCollins.

Bee, H. (1996). *The journey of adulthood* (3rd ed.). Upper Saddle River, NJ: Prentice Hall.

Berkowitz, H. (1994). U. S. Firms Trip Over Their Tongues in Wooing the World. *The Journal Gazette,* June 21, Fort Wayne, IN.

Blair, E. (2003). Culture and leadership: Seven key points for improved safety performance. *Professional Safety, 48*(6), 18–22.

Bordens, K. S., & Abbott, B. B. (2002). *Research design and methods: A process approach* (5th ed.). Mountain View, CA: Mayfield Publishing Company.

Bordens, K. S., & Horowitz, I. A. (2002). *Social psychology* (2nd ed.). Mahwah, NJ: Lawrence Erlbaum Associates.

Bower, G. H. (1972). Mental imagery and associative learning. In L. W. Gregg (Ed.), *Cognition in learning and memory.* New York: Wiley.

Bower, G. H., & Clark, M. C. (1969). Narrative stories as mediators for serial learning. *Psychonomic Science, 14,* 181–182.

Bradley, R. H., & Corwyn, R. F. (2002). Socioeconomic status and child development. *Annual Review of Psychology, 53,* 371–399.

Brislin, R. W. (1993). *Understanding culture's influence on behavior.* Fort Worth, TX: Harcourt Brace.

Brod, M., Stewart, A. L., Sands, L., & Walton, P. (1999). Conceptualization and measurement of quality of life in dementia: The Dementia Quality of Life Instrument (DQoL). *The Gerontologist, 39,* 25–35.

Burchinal, M. R., Roberts, J. E., Riggins, R., Jr., Zisel, S. A., Neebe, E., & Bryant, D. (2000). Relating quality of center-based care to early cognitive and language development longitudinally. *Child Development, 71,* 339–357.

Burger, J. M. (2000). *Personality* (5th ed.). Belmont, CA: Wadsworth.

Burgoon, J. K., & Bacue, A. E. (2003). Nonverbal communication skills. In J. O. Greene & B. R. Burleson (Eds.). *Handbook of communication and social interaction skills.* Mahwah, NJ: Lawrence Erlbaum Associates (pp. 179-220).

Burke, R. J., & Greenglass, E. R. (2001). Hospital restructuring, work-family conflict and psychological burnout among nursing staff. *Community, Work, and Family, 4,* 49–62.

Burn, S. M. (2004). *Groups: Theory and practice.* Belmont, CS: Wadsworth.

Bushman, B. J., & Anderson, C. A. (2001). Media violence and the American public: Scientific facts versus media misinformation. *American Psychologist, 56,* 477–489.

Buss, D. M. (1985). Human mate selection. *American Scientist, 73,* 47-51.

Buss, D. M., Abbott, M., Angleitner, A., Asherian, A., Biaggio, A., Blanco-Villasenor, A., et al. (1990). International preferences in mate selection: A study of 37 cultures. *Journal of Cross-Cultural Psychology, 21,* 5–47.

C

Campion, M. A., Palmer, D. K., & Campion, J. E. (1997). A review of structure in the selection interview. *Personnel Psychology, 50,* 655–702.

Cannon, W. B. (1932). *The wisdom of the body.* New York: Norton.

Carver, C. S. & Scheier, M. F. (1999). Optimism. In C. R. Snyder (Ed.), *Coping: The psychology of what works.* New York: Oxford University Press. (pp. 182–204).

Caspi, A., Sugden, K., Moffitt, T. E., Taylor, A., Craig, I. W., et al. (2003). Influence of life stress on depression: Moderation by a polymorphism in the 5-HTT gene. *Science, 301,* 291–293.

Cattell, R. B. (1973). *Personality and mood by questionnaire.* San Francisco: Jossey-Bass.

Cattell, R. B. (1979). *The structure of personality in its environment.* New York: Springer.

Cavanaugh, J. C., & Blanchard-Fields, F. (2002). *Adult development and aging.* Belmont, CA: Wadsworth.

The Conference Board (2003). *Special consumer survey report: Job satisfaction—September 2003.* Washington, DC: The Conference Board, Inc.

Cooper, D. (1998). *Improving safety culture.* Chichester, UK: Wiley.

Council, J. R. (1993). Context effects in personality research. *Current Directions in Psychological Science, 2,* 3–34.

Coyne, J. C., & Downey, G. (1991). Social factors and psychopathology: Stress, social support, and coping processes. *Annual Review of Psychology, 42,* 401–425.

Cramer, P. (2000). Defense mechanisms in psychology today: Further processes for adaptation. *American Psychologist, 55,* 637–646.

Cushner, K. (1990). Cross-cultural psychology and the formal classroom. In R. W. Brislin (Ed.), *Applied cross-cultural psychology.* Newbury Park, CA: Sage.

D

Darley, J. M., & Schultz, T. R. (1990). Moral rules: Their content and acquisition. *Annual Review of Psychology, 41,* 525–556.

Davidson, R. J., Pizzagalli, D., Nitschke, J. B., & Putnam, K. (2002). Depression: Perspectives from affective neuroscience. *Annual Review of Psychology, 53,* 545–574.

deBoer, C. (1978). The polls: Attitudes toward work. *Public Opinion Quarterly, 42,* 414–423.

DeLongis, A., Folkman, S., & Lazarus, R. S. (1988). The impact of daily stress on health and mood: Psychological and social resources as mediators. *Journal of Personality and Social Psychology, 54,* 486–495.

Dick, D. M., Rose, R. J., Viken, R. J., & Kaprio, J. (2000). Pubertal timing and substance use between and within families across late adolescence. *Developmental Psychology, 36,* 180–189.

Digman, J. M. (1990). Personality structure: Emergence of the five-factor model. *Annual Review of Psychology, 41,* 417–440.

Dillard, J. P. & Marshall, L. (2003). Persuasion as social skill. In J. O. Greene & B. R. Burleson (Eds.). *Handbook of Communication and Social Interaction Skills.* Mahwah, NJ: Lawrence Erlbaum Associates (pp. 479-513).

Dollard, J. Doob, L., Miller, N., Mowrer, O. H., & Sears, R. R. (1939). *Frustration and aggression.* New Haven: Yale University Press.

Donnerstein, E. (2005). Media violence and children: What do we know, what do we do? Paper presented at the 27th National Institute on the Teaching of Psychology, St. Petersburg Beach, FL, January 2-5.

E

Ebstein, R. P., Novick, O., Umansky, R., Priel, B., et al. (1996). Dopamine D4 Receptor (D4DR) Exon III polymorphism associated with the human personality trait of novelty seeking. *Nature Genetics, 12,* 78–80.

Eccles, J. S., & Wigfield, A. (2002). Motivational beliefs, values, and goals. *Annual Review of Psychology, 53,* 109–132.

Ekman, P. (1973). Cross-cultural studies in facial expression. In P. Ekman (Ed.), *Darwin and facial expressions: A century of research in review.* New York: Academic Press.

Ekman, P. (1992). Facial expression and emotion: New findings, new questions. *Psychological Science, 3,* 34–38.

Ekman, P. (1993). Facial expression and emotion. *American Psychologist, 48,* 384–392.

Ekman, P., Levenson, R. W., & Friesen, W. V. (1983). Autonomic nervous system activity distinguishes among emotions. *Science, 221,* 1208–1210.

Elfenbein, H. A., & Ambady, N. (2002). On the universality of cultural specificity of emotional recognition. *Psychological Bulletin, 128,* 203–235.

Elovainio, M., Kivimaeki, M., Sreen, M., & Kalliomaeki-Levanto, T. (2000). Organizational and individual factors affecting mental health and job satisfaction. *Journal of Occupational Health Psychology, 5,* 269–277.

Endler, N. S., Cox, B. J., Parker, J. D. A., & Bagby, R. M. (1992). Self-reports of depression and state-trait-anxiety: Evidence for differential assessment. *Journal of Personality and Social Psychology, 63,* 832–838.

Erikson, E. H. (1963). *Childhood and society.* New York: Norton.

Erikson, E. H. (1968). *Identity: Youth and crisis.* New York: Norton.

Evans, G. W., & Howard, R. B. (1973). Personal space. *Psychological Bulletin, 80,* 334–344.

F

Festinger, L. (1957). *A theory of cognitive dissonance.* Stanford, CA: Stanford University Press.

Foa, E. B. (1995). How do treatments for obsessive-compulsive disorder compare? *The Harvard Mental Health Letter, 12,* 8.

Folkman, S. & Moskowitz, J. T. (2000). Stress, positive emotion, and coping. *Current Directions in Psychological Science, 9,* 115–118.

Ford-Gilboe, M., & Cohen, J. A. (2000). Hardiness: A model of commitment, challenge, and control. In V. R. Rice (Ed.). *Handbook of stress, coping, and health.* Thousand Oaks, CA: Sage.

Forsyth, D. (1990). *Group dynamics* (2nd ed.). Pacific Grove, CA: Brooks/Cole.

Fortner, B. V., & Neimeyer, R. A. (1999). Death anxiety in older adults: A quantitative review. *Death Studies, 23,* 387–411.

Fraley, R. C. (2002). Attachment stability from infancy to adulthood: Meta-analysis and dynamic modeling of developmental mechanisms. *Personality and Social Psychology Review, 6,* 123–151.

Freud, A. (1958). *Adolescence: Psychoanalytic study of the child.* New York: Academic Press.

Freud, S. (1933). *New introductory lectures on psychoanalysis: Standard edition.* New York: Norton.

Friedman, S., & Schonberg, S. K. (1996). Consensus statements. *Pediatrics, 98,* 853.

Funder, D. C. (2001). Personality. *Annual Review of Psychology, 52,* 197–221.

G

Gabbard, G. O., Gunderson, J. G., & Fonagy, P. (2002). The place of psychoanalytic treatments within psychiatry. *Archives of General Psychiatry, 59,* 505–510.

Galanter, E. (1962). Contemporary psychophysics. In R. Brown et al. (Eds.), *New directions in psychology.* New York: Holt, Rinehart & Winston.

Gallup Organization. (1995). *Disciplining children in America: A Gallup poll report.* Princeton, NJ: Author.

Ge, X., Conger, R. D., & Elder, G. H., Jr. (1996). Coming of age too early: Pubertal influences on girls' vulnerability to psychological distress. *Child Development, 67,* 3386–4000.

Gershoff, E. T. (2002). Parental corporal punishment and associated child behaviors and experiences: A meta-analytic and theoretical review. *Psychological Bulletin, 128,* 539–579.

Gerow, J. R. & Gerow, N. S. (2004). *College Decisions: A Practical Guide to Success in College,* Cincinnati: Atomic Dog (pp. 46–47).

Gilligan, C. (1982). *In a different voice.* Cambridge, MA: Harvard University Press.

Gilligan, C. (1993). Adolescent development reconsidered. In A. Garrod (Ed.). *Approaches to moral development: New research and emerging themes.* New York: Teachers College Press.

Giron, S. T., Wang, H. X., Bernsten, C., Thorslund, M., Winblad, B, & Fastbom, J. (2001). The appropriateness of drug use in an older nondemented and demented population. *Journal of the American Geriatrics Society, 49,* 277–283.

Glenn, N. D. (1990). Quantitative research on marital quality in the 1980s: A critical review. *Journal of Marriage and the Family, 52,* 818–831.

Goldstein, I. L. (1991). *Training and development in organizations.* San Francisco: Jossey-Bass.

Goodman, G. S., Ghetti, S., Quas, J. A., Edelstein, R. S., Alexander, K. W., Redlich, A. D., Cordon, I. M., & Jones, D. P. H. (2003). A prospective study of memory for child sexual abuse: New findings relevant to the repressed-memory controversy. *Psychological Science, 14,* 113–118.

Gouran, D. S. (2003). Communication skills for group decision making. In J. O. Greene & B. R. Burleson (Eds.). *Handbook of Communication and Social Interaction Skills.* Mahwah, NJ: Lawrence Erlbaum Associates (pp. 835-870).

Grady, C. L., McIntosh, A. R., Horowitz, B., Maisog, J. M., Ungerleider, L. G., Mentis, M. J., Pietrini, P., Schapiro, M. B., & Haxby, J. V. (1995). Age-related reductions in human recognition memory due to impaired encoding. *Science, 269,* 218–221.

Gray-Little, B., & Hafdahl, A. R. (2000). Factors influencing racial comparisons of self-esteem: A quantitative review. *Psychological Bulletin, 126,* 26–54.

Graziano, A. M., & Raulin, M. L. (1993). *Research methods: A process of inquiry.* New York: HarperCollins.

Grych, J. H., & Clark, R. (1999). Maternal employment and development of the father-infant relationship in the first year. *Developmental Psychology, 35,* 893–903.

Guilford, J. P. (1959a). *Personality.* New York: McGraw-Hill.

H

Haight, J. M. (2003). Human error and the challenge of an aging workforce: Considerations for improving workplace safety. *Professional Safety, 48*(12), 18–24.

Hall, E. T. (1966). *The hidden dimension.* Garden City, NY: Doubleday.

Hall, G. S. (1904). *Adolescence.* Englewood Cliffs, NJ: Prentice-Hall.

Hall, J. A. (1978). Gender effects in decoding nonverbal cues. *Psychological Bulletin, 85,* 845–857.

Harris, T. C. (2003). An instructor's guide for introducing industrial-organizational psychology. *Society for Industrial and Organizational Psychology, Inc.,* from www.siop.org

Hayduk, L. A. (1983). Personal space: Where we now stand. *Psychological Bulletin, 94,* 293–335.

Hays, K. F. (1995). Putting sports psychology into (your) practice. *Professional Psychology: Research and Practice, 26,* 33–40.

Hebb, D. O. (1955). Drives and the C.N.S. (conceptual nervous system). *Psychological Review, 62,* 243–254.

Heshka, S., & Nelson, Y. (1972). Interpersonal speaking distance as a function of age, sex, and relationship. *Sociometry, 35,* 491–498.

Hill, W. F. (1985). *Learning: A survey of psychological interpretations* (4th ed.). New York: HarperCollins.

Holmes, D.S. (2001). *Abnormal psychology* (4th ed.). Boston: Allyn & Bacon.

Holmes, T. S., & Holmes, T. H. (1970). Short-term intrusions into the life-style routine. *Journal of Psychosomatic Research, 14,* 121–132.

Hough, L. M., & Oswald, F. L. (2000). Personnel selection. *Annual Review of Psychology, 51,* 631–664.

Howe, M. L. (2003). Memories from the cradle. *Current Directions in Psychological Science, 12,* 62–65.

Hull, C. L. (1943). *Principles of behavior.* Englewood Cliffs, NJ: Prentice-Hall.

I

Izard, C. E. (1993). Four systems for emotional activation: Cognitive and metacognitive processes. *Psychological Review, 100,* 68–90.

J

Jaffe, M. L. (1998). *Adolescence.* New York: John Wiley & Sons.

James, W. (1890). *Principles of psychology.* New York: Holt, Rinehart & Winston.

Janis, I. L. (1972). *Victims of groupthink.* Boston: Houghton Mifflin.

John, O. P., & Strivastava, S. (1999). The big five trait taxonomy: History, measurement and theoretical perspectives. In L. A. Pervin & O. P. John (Eds.). *Handbook of personality* (2nd ed.). New York: Guilford.

Joint statement on the impact of entertainment violence on children: Congressional Public Health Summit. (2000, July 26). Retrieved July 1, 2003 from http://www.senate.gov/~brownback/violence1.pdf.

Jones, M. C. (1924). A laboratory study of fear: The case of Peter. *Pedagogical Seminary, 31,* 308–315.

K

Kalish, R. A. (1985). The social context of death and dying. In R. H. Binstock & E. Shanas (Eds.), *Handbook of aging and the social sciences* (2nd ed.). New York: Van Nostrand-Reinhold.

Katerndahl, D. A., & Realini, J. P. (1995). Where do panic attack sufferers seek care? *Journal of Family Practice, 40,* 237–243.

Kaya, N., & Weber, M. J. (2003). Cross-cultural differences in the perception of crowding and privacy regulation: American and Turkish students. *Journal of Environmental Psychology, 23,* 301–309.

Kazdin, A. E., & Benjet, C. (2003). Spanking children: Evidence and issues. *Current Directions in Psychological Science, 12,* 99–103.

Kelley, H. H. (1992). Common-sense psychology and scientific psychology. *Annual Review of Psychology, 43,* 1–24.

Kelly, G. A. (1955). *The psychology of personal constructs: A theory of personality* (Vols. 1 & 2). New York: Norton.

Kelly, J. R., Jackson, J. W., & Huston-Comeaux, S. L. (1997). The effects of time pressure and task differences on influence modes and accuracy in decision-making groups. *Personality and Social Psychology Bulletin, 23,* 10–22.

Kessler, R. C., Berglund, P., Demler, O., Jin, R., Koretz, D., et al. (2003). The epidemiology of major depressive disorder: Results from the National Comorbidity Survey Replication (NCS-R). *Journal of the American Medical Association, 289,* 3095–3105.

Kientzle, M. J. (1946). Properties of learning curves under varied distributions of practice. *Journal of Experimental Psychology, 36,* 187–211.

Kim, J. E., & Moen, P. (2001). Is retirement good or bad for subjective well-being? *Current Directions in Psychological Science, 10,* 83–86.

Kim, K., & Smith, P. K. (1998). Childhood stress, behavioral symptoms and mother-daughter pubertal development. *Journal of Adolescence, 21,* 231–240.

Kitayama, S., Markus, H. R., Matsumoto, H., & Norasakkunkit, V. (1997). Individual and collective processes in the construction of the self: Self-enhancement in the United States and self-criticism in Japan. *Journal of Personality and Social Psychology, 72,* 1245–1267.

Kobasa, S. C. (1979). Stressful life events, personality, and health: An inquiry into hardiness. *Journal of Personality and Social Psychology, 37,* 1–11.

Kobasa, S. C. (1987). Stress responses and personality. In R. C. Barnette, L. Beiner, & G. K. Baruch (Eds.), *Gender and stress.* New York: Free Press.

Kohlberg, L. (1963). Moral development and identification. In H. W. Stevenson (Ed.), *Child psychology.* Chicago: University of Chicago Press.

Kohlberg, L. (1985). *The psychology of moral development.* New York: HarperCollins.

Krebs, D. L. (2000). The evolution of moral dispositions in the human species. *Annals of the New York Academy of Sciences, 907,* 132–148.

Kübler-Ross, E. (1969). *On death and dying.* New York: Macmillan.

Kübler-Ross, E. (1981). *Living with death and dying.* New York: Macmillan.

L

Landy, F. J. (1989). *Psychology of work behavior* (2nd ed.). Homewood, IL: Dorsey Press.

Lavond, D. G., Kim, J. J., & Thompson, R. F. (1993). Mammalian brain substrates of aversive classical conditioning. *Annual Review of Psychology, 44,* 317–342.

Lazarus, R. S. (1981). Little hassles can be hazardous to your health. *Psychology Today, 15,* 58–62.

Lazarus, R. S. (1991). Cognition and motivation in emotion. *American Psychologist, 46,* 352–367.

Lazarus, R. S. (1993). From psychological stress to the emotions: A history of changing outlooks. *Annual Review of Psychology, 44,* 1–21.

Lazarus, R. S. (2000). Toward better research on stress and coping. *American Psychologist, 55,* 665–673.

Lazarus, R. S., & Folkman, S. (1984). *Stress, appraisal, and coping.* New York: Springer.

LeDoux, J. E. (1995). Emotion: Clues from the brain. *Annual Review of Psychology, 46,* 209–235.

Leger, D. W. (1992). *Biological foundations of behavior: An integrative approach.* New York: HarperCollins.

Leigh, J. P., Markowitz, S. B., Fahs, M., Shin, C., & Landrigan, P. J. (1997). Occupational injury and illness in the United States: Estimates of costs, morbidity, and mortality. *Archives of Internal Medicine, 157,* 1557–1568.

Leming, M. R., & Dickinson, G. E. (2002). *Understanding dying, death, and bereavement* (5th ed.). Fort Worth, TX: Harcourt College Publishers.

Lempers, J. D., Flavell, E. R., & Flavell, J. H. (1977). The development in very young children of tactile knowledge concerning visual perception. *Genetic Psychology Monographs, 95,* 3–53.

Levine, J. M., & Moreland, R. L. (1990). Progress in small group research. *Annual Review of Psychology, 41,* 585–634.

Levinson, D. J. (1986). A conception of adult development. *American Psychologist, 41,* 3–13.

Lieberman, J., Jody, D., Geisler, S., Alvir, J., Loebel, A., et al. (1993). Time course and biological correlates of treatment response in first-episode schizophrenia. *Archives of General Psychiatry, 50,* 369–376.

Light, K. C. (1997). Stress in employed women: A woman's work is never done if she's a working mom. *Psychosomatic Medicine, 59,* 360–361.

Locke, E. A. (1976). The nature and causes of job satisfaction. In M. D. Dunnette (Ed.), *Handbook of industrial and organizational psychology.* Skokie, IL: Rand McNally.

Loftus, E. (2003). Illusions of memory. Presentation at The 25th Annual National Institute on the Teaching of Psychology. St. Petersburg Beach, FL, January 3.

Loftus, E. F. (1993a). The reality of repressed memories. *American Psychologist, 48,* 518–537.

Loftus, E. F. (1993b). Therapeutic memories of early childhood abuse: Fact or fiction. Paper presented at the Annual Meeting of the American Psychological Association, Toronto.

Loftus, E. F. (1997). Researchers are showing how suggestion and imagination can create memories of events that did not actually occur. *Scientific American,* (September), 71–75.

Lonner, W. J. (1980). The search for psychological universals. In H. C. Triandis & W. W. Lambert (Eds.), *Handbook of cross-cultural psychology* (Vol. I). Boston: Allyn & Bacon.

Lorenz, K. (1969). *On aggression.* New York: Bantam Books.

Lucas, R. E., & Fujita, F. (2000). Factors influencing the relation between extroversion and pleasant affect. *Journal of Personality and Social Psychology, 79,* 1039–1056.

M

Marcia, J. E. (1980). Identity in adolescence. In J. H. Flavell & E. K. Markman (Eds.). *Handbook of adolescent psychology,* New York: John Wiley.

Marengo, J. T., & Harrow, M. (1987). Schizophrenic thought disorder at follow-up. *Archives of General Psychiatry, 44,* 651–659.

Maslach, C. (2003). Job burnout: New directions in research and intervention. *Current Directions in Psychological Science, 12,* 189–192.

Maslow, A. H. (1943). A theory of human motivation. *Psychological Review, 50,* 370–396.

Maslow, A. H. (1970). *Motivation and personality.* (2nd ed.). New York: HarperCollins.

Matthews, K. A., Shumaker, S. A., Bowen, D. J., Langer, R. D., et al., (1997). Women's Health Initiative: Why now? What is it? What's new? *American Psychologist, 52,* 101–116.

McAdams, D. P. (1989). *Intimacy.* New York: Doubleday.

McClelland, D. C. (1985). *Human motivation.* Glenview, IL: Scott, Foresman.

McClelland, D. C., Atkinson, J. W., Clark, R. A., & Lowell, E. L. (1953). *The achievement motive.* Englewood Cliffs, NJ: Prentice-Hall.

McClure, J. (1998). Discounting causes of behavior: Are two reasons better than one? *Journal of Personality and Social Psychology, 74,* 7–20.

McCrae, R. R., & Costa, P. T., Jr. (1990). *Personality in adulthood.* New York: Guilford.

McCrae, R. R., & Costa, P. T. (1997). Personality trait structure as a human universal. *American Psychologist, 52(5),* 509–516.

McCrae, R. R., & Costa, P. T., Jr. (1999). A five-factor theory of personality. In L. A. Pervin & O. P. John (Eds.). *Handbook of personality* (2nd ed.). New York: Guilford.

McDougall, W. (1908). *An introduction to social psychology.* London: Methuen.

McNally, R. J. (2003a). *Remembering trauma.* Cambridge, MA: Belknap Press/ Harvard University Press.

McNally, R. J. (2003b). Progress and controversy in the study of posttraumatic stress disorder. *Annual Review of Psychology, 54,* 229–252.

McNally, R. J. (2003c). Recovering memories of trauma: A view from the laboratory. *Current Directions in Psychological Science, 12,* 32–35.

Meichenbaum, D. (1977). *Cognitive-behavior modification: An integrative approach.* New York: Plenum.

Mick, E., Biederman, J., Faraone, S. V., Sayer, J., & Kleinman, S. (2002). Case-control study of attention-deficit hyperactivity disorder and maternal smoking, alcohol use, and drug use during pregnancy. *Journal of the American Academy of Child and Adolescent Psychiatry, 41,* 378–385.

Milgram, S. (1963). Behavioral studies of obedience. *Journal of Abnormal and Social Psychology, 67,* 371–378.

Milgram, S. (1965). Some conditions of obedience and disobedience to authority. *Human Relations, 18,* 57–76.

Milgram, S. (1974). *Obedience to authority.* New York: Harper-Collins.

Miller, J. G. (1984). Culture and the development of everyday social explanation. *Journal of Personality and Social Psychology, 46,* 961–978.

Mischel, W. (1968). *Personality and assessment.* New York: Wiley.

Mischel, W. (1973). Toward a cognitive social learning re-conceptualization of personality. *Psychological Review, 80,* 252–283.

Mischel, W. (1999). Personality coherence and dispositions in a cognitive-affective personality system (CAPS) approach. In D. Cervone, & Y. Shoda (Eds.). *The coherence of personality: Social-cognitive bases of consistency, variability, and organization.* New York: Guilford.

Mischel, W., Shoda, Y., & Mendoza-Denton, R. (2002). Situation-behavior profiles as a locus of consistency in personality. *Current Directions in Psychological Science, 11,* 50–54.

Mitchell, M. & Jolley, J. (2001). *Research Design Explained* (4th ed.). Belmont, CA: Thomson/Wadsworth.

Moen, P., Kim, J. E., & Hofmeister, H. (2001). Couples' work/retirement transitions, gender, and marital status. *Social Psychology Quarterly, 64,* 55–71.

Montada, L., & Lerner, M. (Eds.). (1998). *Responses to victimizations and belief in a just world.* New York: Plenum.

Muchinsky, P. M. (2000). *Psychology applied to work* (6th ed.). Belmont, CA: Wadsworth.

Muchinsky, P. M., & Tuttle, M. L. (1979). Employee turnover: An empirical and methodological assessment. *Journal of Vocational Behavior, 14,* 43–77.

Murray, H. A. (1938). *Explorations in personality.* New York: Oxford University Press.

N

Neubauer, P. J. (1992). The impact of stress, hardiness, home and work environment on job satisfaction, illness, and absenteeism in critical care nurses. *Medical Psychotherapy, 5,* 109–122.

Neugarten, B. L., & Neugarten, D. A. (1986). Changing meanings of age in the aging society. In A. Piter & L. Bronte (Eds.), *Our aging society: Paradox and promise.* New York: Norton.

NICHD (National Institute on Child Health and Human Development). (2002). Child-care structure → process → outcome: Direct and indirect effects of child-care quality on young children's development. *Psychological Science, 13,* 199–206.

Nickerson, R. S., & Adams, M. J. (1979). Long-term memory for a common object. *Cognitive Psychology, 11,* 287–307.

Nolen-Hoeksema, S. (2001). Gender differences in depression. *Current Directions in Psychological Sciences, 10,* 173–176.

Norenzayan, A., & Nisbett, R. E. (2000). Culture and causal cognition. *Current Directions in Psychological Science, 9,* 132–135.

O

Ortony, A., & Turner, T. J. (1990). What's basic about basic emotions? *Psychological Review, 97,* 315–331.

P

Paivio, A. (1971). *Imagery and verbal processes.* New York: Holt, Rinehart & Winston.

Paivio, A. (1986). *Mental representations: A dual coding approach.* New York: Oxford University Press.

Pandey, J. (1990). The environment, culture, and behavior. In R. W. Brislin (Ed.), *Applied cross-cultural psychology.* Newbury Park, CA: Sage.

Parke, R. D., & Tinsley, B. J. (1987). Family interaction in infancy. In J. D. Osofsky (Ed.), *Handbook of infant development* (2nd ed.). New York: Wiley.

Paunonen, S. V., & Jackson, D. N. (2000). What is beyond the big five? Plenty! *Journal of Personality, 68,* 821–835.

Pearce, J. M., & Bouton, M. E. (2001). Theories of associative learning in animals. *Annual Review of Psychology, 52,* 111–139.

Peplau, L. A., & Perlman, D. (1982). Perspectives on loneliness. In L. A. Peplau & D. Perlman (Eds.), *Loneliness: A sourcebook of current theory, research and therapy.* New York: John Wiley.

Piaget, J. (1932/1948). *The moral judgment of the child.* New York: Free Press.

Piotrowski, C., Belter, R. W., & Keller, J. W. (1998). The impact on "managed care" on the practice of psychological testing: Preliminary findings. *Journal of Personality Assessment, 70,* 441–447.

Plutchik, R. (1980a). *Emotion: A psychoevolutionary synthesis.* New York: HarperCollins.

Plutchik, R. (1994). *The psychology and biology of emotion.* New York: HarperCollins.

Port, C. L., Engdahl, B., & Frazier, P. (2001). A longitudinal and retrospective study of PTSD among older prisoners of war. *American Journal of Psychiatry, 158,* 1474–1479.

Powers, S. I., Hauser, S. T., & Kilner, L. A. (1989). Adolescent mental health. *American Psychologist, 44,* 200–208.

R

Rahe, R. H., & Arthur, R. J. (1978). Life changes and illness reports. In K. E. Gunderson & R. H. Rahe (Eds.), *Life stress and illness.* Springfield, IL: Thomas.

Reddy, M. J. (1979). The conduit metaphor: A case of frame conflict in our language about language. In A. Ortony (Ed.). *Metaphor and thought.* Cambridge, UK: Cambridge University Press.

Rensink, R. A. (2002). Change detection. *Annual Review of Psychology, 53,* 245–277.

Rest, J. R. (1983). Morality. In J. Flavell & E. Markman (Eds.), *Handbook of child development: Cognitive development.* New York: Wiley.

Reynolds, R., & Brannick, M. T. (2001). Is job analysis doing the job? Extending job analysis with cognitive task analysis. *The Industrial-Organizational Psychologist, 39,* from www.siop.org/tip/backissues

Rice, P. L. (1999). *Stress and health* (3rd ed.). Pacific Grove, CA: Brooks/Cole.

Riggio, R. E. (2002). *Introduction to industrial organizational psychology* (4th ed.). New York: Prentice-Hall.

Rochat, F., Maggioni, O., & Modgiliani, A. (2000). The dynamics of obeying and opposing authority: A mathematical model In T. Blass (Ed.). *Obedience to authority: Current perspectives on the Milgram paradigm.* Mahwah, NJ: Lawrence Erlbaum.

Roche, A. F., & Davila, G. H. (1972). Late adolescent growth in stature. *Pediatrics, 50,* 874–880.

Rogers, C. R. (1959). A theory of therapy, personality, and interpersonal relationships as developed in the client-centered framework. In S. Koch (Ed.), *Psychology: A study of science.* New York: McGraw Hill.

Rorschach, H. (1921). *Psychodiagnostics.* Bern: Huber.

Ross, G., Kagan, J., Zelazo, P., & Kotelchuck, M. (1975). Separation protest in infants in home and laboratory. *Developmental Psychology, 11,* 256–257.

Rowe, J. W., & Kahn, R. L. (1987). Human aging: Usual and successful. *Science, 237,* 143–149.

Russell, J. A. (2003). Core affect and the psychological construction of emotion. *Psychological Review, 110,* 145-172.

Russell, J. A., Bachorowski, J., & Fernández-Dols, J. (2003). Facial and vocal expressions of emotion. *Annual Review of Psychology, 54,* 329–349.

Ryan, A. M. (2003). Defining ourselves: I-O psychology's identity quest. *The Industrial-Organizational Psychologist, 41,* 21–33.

S

Salas, E., & Cannon-Bowers, J. A. (2001). The science of training: A decade of progress. *Annual Review of Psychology, 52,* 471–499.

Samuelson, F. J. B. (1980). Watson's Little Albert, Cyril Burt's twins, and the need for a critical science. *American Psychologist, 35,* 619–625.

Sarkus, D. J. (2003). Safety and psychology: Where do we go from here? *Professional Safety, 48*(1), 18–25

Schacter, D. L., Norman, K. A., & Koutstaal, W. (1998). The cognitive neuroscience of constructive memory. *Annual Review of Psychology, 48,* 289–318.

Scheier, M. F., & Carver, C. S. (1993). On the power of positive thinking: The benefits of being optimistic. *Current Directions in Psychological Science, 2,* 26–30.

Schultz, D. P., & Schultz, S. E. (1998). *Psychology and work today: An introduction to industrial and organizational psychology* (7th ed.). Belmont, CA: Wadsworth.

Shaffer, D. (1999). *Developmental psychology: Childhood and adolescence* (5th ed.). Pacific Grove, CA: Brooks/Cole.

Shaffer, D. R. (2000). *Social and personality development* (4th ed.). Belmont, CA: Wadsworth.

Shaffer, D. R. (2002). *Developmental psychology: Childhood & Adolescence* (6th ed.). Belmont, CA: Wadsworth.

Shannon, C. E. & Weaver, W. (1949). *A Mathematical Model of Communication.* Urbana, IL: University of Illinois Press.

Sheridan, C. L., & Perkins, A. (1992). Cross-validation of an inventory of stressors for teenagers. *Medical Psychotherapy, 5,* 103–108.

Silver, E., Cirincione, C., & Steadman, H. J. (1994). Demythologizing inaccurate perceptions of the insanity defense. *Law and Human Behavior, 18,* 63–70.

Sinai, M. J., Ooi, T. L., & He, Z, J. (1998). Terrain influences the accurate judgment of distance. *Nature, 395,* 497–500.

Skinner, B. F. (1983). Intellectual self-management in old age. *American Psychologist, 38,* 239–244.

Skinner, B. F. (1989). The origins of cognitive thought. *American Psychologist, 44,* 13–18.

Smetna, J. G., & Gaines, C. (1999). Adolescent-parent conflict in middle-class African-American families. *Child Development, 70,* 1447–1463.

Smith, P. C. (1976). Behavior, results, and organizational effectiveness: The problem of criteria. In M. D. Dunnette (Ed.), *Handbook of industrial and organizational psychology.* Skokie, IL: Rand McNally.

Smith, S. (2003). The top 10 ways to improve safety management. *Occupational Hazards.* From www.occupationalhazards.com

Snarey, J. (1987). A question of morality. *Psychology Today, 21,* 6–8.

Somerfield, M. R. & McCrae, R. R. (2000). Stress and coping research: Methodological challenges, theoretical advances, and clinical applications. *American Psychologist, 55,* 620–625.

Sommer, R. (1969). *Personal space: The behavioral basis of designs.* Englewood Cliffs, NJ: Prentice-Hall.

Staddon, J. E. R., & Cerutti, D. Y. (2003). Operant conditioning. *Annual Review of Psychology, 54,* 115–144.

Stein, J. A., Newcomb, M. D., & Bentler, P. M. (1990). The relative influence of vocational behavior and family involvement on self-esteem: Longitudinal analyses of young adult women and men. *Journal of Vocational Behavior, 36,* 320–328.

Steinberg, L. (1999). *Adolescence* (5th ed.). Boston: McGraw-Hill.

Stephan, W. (1985). Intergroup relations. In G. Lindsey & E. Aronson (Eds.), *Handbook of social psychology* (3rd ed.). New York: Random House.

Stoner, J. A. F. (1961). A comparison of individual and group decisions involving risk. Unpublished master's thesis, Massachusetts Institute of Technology, Cambridge.

Strayer, D. L., & Johnston, W. A. (2001). Driven to distraction: Dual-task studies of simulated driving and conversing on a cellular telephone. *Psychological Science, 12,* 462–466.

Straus, M. A., Sugarman, D. B., & Giles-Sims J. (1997). Corporal punishment by parents and subsequent antisocial behavior in children. *Archives of Pediatrics and Adolescent Medicine, 155,* 761–767.

T

Tanner, J. M. (1981). Growth and maturation during adolescence. *Nutrition Review, 39,* 43–55.

Taylor, S. E., Klein, L. C., Lewis, B. P., Gruenewald, T. L., Gurung, R. A. R., & Updegraff, J. A. (2000). Biobehavioral responses to stress in females: Tend-and-befriend, not fight or flight. *Psychological Review, 107,* 411–429.

Tenopyr, M. L. (1981). The realities of employment testing. *American Psychologist, 36,* 1120–1127.

Thoma, S. J., & Rest, J. R. (1999). The relationship between moral decision making and patterns of consolidation and transition in moral judgment development. *Developmental Psychology, 35,* 323–334.

Tice, D. M., & Baumeister, R. F. (1997). Longitudinal study of procrastination, performance, stress, and health: The costs and benefits of dawdling. *Psychological Science, 8,* 454–458.

Tolman, E. C., & Honzik, C. H. (1930). Introduction and removal of reward and maze performance in rats. *University of California Publication in Psychology, 4,* 257–275.

Triandis, H. C. (1990). Theoretical concepts that are applicable to the analysis of ethnocentrism. In R. W. Brislin (Ed.), *Applied Cross-cultural Psychology.* Newbury Park, CA: Sage.

Triandis, H. C. (1993). Collectivism and individualism as cultural syndromes. *Cross-Cultural Research, 27,* 155–180.

Tuckman, B. (1965). Developmental sequence in small groups. *Psychological Bulletin, 63,* 384–399.

Tuckman, B., & Jensen, M. (1977). Stages of small group development. *Group and Organizational Studies, 2,* 419–427.

Tulving, E., & Thompson, D. M. (1973). Encoding specificity and retrieval processes in episodic memory. *Journal of Experimental Psychology: Learning, Memory, and Cognition, 8,* 336–342.

Tune, L. E. (2001). Anticholinergic effects of medication in elderly patients. *Journal of Clinical Psychiatry, 62,* (Supplement 21), 11–14.

Turnbull, C. (1961). Some observations regarding the experiences and behaviors of the Bambuti pygmies. *American Journal of Psychology, 74,* 304–308.

Turner, J. S., & Helms, D. B. (1987). *Contemporary adulthood.* New York: Holt, Rinehart & Winston.

V

van der Pompe, G., Antoni, M. H., & Heijen, C. (1998). The effects of surgical stress and psychological stress on the immune function of operative cancer patients. *Psychological Health, 13,* 1015–1026.

van Ijzendoorn, M. H., & Kroonenberg, P. M. (1988). Cross-cultural patterns of attachment: A meta-analysis. *Child Development, 59,* 147–156.

Vander Wall, S. B. (1982). An experimental analysis of cache recovery in the Clark's nutcracker. *Animal Behavior, 30,* 84–94.

Vansteelandt, K., & Van Mechelen, I. (1998). Individual differences in situation-behavior profiles: A triple typology model. *Journal of Personality and Social Psychology, 75,* 751–765.

Vroom, V. (1964). *Work and motivation.* New York: Wiley.

W

Walster, E., Aronson, V., Abrahams, D., & Rottman, L. (1966). Importance of physical attractiveness in dating behavior. *Journal of Personality and Social Psychology, 4,* 508–516.

Wamboldt, F. S., & Reiss, D. (1989). Defining a family heritage and a new relationship identity: Two central tasks in making of a marriage. *Family Process, 28,* 317–335.

Waterman, A. S. (1985). Identity in the context of adolescent psychology. *New Directions in Child Development, 30,* 5–24.

Watson, J. B. (1919). *Psychology from the standpoint of a behaviorist.* Philadelphia: Lippincott.

Watson, J. B. (1925). *Behaviorism.* New York: Norton.

Watson, J. B. & Rayner, R. (1920). Conditioned emotional reactions. *Journal of Experimental Psychology, 3,* 1–14.

Weintraub, Z., Bental, Y., Olivan, A., & Rotschild, A. (1998). Neonatal withdrawal syndrome and behavioral effects produced by maternal drug use. *Addiction Biology, 3*(21), 159–170.

Westen, D. (1998). The scientific legacy of Sigmund Freud: Toward a psychodynamically informed psychological science. *Psychological Bulletin, 124,* 333–371.

Widiger, T. A., & Sankis, L. M. (2000). Adult psychopathology: Issues and controversies. *Annual Review of Psychology, 51,* 377–404.

Williams, J. M., & Dunlap, L. C. (1999). Pubertal timing and self-reported delinquency among male adolescents. *Journal of Adolescence, 22,* 157–171.

Wolpe, J. (1958). *Psychotherapy by reciprocal inhibition.* Stanford, CA: Stanford University Press.

Wolpe, J. (1981). Behavior therapy versus psychoanalysis. *American Psychologist, 36,* 159–164.

Wolpe, J. (1997). Thirty years of behavior therapy. *Behavior Therapy, 28,* 633–635.

Wood, J. M., Garb, H. N., Lilienfeld, S. O., & Nezworski, M. T. (2002). Clinical assessment. *Annual Review of Psychology, 53,* 519–543.

Worchel, S., Cooper, J., Goethals, G. R., & Olson, J. M. (2000). *Social psychology.* Belmont, CA: Wadsworth.

Wyer, R. S. Jr. & Adaval, R. (2003). Message reception skills in social communication. In J. O. Greene & B. R. Burleson (Eds.). *Handbook of Communication and Social Interaction Skills.* Mahwah, NJ: Lawrence Erlbaum Associates (pp. 291–355).

Z

Zuckerman, M. (1978). Sensation seeking and psychopathology. In R. D. Hare & D. Shalling (Eds.), *Psychopathic behavior.* New York: Wiley.

Zuckerman, M., Buchsbaum, M. S., & Murphy, D. L. (1980). Sensation seeking and its biological correlates. *Psychological Bulletin, 88,* 187–214.

Marginal glossary items, defined upon their first appearance unless noted otherwise, are in bold type. Chapter Summaries, Study Checks and Guides, Cyber Psych, and review questions are not indexed.